ABOUT THE AUTHOR

After graduating from the Eastman School of Music, Jim Willis became a high school band and orchestra teacher during the week, a symphony trombonist on the weekends, a jazz musician at night, and a choral conductor on Sunday mornings. The author of seven books on religion and spirituality, he has been an ordained minister for over forty years, while working part time as a carpenter, the host of his own drive-time radio show, an arts council director, and an adjunct college professor in the fields of world religions and instrumental music. His teaching career produced both the comprehensive one-volume encyclopedia of religion, *The Religion Book*, and *Armageddon Now: The End of the World A to Z*, written with his wife, Barbara. Both were published by Visible Ink Press. Concern for spiritual growth in contemporary society prompted his book *Faith, Trust & Belief: A Trilogy of the Spirit*, while his love for long-distance bicycling led him to make several cross-country bike trips and inspired his first book, *Journey Home: The Inner Life of a Long Distance Bicycle Rider* and its sequel, *Snapshots and Visions: A View from the Now*. *Savannah: A Bicycle Journey through Time and Space* continued in that tradition. His current residence in the woods of South Carolina inspired his book *The Dragon Awakes: Rediscovering Earth Energy in the Age Of Science*.

ALSO FROM VISIBLE INK PRESS

Real Visitors, Voices from Beyond, and
  Parallel Dimensions
By Brad Steiger and Sherry Hansen Steiger
ISBN: 978-1-57859-541-9

Real Zombies, the Living Dead, and Creatures
  of the Apocalypse
by Brad Steiger
ISBN: 978-1-57859-296-8

The Religion Book: Places, Prophets, Saints,
  and Seers
by Jim Willis
ISBN: 978-1-57859-151-0

The Sci-Fi Movie Guide: The Universe of Film from
  Alien to Zardoz
By Chris Barsanti
ISBN: 978-1-57859-503-7

Secret History: Conspiracies from Ancient Aliens to
  the New World Order
By Nick Redfern
ISBN: 978-1-57859-479-5

Secret Societies: The Complete Guide to Histories,
  Rites, and Rituals
By Nick Redfern
ISBN: 978-1-57859-483-2

The Spirit Book: The Encyclopedia of Clairvoyance,
  Channeling, and Spirit Communication
by Raymond Buckland
ISBN: 978-1-57859-172-5

UFO Dossier: 100 Years of Government Secrets,
  Conspiracies, and Cover-Ups
By Kevin D. Randle
ISBN: 978-1-57859-564-8

Unexplained! Strange Sightings, Incredible
  Occurrences, and Puzzling Physical Phenomena,
  3rd edition
by Jerome Clark
ISBN: 978-1-57859-344-6

The Vampire Book: The Encyclopedia of the
  Undead, 3rd edition
by J. Gordon Melton
ISBN: 978-1-57859-281-4

The Werewolf Book: The Encyclopedia of Shape-
  Shifting Beings, 2nd edition
by Brad Steiger
ISBN: 978-1-57859-367-5

The Witch Book: The Encyclopedia of Witchcraft,
  Wicca, and Neo-paganism
by Raymond Buckland
ISBN: 978-1-57859-114-5

The Zombie Book: The Encyclopedia of the
  Living Dead
By Nick Redfern and Brad Steiger
ISBN: 978-1-57859-504-4

"REAL NIGHTMARES" E-BOOKS BY BRAD STEIGER

Book 1: True and Truly Scary Unexplained Phenomenon

Book 2: The Unexplained Phenomena and Tales of
  the Unknown

Book 3: Things That Go Bump in the Night

Book 4: Things That Prowl and Growl in the Night

Book 5: Fiends That Want Your Blood

Book 6: Unexpected Visitors and Unwanted Guests

Book 7: Dark and Deadly Demons

Book 8: Phantoms, Apparitions, and Ghosts

PLEASE VISIT US AT VISIBLEINKPRESS.COM

DEDICATION

Sobuko
May I someday prove as helpful …
and as worthy.

ANCIENT GODS

LOST HISTORIES,
HIDDEN TRUTHS,
AND THE CONSPIRACY OF SILENCE

Jim Willis

VISIBLE
INK
PRESS

Detroit

Visible Ink Press®
43311 Joy Rd., #414
Canton, MI 48187-2075

Visible Ink Press is a registered trademark of Visible Ink Press LLC.

Most Visible Ink Press books are available at special quantity discounts when purchased in bulk by corporations, organizations, or groups. Customized printings, special imprints, messages, and excerpts can be produced to meet your needs. For more information, contact Special Markets Director, Visible Ink Press, www.visibleink.com, or 734-667-3211.

Managing Editor: Kevin S. Hile
Art Director: Mary Claire Krzewinski
Typesetting: Marco DiVita
Proofreaders: Janet L. Hile and Barbara Lyon
Indexer: Larry Baker

Cover images: Shutterstock

Cataloging-in-Publication data is on file at the Library of Congress.

10 9 8 7 6 5 4 3 2 1

CONTENTS

Prologue   [xiii]

Introduction   [xix]

WHERE DO WE COME FROM?

SEARCHING FOR CLUES

Photo Sources

Arp (Wikicommons): p. 332.

BabelStone (Wikicommons): p. 11.

Simon Burchell: p. 207.

Chatsam (Wikicommons): p. 116.

Bruno Comby: p. 237 (right).

Gavin Collins: p. 60.

Cpt. Muji (Wikicommons): p. 96.

Crates (Wikicommons): p. 184.

John D. Croft: p. 15.

Daderot (Wikicommons): pp. 170, 225.

Jeff Dahl: p. 152.

Didier Descouens: p. 19.

Elliot & Fry: p. 45.

Eric Ewing: p. 145.

Mohammad Fadli: p. 165.

Lörincz Gabriella: p. 299.

CGP Grey: p. 151.

Kevin Hile: p. 302.

HJPD (Wikicommons): p. 148.

Jibowks (Wikicommons): p. 12.

Jpedreira (Wikicommons): p. 237 (left).

JRodSilva (Wikicommons): p. 73.

Khoufou (Wikicommons): p. 256.

Simon Ledingham: p. 335.

Library of Congress: pp. 7,

Morio (Wikicommons): p. 172.

D. Mukherjee: p. 1216.

NASA: pp. 109, 119.

National Library of Austria: p. 311.

NOAA: p. 132.

Bengt Nyman: p. 327.

Offthemapz (Wikicomons): p. 99.

Pelloosah (Wikicommons): p. 21.

Pirouettewp (Wikicommons): p. 218.

Rémih (Wikicommons): p. 190.

Roblespepe (Wikicommons): p. 121.

SeriouslySerious (Wikicommons): p. 43.

Stan Shebs: p. 71.

Shutterstock: pp. 28, 35, 51, 52, 56, 66, 75, 77, 79, 83, 86, 101, 103, 117, 124, 128, 130, 135, 140, 142, 167, 174, 176, 181, 187, 192, 227, 229, 232, 239, 241, 247, 249, 251, 261, 264, 273, 279, 282, 284, 288, 292, 294, 297, 301, 305, 309, 314, 329, 338, 346, 350, 354, 357, 359, 363, 366, 369, 374, 379, 381, 382, 385.

Ephraim George Squier and Edwin Hamilton Davis: p. 146.

Martin St.-Amant: p. 277.

Stanford University School of Medicine: p. 307.

UNESCO: p. 64.

Rita Willaert: p. 62.

Jim Willis: pp. 88, 91, 220, 244, 253.

World Imaging: p. 39.

Xjunajpù (Wikicommons): p. 179.

Zhengan (Wikicommons): p. 158.

Public domain: pp. 9, 24, 32, 105, 111, 114, 144, 155, 160, 161, 177, 205, 211, 213, 216, 221, 234, 267, 270, 316, 320, 322, 324, 370, 372.

ACKNOWLEDGMENTS

First and foremost, a big thank you to my wife, Barbara. None of my books could have been written without her. People sometimes ask us what we talk about all day, all alone and living in the woods by ourselves. Well, we talk about stuff like this.… And a whole lot more!

I have many "mentors whom I have never met." Two of them are Andrew Collins and Graham Hancock. Their meticulously detailed, thoroughly researched, "boots on the ground" authenticity led them to write books that ask the kinds of questions that have no doubt barred them from many an archeological dig. They have no tolerance for the *Conspiracy of Silence*. When I needed help on a project I was working on while researching this book, I wrote to Andrew to ask him a question. He got back to me within the hour. Although traditional "experts" often banish them both to the "fringe," I have come to believe they are holding aloft the torch of truth by asking penetrating questions and daring to go where the facts lead instead of pleasing the establishment. May their kind always be with us!

Albert Goodyear is a respected archeologist who risked his reputation by daring to take the Topper Site in South Carolina to new heights. Or should I say depths? By delving beneath the Clovis layer, he pushed open the door to some amazing insights into who we really are. He has been an inspiration to many of us.

Dean Radin, Ph.D., is the chief scientist at the Institute of Noetic Sciences. One Sunday afternoon, I wrote to him concerning a technical question I had about Transcendental Monism. He responded that very afternoon. The good ones always seem open and welcoming, even to unknown writers from a small town in South Carolina. He, and others like him, continue to inspire me.

Likewise, the work of Ervin Laszlo involving Akashic field studies, and William Buhlman's books and seminars on the topic of out-of-body experiences, have been extremely helpful.

Sandra Kransi is a good friend who patiently keeps me on the right track when I'm writing about things like DNA and mitochondrial research, which she understands and teaches to people such as me who don't. Denise Chrislip is my go-to for all things Mayan, and Ben Erwin helped me remember things I didn't know I knew about Charles Hapgood. Thanks to you all!

Thanks also to Darrell Newby, who generously gave of his time, experience, and high-tech equipment when I needed help plotting and researching historical landmarks in the area. His interest in the subject is contagious!

Jeffrey Rich and his husband, Jeff Wright (a.k.a. "OneTree"), are shamanic practitioners and good friends of ours, so I felt in capable hands when I consulted them concerning chapters about shamanism. Jeffrey has studied extensively in a variety of shamanic traditions and teaches workshops in Alabama, a historically notorious hotbed of shamanistic practice! He's also a great tenor. You can find more about him on his website: http://waterwillowmoon.com/.

To Roger Jänecke and the folks at VIP, this is our third project together. It's been a good journey. Thanks for your faith in the importance of print media. People like you will help preserve human wisdom long after the electricity goes out!

Prologue

An Emergence Legend of the Hopi

A respected elder sat before the dying embers of a fire, holding with loving care a long-stemmed pipe. Carefully shaped and decorated with feathers and beads, the pipe appeared to be carved out of wood that might have served as a model for the dark creases and curves of the old man's leathery face. Only his eyes, dark and deep pools of both mirth and concern, appeared alive. It seemed to those who had joined the fire circle that if anyone had tried to lift the man up, the ground would have come with him. He appeared to be immensely heavy and solid, yet fragile as old parchment. Utterly without movement, as if remembering stories of long ago, he stared at the pipe, worn smooth by the caress of many hands.

It would have seemed the height of blasphemy to interrupt his reverie, so the disparate group that gathered that evening simply sat, caught up in the old man's spiritual focus. They were of all ages and walks of life: traditionalists and futurists, formally educated and self-taught, men and women, professionals and non-professionals. In most cases, they didn't know the names of the others who sat in this circle, or how they had come to be here. They hadn't yet shared their stories. That might come later.

There was no question as to who was at the center of this evening's gathering. The old man, without saying a word or making a movement, simply waited. He radiated an energy that was at once powerful and peaceful. If anything were to happen tonight, he would be the focus of it.

There finally came a time when the waiting seemed over. No one else walked in from the darkness. The circle was unbroken. Only then did the old man reach purposefully for tobacco, place it in the pipe, and begin to slowly tamp it into place. As he lit the charred and blackened bowl with a small twig from the fading fire, each movement seemed to be made with resolute purpose, as if the ancient one was concerned only with the particular motion required for each task. Did the process take a few seconds, a few minutes, or an hour? No one could really tell. It seemed that each movement occupied the entire concentration of every person who sat around the fire. Every motion was a ritual, each act a sacrament.

Only after he had exhaled a puff of smoke in each of the four directions, only after he allowed it to frame his weathered face, did the old man speak. His voice seemed to come from the earth itself. It was soft, every word distinct. It wasn't powerful, but it commanded attention. It was not what many would call authoritative, but it rang with truth. It was directed at each individual who sat in the circle that night, conveying ideas and insights each of them heard as if for the first time but, once digested, seemed to be that which each of them already knew, and had known for a long, long time.

The Elder's Story

"It might not have happened in just this way," he began, "but this is a true story just the same.

"The world we see, this world we know, the world in which we now live, is not the only world that has been. They say others have come before. And perhaps more will follow. Who can say? But the old ones who tell the stories remember other places, other times, other people."

The First World: Tokpela

When the first people awakened to life they were instructed by Sotuknang and Spider Woman to respect both Taiowa, the Creator, and the land they were given for their home. Spider Woman had formed it for them and they were nurtured by its bounty. They discovered vibration centers spread throughout the earth that echoed in similar centers within their own bodies and sang in resonance with the music of the stars in the heavens. The purpose of these centers was to help keep the people in tune with the Creator as they followed his ways.

The people forgot to listen. Ignoring the music of the stars that rang in their hearts they no longer followed the Way and began to quarrel amongst themselves. It got to be so bad that Sotuknang decided he must destroy the people before they ruined everything they had been given.

But some of the old ones still remembered how to act correctly and show proper respect, so Sotuknang appeared to them with the sound of a mighty wind and said he would lead them to safety if they followed him and obeyed his instructions. And so it was that a few of the ancient ones took refuge among the Ant People as the First World was destroyed by fire. Sotuknang caused the earth to bellow forth smoke and flame. Volcanoes erupted from deep below the surface of the land. A Second World was then prepared for the people.

The Second World: Tokpa

The Second World was almost as beautiful as the first, but in this world the animals no longer trusted humans. They kept themselves separate and ran away whenever the people came upon them. Still, it was a good place to live. It was so good, in fact, that the people once again began to think they knew more than the Creator and ignored his plan for them. Life was too easy. They had everything they needed but they wanted more. They thought they could live any way they chose, even if it was disrespectful and selfish, and it soon became apparent that Sotuknang would have to destroy them again.

Once again, Sotuknang called on the Ant People to open their kivas to those who remembered, to those who still sang the songs of Taiowa. He led them again to safety in the underground world.

This time, Poqanghoya and Palongawhoya, the Twins who guarded the poles of the earth, left their posts and the world spun off its axis and went out of control, whirling through space. It soon became covered with ice and was frozen until the Twins once again took up their stations and restored life to the earth. The ice melted and the people could once again return to their new home. This was the home the wise ones called Kuskurza, the Third World.

The Third World: Kuskurza

In this third world, the people quickly multiplied. They created cities and countries—a whole new civilization. Sotuknang and Spider Woman despaired. The people could not sing the praises of Taiowa, the Creator, when they were too busy being occupied by their earthly plans and selfish dreams.

Some, of course, remembered the old ways. They knew that the further people traveled on the Road of Life, the harder it was to remain faithful and true. They tried to teach the young people the old ways, but the young people refused to listen. Instead, they found new ways to destroy and conquer. They sought to enhance their personal power at the expense of others. Some even invented flying shields, capable of carrying them to villages far away, where they could attack, pillage, and return so quickly that no one knew where they had gone.

Sotuknang knew he could not allow this way of life to continue. So he warned Spider Woman that he would again destroy the people, this time with a great flood.

Spider Woman knew of the few people who still listened—who still tried to teach the people the ways of the Creator. But this time she didn't know how to save them. In a great flood, even the home of the Ant People would be destroyed. The people searched long and hard for a solution, for a way of salvation. Finally, they hid themselves inside the hollow stems of bamboo trees while their world was drowned.

The Fourth World: Tuwaqachi

When the flood waters calmed, the people came out and began again. They made what seemed an endless journey by boat, paddling uphill all the way. But the earth was covered with water. From time to time, they would send out birds to scout for a place of safety, but the birds always returned. Finally, they began to find land. Islands appeared, like stepping stones, and they offered good places to live. But each time Spider Woman told them they must move on. The places they stopped were too easy, she said. They would soon fall again into their evil ways.

Finally, the people were too exhausted to continue on their own. All they could do was open the doors of their hearts and allow Spider Woman to guide them. They were forced to submit to her wisdom.

At long last they came to a sandy shore where they were greeted by Sotuknang, who gave them instructions. They were to separate into different groups, each group following its own star by night and pillar of cloud by day, until they came to a place where the earth met the sea. Each group would keep track of their migration on a tablet of stone, and record in symbol the representation of their journeys. At long last they would be brought together again, but only after much travail. In this way, they would finally come to remember what they had forgotten—to obey Taiowa, the Creator, and live according to his plan for them.

Hear the words of Sotuknang, spoken at the beginning of the fourth world: "I have washed away even the footprints of your Emergence; the stepping-stones which I left for you. Down on the bottom of the seas lie all the proud cities, the flying shields, and the worldly treasures corrupted with evil, and those people who found no time to sing praises to the Creator from the tops of their hills. But the day will come, if you preserve the memory and the meaning of your Emergence, when these stepping-stones will emerge again to prove the truth you speak."

Conclusion

The respected elder, having finished his story, sat again in silence, staring at the cold pipe he still held lovingly in his hands. The fire had long since died out and was now reduced to a few burning embers, leaving the assembled sojourners in darkness. On the eastern horizon there appeared a thin line of gray, harbinger of the coming dawn. The night of magic had passed. And from high above sounded forth the shrill "Kree!" of a circling hawk, joyously greeting the dawn of a new day.

(Adapted from: Waters, Frank. *Book of the Hopi*. New York, NY: Penguin Books, 1977, and Willis, Jim. *The Dragon Awakes: Rediscovering Earth Energy in the Age of Science*. Daytona Beach, FL: Dragon Publishing Co., 2014.)

INTRODUCTION

It strikes me how arrogant we are to assume we know anything.
We, who don't know what we are, why we're here, or even where
we go, consider ourselves the dominant, intelligent rulers of the
world. It's truly ironic just how deceived we are.

William Buhlman in *Adventures Beyond the Body*

What If?

For thirteen days in October of 1962, our civilization was poised on the
edge of nuclear destruction. American president John F. Kennedy and Soviet
premier Nikita Khrushchev engaged in a faceoff that has since been labeled,
on this side of the Atlantic, the Cuban Missile Crisis. The world watched as
the Cold War escalated precariously toward the brink of what was then called
the doctrine of Mutual Assured Destruction. That was the tactic employed by
both super powers, called Second Strike Capability, that would enable them to
destroy each other with intercontinental ballistic missiles, no matter who fired
first. In the last 12,000 years, it was the closest human civilization has ever
come to complete annihilation.

What if the Soviet Union had not backed down?

Imagine, for a moment, that during those tumultuous days you had
lived in a small, remote village, perhaps high up in a distant mountain range or
off on a small island somewhere in the midst of the sea. What if things had
gone differently?

One day you are simply living your life, normal in every way. Then
things suddenly change forever. One moment you are walking down a well-
trodden pathway, thinking about whatever it is that occupies your days. The

next moment, a far-off war of which you are not even aware, fought by countries you never heard of, changes your world forever. The effects of nuclear winter alter the climate, perhaps even the very air you breathe. Smoke and ash circulating through the upper atmosphere blot out the sun and your crops fail. A strange sickness devastates your family and the small community of which you are a part. How will you grow vegetables? How will you find food? How will you survive?

Worse yet, if you are of a religious mind, are the spiritual questions. Can you trust that this was just a cosmic accident or has something you have done here on Earth somehow influenced how you were treated by the gods of the universe? What did you do to deserve this? How do appease your deities so this won't happen again? Should you build an altar or a temple of worship?

All around you there are signs and signals that things will never be the same. As far as you know, your life is starting over again. Even though you don't fully understand the immense repercussions, even though you may have never been aware of the majority of humankind who were once familiar with cars and telephones, who once flew the friendly skies and traversed the globe, who once gathered around TV sets and radios, who once took the good life for granted, much of that human population is now gone. The ones who are left suffer from what amounts to cultural amnesia. The technical benefits of a civilization that once formed a world-wide infrastructure are gone, buried under the fires and ash of a nuclear holocaust. Those who remain must begin again.

A Case of Cultural Amnesia

Now, back in the present for a moment, ask another question. Has something like this happened before? Substitute a comet or asteroid colliding with the earth for the nuclear explosion we just postulated. Insert a devastating episode of volcanic eruptions over a vast area of the planet. Think about a sudden shift in plate tectonics, shuffling huge land masses into climate zones which are now either suddenly frigid or temperate, depending on their latitude, resulting in freezes or mass floods. What might be the result?

Consider the thought that what we call "civilization" did not really arise in Mesopotamia or Sumer or Egypt or anywhere else in the Middle East. Suppose that what we call the "beginning" is really a "re-beginning," a rebirth. What if we *are* suffering from cultural amnesia brought on by a great catastrophe that, in one brief moment of time, obliterated a large proportion of human culture, leaving only a few fortunate survivors to tell the tale? The children of their children would have no historical memory of what happened. All they would be able to draw upon would be the tales of their elders and physical remnants left over from the catastrophe. Without help from those who remember, they would be forced to start over again, reinventing such things as writing, mathematics, and technical skills that once were commonplace but are now long forgotten, buried by the dust of time.

Think about it this way. Archeologists in America sometimes discover homes from relatively recent colonial days in places where no one now alive knew anyone ever lived. We wonder what happened. Perhaps a fire blazed out of control. Perhaps sickness took its quiet toll. We may find tools and implements, but no one recalls any names or faces. No one recorded the hopes and dreams of those who lived and loved there. We can't even really tell what the homeowners did for a living unless we are lucky enough to find some tools or other evidence of whatever occupied their days. Even then, we can really only guess. After all, only the most durable evidence survives. Everything else, including that which is most important, disintegrates. Their unique knowledge and experience lies buried with them.

And this is an example of only a single family who lived in an age of writing, surrounded by others who lived on after them. History is rife with examples of people such as the Anasazi or, more recently, the Lost Colony of Roanoke, who seem to have just disappeared. One day they were living, thriving, and building a legacy. The next day they were gone. What if the catastrophe that claimed them struck a much larger area, perhaps a whole continent or even a whole planet?

It has happened before. In this book we will explore all sorts of historical oddities that offer very real and tangible evidence of past cataclysms. Sixty-five million years ago an asteroid wiped out the dinosaurs and ushered in an era of unprecedented volcanic destruction. This we know to be true. We've even found the crater it left behind in the Yucatan Peninsula. But, as we will discover in the following pages, it is very probable that within the last 12,000 years, a time period during which modern humans existed on Earth, a segmented comet brought the reign of mastodons and mammoths to an end. Silent cities now slumber beneath rising seas off the shores of almost every continent on earth. If climate scientists who study such things are correct, Miami and New York might join their ranks in the next hundred years. Buried temples in Turkey that have not seen the light of day for millennia are coming to life, thanks to the work of careful archeologists. Unexplored pyramids still lie hidden beneath dense undergrowth in Peru and Central America, while some enigmatic building projects, such as the Sphinx and Stonehenge, have been hiding in plain sight for thousands of years. We have forgotten how, when, and why they were ever built.

Here's the point: if our species is capable of developing cultural amnesia over the course of just a few hundred years, what about a few thousand? What about ten thousand? Or fifty thousand?

Creating Ancient Gods

Go back, for a moment, to our earlier example of your personal fate resulting from cultural amnesia following a nuclear holocaust. You are still living in your isolated village. Now add another layer of intrigue.

One day, while you are still in shock, trying to figure out what happened, while you are trying to decide what to do next and how you are going to survive the effects, someone else appears on the scene. He witnessed the whole catastrophe. He was there. He remembers. He somehow lived through it and escaped unscathed. He can tell you how to rebuild your life. He remembers former skills. He knows!

And he is willing to help. Slowly he teaches you the rudiments of how to rebuild your lost life. To you, everything seems new and fresh. You learn what seem like new skills and exciting ways of living that far surpass the primitive existence you once knew. To your new friend, this is all old stuff. But he is patient with you, teaching you only as much as you can absorb. As you pass his knowledge on to your children, as they learn how to excel and thrive in their own lives, and then teach their children, your community rebuilds what was familiar to others who once lived far away. You never before heard of these skills. To you, this is a journey of discovery. It is fresh, entrepreneurial, and challenging. Each day is an adventure. You are building what amounts to a new civilization.

Eventually, however, your new friend dies. Your children may have met him, but their children have not. To the children of your grandchildren he is only a distant family memory, remembered with great fondness as the one who taught you a level of life undreamed. He couldn't build an airplane or an automobile by himself. He didn't have the resources. But he could tell you about them and get you thinking along those lines so that a few hundred years in the future your descendants could build them, or something similar that may even surpass them. After a few generations, your friend will probably be remembered only through the telling of myths that have grown to epic proportions. The stories may even mold him into an ancient godlike figure who arrived at just the right time to set your family on a new, straight path. As the years go by, the myth will grow until he didn't just know a lot—he knew everything. He didn't just roll up his sleeves and help out. He accomplished miracles. He arrived by magic. He could leap tall buildings with a single bound. He could fly through the air. He told tales of forgotten cities where miracles happened every day. He was part of an ancient golden age that becomes more thrilling with each rendition of the story. He was the one who brought about what you now call "the beginning!"

We could continue. But the point is this: the accomplishments of heroes grow with the telling. We all know that. It's human nature.

Heroes of Old

Don't treat this too lightly. It's a familiar tale. The early texts about Jesus of Nazareth, for instance, don't mention anything about a virgin birth or raising the dead. All that came years later. He wasn't declared to be equal with God until the Council of Nicea, more than three hundred years after his birth.

The Buddha, according to his own testimony, was simply an enlightened human being until many years after his death. It was only then that his followers began to deify him.

Chinese children didn't start offering sacrifices to Confucius until 56 C.E., and he wasn't declared to be "equal with heaven and earth" until 1908!

Quetzalcoatl, the Plumed Serpent, was first described as a blue-eyed white man with a beard who looked nothing like the Mesoamerican people to whom he appeared. Many years later, they recalled him so vividly that they illustrated him with the feathers of a bird and scales of a serpent.

On and on it goes. After many years pass, heroes are remembered to have done amazing things. When he was safely dead, for instance, the story circulated that George Washington threw a silver dollar all the way across the Potomac river. Respected Roman Catholic figures are never granted the status of miracle-working saints until they are tucked away in their graves for a few centuries (an exception being St. Mother Teresa). A shadowy figure like Merlin had to wait until the Middle Ages, long after Arthur and his court, if they ever existed, had passed into memory before he could become a real practitioner of magic.

Earthly, godlike figures exist only in long-ago, ancient times. That's what keeps them heroic. We don't have to deal with them ourselves. All we have to do is tell their story. Tales of ancient glory all happen "once upon a time." Even Yoda, Darth Vader, and his minions existed "long, long ago, in a galaxy far away." Thus, we keep our heroes safely at arm's length.

But what if, in some cases, the stories have grown from a kernel of truth?

Lost Histories and Hidden Truths

All around the world, we find enigmatic structures, archeological wonders, and geographic anomalies that stand in the way of a uniform understanding of who we are as a people. They raise nagging questions:

- 40,000 years ago, across Europe and Asia, our ancestors felt the need to crawl deep underground, sometimes as much as a mile, braving the depths and darkness, to paint magnificent images on the walls of caves. Why?

- Six miles from Urfa, an ancient city in southeastern Turkey, stand the ruins of a megalithic temple site called Göbekli Tepe. Built 11,600 years ago, before the agricultural revolution, before humans had discovered how to grow their own food to support such an endeavor, it begs the question, "Why?"

- Six thousand years later, humans dragged stones, weighing up to four tons, 140 miles across England to build a monument called Stonehenge. Why?

- On an equatorial band circling Earth our ancestors felt the need to build pyramids. Why?

- Over the course of three thousand years no less than five world religions were born that are still a source of faith and practice to billions of people around the world. Why?

- The great questions of humanity have been the same for as long as there have been humans around to ask them: "Who are we?" … "Where did we come from?" … "Why are we here?" … "What is our purpose?" … "Is there more?"

In short, we seem to be a species with cultural amnesia. Is it possible that we have forgotten who we are? Is there a lost history out there, hidden truths that can teach us something important about our past? If we can recover even a *portion* of that forgotten history and probe *some* of those hidden truths, will it help answer pressing questions that now seem to threaten the future of our very existence? Can recovering even *some* of our story lead us out of the quagmire of human-induced calamity that today dominates the headlines and threatens our planet?

A Radical Concept

This book proposes a rather radical concept for us to consider. We, the current ruling species on the planet, *have* indeed suffered a catastrophic accident. Maybe several. We are *not* the first civilization to come down the pike. We *have* developed cultural amnesia. What we call *the* beginning is really a *new* beginning, built on the ruins of what came before.

Could it be that our civilization is not the first? Could it be that other "worlds," just as in the Hopi myth that forms the Prologue of this book, have come before us? Could the Hopi-inspired legend about the destruction of former "worlds" by fire, ice, and water be more than a tale told around an evening campfire? Could the myth be a poetic description of events that really took place? Were there people alive who were eyewitnesses? Did they survive to become the heroes of old, the ancient gods of renown? Did they pass on wisdom from a former time, thus shaping the future of the human race?

The Conspiracy of Silence

In today's politically and academically correct climate, it is difficult to seriously raise such questions because we live in a culture that worships at the altar of *Uniformitarianism*—that is, the belief that our evolution, both at the level of planetary geology and species biology, continues on in a relatively uninterrupted manner in the sense that things happening today are similar to things that happened yesterday. Forces at work today are the forces that will be at work tomorrow.

According to this belief system, the human race has evolved slowly and steadily, aided by occasional mutational jumps, from one-cell organisms to amphibians to apelike mammals to *Homo sapiens*. It's the formula most of us learned in school, backed up by the supposedly rock-hard, scientific facts gleaned from archeology, biology, physiology, historical research, carbon dating, and common sense.

The technique has remained the same for hundreds of years: *Find an artifact, determine its age, plug it into the existing chart, and continue on.*

But what happens when you uncover something that doesn't fit the existing chart?

- What if you find an anomaly—something that seems to refute the existing formula—something that, indeed, might call into question the very structure of so-called "scientific" knowledge?

- What if it were to be proven that, maybe even in the not-so-distant past, natural cataclysms, be they volcanic eruptions, comets from space, sudden melting of glacial ice caps, earthquakes, or something similar, had punctuated the equilibrium of the natural flow of evolution?

- What if these things had happened within the time frame of human existence on the planet? In other words, what if people were alive at the time, a few of whom survived to tell the tale?

- What if the human race is no different from the thousands of other species that have gone extinct, or nearly so?

More and more, with each passing day, the reports of field archeology from all over the world indicate that this might be the case. More and more it seems as if this is the only story that will make sense of *all* the existing facts.

But accepting these new findings is difficult. It upsets the apple cart of history's plodding story. It discredits former beloved teachers and requires the rewriting of textbooks. It poses more questions than it answers. Who wants to teach a high school or college course consisting of questions? Academia, it is thought, is a place for answers, not questions! It's uncomfortable to stand in front of a room full of students and say, "We just don't know!"

So it's far easier to become an academic fundamentalist—to simply take refuge in traditional doctrine and the accepted "text," sweep inconvenient facts under the rug, declare them to be "interesting anomalies," and hope no one notices.

There is a wonderful, no doubt apocryphal, story about an old religious fundamentalist woman, who, when told about Darwin's theory of evolution, prayed fervently, "God, make it not true. And if it is true, don't let anyone find out about it!"

This is what happens when a popular archeological professor from a midwestern university, confronted by an irrefutable fact of historical evidence that questions the identity of the first Americans, appears on national television and says, "I don't want just one fact. I want many facts!" And slams the proverbial door shut behind him.

This is what happens when a highly accredited teacher of archaeology feels pressured to tell his students, "If you find artifacts that are older than the standard model accepts, cover them up and don't tell anyone. You'll ruin your career!"

This is what happens when a controversial author of great repute and popular appeal finds his lectures pulled from a large YouTube forum when they don't fit existing theory.

We will look into their stories in depth in the following pages. They are all victims of a conspiracy of silence. No one person is to blame. There is no sinister organization that orchestrates their ostracism. It is simply the method by which ingrained, institutional thinking tends to operate.

In November 2015, Volume 61 of the *Journal of Experimental Social Psychology* condensed the results of six experiments that might well serve as a commentary explaining the conspiracy of silence. The studies investigated how people behaved when they were told they were "experts" on a particular subject, whether or not they actually were. The results of the experiments showed that perceived experts tended to be more closed-minded and less open to arguments than members of the control groups. It didn't make any difference whether they were really experts or not. As long as they thought they were, they acted as though they knew the answers. They exhibited what the study labeled the "Earned Dogmatism Effect". What that means, according to the study, is that the more a person knew, or thought he or she knew, about a particular subject, the more they were apt to ignore someone with a different opinion, whether or not that opinion was based on fact. It took a tremendous effort for the experts to reconsider their views.

The results of the study were thus summarized:

- Social norms entitle experts to be more closed-minded or dogmatic.

- Self-perception of high expertise increased closed-mindedness.

The final conclusion?

Although cultural values generally prescribe open-mindedness, open-minded cognition systematically varies across individuals and situations. According to the *Earned Dogmatism Hypothesis*, social norms dictate that experts are entitled to adopt a relatively dogmatic, closed-minded orientation. As a consequence, situations that engender self-perceptions of high expertise elicit a more closed-minded cognitive style. These predictions are confirmed in six experiments.

How easy it is for us to ignore the words here condensed from a text written almost two thousand years ago:

In the last days, scoffers will come.... They will say ... "Ever since our fathers died, everything goes on as it has since the beginning of creation." But they deliberately forget that long ago ... the heavens existed and the earth was formed out of water and with water. By water also the world of that time was deluged and destroyed. By the same word the present heavens and earth are reserved for fire, being kept for the day of ... destruction....

2 Peter 3:3–7—New International Version of the Bible

This passage is taken out of context, of course, and paraphrased. But it illustrates the fact that people have been thinking along these lines for a long time. It's human nature.

With no support and encouragement, with no fresh and open minds willing to probe and push, with no funds available for research, new and compelling facts wither on the vine. And our cultural amnesia continues. Again and again we repeat the mistakes of our forgotten ancestors. What they learned through hard work and experiment is lost. And we are forced to begin again.

New Beginnings

So we repeat our opening question. If most of the human race were suddenly wiped off the face of the earth, leaving only you and a few others left to carry on, would you be able to instruct your children and perhaps some primitive folk who survived the cataclysm because they lived deep in the rain forest or high in the mountains about the "magic" of electricity or internal combustion engine? You could tell wondrous tales of what they accomplished. But could you produce their effects given the limited technology of the surviving world?

No, you couldn't. All you could do would be to talk about them and hope someone, someday, rediscovers them. You would have to await their reinvention thousands of years in the future. And, over the course of millennia, all evidence of them would rot away and be buried under a rising sea, a mile-high glacier or drifting desert sands.

But maybe by that time something you never dreamed of would take their place. Electricity and gas-powered vehicles might become forgotten wonders, but they might be replaced by inventions you did not even imagine. After all, the "necessities" we take for granted, the ones that dominate our waking lives, are all new. Two hundred years ago—in some cases even thirty years ago—they were not a part of human life. Smart phones, computers, video games, televisions—even plastic—all of them are brand new, unknown to our great-great grandparents. Maybe, if an asteroid blasted the planet and the human race were to be forced to start all over, all that we hold dear would exist forever only in myth and legend, the toys of forgotten gods—us. And most people then living would believe such things were only stories told around the campfires of a forgotten race—until some future archeologist discovered the remains of a buried laptop and began to wonder.

You Be the Judge

Is all this farfetched? Is it impossible? Is it the fitful imagination of a dreamer with too much time on his hands? The evidence is piling up that the era of our cultural amnesia is coming to an end. There are simply too many anomalies to consider, too many riddles being unearthed, too many enigmatic wonders of the past to consider. As unlikely as it once seemed, daring archeologists, far-seeing scientists, and courageous academics are now asking questions that have been ignored for too long. Relevant television shows are multiplying. Controversial books are coming off the presses. Papers are being published and discussed.

And if you still think that all this is nothing more than an entertaining illusion, consider the following: Are you sitting in a chair right now, holding this book in your hands, quietly reading these words? Do you feel that you are comfortable, still, and immovable, a solid fixture in time and space? Well, although your great-grandparents would never believe it, remember that in the time it took you to read this paragraph we now know that you hurtled some five hundred miles through space in a mad, orbital dash around the sun.

Talk about an illusion! And there are many more. Obviously, life is not always as secure and stable as it appears to be. There are wonders to behold of which we are hardly ever aware, in the course of our day-to-day lives. Maybe it's time to consider some more "impossible" truths that may seem radical from the comfort of your armchair but appear to stand up to scrutiny in the hard, exacting court of science. Then decide for yourself.

A Final Caution

There is one more important issue to address, and it is by no means a trivial adjunct to the discussion. When two people with differing ideas confront each other face to face, conventions of courtesy usually apply. By that we mean that a level of civil discourse and argument is expected. Unfortunately, the computer has changed many of those conventions. It is now too easy for uninformed people to sit in a darkened room, type all sorts of unfounded allegations and accusations onto an impersonal screen, punch the "send" button, and ridicule an unseen opponent before the whole world. There is probably not one subject covered in this book that has not been scathingly attacked in print and engraved forever in the cloud of the Internet cosmos. Often the only source of intellectual criticism found in such articles is that "so-and-so" appeared on some TV show with "what's his name" and is therefore a "fool," not to be trusted.

Such activity, sad to say, is common these days. Civil, constructive discourse, be it religious, academic, or political, can still be found in face-to-face seminars and classrooms, but it is often lacking on news programs, TV, and talk radio, and, of course, the Internet.

We live in an age of unprecedented opportunity to expose ourselves to exciting ideas concerning evidence both new and familiar. An open and inquiring mind is essential. Neither amateurs nor accepted authorities are above suspicion. In the end, the only ones on whom we can really depend for answers are those seekers who are open-minded, careful with their claims, and ready to learn.

A journey of discovery awaits!

WHERE DO WE COME FROM?

INTRODUCTION

The time will come when diligent research over long periods will bring to light things which now lay hidden. A single lifetime would not be enough for the investigation of so vast a subject, so this knowledge will be unfolded only through long successive ages. There will come a time when our descendants will be amazed that we did not know things that are so plain to them. Many discoveries are reserved for ages still to come, when memory of us will have been effaced. Our universe is a sorry little affair unless it has in it something for every age to investigate.... Nature does not reveal her mysteries once and for all.

Seneca in *Natural Questions*, Book 7. First Century C.E.

Answers do not drive the evolution of knowledge. The engine that propels us forward lies in questions. When we ask questions, we are moved to seek out truths that are hidden tantalizingly close, it would seem, in the mists shrouding the eyes of our intellect. We want to know. We want to learn. We want to understand. So we ask questions. And the journey begins. We stop standing still. We begin to move forward.

The answers come, to be sure. But they are often mere incentives grasped along the way. They serve to motivate us, to reward us and keep us moving ahead.

Some people, sad to say, seem to think that finding answers are a reason to stop. Having seemingly arrived at their destination, such people think the journey is over. They don't realize that a good answer merely opens up more questions. So they enshrine their answers, preserve them in amber, print them in textbooks and turn them into doctrines, dogmas, and doctorates. Such people often become professors and priests. They teach their answers to students and act as though the matter was settled for all time. "As it was in the beginning, is now and ever shall be, world without end!" Amen! It is finished!

If you prefer your history wrapped up in a neat ribbon, signed, sealed, and delivered in dogmatism, you can put this book down and stop reading. What follows won't interest you.

But if you'd like to break out of the conspiracy of silence that surrounds so much of what passes for "certified and proven" history, if you are more interested in history's questions than in supposed answers, read on. This is for you.

In Part 1 of this book we're going to ask one of the most profound questions anyone can ask: "Where do we come from?"

There are many questions imbedded in this query. Who are we? Who are our ancestral parents? What made them tick? Why is the world the way it is? What, and who, came before us?

In the course of seeking some answers, we're going to go in search of our ancient ancestors. We're going to discover that they had a fascination for the night sky. They were, indeed, ancient astronomers. But this raises more questions. Why? Was there something in the cosmos that called to them? Was there a memory of something great, something awesome, maybe even terrible, that once reached out from the great beyond and changed them forever? Was their fascination with the heavens due to the fact that they had once witnessed ancient catastrophes which they interpreted as coming from the gods who ruled from on high? Did they then have to go about the task of recreating their lives anew by building ancient civilizations? Do we, in fact, inhabit a new civilization they built?

And even more important for us living today, did these folks, recognizing the errors inherent in their culture, seek to warn us, their children, so we won't follow in their footsteps? We don't have to believe a cosmic catastrophe was really punishment from God. The important thing is that they did. The ones who survived "Noah's flood," the destruction of "Atlantis," the devastation of the Ojibwa "low-flying comet with the fiery tail," or the "watery grave" described by Gilgamesh all had plenty of time to consider what had happened. Being human, they asked questions: "Why? What did we do wrong? Is God punishing us?"

As always, the questions kicked in and led them to seek answers. In their case, they turned inward, analyzing their society and culture to determine how they could do it differently next time. They sought to better humanity.

Did they encode their wisdom in what they left behind? Do their very architecture and lost histories preserve hidden truths they had gained from asking the right questions?

If so, their questions led them to leave for us, their children, the benefits of their wisdom. Which leads to another question. Are we listening?

ANCIENT ANCESTORS

In the mystic sense of the creation around us, in the expression of art, in a yearning towards God, the soul grows upward and finds the fulfillment of something implanted in its nature.... The pursuit of science [also] springs from a striving which the mind is impelled to follow, a questioning that will not be suppressed. Whether in the intellectual pursuits of science or in the mystical pursuits of the spirit, the light beckons ahead and the purpose surging in our nature responds.

Sir Arthur Eddington in *The Nature of the Physical World*

When I was born and saw the light
I was no stranger in this world.
Something inscrutable, shapeless, and without words
Appeared in the form of my mother.

Rabindranath Tagore

Who Are We?

It has been said that whenever you call a friend and listen to the voice on her answering machine, whatever the recorded message says, it conveys a variation of two profound questions.

The first is, "Who are you?"

The second is, "What do you want?"

Philosophical humor aside, if, in your life's journey, you answer these two questions satisfactorily, your life has been successful.

This simple truth has sparked a plethora of book titles, song lyrics, and published articles. It obviously provokes thought in those who are so inclined.

The first important question asked by every child is usually, "Where do I come from?" For most parents it generally causes either embarrassment or confusion. It's not that sex education is that difficult. It's that phrasing an answer in words appropriate to the experience and understanding of a five-year-old is tricky. Given the number of books devoted to this very question—books centered on a level other than biology, of course—it can be said that when it comes to a competent philosophical answer, we are all five-year-olds.

This chapter begins with basic questions. They are about origins. Who are we? Where do we come from? How did we get here? Is there anything or anyone working behind the scenes? When did our ancient ancestors arrive at a point where they could begin to ask these questions for themselves? For that matter, who are our ancestors? Could it be that ancient beings now remembered as "gods" were, in fact, flesh and blood people? Did the knowledge they bequeathed to us come from the heavens? Or was it the product of our very human ancestors who struggled, just as we do, to discover more about the world in which we live?

Common Theories

Until relatively recently, and by that I mean the last few hundred years or so, questions about origins were handled, at least in European/American circles, by religious folks who declared that we are the product of divine fiat: "God said … and it was so!" Many indigenous cultures around the world held similar beliefs, but described their particular divinity and the nature of His/Her/Its *modus operandi* in different terms than Judeo-Christian theologians.

Ever since Darwin, however, the prevailing and constantly developing answer from the world of traditional anthropology and DNA research held forth that modern humans, *Homo sapiens sapiens*, descended from an African woman (now appropriately nicknamed "Eve") who gave birth to the species some 200,000 years ago, probably in Ethiopia. But new discoveries are now being published that add fresh information and seem to push back the date of our birthday with disturbing frequency.

Some anthropologists are not even happy about starting with "Eve." They point to earlier species such as *Homo floresiensis* that appear to be our antecedents and wonder if our human predecessors were as primitive as we usually portray them, especially since evidence is piling up that they left behind structures and artifacts that point to quite a different kind of people than the ones described in traditional textbooks.

Others, most notably those from the Ancient Aliens school, wonder if we are the seed of beings from other planets, other dimensions, or future periods of time. As we shall soon discover, even the revered text of the Bible offers tantalizing hints about this possibility.

Still others wonder if a combination of the second two theories is most accurate, putting forth the suggestion that our earthly, biological ancestors were helped along by some judicious DNA manipulation by ancient visitors from other worlds. That view, too, is heralded by some indigenous cultures who retain memories of star people coming to Earth to aid in our development.

Archeologists generally feel most comfortable dealing with a specific group of people. "Where did they come from?" as opposed to "Where did we come from?" By that they mean, "How did a particular group of people get to where we now find their artifacts or remains?" "Who were the first Americans?" "When did the first Australians arrive on their continent?" "Who first settled the British Isles?" That sort of thing.

Charles Darwin, while not the inventor of the theory, is famous for his writings on evolution, a concept that is accepted by most scientists today to explain how human beings came to be.

It's a defining trait of science to separate, divide, and study parts rather than the whole. So the tendency to divide humans into opposing groups seems to be an ingrained habit of the ones doing the investigating. In short, the methods of scientists, while professing objectivity, instead produce a subjective result that all too often produces modern headlines about race, sex, and nationality—us against them.

Questions about differences are important and interesting, to be sure, but it is important to remember that they talk about our distinctions rather than our similarities. They separate, rather than unify. They don't go back to the very beginning of the human race, which is a starting point we must at least explore before we can even begin to question whether former civilizations may have since disappeared.

By following the so-called objective, scientific method of study by separation, archeologists can leave questions of origins to the biologists and anthropologists. They, in turn, find it convenient to retreat into their specialties and pass the burden of our beginnings on to the philosophers. And so it goes, on down the line.

Sometimes it's safer and easier to retreat into specialization.

Time's Arrow

One thing is important to remember, even though it's a very difficult concept to grasp for most of us born and raised in what is commonly called the West, meaning contemporary Europe and America. That is the concept of time.

It's very difficult for us to think in terms of time being anything other than a straight line. We speak of Time's Arrow, as the astrophysicist Arthur Eddington first called it in 1927, or the river of time. To most of us, time flows from the past through the present into the future in a straight line. We just can't escape it. That's the way our minds have been programmed. But many Native American peoples, along with folks raised in cultures commonly associated with the East who claim Buddhist, Hindu, or Shinto backgrounds, don't think in those terms. When we ask them where their people came from, they answer, "We've always been here." When we ask them, "Where have your ancestors gone?" they say, "Nowhere. They're still here."

> **B**ut cutting-edge, scientific thinking about the nature of time is changing in the West.

When confronted by answers such as these, many Westerners nod their heads in sympathy, as if in agreement, while keeping patronizing thoughts to themselves. Such thinking seems simplistic and naive to them. They may be too polite to say anything, but their feeling is usually that any other concept of time different from their own is rather primitive, perhaps even childish.

But cutting-edge, scientific thinking about the nature of time is changing in the West. Although it hasn't yet fully filtered down to laypeople, it might prove that our Western concept of time flowing from past to future is simply a very powerful illusion. It might not work that way at all. Julian Barbour, for instance, has helped make popular the idea that time consists of a series of nows, a word that simply indicates where everything in the universe happens to be at any given moment. Although it is an almost impossible concept for those of us in America and Europe to grasp and accept, given our culture, education, and language restraints consisting of past, present, and future tenses, it might be that tracing our ancestors back through time will turn out to be a futile endeavor for us, better understood by other approaches that simply shelve the whole matter as irrelevant.

If this turns out to be the case, the idea of a cyclic progression of civilization followed by cataclysm, followed by a new civilization and yet another cataclysm, on and on, might be the most fruitful way of understanding the past.

This is not a new idea, by any means. It is exactly what the classic Hindu *rishis*, wise men, taught five thousand years ago.

Where did we come from? We don't know. But what follows is a broad spectrum of theories to consider.

ANUNNAKI

You are gods, you are all sons of the Most High.

Psalm 82:6

Jesus said to them, "Is it not written in your law, 'I have said that you are gods'?"

John 10:34

Ancient Texts That Few Ever Read

In 1853, Hormuzd Rassam discovered fragments of an ancient Sumerian text which is now considered to be the first great work of literature our civilization ever produced. After its translation it was published in 1870 by George Smith. Although known by serious Mesopotamian scholars far and wide, it was generally consigned to oblivion in the popular press. As a matter of fact, it took an episode of *Star Trek: The Next Generation* to really spark any real public interest in the work. When, in the fifth season of the popular show, the second episode, titled "Darmok," called for Patrick Stuart's character to quote the lines, "He who was my companion through adventure and hardship is gone forever," people all over the world rushed to read *The Epic of Gilgamesh* to learn more about the heroes Gilgamesh, king of Uruk, and Enkidu, a wild man who was created by the gods. It was another triumph for those who trumpet the enormous impact, and resulting responsibility, of popular television shows.

Flood Parallels

Part of the reason the conspiracy of silence condemned this work to obscurity was that most college professors and students of religious history simply didn't know about it in those pre-Internet days. But there was a darker issue that, while some-

Assyrian archeologist Hormuzd Rassam discovered the tablet fragments of *The Epic of Gilgamesh.*

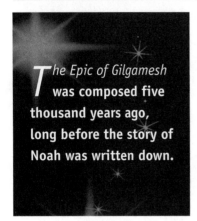

The Epic of Gilgamesh was composed five thousand years ago, long before the story of Noah was written down.

times brought up in seminaries or ministerial study sessions, few mentioned in public. *The Epic of Gilgamesh* told the story of a great worldwide flood that destroyed most of humanity. The only survivors were a god-fearing family led by a patriarch named Utnapishtim. They managed to ride out the deluge by building a boat. That sounds suspiciously like the biblical story of Noah and the Ark.

Here's the problem: *The Epic of Gilgamesh* was composed five thousand years ago, long before the story of Noah was written down. And although they were very similar in some respects, they differed in others. That cast doubt on a sacred text of Jews, Christians, and Muslims, many of whom would not have been happy to discover that their beloved bible story was simply a copy of an earlier record.

The issue was recently addressed by Frank Lorey, a creationist scholar, in an article written for the Institute for Creation Research:

> *The Epic of Gilgamesh* has been of interest to Christians ever since its discovery in the mid-nineteenth century in the ruins of the great library at Nineveh, with its account of a universal flood with significant parallels to the Flood of Noah's Ark. The rest of the *Epic*, which dates back to possibly the third millennium B.C., contains little of value for Christians, since it concerns typical polytheistic myths associated with the pagan peoples of the time.
>
> (http://www.icr.org/article/noah-flood-gilgamesh/)

In other words, because the text, aside from the flood narrative, contains "polytheistic myths associated with pagans," why offer conflicting literary options when you are fighting for the souls of your neighborhood congregation? After all, if they start to distrust Noah and the flood, what sacred myth might fall next? Will they start to doubt the crucifixion accounts (which, by the way, were preceded by Egyptian stories), or even the Christmas story (which arose shortly after a similar Mithraic version)? Far better to simply pick and choose what fits best into your preconceived doctrine, ignore the rest, and let the conspiracy of silence hold sway.

As a result, when the problem was brought up at Bible study by the few congregants who read outside the lines of established and approved lists, the easiest way to handle it was with scorn.

Haven't you read Matthew 24:39? Listen to the words of Jesus:"

"As it was in the days of Noah, so it will be at the coming of the Son of Man. For in the days before the flood, people were eating and drinking, marrying and giving in marriage, up to the day Noah entered the ark; they knew nothing about what would happen until the flood came and took them all away."

Obviously Jesus believed in Noah's flood. He must have known more than a few liberal archeologists who are trying to undermine your faith! Are you going to believe them or Jesus? *Gilgamesh* is probably a Satanic counterfeit. End of discussion!

Judges of Hell

The Epic of Gilgamesh also contained a hidden time bomb that wouldn't explode until more than 150 years had passed. It told of seven "judges of hell" who set the land aflame in advance of the great flood. They were called Anunnaki.

This clay tablet containing text from *The Epic of Gilgamesh* is preserved at the British Museum.

In 1849, four years before the *Gilgamesh* discovery, Austen Henry Layard had discovered, hidden away in the Library of Ashurbanipal in what is now Mosul, Iraq, fragments of a 3,800-year-old manuscript containing a Babylonian creation epic called *Enuma Elish*. Twenty-seven years later it was published by the same George Smith who published *The Epic of Gilgamesh*. It told the story of the god Marduk (also called Nibiru), who created humans as a slave race in order to serve the gods. To oversee this workforce he created a team of six hundred Watchers or Holy Ones, also called Anunnaki, three hundred of whom served in heaven and three hundred on Earth. Marduk was the son of the god named either Enki or Ea, the "God of the Waters."

This made the case of the Anunnaki more confusing. Were there seven or six hundred? Some versions even featured fifty or nine hundred! And what exactly did they do?

Is it any wonder that the conspiracy of silence found it easier to hold the whole issue at length and declare it to be simply an ancient myth with no basis in historical fact? That was, and still is, the primary position of most scholars of early mythology. Anunnaki, we are told, is simply a generic term meaning "gods (angels) of heaven and Earth." There is no need to take it to extremes.

The Anunnaki were even officially baptized and embraced by Christians when the publication of a now well-known hymn, "Ye Watchers and Ye Holy Ones," written by Athelstan Riley, placed them right in the heavenly choir alongside seraphs and cherubim. This hymn is found in almost every denomination's hymnbook, even though most Christians don't realize they are honoring the Anunnaki of the *Enuma Elish* when they sing it.

Enter the Aliens

That is probably where the whole matter would have stayed were it not for the work of the late Zecharia Sitchin. He insisted that the name Anunnaki didn't mean "gods of heaven and Earth." He said it was better translated, "those who from heaven to Earth came." He even located their home world on a planet named Nibiru, which he claimed comes within traveling distance of Earth from time to time as it follows its long orbital path through the heavens. (Nibiru, remember, was another name for the god Marduk.) The inhabitants of Nibiru, he wrote, were having trouble with their atmosphere and needed to seed it with gold in order to save themselves. Our planet had plenty of gold to spare, but in order to mine it the Nibirueans needed a slave race. Thus, with a little genetic manipulation, the human race came into existence, coaxed from existing life forms by tweaking their DNA.

This story took on added significance in January 2016. Scientists discovered evidence of a new, massive planet in our solar system, orbiting our sun out beyond Pluto. Pluto had, a few years earlier, been downsized to dwarf-planet status, much to the dismay of many who had memorized the planets in their order and found it disconcerting that a small group of astronomers could arbitrarily disrupt our whole idea of the solar system. Although as of January they had not yet physically observed the planet, by computing the number of objects around it (possible moons that it had captured with its gravitational pull), scientists knew it must be big. It certainly seemed as though it was a worthy candidate to replace Pluto as our ninth planet.

Because it exists way out beyond the Goldilocks Zone, an area neither too hot nor too cold to support life, it certainly doesn't seem to be a suitable candidate for the mythical planet Nibiru. But the fact that it's there, has remained hidden for all these years, is mysterious, and that it seems to be a long way off, but possibly coming closer, is certainly bound to set off some speculation, especially

The Russian-born author Zecharia Sitchin averred that humans were descended from ancient aliens.

because there are those who trace the entire Ancient Aliens theory back to that simple translation—Anunnaki: those who from heaven to Earth came.

Has their home planet finally showed itself on our radar screen? Only time will tell.

The Ancient Alien theory may have been popularized by Erich von Däniken (*Chariots of the Gods*), but Sitchin was "The Main Man!" First of all, he was a scholar, albeit one who operated outside his field of training. He was one of a small handful of people who could actually read Sumerian, so it was assumed by his followers that he could be trusted when it came to translations of esoteric texts.

> The Ancient Alien theory may have been popularized by Erich von Däniken (*Chariots of the Gods*), but Sitchin was "The Main Man!"

While Däniken was ridiculed and blasted by a conservative establishment when he dared to suggest that we may have been visited by ancient aliens, including the Anunnaki, Sitchin was given a bit more credence. But his book, *Genesis Revisited*, which sought to shed light on ancient mythology and the profusion of megalithic ruins scattered around the globe, never quite caught on like Däniken's, so he could be more easily ignored.

With the advent of the History Channel, things changed. Ancient aliens became a household phrase. Although neither Sitchin nor Däniken coined the phrase Ancient Alien theory, it, along with the name Anunnaki, is now well known.

In short, the theory proposes that mythical gods and goddesses were not simply made-up beings or figments of the fertile imaginations of an ancient priestly class. Instead, they were physical kings and rulers from other planets, dimensions or time zones, elevated to the status of gods after centuries of myth-telling and the resultant expansion of legends and stories. Their means of travel became, of course, *Chariots of the Gods*.

But did Anunnaki come from outer space, or were they human survivors of a great cataclysm that destroyed their civilization here on Earth, as is claimed by scholars such as Andrew Collins, who traces them to ancestral Solutreans, a very earthbound human culture who survived the great cataclysm of the Younger Dryas Event?

It is difficult to ignore the texts. Even the ancient religious literature seems to take them very literally. Take this passage, for instance, from the beloved book of Genesis:

> When men began to increase in number on the earth, the sons of God saw that the daughters of men were beautiful, and they married any of them they chose…. The Nephilim (some translations use the word "Giants") were on the earth in those days—and

also afterward—when the sons of God went to the daughters of men and had children by them. They were the heroes of old, men of renown. The Lord saw how great man's wickedness on the earth had become, and that every inclination of the thoughts of his heart was only evil all the time. The Lord God was grieved that he had made man on the earth, and his heart was filled with pain. So the Lord said, I will wipe mankind, whom I have created, from the face of the earth.

Genesis 6:1–7)

Who were these "Nephilim," fathered by the mysterious sons of God? Were they the Anunnaki, the "heroes of old, men of renown?" The Old Testament text comes from roughly the same geographical location as the earlier Babylonian and Sumerian stories. Were they all related? Are they religious myths or historical legends based on fact?

We may never know for sure, but the debate goes on.

The Hopi Connection

We cannot leave this discussion without a quick trip halfway around the world to the homeland of the Hopi Indians of the American Southwest.

Read again the Hopi legend in the prologue of this book. Notice that the ancient Hopi ancestors are saved from the first and second catastrophes that overcame their world by their friends, the Ant People, who give them shelter and see them through the worst of the destruction. In Hopi, the word translated as "ant" is *anu*. The root word of "friends" is *naki*. Thus, "ant friends" can be translated "Anu-Naki," which is suspiciously close to the Sumerian Anunnaki.

Is this just coincidence? Or were the Anunnaki, the "heroes of old, the men of renown," more widespread than we have been taught?

DNA RESEARCH AND THE OUT OF AFRICA THEORY

The Multiregional Continuity Model contends that after *Homo erectus* left Africa and dispersed into other portions of the Old World, regional populations slowly evolved into modern humans…. In contrast, the Out of Africa Model asserts that modern humans evolved relatively recently in Africa, migrated into Eurasia and replaced all populations which had descended from *Homo erectus*.

www.actionbioscience.org/evolution/johanson.html

Who Are We?

First: what makes us human? Second: how did we get that way?

A full study of this topic would, and does, fill books and even libraries. Most of us soon get rather glassy-eyed when technical articles start talking about the difference between *Homo heidelbergensis* and *Neanderthalensis*, and we don't really know our *Homo sapiens* from our *Denisova hominins*. That's probably why many magazines written for public consumption usually just differentiate "Modern Humans" and leave it at that. Unfortunately, though, that leaves the impression that there are experts out there who, given enough verbiage, can answer these two questions about our origins. We trust that somebody, somewhere, has it all figured out.

That is where we make our mistake. The truth is, no one really knows. The best we can do is guess. Here's just one example.

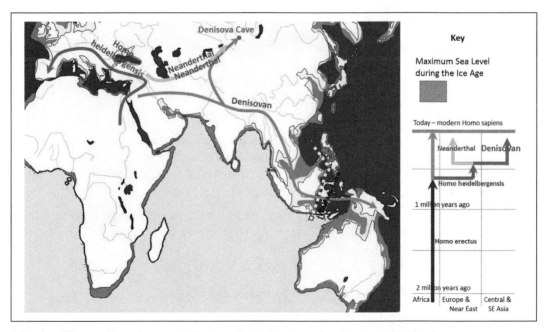

This map illustrates how the species *Denisova hominin* migrated and interacted with other hominid species (the Wallace Line is a faunal boundary line between Asia and Australia).

In March of 2010 an announcement about a discovery of a new human species from Siberia called *Denisova hominin* took the scientific community by storm. These ancient folks lived about 41,000 years ago and were contemporaries with both Neanderthals and so-called "modern" humans. As a matter of fact, bones from all three species were discovered in the same cave. Scientists were able to tease out some mitochondrial DNA samples and determined that the new species shared a common ancestor with Neanderthals and may have interbred with ancestors of modern humans. As a matter of fact, between three to five percent of Aboriginal Australians also carried their DNA and there is evidence that as long as 400,000 years ago, *Denisovans* were mating with *Homo heidelbergensis* all the way over in Spain at a time when only Neanderthals were thought to have lived there.

The world of anthropology was thrilled and magazines galore carried the news.

But how much evidence had archeologists uncovered to deduce this earthshaking find? One finger bone!

Let's not disparage the science of anthropological DNA studies. It produces amazing results. But one finger bone does not exactly a fully packed theory make. The headlines, easily read and digested, looked great. "NEW ANCESTRAL HUMAN SPECIES!" But it's not a very convincing hypothesis once we dig in, read the small print and uncover what a miniscule sample they're getting excited about.

This story took a new twist in November of 2015, when Carl Zimmer, writing an article for *The New York Times*, ("In a tooth, DNA from some very old cousins, the *Denisovans*") revealed that new DNA evidence, discovered in a tooth found in a Siberian cave, pushed back the accepted dates another sixty thousand years. Now we have both a finger bone and a tooth.

To quote Todd Disotell, a molecular anthropologist at New York University, "our species kept company with many near relatives over the past million years. The world was a lot like Middle Earth. There you've got elves and dwarves and hobbits and orcs." He continued that on the real Earth "we had a ton of hominins that are closely related to us."

A tooth and a finger bone, and now we've got Middle Earth revisited. Obviously, there is a lot more work to do before we set our ancient ancestors' history in doctrinal stone.

Mitochondrial Eve

Human genetics is a fascinating science. Accepted current research suggests that every human being on Earth is descended in an unbroken line, traced through our mothers in a genetic system called matrilineal descent, from one woman who lived in western Africa some 200,000 years ago. She was given the rather catchy nickname, "Mitochondrial Eve," named after her biblical counterpart. Unlike her counterpart, however, no one suggests that she was the only woman who lived at the time. The human population numbered in the tens of thousands back then. Other women alive at the time no doubt passed on their lineage to people living today who carry their genes. But at some point in the long human history since then, each of their lines of descent failed to generate a reproducing female, thus breaking the mitochondrial line. In order for the genes carrying this mitochondrial material to continue into the future, the offspring of these women had to, at some point, mate with the descendants of Mitochondrial Eve, the African matriarch of us all. Mutations have occurred, obviously. We share different color skin and eyes, for instance. But according to the Out of Africa theory, every person alive on planet Earth today is, in one sense, African beneath the surface.

> The offspring of these women had to, at some point, mate with the descendants of Mitochondrial Eve, the African matriarch of us all.

(There is a parallel line traced through the male Y-chromosome back to a man named Y-Chromosome Adam who lived at a time estimated anywhere from 120,000 to 156,000 years ago. But probably the only people still with me here are anthropology nerds.)

All this biological talk, however, still doesn't answer our two questions. What makes us human, and how did we get that way?

Is the answer to be found in our biology or our physical actions? In other words, are we human because of what we are or what we do?

Theories Abound

If we became human when we started to walk upright, then it can be said that our transition from ape to human took place some six million years ago. But if we became human when ancient upright walkers started to have legs mechanically similar to ours, then, according to Smithsonian studies, that would make us some three million years old.

If we became human when we tamed and utilized fire, we are about 350,000 years old.

If we became human when we started to bury our dead with grave implements, signifying religious thought or a belief in an afterlife, then we are about 100,000 years old as a species. If we search out the very earliest example of symbolic thought, meaning cave paintings and rock art, it was only about 40,000 years ago when we began to hit our stride.

So what makes us human, and how did we get that way? It depends entirely on who is asking the questions.

The interesting thing is this. Recent discoveries always seem to push the dates back further in time. Anthropologists today think our species is much older than did their counterparts of a hundred years ago, or fifty years ago, or even twenty years ago.

What that implies is that if we were sitting, perhaps even dancing, around a fire in the Middle East at least 350,000 years ago, if we were building boats and making voyages across large expanses of water 130,000 years ago, if we were using tools and depositing them all over the world at least 100,000 years ago, we have had plenty of time to develop cultures that are now lost to history. We are an amazing species! What might those lost cultures, perhaps even whole civilizations, have been able to teach us?

ELONGATED SKULLS FROM AROUND THE WORLD

Many of you may remember the old *Saturday Night Live* routine with Dan Aykroyd and gang as the strange family of "Coneheads." … As funny and bizarre as [they may have] appeared … such "coneheads" did, and do, exist! In fact, the remains of "coneheads" of various shapes and sizes have been found all over the world, from Peru and Mexico and the Pacific Northwest to ancient Egypt and China and beyond.

David Childress and Brien Foerster in
The Enigma of Cranial Deformation

An Ancient Mystery

From ancient Sumer and Egypt, from the land of the Mayans and Incas, from the Bahamas and Australia, from "Russia's Stonehenge" in the Ukraine, dating back some three thousand years, comes the evidence of a practice called Cranial Deformation.

It was first mentioned by Hippocrates some 2,400 years ago and seems to involve the practice of deliberately binding the heads of infants with boards and ropes so that they grow into what can only be described as elongated skulls. Surprisingly, it was a fairly common practice. Even Native American tribes such as the Choctaw flattened the heads of some of their infants in this way. (Although, curiously, the "Flathead" Indians didn't.)

The practice probably spread throughout Europe with the advancement of the Huns. The folks they dominated might have wanted to emulate their new rulers, and the Huns apparently picked up the practice from the Alan people of Turkey. If that was the case, the idea might have been to project children into some kind of upper class social strata.

Still, it seems somewhat bizarre for parents to deliberately disfigure their children in this way, so the temptation to wonder if archeologists are missing something is strong. It only grows when we learn that some fetus remains are found with this condition, obviously long before any outside parental pressure could have been applied.

So what's going on? Is this simply a custom totally foreign to us moderns and thus outside our ability to understand? Or is there something else mysteriously at work?

The Paracas Skulls

The Paracas people of Peru lived in the area now made famous by the Nazca Lines. They were the first, as a matter of fact, to carve lines into the Nazca plateau. For a thousand years they plied their trade in this hot, dry climate until they were defeated by the vigorous Nazca people who absorbed their culture and customs.

In 1928, the elongated Paracas Skulls were discovered in Peru by Julio Tello. They sat on a shelf, considered merely an oddity, until Brien Foerster decided to do a little digging. The results of his research were unveiled in 2012 in a book co-written with David Childress, called *The Enigma of Cranial Deformation: Elongated Skulls of the Ancients* In it he claimed to have sponsored DNA testing which revealed that the skulls belonged to a species completely divorced from any human antecedent. The researcher who did the testing even questioned whether or not the former owners of the skulls could have reproduced with humans at all. Because the skulls were found in the same general area as the famous Nazca Lines, and because Foerster's research was co-authored with David Childress of ancient astronauts fame, the idea quickly spread that the skulls consisted of an alien species. This immediately opened up the possibility that other mysterious elongated skulls from around the world were also the result of alien contact.

But then some nagging questions began to surface. Foerster would not reveal

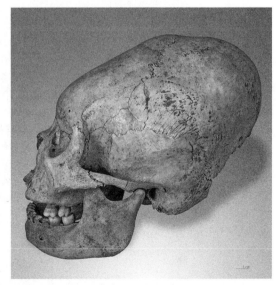

This preserved skull dating from 200 to 100 B.C.E. was found in Peru and is an example of the culture there deliberately changing the shape of a person's head.

what DNA lab had done the testing. He claimed that the researcher wanted to remain silent until more results were in. The museum that Foerster worked for was said to be a "front" for his day job, described on his website as leading "Hidden Inca Tours: Exploring Ancient Peru & Beyond."

It seemed suspicious to reviewers that he and Childress would publish a book with such groundbreaking claims without first submitting their research to at least some peer review, especially because, given Childress's success on the *Ancient Aliens* television show and his need to fill up more and more time slots with more and more ancient alien speculations, the eyes of the commercial world would be on them both.

Despite all this negative publicity, mostly on the Internet and some rather spectacular TV shows, there are those who believe elongated skulls are proof that ancient aliens visited Earth in the past and disappeared after doing whatever task they had come to do. Others wonder if our early human ancestors were somehow moved to imitate or copy the physical characteristics of those aliens who they considered to be gods. Still others, with no real evidence at all, simply believe that, for whatever bizarre reasons, humans somehow decided it would be cute to change the appearance of their offspring. And some believe that an elongated head is a genetic anomaly that appears in some human children.

Whatever the answers may someday prove to be, the questions are profound. Why? And when? And how? Are they the definitive evidence of alien influence on a forgotten human civilization? We may never know.

Homo Aquaticus

My thesis is that a branch of primitive ape-stock was forced by competition from life in the trees to feed on the sea-shores and to hunt for food, shell fish, sea-urchins etc., in the shallow waters off the coast. I suppose that they were forced into the water just as we have seen happen in so many other groups of terrestrial animals. I am imagining this happening in the warmer parts of the world, in the tropical seas where Man could stand being in the water for relatively long periods, that is, several hours at a stretch.

Sir Allister Clavering Hardy in *New Scientist*, March 17, 1960

Our Aquatic Past?

Any search for lost histories and hidden truths, as well as any examination of a conspiracy of silence, has to include a look at *Homo aquaticus*, or the

Aquatic Ape hypothesis. It's a controversial theory that vividly demonstrates all three.

The story begins with the man generally acknowledged to be the world's first scientist and the father of evolutionary theory, the sixth century B.C.E. pre-Socratic Greek, Anaximander of Miletus. As far as we know, he was the first to take a non-mythic approach to human origins. Anaximander thought that humans must have developed in the sea, evolving from aquatic, primitive life forms. His ideas held sway until the fall of classical Greek civilization and were eventually superseded, after a long period in which creation by divine fiat was the only accepted theory in Europe and America, until the publication of Darwin's *The Descent of Man* opened up the evolutionary argument again.

There were gaps in Darwin's theory, of course, but his general ideas were unequivocally accepted by a large portion of the scientific establishment until 1926. That was the year Dr. Max Westenhöfer delivered a paper at the Anthropological Congress at Salzburg, Austria. Dr. Westenhöfer was disturbed about some of Darwin's generalities that he felt overlooked some very important details about human physiology.

Why didn't the human sense of smell develop along the lines of other mammals when they relocated from the trees to the ground? Why do we, alone among the primates, cry salt tears? Such developments would have been a disadvantage, not an advantage. Why do human embryos develop what amounts to gills while they are still in the womb? A few babies in every generation are even born with them. Babies don't breathe air until they are born. So what's the evolutionary advantage of gills in the womb? For that matter, why do babies develop webs between their fingers and toes? They don't need them. It's not like they are swimming before birth, even though they do develop quickly to an aquatic environment and respond with elementary swimming strokes if they are immersed in water soon enough. What's the advantage of standing upright on the savannah? It's true that you can see better. But you can also be spotted more easily by prey.

German biologist and pathologist Dr. Max Westenhöfer believed that biological and physiological aspects of human beings bore evidence of a recent aquatic past.

These and many other questions caused him to wonder if humans had entertained an aquatic interval sometime in their evolutionary past. Whales and dolphins were land creatures before they returned to the sea. Westenhöfer asked if a similar thing could have happened to us. "Primitive, surviving features from an aquatic phase," he wrote in his paper, "are preserved in man's anatomy today. The postulate of an aquatic mode of life during an early stage of human evolution is a tenable hypothesis, for which further inquiry may produce additional supporting evidence."

His book *Der Eigenweg des Menschen* (*The Singular Way to Mankind*) was received quite favorably, and might have had more of an impact were it not for the interruption of World War II. But after his death his research was picked up and amplified by Sir Alister Clavering Hardy, whose thesis is quoted at the beginning of this entry. Sir Hardy was a respected professor of zoology and natural history. Even still, he waited until he was safely retired before he published his findings. "It is in the gap of some ten million years or so, between *Proconsul* (an 18-million-year-old fossil thought to have been an ancestor of apes and humans) and *Australopithecus* (a progenitor of the *Homo* species) that I suppose Man to have been cradled in the sea."

Breaking the Conspiracy of Silence

Hardy wrote for scientists. His work, scorned by some and cautiously considered by others, probably would have died on the public vine were it not for a popular book written in 1982 by Elaine Morgan called *The Aquatic Ape Hypothesis*. This was the book, still in print and readily accessible, that moved the aquatic ape theory onto the public radar. Only *The Naked Ape*, written by Desmond Morris in 1967, attracted the kind of attention Morgan received. Morris, speaking about our early ancestors, had written, "At this point the zoologist is forced to the conclusion that either he is dealing with a burrowing or an aquatic mammal, or there is something very odd about the evolutionary history of the naked ape." But the implication of his words hadn't really resonated with the public.

Elaine Morgan changed all that. In her carefully reasoned but very readable book, she brought out into the open facts that anthropologists found challenging—facts they simply buried deep in the pages of technical literature or otherwise condemned to the conspiracy of silence. She shed the light of public scrutiny on otherwise ignored questions concerning the since-discredited but then-accepted Savannah theory. That was the theory that claimed our upright walking posture arose from the fact that when we left the trees and moved out on the Savannah, we needed to see above the grasses.

If that was the case, she asked, why were all of the 3.5-million-year-old fossils, including our famous ancestor Lucy (named after the Beatles song that was playing in camp the day she was discovered), found to inhabit areas which were then flooded? Why did Lucy's last supper, given the fossils discovered with her body, undoubtedly consist of sea food? Why did all the experts know about this but refuse to talk about it?

She offered many more detailed and embarrassing questions, of course, to the point which Daniel Dennett, in his book *Darwin's Dangerous Idea*, was forced to offer this admission:

> During the last few years, when I have found myself in the company of distinguished biologists, evolutionary theorists, paleoanthropologists and other experts, I have often asked them to tell me, please, exactly why Elaine Morgan must be wrong about the aquatic theory. I haven't yet had a reply worth mentioning, aside from those who admit, with a twinkle in their eyes, that they have wondered the same thing.

Thus the conspiracy of silence again rears its ugly head, aided and abetted by the very experts who carry the responsibility of enlightening us and moving forward our search for knowledge about who we are.

The Hypothesis Hits the Airwaves

It's possible, though, that even Morgan's The Aquatic Ape Hypothesis might not have achieved the success it did were the theory not taken up by none other than television's The Animal Planet network (*Mermaid: The Body Found* [2012] and *Mermaids: The New Evidence* [2013]). These shows (The Harry Potter and Little Mermaid movies probably didn't hurt, either!) not only postulated a branch of human ancestry originating from the sea, but went on to offer alleged visual proof that remnants of this early species stayed in the sea and never returned. Although the network has since described these episodes as entertaining but fake documentaries, they still run from time to time, along with their conspiracy claims that "government officials" associated with the US Navy know about it, but are covering up the evidence for reasons known only to them, probably having to do with the fact that their sonar scans, enacted for public safety, are reaping havoc upon an unknown species.

Jerome Clark, in his book *Unexplained!*, devotes a whole chapter to published reports from contemporary sightings as well as those recorded by no less a luminary than Christopher Columbus, and many more dating back hundreds of years.

What this means is that conspiracy theorists now have a new playground. They can accuse the government of covering up evidence of our aquatic cousins as well as

What this means is that conspiracy theorists now have a new playground. They can accuse the government of covering up evidence of our aquatic cousins as well as alien visitors.

alien visitors. "Could it be," they ask, "that when the world was inundated by water as a result of floods of historic proportions, a heretofore unknown human species was able to flourish, only to be wiped out in our day by technology that pollutes, theatens, and otherwise destroys what could be a whole new (or perhaps "old") previous civilization?"

Talk such as this, of course, prompted a new wave of Internet scorn from the life-science community. Elaine Morgan was ridiculed, but still perseveres. Animal Planet's TV series about merbeings has been vilified by supposed experts. But still, most of the arguments about the whole idea of an aquatic phase in human evolution, once taken quite seriously by those who listened to men such as Westenhöfer and Hardy, have been largely ignored.

The scorn seems to be subjective, rather than objective. There are some very well-respected scholars who still refuse to close the door on the subject, but most of the objections are more along the lines of, "Why go on TV? Why not offer peer-reviewed papers?" In other words, "Please run it by us first before you go public."

Unexplained Mythology

All in all, thanks to a commercial media set apart from the shackles of academically controlled financial influence, and thus able to do an end-run around the conspiracy of silence, the whole idea of an aquatic chapter being part of our evolutionary story remains a highly controversial topic that seems to be far from going away any time soon, especially when you consider the implications of mythology from around the world, backed up by pictures and statues of beings that seem to be half human, half fish.

Consider, for instance, the mysterious ruins at Tiahuanaco in western Bolivia. There stands an enigmatic statue of a figure who seems to be garbed in the scales of a fish. Graham Hancock, writing in *Fingerprints of the Gods*, comments that:

An illustration (published in a 1906 Russian book) of Oannes, a half-fish figure from Mesopotamian mythology.

I had learned of one local tradition I thought might shed light on the matter. It was very ancient and spoke of the 'gods of the lake, with fish tails, called Chullua and Umantua.' In this, and in the fish-garbed figures, it seemed that there was a curious out-of-place echo of Mesopotamian myths, which spoke strangely, and at length, about amphibious beings, 'endowed with reason,' who had visited the land of Sumer in remote prehistory. The leader of these beings was named Oannes.

According to *The Sirius Mystery*, by Robert Temple, Oannes cut quite a figure:

> [His] whole body was like a fish; and had under a fish's head another head, and also feet below, similar to those of a man, sub-joined to the fish's tail. His voice, too, was articulate and human; and a representation of him is preserved even to this day.... When the sun set, it was the custom of this Being to plunge into the sea, and abide all night in the deep; for he was amphibious.

How do cultures all over the world come up with this stuff? Where did they get the idea? How is it that both Bolivian and Mesopotamian craftsmen sculpt the same images?

Did they share a common memory? Are they portraying a common story? Is there more here than meets the eye?

PANSPERMIA AND THE MANY WORLDS THEORY

A funny thing happened recently on the way to Mars. A few days after the successful launch of NASA's behemoth Curiosity rover with its Mars Science Laboratory instruments on November 26th 2011, a somewhat muted piece of news came out admitting that the strict biological planetary protection rules had not been adhered to quite as everyone expected. What this meant in practical terms was that the rover's drill bits were not sealed up for launch with quite the same protocols for sterility as everyone had expected. Thus there is an added possibility that alien invaders from Earth are heading for Mars.

Caleb A. Scharf in
"Astrobiology: We Are the Aliens," *Scientific American*

Any speculation about how life ultimately began has to include two theories, both of which are currently hot topics of discussion in the science community. The first concerns the origin of life on Earth. The second, how life began at all in a young universe of unimaginable chaos and violence. Both speak to the theme of this book.

Let's take them one at a time, beginning right here on our home planet.

Panspermia

There are only two ways life could have begun on Earth. Either it originated here or it was brought here.

Most scientists who study such things operate on the assumption that somehow, someway, something happened right here on Earth that managed to work the magic. It must have been part of a universal process, eventually understandable to science, built into the very fabric of the cosmos, thus capable of repeating itself on planet after planet throughout the universe.

There are current theories, of course, that attempt to explain it. But the simple truth is that no one really knows how it came to pass that, one day, inorganic material suddenly developed the capacity to manufacture reproducing cells complete with DNA that could guide the course of evolution. Although there have been many experiments that seek to unlock the mystery of life, we just don't have any clear, definitive explanation yet.

So the easiest way, or perhaps we should say the most comfortable way, to explain our ultimate origins is to theorize that life here was seeded from life out there. In other words, cellular life developed somewhere, somehow in the universe and was then brought here on some interplanetary transport, be it comet, asteroid, or even space dust. Once it arrived on a suitable planet, full of all the right building blocks that could nurture and sustain its existence, it began to flourish, evolving from single cells to what we see all around us today.

This theory is called Panspermia, meaning "seeds everywhere." Probably the first to think along these lines was Anaxagoras, a Greek contemporary of Socrates. But Aristotle, part of the same crowd, disagreed. He thought life came about by a process he called "spontaneous generation." Science sided with Aristotle for more than two thousand years, until Louis Pasteur performed an experiment in 1864 that proved Aristotle and everyone else had been wrong for all this time. Although a few diehards tried to hold on by saying life had begun on Earth spontaneously one time by accident before settling down into an observable process, they couldn't save the theory. It died a quick death even though there were no other ideas around that could better explain the problem.

So what to do? Where and how had life come from non-life?

There is always the religious hypothesis, of course. "God did it and that settles it!" But science is understandably reluctant to go there.

So the path of least resistance seems to involve kicking the can down the road, or at least off the planet. In other words, we may not know how life developed out there, but we can guess how it came to be here. Life arrived on an interplanetary visitor that collided with Earth in the distant past after surviving a long journey during which it lay dormant, awaiting a good environment. The theory works because it seems a logical, safe way to explain things. After all, no one was around billions of years ago to check it out. So why not?

That's a good middle-of-the-road theory halfway between "God did it" and "ancient aliens produced it," or some such thing. It's feasible and it works. It seemingly solves the problem of life on our planet in the same way anthropologists solve the problem of how a particular continent became home to a particular group of people. "We're not going to discuss human origins in general," they say. "We're just going to talk about how humans got *here*."

This leads to another fascinating thought. What if DNA-carrying bacteria were deliberately sent here? What if an ancient civilization faced extinction because of, for instance, its star going nova or another cosmic catastrophe? Such a scenario is usually confined to the sci-fi genre, such as a famous *Star Trek: The Next Generation* episode ("The Inner Light") wherein Captain Jean-Luc Picard finds himself living an earlier, parallel life on a planet that is about to be destroyed. The inhabitants send out a "message in a bottle" to whomever might come across it so that they won't be forgotten.

> What if DNA-carrying bacteria were deliberately sent here? What if an ancient civilization faced extinction due to, for instance, its star going nova or another cosmic catastrophe?

A surprising number of scientists are willing to consider such a thing. They reason that our so-called "junk DNA," the 97% of DNA that we can't figure out, really contains coded messages that tell us who we are and why we are here. In other words, we are the aliens.

If this turns out to be true, it's no different than that of a cosmic Atlantis scenario that we will soon be considering, wherein a civilization here on Earth is destroyed, leaving the survivors to spread the seed of their lost culture throughout the world.

All this is fun, but it doesn't really solve the primary question. How did life begin?

Quantum Theory

Another way to approach the problem is to delve into the wacky, wonderful world of quantum physics. This gets tricky and takes us into some pretty speculative philosophical territory, so hold on to your hats.

In all of quantum theory there is one concept that has probably generated more public familiarity than any other. That involves a now-famous and fully accepted concept involving waves and particles.

Light, for instance, turns out to be a fascinating thing. According to physicists, it is both a wave and a particle—at the same time. It's not that sometimes it's a wave and sometimes it's a particle. It's not even that it turns into one or the other. It is both a wave *and* a particle at the same time, and the only thing that determines which you're going to see when you look at it is what mood you happen to be in and what equipment you are using. If you look for a wave, you're going to find that light is a wave. If you look for a particle, you're going to find a particle. If you want to determine light's position in space and time, you're going to find a particle. But if you look for light's possible manifestations, its probability quotient, you're going to find a wave. As a matter of fact, if you don't look for it at all, it won't be there until you do.

That's right. As strange as it may seem, light exists only in potential until you decide to look. Then it appears in the form you are looking for.

Weird, huh?

I won't go into all the particulars because I have seen too many eyes turn glassy at seminars in which I did just that. If you want to know more, check out the Copenhagen interpretation of quantum theory. You'll find enough material to keep you busy for a lifetime. That's the world of quantum reality.

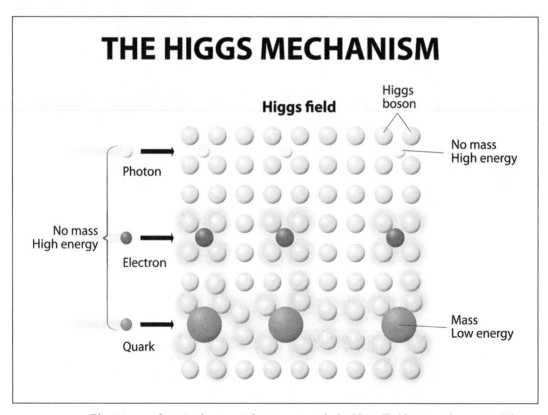

THE HIGGS MECHANISM

Higgs field

Higgs boson

No mass
High energy

Photon

No mass
High energy

Electron

Mass
Low energy

Quark

Physicists are learning how particles interact with the Higgs Field, giving them mass. The more particles interact with the Higgs boson, the more mass they obtain.

But to make a long story short, this process of seek and ye shall find results in a wave of energy collapsing through the newly discovered Higgs Field into material particles with mass. Energy enters into our material existence, our world, so to speak, and forms physical mass. The official title for this is wave function collapse.

Before physicists came to understand all this, they thought that reality consisted of a story unfolding in a single, uniform manner. What happened, happened. What we see is what there is. There is only one reality, and we're living in it.

But with the philosophical concept of wave function collapse, all that changed. Instead of there being only one reality—ours—it now appeared, backed up by the mathematical computations of physicists, that what we experience as reality is an illusion—that there are, in fact, many realities. We see what we see because we are part of the reality in which we live. When we observe the material world around us we are, by the very act of observing, collapsing the wave function into our physical environment. It looks the way it does because that's the way we see it. Physicists refer to it as a subjective appearance of wave collapse rather than an objective reality.

But somehow, hidden from our view in parallel universes, there are other ways of seeing it. There are other waves collapsing into other realities.

The Many Worlds Theory

This brings us to a concept that is very difficult to imagine even though it mathematically seems to be possible, perhaps even probable, whether or not we choose to believe in it. It's called the Many Worlds theory. What this theory says is that, according to quantum physics, every possible outcome of subjective reality occurs. Every possible world is created. In an infinite number of worlds and an infinite number of universes, an infinite number of people who all think they are "you" observe the particular universe they inhabit and think it's the only physical reality possible.

So why is there life in our universe? Because we happen to inhabit one of an infinite number of universes in which life was formed as part of the wave function collapse which produced this particular environment.

In other words, everything, including the creation of life, that could possibly happen, everywhere and anywhere, has indeed happened somewhere. But because we, as observers, only see it from our small, physical perspective, we think this is the sum total of everything. We call it reality. But it is only one of an infinite number of realities. They all exist. They are all real.

Think about the implications! Everything we think we missed out on in life did, in fact, occur. Some other "you" did it, and probably regrets missing out on things that you did but he or she didn't. There are universes in which life never began at all. And there are universes where it did, but evolved in a totally different way. All we know is our own, so we feel a subjective experience of uniqueness.

Hugh Everett III, back in 1957, was the first to speculate seriously about all this. Bryce DeWitt gave it the Many Worlds name and popularized it throughout the '60s and '70s. It was soon given an official title, "decoherence," and although there are many different variations on wave collapse theories, the general parameters of it are now considered mainstream, even if physicists will argue interminably about what the term means.

Avoiding the Issues

As interesting as theories such as these are, they still avoid the main issue. It sounds intellectually satisfying, even though a bit circular, to say that life originated in this universe because we exist in a universe in which it did. But, in the long run, that's really not much different from declaring that, "In the beginning, God created the heavens and the earth." Both are faith statements. One declares a belief in physics, the other a belief in a supreme being. We are faced with the prospect of two ardent believers, the scientist and the religionist, standing across a great divide and shouting affirmations at one another.

The reason we include this discussion in a book that seeks to explore lost histories and hidden truths is this: There are a great many things in this world that we simply cannot explain. There are a great many possibilities that we may never realize. There are a great many experiences we have never had.

> If there is any possibility, no matter how remote, that the universe is somehow conscious and living a material life through our evolution, that is, through us and our physical experience?

Or have we? Is there any possibility, no matter how remote, that the universe is somehow conscious and living a material life through our evolution, that is, through us and our physical experience? If there is any possibility, no matter how remote, that purpose is winding its way through time, then we have to at least consider that previous civilizations had their day in the sun, learned, to see objective reality through their own subjective lenses, and then, their time over, disappeared into oblivion and were forgotten. Perhaps that process is what is known as the search for the meaning of life.

If any of this is true, then according to some cosmic clock, ticking out the seconds of eternity, other civilizations might have lived, learned and died after depositing their experience in the memory banks of some cosmic computer. Maybe, just maybe, we will join them someday. But before we do, maybe we can learn to access their experiences. That would certainly be an evolutionary leap forward!

SEAFARERS OF OLD

We're just going to have to accept that, as soon as hominids left Africa, they were long-distance seafarers and rapidly spread all over the place," [archeologist Thomas] Strasser says. The traditional view has been that hominids (specifically, *H. erectus*) left Africa via land routes that ran from the Middle East to Europe and Asia. Other researchers have controversially suggested that *H. erectus* navigated rafts across short stretches of sea in Indonesia around 800,000 years ago and that Neanderthals crossed the Strait of Gibraltar perhaps 60,000 years ago.

Science News, January 11, 2010

Across the Vast Oceans

In 1976, to coincide with America's bicentennial, Barry Fell, a Harvard professor of invertebrate zoology whose hobby was the study of ancient writing (epigraphy), published a book called *America B.C.: Ancient Settlers in the New World*. It was followed by two sequels, *Saga America* and *Bronze Age America*. All three books argued the same message: America was colonized early and often, and the primary way of getting there was by boat.

To say that he was ridiculed by the academic establishment would be an understatement. He was vilified in articles that attacked him personally as well as his work. The backlash consisted of one of the truly great smear campaigns in academic history. Some things that were said included "No evidence" … "Shoddy scholarship" … "Ignores peer review" … "Seeks too much publicity…." And those are just the most printable.

But Fell kept at it until his death and, if the truth were known, even after. Slowly, little by little, his work exposed mysterious oddities that experts knew about but largely ignored because the facts didn't fit the accepted party line of what had come to be known as the Clovis First theory, which is explained more fully in the chapter "Ancient Catastrophes: Topper Site of South Carolina."

Eventually the conspiracy of silence concerning America's first settlers began to unravel. Even archeologist David Kelley from the University of Calgary, best known for his work on Mayan glyphs but a fervent opponent of Fell, was forced to admit in 1990:

> Fell's work [contains] major academic sins, the three worst being distortion of data, inadequate acknowledgment of predecessors, and lack of presentation of alternative views.... I have no personal doubts that some of the inscriptions which have been reported are genuine Celtic ogham ... [but] despite my occasional harsh criticism of Fell's treatment of individual inscriptions, it should be recognized that without Fell's work there would be no [North American] ogham problem to perplex us. We need to ask not only what Fell has done wrong in his epigraphy, but also where we have gone wrong as archeologists in not recognizing such an extensive European presence in the New World.
>
> *The Review of Archeology, 1990*

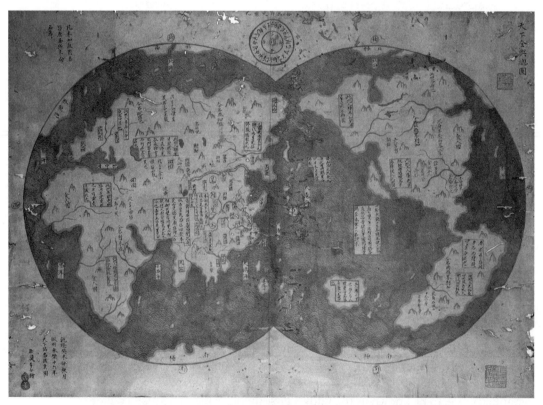

This 1763 Chinese map is reportedly a reproduction of a 1418 map from the travels of the explorer Zheng He. If real, it would mean the Chinese explored North America before Columbus arrived. The late Barry Fell argued that there were many such explorers long before the Spanish and English arrived.

Ten years later there was no more denying it. The diffusionists, those who believe cultures and civilizations spread and affect others even across vast distances, had won the fight. In the January 2000 issue of *The Atlantic* magazine, author Mark Stengel in an article titled "The Diffusionists Have Landed," was forced to admit, "You've probably heard of those crackpot theories about ancient Phoenicians or Chinese in the New World. Maybe it's time to start paying attention."

These days, with no less a prestigious archeologist than Dennis Stanford of the Smithsonian leading the charge (*Across Atlantic Ice: The Origin of America's Clovis Culture*), there is no doubt whatsoever that ancient people had boats, knew how to use them, and traversed the globe.

The question became, when and to what extent? What did they accomplish and why don't we know anything about it? Once people began to look, the answers turned out to be nothing short of amazing.

An article by Heather Pringle in the May 2008 issue of *Discover* magazine summed up the arguments nicely:

> Until recently most researchers would have dismissed such talk of Ice Age mariners and coastal migrations. Nobody, after all, has ever unearthed an Ice Age boat or happened upon a single clear depiction of an Ice Age dugout or canoe. Nor have archeologists found many coastal campsites dating back more than 15,000 years. So most scientists believed that *Homo sapiens* evolved as terrestrial hunters and gatherers and stubbornly remained so, trekking out of their African homeland by foot and spreading around the world by now-vanished land bridges. Only when the Ice Age ended 12,000 to 13,000 years ago and mammoths and other large prey vanished, archeologists theorized, did humans systematically take up seashore living—eating shellfish, devising fishing gear, and venturing offshore in small boats.
>
> But that picture … is badly flawed, due to something researchers once rarely considered: the changes in sea level over time. Some 20,000 years ago, for example, ice sheets locked up much of the world's water, lowering the oceans and laying bare vast coastal plains—attractive hunting grounds and harbors for maritime people. Today these plains lie beneath almost 400 feet of water, out of reach of all but a handful of underwater archeologists. "So this shines a spotlight on a huge area of ignorance: what people were doing when sea level was lower than at present," says Geoff Bailey, a coastal archeologist at the University of York in England. "And that is especially problematic, given that sea level was low for most of prehistory." Concerned that evidence of

human settlement and migration may be lost under the sea, researchers are finding new ways of tracking ancient mariners.

Questions

When framed as succinctly as that, the questions pile up:

- Who were those seafaring people?
- What happened to them?
- When did they live?
- How extensive was their cultural network?
- Could the old legends of Atlantis and similar stories actually have a kernel of truth to them?

Some of the answers will probably remain hidden for a long time. We may never be able to answer all of them. But a picture is emerging, given the blending of many disciplines and people who are now willing to work together to break the conspiracy of silence.

But to sum up the broader topic of seafarers of old, what archeologists have learned in the past few years, or perhaps it would be better to say that what has come into the public sphere from out of the conspiracy of silence, is that until recently much of what we have been taught about history, especially seafaring history, is, quite simply, wrong. Humanity has been going to sea for thousands of years. It is now accepted as a working hypothesis that it is possible that Europe was not settled by humans walking around the Mediterranean coastline but by Neanderthals who used rafts to cross the Strait of Gibraltar some 60,000 years ago. And chances are they weren't the first.

By studying remote islands and observing evidence from computer simulations depicting rising and lowering sea levels, it is possible to imagine voyages from Asia to the Americas that took place some 15,000 years ago, and from southern France to the Americas anywhere from 25,000 to 50,000 years ago. The short hop from Japan to Okinawa some 30,000 years ago is a distinct possibility, as well as the journey from Southeast Asia to Australia 50,000 years ago.

Perhaps Dennis Stanford was right when he said, on a number of popular TV shows, "Once you have a boat, rivers and oceans cease to become barriers. They become highways."

If these theories prove correct, it is entirely possible that our ancestors left Africa and populated the whole world as quickly as they did because they were sailors, not hikers.

> By studying remote islands and observing evidence from computer simulations depicting rising and lowering sea levels, it is possible to imagine voyages from Asia to the Americas that took place some 15,000 years ago....

Ego and the Conspiracy of Silence

Why did it take so long to seriously consider these things? Why was the archeological establishment so vocal, uncivil, and downright rude in its public attacks against those who dared to voice this alternative theory?

In a word, ego. It is just too hard for people, even professional people, to consider and identify with an experience unlike their own. For most landlubbers, a voyage across an ocean such as the North Atlantic is terrifying. And it is! It's dangerous. But the question shouldn't be, "Is it dangerous?" The question should be, "Is it possible?"

When Thor Heyerdahl theorized that Easter Island was settled by men on rafts from South America, he was ridiculed.

This is a replica of *Kon-Tiki,* the raft that Norwegian Thor Heyerdahl built to prove that people could have settled Easter Island by sailing boats from America.

"If you think it's possible to cross the Pacific on a raft, why don't you build one and try it!"

So he built *Kon-Tiki* and did just that.

When he was told reed boats from the Tigris valley couldn't cross the Atlantic, he did it. Yes, it was dangerous. It took him two tries. But he made it.

We simply don't give the Ancient Ones enough credit. Our ancestors were not dull and simple people. They were adventurous, brave, and resourceful. They were just as smart as we are. Maybe more so. They couldn't program computers, but they could undertake dangerous journeys in an Ice Age climate, surviving with only stone tools. How many computer programmers can do that?

Light in the Darkness

Theories involving ancient seafarers explain a lot.

- They explain ancient maps that curiously describe the world in much the same way as modern maps do today even though, in the case of Antarctica, the lands they depict have been covered with glacial ice caps for thousands of years, way before modern humans were thought to have been around to see them.

- They explain how humans could have traveled to remote islands using navigational techniques we can't duplicate today without highly technical equipment and skill.

- They explain how construction techniques such as pyramid and megalithic building projects can be so similar in different countries, even though they are separated by thousands of miles of oceans.

- And most important of all, they explain how humans could have survived great catastrophes, even floods of biblical proportions, and passed on knowledge that would otherwise have been lost.

One can easily imagine a seafaring culture, devastated by a worldwide calamity, sailing through the storm and arriving in places as far apart as Egypt and Peru, there to pass on to primitive survivors what they had so painstakingly learned down through the ages. Their civilization may have been destroyed, but much of its wisdom could be preserved in the language of mathematically coded building projects, awaiting a day when a civilization would arise that would be intelligent enough to interpret the ancient secrets. Why else would a boat be preserved in the deserts of the Giza Plateau? It is called the Khufu Ship and was buried at the foot of the Great Pyramid around 4,500 years ago. Its presence screams, "We were here!" After a few generations, such mysterious immigrants would probably have been remembered as ancient gods.

> One can easily imagine a seafaring culture, devastated by a worldwide calamity, sailing through the storm and arriving in places as far apart as Egypt and Peru....

Indeed, this is exactly the scenario presented in some of the most ancient texts of Egypt, the *Edfu Building Texts*, that tell the story of a group of sages who, after seeing their homeland destroyed by a ferocious flood, wandered the earth in their great ships, trying to help what we now call stone-age peoples dig out from the rubble and begin civilization anew. All this happened, according to the texts, during the Zep Tepi, the "First Time," when the ancient Egyptians believed that gods walked the earth.

Objections

To take these myths seriously, or perhaps "historically" is a better word, is to invite scorn from traditional archeologists. The objections come, one after another.

"Where is the evidence of harbors and boat building?"

Buried offshore, beneath the rising seas. As a matter of fact, in places as far apart as the Bahamas, Egypt, Malta, India, and Japan, we are now discovering them!

"Why didn't the tradition continue?"

Think of it this way. If you managed to drive your way out of a catastrophe that destroyed the known world, the people who welcomed you on the other side might admire your car. But without a lot of infrastructure, you couldn't build one yourself. You wouldn't have the resources. And besides, who is to say the tradition didn't continue, after a long and painful period of renewed startup?

"Why don't we have an oral history of all this?"

We do. They're called myths.

On and on it goes. The evidence, however, is mounting. Now that we are beginning to look in the right places and asking the right questions, who knows where it will lead?

SOLUTREAN CULTURE

It is abundantly clear that the Solutrean was highly variable through space and time.

Dennis Stanford and Bruce Bradley in *Across Atlantic Ice*

The Name and the People

From 25,000 years ago until about 16,500 years ago (some say 12,000 years ago), during the last Ice Age, an enigmatic culture called Solutrean thrived in southwestern France and northern Spain, eventually spreading farther east into Europe.

Because they wander in and out of a number of entries in this book, we will have to deal with them by doing some jumping around. To read theories about them influencing various far-flung areas following cataclysmic conditions, possibly even generating myths about ancient gods, see the entries on Anunnaki / Seafarers of Old, Topper Site of South Carolina / Younger Dryas Event, Ancient Civilizations: Göbekli Tepe.

In this entry, we will set the stage for their story by unraveling a little of their history.

Their name comes from Solutré, near Dijon, France, where their distinctive stone artifacts were first described in the systematic fashion required by contemporary archeology. For a people who figure so prominently in the human story, they have suffered from very bad publicity.

- First of all, where they came from and where they went before they disappeared is a matter of considerable debate. Some archeologists believe they evolved "on site," as it were, eventually fading from history after being absorbed into similar local cultures. Others trace their roots back into eastern Europe and even Africa before, as we shall see, attempting to follow their progress west to America and east to Turkey.

- Second, virtually all the evidence of their culture has been discovered under cliff overhangs and in caves. If they lived in caves, so the thinking goes, they must have been "cave men." And everyone knows that cavemen are big, hairy, shaggy brutes who carry clubs, wear skins, and are not very smart. That's the image that has been with us ever since "Alley Oop" was a feature in the Sunday comics of the 1930s, and Hollywood has not done much to change that impression. The pejorative phrase, "He's a Neanderthal," might even apply, because some scholars believe them to be a Neanderthal/human hybrid cross. But none of this thinking comes anywhere close to describing them.

- Third, archeologists have found hardly any open terrain settlements, no burials, and hardly any remains except for animal bones left behind at midden (refuse) sites, or domestic waste dumps, so there's really no way to build a museum display showing how they lived. It's hard to feel close to, let alone try to understand, a ghost culture such as this.

- Fourth, they were a marine people who made a good living partly by exploiting the bounty of the sea during a time when a lot of the earth's water was tied up in glaciers. Later, when the ice age began to wane and all that water returned to the oceans, the rising water no doubt drowned a lot of the evidence of their civilization, which was located near shorelines.

All that being said, what they did leave behind is nothing short of amazing.

The Stonework

The Solutreans were some of the most innovative and gifted flintknappers the world has ever known. Their stone artifacts, tools, and projectile points, a superb example of Paleolithic craft surpassed only by the American Clovis culture, which may very well have been a Solutrean-based culture, were in so much demand that prior to World War I hundreds of sites were dug out and looted, forever spoiling any possibility of recovery, let alone the means of studying them in context with their environment.

Their technique consisted of bifacial flake technology. That means that both sides of a stone flake, struck from a prepared blank, were sharpened in a serrated fashion that produced a very sharp tool, similar to a modern bread knife. There is also evidence that the Solutreans either invented or perfected a method of heat treatment used in their stone work, which employed beautiful examples of chert that went far beyond simple necessity. (According to the dictionary, chert is "a fine-grained silica-rich microcrystalline, cryptocrystalline or microfibrous sedimentary rock," which is probably more information than most of us want to know. Suffice it to say that they used it for tools, including projectile points, and it was beautifully colored and artistically fashioned.)

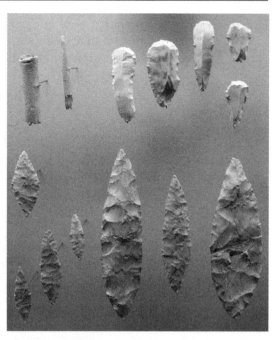

A sampling of Solutrean tools found near Loire, France, show that, for a culture some 20,000 years old, the people who made these were quite advanced.

It was no accident that when Jean Auel wrote her now-famous series of novels about this time of history, culminating in *The Shelters of Stone* in 2002 and *The Land of the Painted Caves* in 2010, she had her heroine, Ayla, hook up with Jondalar, a man of this period and place, who was a talented flintknapper. Much of the material she drew on for her novels was based on conclusions drawn from Solutrean archeological studies.

Cave Art and More

Besides their stone tool work, the Solutreans left behind some beautiful examples of rock art. From the famous Venus figurines, probably Earth Mother icons, to the murals on their cave walls, it is safe to say that Solutreans were world-class artisans. Although the most famous examples of this art came later, in the magnificent work in Lascaux and the caves of southern France and northern Spain during the time period called Magdalenian (16,500 to 13,000 years ago), the Solutreans certainly were no amateurs. Their paintings depict great auks, walrus and bearded seals, but also salmon, tuna, and deep water marine species. They obviously didn't encounter many of these species by fishing from the beach. They must have had boats in order to hunt the edges of the ice flows. That, coupled with evidence that they made ropes and were accomplished tailors, given the delicate-eyed needles they left behind, indicates they were probably a seafaring culture of accomplished sailors, familiar with both the Mediterranean and the ice flows of the North Atlantic.

If that were not enough, there is evidence suggesting that it was the Solutreans who invented the spear thrower now called the *atlatl*, and possibly even the Mediterranean version of the bow and arrow.

The End of a Culture

If this was all we knew about the Solutrean culture, these people would be interesting enough, but wouldn't warrant an entry in a book of this type. No, what earns the Solutreans their place here is what happened to them after their culture supposedly disappeared about 12,000 years ago.

Where did they go? Various experts from differing academic and scientific disciplines have contributed to the discussion and if only some of their theories are true, the Solutreans could well be the genesis of the legends concerning the gods who survived the great cataclysm of the Younger Dryas comet event and helped shape the nature of the survivors' new world.

First, though, it's important to get straight in our minds both the wonders and the pitfalls of archeology.

The Pitfalls of Archeology

When we say "The Solutrean people of Southeastern Europe," we are apt to form a mental image of unified stability that is simply not helpful. Remember that we are talking about a period of history that lasted for more than 12,000 years, more than twice as long a time as that which stands between us and the pyramids of Egypt! That's a long, long time—plenty of time for them to change and evolve. And most of what we know about these people is what we accept from experts who base their findings on what they call lithic technology. By that they mean hard evidence that consists of finding stone tools that are made in similar fashion, dating the soil in which they are found, checking their findings against similarly dated sites and then making their pronouncements.

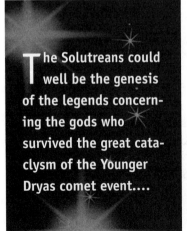

The Solutreans could well be the genesis of the legends concerning the gods who survived the great cataclysm of the Younger Dryas comet event....

We can well be in awe of archeologists and what they do. But that's pretty slim methodology.

Look at it this way. Suppose that some archeologist from 20,000 years in the future brings his grad students and volunteers to my home in South Carolina and starts a dig that eventually unearths the home of a young Civil War veteran who marched with General Lee to Gettysburg.

First of all, it is extremely improbable that they will find anything other than the rock foundation of his house. Everything else would long ago have rotted away. But suppose they do? Maybe they unearth some mementos or artifacts that help them determine what kind of life the man lived. Maybe they learn enough to deduce that the man lived in a small shack without heat or electric lights and traveled everywhere either on foot or by horseback. All this could very well be possible.

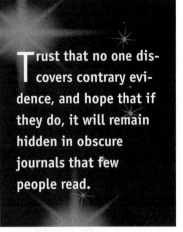

Trust that no one discovers contrary evidence, and hope that if they do, it will remain hidden in obscure journals that few people read.

But then another archeology team comes along a few years later and digs some more. They discover that this same young man died in a now fully electrified house and traveled around the countryside in a Packard Twelve automobile!

This actually happened. Technology changed drastically over the course of this young soldier's life. His lifestyle was completely altered. From the perspective of 20,000 years in the future, this might seem a miracle. Undoubtedly our two hypothetical archeologists will publish papers that are quite different from each other. Each will insist he is right. And each will be. If technology can grow, multiply exponentially, and completely change a single human life within a period of fifty or sixty years, imagine how much it can change a culture over a period of 20,000 years!

"But where is the evidence of that change?" we might ask. "Show us the particulars!"

Returning to our example, if we dig in the vicinity of our young man's South Carolina home we might find evidence of an automobile. But unless we are lucky enough to uncover a factory in Detroit and a dealership in Columbia, we won't know where it came from. For that matter, if the car finds its final resting place in a junkyard a few miles away, we won't find it at all.

Such is the plight of the science of archeology. Without written accounts, and sometimes even with them, we can never really be sure what we are discovering. And, human nature being what it is, it is all too easy for even experts to become wedded to a particular interpretation and enter into the conspiracy of silence: Trust that no one discovers contrary evidence, and hope that if they do, it will remain hidden in obscure journals that few people read.

That being said, it's time to consider the claims of those who believe the Solutreans helped shape the world that emerged after their demise.

The Solutrean Hypothesis

In 2012, Dennis Stanford and Bruce Bradley published a book called *Across Atlantic Ice: The Origin of America's Clovis Culture*. It was, as expected, immediately the subject of controversy. In this book they carefully put forth what is now called the Solutrean hypothesis. Archeologists, being the scientists that they are, depend on precise language. So here is the Solutrean hypothesis in their words:

> Who were the first Americans? The Solutrean hypothesis, in simple outline form, is that during the Last Glacial Maximum, sometime between 25,000 and 13,000 years ago, members of the Solutrean Culture in the Southwest coastal regions of Europe were led by subsistence behavior appropriate to their time and place to exploit the ice-edge environment of the polar front across the North Atlantic and colonize North America to become—after several millennia—what we know as the Clovis peoples, who eventually spread far and wide across the Americas. This does not necessarily mean that the Clovis people were the ancestors—or the only ancestors—of contemporary Native Americans, and it does not mean that Paleolithic northeast Asians did not also colonize the Americas. It does mean, in concert with other strands of evidence, that Clovis is part of the rich, complex, and wonderful story of the ebb and flow of people whose descendants are what we call Native Americans.

> Dennis J. Stanford and Bruce A. Bradley.
> *Across Atlantic Ice: The Origin of America's Clovis Culture.*

Because this is discussed in more detail in the chapter "Ancient Catastrophes: Topper Site of South Carolina," we will simply summarize their conclusions by saying that in their view, representatives of the Solutrean culture migrated west across the Atlantic, possibly becoming the first people to ever set foot on the continent. There they settled for thousands of years, spreading out across the land, eventually evolving their finely honed stone craft into what is now known as the Rolls Royce of stone technology, the beautifully fluted Clovis Point. As is more fully described in the entry on the Topper Site, when their civilization, the Clovis Culture, was destroyed by a comet that brought about the Younger Dryas Ice Age, the survivors of the dramatic climate change managed to pass their skills on to the people who had arrived in America from another direction. Those who crossed on foot across the Beringia land bridge reaped the benefits of the Solutrean bifacial stone technology, producing a serviceable point called the Folsom Point. It was smaller and easier to make than the Clovis, but that was acceptable because the mega fauna, mastodons and mammoths among them, were now extinct, leaving a game supply that was less difficult to bring down. As these Folsom people gradually spread back into the lands previously made

This gets interesting when we note that the skull and bone fragments of these people bear evidence of their being Neanderthal/human hybrids.

uninhabitable by the comet impact, they eventually became the ancestors of many Native American Indian tribes, possibly carrying with them stories about the Ancient Ones who survived the destruction of their previous world and emerged to tell the tale.

If all this is true, whenever you pick up a typical bifacial Indian arrow head, you are holding in your hand the legacy of the Solutrean people of western Europe.

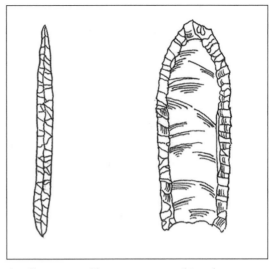

An illustration of how stones were chipped to create the "Folsom Point," an easier way to make spear- and arrowheads for hunting.

The Watchers of Eden

There is another theory involving the Solutrean culture that follows their migration after the comet impact event that set off the Younger Dryas Ice Age. This theory traces them east across Europe rather than west to America.

In 2014, Andrew Collins published a book titled *Göbekli Tepe: Genesis of the Gods: The Temple of the Watchers and the Discovery of Eden.* In it he attempts to discover the identity of a mysterious race of mythical god-like human beings who, by their superior knowledge and technical information, brought about the beginning of the Neolithic (Agricultural) Revolution and the building of the now-famous archeological work being uncovered at Göbekli Tepe. They were called by various names, but the most popular are Anunnaki and Watchers of Eden.

By closely following similar stone-crafting techniques, Collins traces the Solutrean tradition east into Europe, where it evolves or merges into a culture called Swiderian. In this migration, he believes the Solutreans were coming home, so to speak, having originally evolved here in the first place. He believes, along with Bruce Bradley who co-authored the Solutrean hypothesis, that the roots of the Solutrean come from the cold forest steppes north and northeast of the Black Sea and as far as the Russian Plain.

This gets interesting when we note that the skull and bone fragments of these people bear evidence of their being Neanderthal/human hybrids. In the rock art and cave paintings on their route east, he even finds evidence of a hypothetical Solutrean Bird-Cult, that seems to imply attachment to the sky similar to Native American myths concerning Sky People.

If all this is true, then according to Collins, the Swiderian people, who were descendants of the Solutreans, carried the genes and thus the physiology of a Neanderthal/human hybrid, might have been the people who, following the Younger Dryas comet impact, were the genesis of the mysterious gods who organized the builders of Göbekli Tepe, convincing them to turn from their hunter-gatherer ways in order to build the earliest and one of the greatest temples yet discovered, inaugurate the Agricultural Revolution and bring about a new civilization on a planet recovering from a devastating catastrophe.

This is, of course, an oversimplification. To read further into this theory will require reading each individual entry we've marked in bold text.

Suffice it to say that the Solutrean culture is fascinating. It could be that we owe much of what we call our civilization to these hardy survivors.

Children of the Stars

Twinkle, twinkle little star.
How I wonder what you are!

Traditional—Author Unknown

A popular New Age teaching involves children "from the stars" who have come to Earth in order to teach and protect humankind from itself. Perhaps it is most succinctly summarized by *Children of the Stars* author, Nikki Pattillo:

Star Children are children who have been sent here from all areas of the Universe to help our Earth including all living and non-living things on it. They possess psychic, spiritual and other extra sensory abilities. The Star Children are here to bring peace, topple corrupt systems, and shift dimensional consciousness. They have come here on special assignment in a rebirth into a higher dimensional Earth.

http://omtimes.com/2015/03/identifying-star-children/

This concept isn't really much different from many Native American beliefs. The Hopi, for instance, believe their ancestors came from the Pleiades cluster of seven stars. This belief is echoed in stories from the Dakota people.

Both Cree and Zuni stories teach that our ancestors came from the stars to the earth, where they then became human. Other native traditions believe that mysterious beings, spheres of light, came from the stars to teach us. In some cases they even abduct children to take back with them for reasons unknown.

The Oglala Sioux holy man Black Elk, who once toured with Buffalo Bill's Wild West Show, received a spurt of publicity when Joseph Campbell talked about him with Bill Moyers in a popular PBS interview. Campbell mentioned the book written by John Neihardt, *Black Elk Speaks*, and sparked a revival of interest in Indian culture. The following passage from *Black Elk: The*

Sacred Ways of a Lakota, by Wallace Black Elk and William Lyon quotes the holy man as saying:

> So when I went to vision quest, a disk came from above. The scientists call that an Unidentified Flying Object, but that's a joke, see? Because they are not trained, they lost contact with the wisdom, power and gift…. So that disk landed on top of me. It was concave, and there was another one on top of that. It was silent, but it lit and luminesced like neon lights. Even the sacred robes there were luminesced, and those tobacco ties lying there lit up like little light bulbs. Then these little people came, but each little group spoke a different language. They could read minds, and I could read their minds. I could read them. So there was silent communication. You could read it, like when you read silent symbols in a book. So we were able to communicate…. They are human, so I welcomed them. I said, "Welcome, Welcome…."

Black Elk (shown at right in a photo taken during his Wild West Show days) was a Sioux Indian who was interviewed for the book *Black Elk: The Sacred Ways of a Lakota,* which sparked new interest in Native American culture.

Apart from the fascinating questions concerning aliens that arise from these stories, at the very least they remind us that we are all children of the stars. Every particle in our body was forged in a distant sun. In that sense, the answer to the question that began this chapter, "Who are we?" is that we are conscious, sentient beings, conceived in mystery, who have evolved to the point at which we can begin to ask questions about our origins.

Was our planet seeded with life from outer space, as the panspermia theory holds? Is this just one of many worlds hidden in the recesses of quantum thought?

If these questions prove unanswerable, and thus unsatisfying, can we search for origins close to home? Has DNA research proved that we all came out of Africa to populate the world, perhaps sending cousins to spend time in and near the sea, as the *Homo aquaticus* theory holds? Did ancient seafarers of old, such as the Solutrean culture or the mythical Anunnaki, manage to survive an ancient cataclysm and preserve both our genes and knowledge so we

W as our planet seeded with life from outer space, as the panspermia theory holds? Is this just one of many worlds hidden in the recesses of quantum thought?

would not go the way of the dinosaurs? Do elongated skulls from around the world reveal missing pieces of our genealogical history?

Without questions, knowledge stagnates. Questions spur the quest for intellectual progress. Each of these topics raises legitimate questions that are, as yet, unanswered. The fact that they are threatening and uncomfortable is demonstrated by the vociferous response they generate. People don't strike out in anger unless they are threatened. And by the cacophony of rhetoric sounding forth from the halls of academia, drowning out the long-established conspiracy of silence, it appears things are changing. Our culture of amnesia may be breaking forth into the sunlight. Maybe we are beginning to remember who we are.

In the quest for knowledge about our past, it isn't important that we agree. It is important, however, that we respect those with whom we disagree.

Here's one example:

Navajo culture doesn't have much respect for ego. Children are taught not to push themselves forward to try to be number one. As a result, when a Navajo child, sitting in a school classroom, is asked the question by his white teacher, "Who discovered America?" he isn't comfortable jumping to his feet and declaring the answer he knew the teacher wanted—"Christopher Columbus!" That would certainly have brought praise. It would have elicited, at the very least, a "Good for you!" response.

Instead, out of respect for his culture, his teacher, and his classmates, he would probably defer, in polite Navajo fashion, by refusing to take credit himself for knowledge. He would answer, "They say it was Christopher Columbus." That way, "they" would receive the credit rather than himself, avoiding an ego-boosting "I know the answer."

The teacher, however, wouldn't know anything about this modest Navaho trait. Coming from her totally different experience as a product of a white culture that values pushing oneself forward, she would completely misunderstand what the student was saying. She would interpret his "They say it was Christopher Columbus" as implying that the student was criticizing white culture's insistence that a European explorer "discovered" a new world that was inhabited by people who had discovered it long ago. Mistaking humility for racial arrogance, she would probably punish the child severely. Instead of initiating a conversation that might be helpful, her response would further alienate everyone and send them all deeper into mutual distrust.

Dare we say that much the same thing is happening today in the world of science and religion? When it comes to human origins, scientists distrust religion, often rightfully so, because they assume religionists refuse to look at proven biological and anthropological evidence. And religionists circle the wagons against scientists, often rightfully so, because they perceive an arrogance and closed-mindedness toward any answers that seem to imply something other out there beyond the Higgs Field.

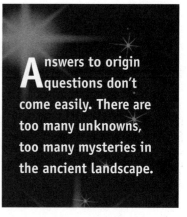

Answers to origin questions don't come easily. There are too many unknowns, too many mysteries in the ancient landscape. To fully explore these realms requires a lot of mutual respect, openness, and broad-based synthesis.

So who are we? We don't know. Yet! But if we remain open in our investigation, we might discover hints about who we are by studying what we do. We may even discover some lost histories and hidden truths. This first chapter, "Ancient Ancestors," raised some questions. Now it's time to move on by observing our ancient ancestors at work pursuing answers. They began by looking at the stars. That's where we'll go next.

ANCIENT ASTRONOMERS

And God said, "Let there be lights in the expanse of the sky to separate the day from the night, and let them serve as signs to mark seasons and days and years.…"

Genesis 1:14

I feel that ley-man, astronomer-priest, druid, bard, witch, palmer, and hermit, were all more or less linked by one thread of ancient knowledge and power, however degenerate it became in the end.

Alfred Watkins in *The Old Straight Track*

For a long time, megaliths were considered to have had primarily funerary purposes, which is reflected in the names given them such as "Chamber tombs," "Burial-mounds," "Passage graves," "Gallery graves," etc. This assumption is now in question.…

Alex Whitaker on the website *Ancient-Wisdom*

Ancient Gods of the Heavens

The ancient gods of humanity probably lived first in the heavens. The Sun God, the Moon Goddess, and the clusters of stars forming the bodies of Orion the Hunter, Cygnus the Swan, Draco the Dragon, and Leo the Lion were familiar to our ancestors. Although it was the Babylonians who first immortalized them in writing, there is megalithic evidence written in stone that suggests they were recognized long before the Babylonians arrived on the scene. Planets must have appeared to be wandering stars that didn't quite fit the pattern. Comets and shooting stars, mystifying in themselves, and eclipses, which were probably terrifying, were almost certainly seen as divine portents from the beyond.

There is no doubt that our ancestors saw the world through quite different eyes than we do. Take a nighttime flight along the coastline of America. See the millions upon millions of lights illuminating the landscape, outlining the continent while turning night into day, and it's easy to understand how we moderns have cut ourselves off from what was once sacred space, full of mystery and wonder.

In this chapter we're going to examine the evidence left behind by those who preceded us; clues that indicate clearly and unequivocally that they were obsessed with the heavens. Then, in the "Ancient Catastrophes" chapter, we're going to offer hints as to why. There may have been more than ancient curiosity and religion involved.

Even though we have forgotten much of their worldview, they bequeathed their fascination down to us in artifacts of stone, language, mythology and religion. As we shall see, it could even be that they left us messages which, until relatively recently, have been hiding in plain sight from most of humanity.

But first we need to relearn much of what they accepted as a matter of course. Before they can speak to us, we have to learn the basic vocabulary of their language.

It wouldn't be surprising to discover that no one reading these words knows the current phase of the moon, let alone the subtle variances about which house the sun rose in this morning. So let's begin with a basic primer in the ancient language of the night skies.

The Zodiac

As the earth makes both its daily rotation around its axis and its yearly trip around the sun, it slowly wobbles a bit. The tilt is called the elliptic. The wobble refers to precession. If you picture the sun, with the earth next to it, we are tipped about 23.5 degrees away from being perfectly upright. What that means is that as we follow our orbital path around the sun it appears higher and lower in the sky, depending on what season we are in. In summer, those in the northern hemisphere see the sun higher in the sky than they do in the winter. For those in the southern hemisphere it's just the opposite. (That's why "I'm Dreaming of a White Christmas" doesn't resonate much with folks in New Zealand. One of their favorite seasonal hymns is called "Upside Down Christmas" by Shirley Erera Murray.)

Ancient Astronomers

This also affects the position of the stars in the sky when we first see them every night. As we wobble around in our orbit they appear to slowly change locations.

Now, what follows isn't exact. Our elliptic and our orbit, to say nothing of what we have called our slow wobble, don't quite fit our western calendar, so we have to generalize and simplify a bit.

Most of our clocks are built around the perceived course of the sun each day. Hebrew, Muslim, and Phoenician cultures say the day starts at sunset. Taoist and Gregorian clocks are keyed into midnight. By that we mean that 12:00 A.M. is the beginning of a new day. Hence, Americans, following a Gregorian calendar, stay up until midnight to celebrate the new year. If we were to follow a Hindu, Babylonian, or Egyptian system, we would get up at dawn to do the same thing because their day starts at sunrise.

But let's stick to the Gregorian calendar most of us use, named after Pope Gregory XIII, who authorized it back in 1582. It divides the year into 365 days. (But because time doesn't take orders even from a Pope, we have to add a day every four years in order to keep things in sync between our wobble and the sun's relative position. We call it leap year.)

Now things start to get complicated. We see the moon because it reflects the sun's light back at us. It doesn't generate any illumination of its own. So as it orbits around the earth, it appears different every night. It goes through phases, sometimes appearing full and round, sometimes crescent shaped, and sometimes disappearing entirely, depending on where it is in relation to the sun and our eyes. Twelve times a year it appears full. We measure its progress by months. (Although it doesn't quite work out that way. In a perfect world, the first of every month would feature a full moon. But because our calendars are based more on approximations than exact placements, the full moon hardly ever corresponds to the first day of the new month. Sometimes it even appears twice in a month. We call that a blue moon.)

We thus begin to see the problems inherent with designing a calendar. We

Pope Gregory XIII came up with what is now called the Gregorian calendar, which divides the year into 365 days and twelve months. Because there are actually 365 and a quarter days in a year, a leap day was later added every four years.

need to tie it to the sun in order to mark seasons of the year with their differing temperatures and tasks such as planting and harvesting. But the waxing and waning of the moon, with its apparent influence on everything from tides to menstrual cycles, is so dramatic that we can't ignore it. So we need to compromise between moon cycles and sun cycles. What's a poor astronomer to do, especially when it comes to expending time and human resources in building a megalithic monster of a standing-stone astronomical calendar?

Well, he tries for the best of both worlds. He honors the sun and the moon together.

Let's start with the moon's nightly journey.

The Twelve Stations of the Full Moon

Given clear skies and an unimpeded horizon, you see a full moon once every twenty-nine or thirty nights. When it rises it does so against a pattern of stars. Every month or so, that pattern appears to change by a little less than thirty degrees to the east because, due to Earth wobble, the moon appears to have moved along the horizon. So over the course of a lunar year, the pattern of stars behind the full moon will have changed twelve times. (Remember, this is an approximation.)

In other words, over the course of a lunar year, the full moon will have risen in front of twelve patterns of stars, each of which makes up one compartment, or house, about thirty degrees wide. To assist astronomers in identifying each house, the ancient Babylonians superimposed an image of a different animal over the stars that formed that particular compartment. One was a lion (Leo), one was a fish (Pisces), one a dragon (Draco), one a bull (Taurus), etc. This system was taken over by the Greeks. The Greek word for animal, or "living being," is spelled, in English, zoon (from which we get our word "zoo"). The twelve animals together formed, in Greek, a *zodia*. It means "animal circle." In English we spell it zodiac. Although different cultures and civilizations saw different animals, there were always twelve compartments, or twelve houses.

The twelve signs of the zodiac are well known in popular culture these days. The signs are derived from constellations that appear prominently during the different months of the year.

It wasn't long before these animal figures were given god-like qualities, seemingly affecting life on the planet. Sometimes we even honor that principle today. Hence:

When the moon is in the seventh house
And Jupiter aligns with Mars
Then peace will guide the planets
And love will steer the stars
This is the dawning of the age of Aquarius....

"Age of Aquarius" from the musical *Hair*
by James Rado and Gerome Ragni

The Great Year of the Sun

If the moon rises in each of these houses, obviously the sun does too. But it takes a lot longer to run its course. As a matter of fact, if you measure the sun rise only on the spring equinox, which traditionally is when the year begins, it makes the full circle of the zodiac approximately every 26,000 years, spending some 2,160 years in each "house" before returning back to the beginning. This time period is called a great year. Those of us who lived through all the hoopla on December 21, 2012, well remember that the Mayans were especially good at keeping track of this very long period of time. That's when their great year ended and a new one began.

The ironic thing is that if you look up your birth month, named after one of these animals, and try to match it to your actual horoscope dates according to a western calendar, you will discover that the sun didn't rise in that particular house the day you were born. That's where it was several thousand years ago when the system was first invented. By now everything appears to have moved. Thanks to Earth wobble, things have changed quite a bit since then.

As Above, So Below

Here's the point of all this background information. Our ancient ancestors knew all this. They developed it. But probably not all of them. Only those with an astronomical education, consisting of a lot of late-night sessions and years of study, could really understand the whole system, see the changes and infer what was happening in the night sky. They probably formed the first class of what we now call priests. They were the ones who studied the mysterious realm of the gods. They interpreted the omens and the messages. They learned to predict when the next eclipse would come. They knew when you could safely plant your crops. They had the power to speak for the gods! Thus, they controlled the people.

The most famous of this class of priests are remembered every year at Christmas time. The Magi, three Wise Men who, while studying the stars, learned about big doings going on in Israel, are said to have made a journey that catapulted them into their fifteen minutes of fame. They probably never expected to be remembered each year by boys dressed up in bathrobes at Sunday School pageants, but their theme song is catchy.

What happened when something terrible came from the skies to disrupt things on Earth? What happened when the rains were withheld? What happened when a storm flooded the village? What happed when an asteroid slammed into the planet? What was the meaning of a fiery comet with a long tail?

It took a special class of learned people to interpret all this. They were the ones who decided what the people below had done to anger the deities above. They were the ones who decided what you had to do to appease the gods. Maybe it meant offering a sacrifice at a special place of worship. Maybe it meant building a temple or ziggurat, the better to both observe the heavens and serve as a place for the people to meet in cyclical festivals.

When the study of a mystery becomes organized, we call it religion. A religion consists of three things:

- A priestly class who stand between deities and faithful congregants.
- Rules to live by and an organization to enforce them.
- A central place to worship.

Of such activities, civilizations are born. When the people supported the priests, they built magnificent structures for study and worship. As we shall see, this was probably the impetus behind such places as Stonehenge and Göbekli Tepe.

But when the priests lost the confidence of the people, or when they abused their position, the people sometimes revolted. That is what probably happened to the world of the Anasazi.

In this chapter, we will look at some of the structures, artifacts, religions, and mythologies that were once built to honor ancient gods who were believed to exist in the heavens but who sometimes were said to have come down to Earth. In doing so, we may discover clues leading to more than a few lost histories while uncovering some hidden truths along the way.

Arth Vawr and the Pendragon

O Merlin in your crystal cave
Deep in the diamond of the day,

Will there ever be a singer
Whose music will smooth away
The furrow drawn by Adam's finger
Across the meadow and the wave?
Or a runner who'll outrun
Man's long shadow driving on,
Burst through the gates of history, and hang the apple on the tree?
Will your sorcery ever show
The sleeping bride shut in her bower,
The day wreathed in its mound of snow,
And time locked in his tower?

Merlin, by Edwin Muir

Mythic Evidence of Forgotten Days

From Mystery Hill and the spot dubbed Calendar Hill in New England to the venerable Stonehenge, from Aztec pyramids to the Australian outback, from the windswept northern islands of Great Britain to sun-washed Egyptian ruins, the findings all are similar. There seems to be plenty of evidence that most, if not all, megalithic monuments had an astrological connection that pointed to something in the heavens. On the morning of a solstice, stand in the center of Stonehenge, visit Newgrange, climb a watchtower at Mystery Hill, or trek back into the Peruvian jungle to one of the great pyramids, and you will certainly understand that there is as much mathematical precision at any of those age-old places as you will find in the most complicated observatory built today, possibly even more. Contemporary astronomers have sophisticated computers and telescopes at their disposal. If challenged, however, not many of them could duplicate our ancestors' work if all they were given to work with was stone.

But the astrology of the time is hidden away in other disciplines besides stone. Katherine Maltwood, for instance, wrote a book in 1929 called *A Guide to Glastonbury's Temple of the Stars*. It caused an immediate stir because she claimed to have discovered, in the very face of the landscape which was, in her time, covered by fields and seemingly natural folds of the ground, a series of huge figures that were literally carved into the earth. She recognized in them the signs of the zodiac, each figure constructed beneath its parent constellation.

At the time of her discovery, she was diligently at work illustrating *The High History of the Holy Graal*, a work that had been translated from old French by a Dr. Sebastian Evans. On the final page of that book were written these words:

> The Latin from whence this History was drawn into Romance,
> was taken in the Isle of Avalon, in a holy house of religion that

standeth at the head of the Moors Adventurous, there where King Arthur and Queen Guinevere lie.

Avalon? That was right there at Glastonbury! Could there be a connection between the Arthurian saga and astrology? In other words, could the saga itself, sometimes called the Matter of Britain, which was first spoken and later written down many hundreds of years later, contain an astrological message that duplicated the work of ancient Neolithic workers in stone?

Stick with this, now, because it's worth a little struggle.

First, as we noted in the introduction to this chapter, as the earth spins on its axis, it wobbles a little bit. Slowly, over the course of thousands of years, the constellations appear to change places. Our present North Star, Polaris, wasn't always located in the true north. (As a matter of fact, it still isn't, and won't be until the year 2100.)

Second, the dragon is an Eastern symbol for Earth energy, or pagan religion. Its sign in the zodiac is the constellation Draco.

Here's the point. During the centuries when the great stone monuments were being built all over England, there were actually two north stars, both located in the constellation Draco—the dragon.

Now it starts to get interesting. Back at that time, the stars pointing to true north were already being apparently pushed out of the way by the constellation called in Welsh, and phonetically in Old Celtic, *Arth Vawr*. It means "Great Bear." (Although in modern America we see a big dipper, virtually every other culture, from the Native Americans to the Chinese, from south to north and around the world, see a bear. Most Americans really have trouble with this. We stare and stare, and all we see is a dipper. But that's our problem.)

Part of what is seen in many cultures as the Great Bear constellation is viewed as the Big Dipper by Americans, who are considering only the stars in the tail and hindquarters.

Anyway, Arth Vawr, transliterated into modern English, is, of course, Arthur. And who was Arthur's (the Great Bear's) father? In the sagas, he is called Uthyr or Uther (which might mean either "Wonderful" or "Terrible") Pendragon, or "Head of the Dragon." And what was a prime activity for Arthur (the Bear), who succeeded Uther (the Dragon), and his knights? Slaying dragons, of course.

Thus it is that at precisely the same time in history that the megalithic stone structures across the countryside were being built, the North Star, which had been in the constellation Draco the Dragon, was being superseded by a new star, pointed to by the constellation named for the Great Bear.

Much later, when it came time to tell the Arthurian stories, Arthur, the Great Bear himself, who was born a pagan but raised by Christians, was pushing out the Dragon—the old, pagan religion. In this reading of the saga, the Church Triumphant, championed by both Arthur and his famous, pure-of-heart and dedicated Christian Knights of the Round Table, went about the countryside searching for Holy Grails and the like, while Merlin, the part-Druid, part-pagan and generally mysterious magician of the old ways, sadly slipped into his cave, just like Puff the Magic Dragon.

The Myth of the Victors

When you understand the story in these terms, it makes perfect sense. History, after all, is written by the victors. In this case it was written by the Christian Church, which had a vested (pardon the pun) interest in putting to rest the old Dragon religions that pointed to the stars rather than Heaven, and derived its strength from Mother Earth instead of the Sun (or rather, Son. Again, pardon the pun). The time of the Dragon was dead. Long live the new age!

> In Japan, where the Ainu people believed they were descended from the original inhabitants of the land, the bear was worshipped before all gods.

This didn't happen only in the West. In China the supreme god of this time was T'ien. His totem was the Great Bear. In Japan, where the Ainu people believed they were descended from the original inhabitants of the land, the bear was worshipped before all gods. In India, the mythical mountain Meru is the place where the gods reside. It is located, according to their stories, at the North Pole. New England native tribes used to celebrate certain auspicious days of the year by serving a captive bear a portion of his own flesh—symbolically, of course. They would feast on the meat of the bear and place a leg bone in the mouth of the bear's skull, after which it would be buried with honor and dignity.

The Arthurian sagas offer only one example of how mythology points to ancient astronomers. Sometimes the teaching was built into huge megalithic stone structures. Sometimes it was built into their stories. But no matter what the medium, it is there for future generations to ponder. They understood something we have forgotten. Theirs is a lost culture. We don't really understand the depths of their philosophical and religious thought. But if we ask the right questions and apply some thought to the problem, we may yet come to understand hidden truths that might affect us today.

BABYLONIAN ASTRONOMY

The Ancient Babylonians once lived in what is now Iraq and Syria. The civilization emerged in about 1800 B.C.E. Clay tablets engraved with their cuneiform writing system have already shown these people were advanced in astronomy. "They wrote reports about what they saw in the sky," Professor Mathieu Ossendrijver told the BBC World Service's *Science in Action* program. "And they did this over a very long period of time, over centuries." But this latest research shows they were also way ahead when it came to math. It had been thought that complex geometry was first used by scholars in Oxford and Paris in medieval times. They used curves to trace the position and velocity of moving objects. But now scientists believe the Babylonians developed this technique around 350 B.C.

Sandee Taylor: http://www.discreetnations.com/signs-of-modern-astronomy-seen-in-ancient-babylon/

Pushing Back Dates Again!

Babylon is an ancient land, described in early texts such as the Bible. It is steeped in tradition. The famous Hanging Gardens, the Tower of Babel, the Jewish Babylonian Captivity, and the Code of Hammurabi are only a few of the immortal images that were brought again into American homes during the press coverage of the Gulf War.

Less known is the history involving the talented scribes who practiced extremely sophisticated astronomy. Their cult is immortalized every Christmas when the three most famous of the order are said to have observed a star in the east and followed it to Bethlehem. If you were a Babylonian astronomer, you watched the heavens. That's just what you did all night. Your job was to report to the king about what the stars foretold so he wouldn't be caught by surprise when unusual events took place.

Naked eye astronomy takes years, even centuries, to practice correctly. Stars and planets move so slowly through their precession that it takes intense observation over long periods of time to record changes. It appears it also takes some pretty complex math. A recent discovery

Babylonians employed a set of pre-calculus 1,500 years before Isaac Newton and Gottfried Leibniz independently "invented" it in Europe.

indicates that in the course of their observations, Babylonians employed a set of pre-calculus 1,500 years before Isaac Newton and Gottfried Leibniz independently "invented" it in Europe. According to an article in the *New York Times*, written by Kenneth Chang and published on January 28, 2016, Babylonians were using advanced geometry as well to calculate the orbit of the planet Jupiter. This would not be a surprising choice of astronomical targets for them. They associated Jupiter with their principal god, Marduk. Jupiter was to the Babylonians what Orion was to the Egyptians—a heavenly manifestation of their principal deity. And 2,500 years ago they had already developed a sophisticated mathematical system to track his movements.

The Quality of Humanness

Why is this important? Why should we care that human beings were so smart so long ago?

Here's one reason. Almost all of us carry undefined, and thus unacknowledged, points of view around with us. Most of us have been subtly force-fed the prejudicial opinion that evolution has continued since our emergence on an uninterrupted path that led from primitive ancestors to sophisticated moderns. We are smarter than the Old Ones. We know more. Our science is better. Our toys are more sophisticated. We are, in other words, on the cutting edge of evolutionary development.

It's probably natural that most of us, without ever examining this idea, accept it as a given. We associate technological superiority with the advancement of civilization. We remember how our grandparents back on the farm lived, we compare it to our lives today, and consider ourselves more advanced. We view with aloof amusement the "woo-woo voodoo" of a primitive shaman and assume we know more than he does so we're better than he is. We consider it our duty to help poor countries so as to bring them up to our standards. (The emphasis here is on the word "up.") We divide the world into First World and Third World countries almost entirely by judging what we consider to be the ultimate criteria—living conditions which include cars, computers, and cell phones.

What we forget is that our grandparents, and even our parents, never had computers and cell phones, and some of them never even had cars. Those are brand new inventions less than two generations old. But they have become the gold standard of judging intelligence, worldliness, and sophistication.

To put it bluntly: Isaac Newton and Nicolaus Copernicus never even had electricity at their disposal, but do you honestly think you're smarter than they were? Technology has very little to do with intelligence and understanding. Fancy hand-held toys do not equal genius. When we equate the two, we are merely revealing our unexamined prejudices.

Learning from the Old Ones

Here's the point. The ancient Babylonian astronomers discovered and utilized a sophisticated mathematics that was later lost and forgotten. Fifteen hundred years went by before it was rediscovered. And it wasn't until the year 2016 that we woke up from our amnesia to discover that by Isaac Newton's time, calculus was already old.

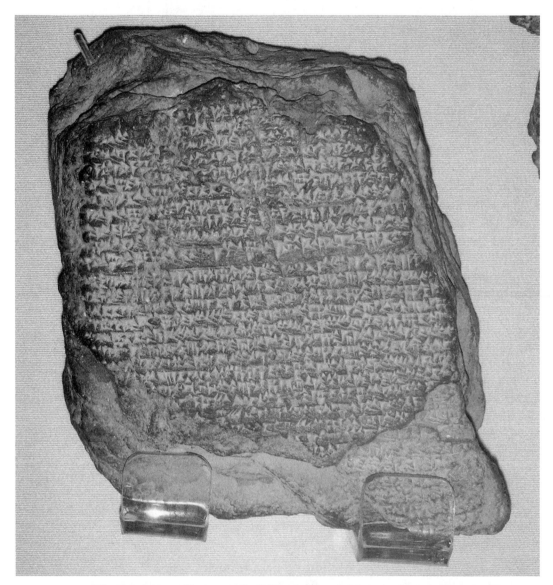

This Babylonian tablet, currently held at the British Museum, dates to 164 B.C.E. The cuneiform writing describes a sighting of Halley's Comet, evidence that the Babylonians were sophisticated astronomers.

If we can develop cultural and historical amnesia in just a few thousand years, what else have we forgotten? What else can the Old Ones teach us?

We face some great perils in our day. Did the ancients face the same perils? Can we awake from our amnesia and discover that maybe the answers we seek have already been found?

If not, than we are no better than children who think their parents don't know anything so can't possibly give them good advice about how to live.

Mark Twain once observed that when he was a child, his father didn't know anything. But he went on to say that he was amazed how much his father had learned by the time young Mark Twain had turned twenty-one.

If we think we can't learn from our ancestors just because they didn't have iPods, we are acting like children. It's time to pay more attention, not less, to the wisdom of the ancients.

KARAHUNJ

They sit like soldiers on a hill, huddled in formation. The 204 stones have been ascribed with mystical, fertility and cosmic powers, but rarely have ancient monuments caused such a sensation in astronomical circles.

Cyrus Shahmiri in *An Empire History Forum*

Cradle of Our Civilization?

Is the cradle of our civilization to be found in ancient Armenia, rather than the Fertile Crescent of Mesopotamia, as is widely taught? Some students of archeology believe that is a very distinct possibility. On the plains outside the Armenian city of Sisian, near the site of a Bronze Age settlement and cemetery called Zorakarer, stand 204 stones that, although not as refined and complex, echo the measurements and mathematical proportions of England's Stonehenge. But according to a distinguished professor and megalithic specialist named Gerald Hawkins, Armenia's Stonehenge, called Karahunj, or Carahunge, is some 3,500 years older than Britain's attraction. Until the discovery of Göbekli Tepe in Turkey, Karahunj was considered to be the oldest such monument in the world. It predates the Carnac stones in France and Newgrange in Ireland. Although this area is rich in standing stones and monuments, labeled *dolmens* and *menhirs*, many of them thought to be burial sites,

Karahunj is unique in that it appears to be a megalithic observatory, built to study the night skies.

In the Armenian language, *kar* means "stone." *Hunj* means "henge." Hence, Karahunj can be translated as Stonehenge. And the similarities between the two ancient observatories aren't limited to language. Some of the earliest Anglo-Saxon chronicles that still survive claim that the very first inhabitants of the British Isles came from Armenia. If this is, indeed, the case, was Karahunj an early warmup for what eventually came to be known as Stonehenge?

The Armenian sun god is Ari, translated as "sun." So it stands to reason that many of the alignments found there are situated in ways that measure the sun's path through the heavens. They also feature a temple within the Karahunj complex consisting of forty stones, some of which have holes drilled through them so that certain stars and the moon can be observed at special times as well. Sightings seem to infer that these early astronomers might have been able to accurately measure latitude, so they probably knew that the earth was round, and arranged an accurate calendar on the landscape.

The megalithic menhirs of Carahunge (Karahunj) in Armenia predate Stonehenge by some 3,500 years.

Speculations

All this raises some interesting questions. Karahunj is far cruder than Göbekli Tepe, which was built about 11,500 years ago in Turkey. One would think that the earliest monument, Göbekli Tepe, would be the simplest. But this is not the case. It begs the question, why is the order reversed in this case? Why is Göbekli Tepe the more sophisticated, even though it is 3,000 years older?

And is there really a connection between Armenia and England? Did an Armenian culture transport itself across all of the Middle East and Europe, bringing its religion and stone technology with it? If so, why? Or were they connected in some other way?

Speculation is fun, but until more hard evidence is discovered, the questions remain unanswered. All we have now is a circle of standing stones that point to the heavens, suggestive hints pointing to a very mature, sophisticated people that must have been quite different from the caveman image we have been taught, and a lost civilization that seems to be keeping its secrets.

LASCAUX: UNDERGROUND ASTRONOMY

> We will probably never understand completely what Cro-Magnon man had in mind when he painted the Lascaux caves. The images of the animals seem obvious but what are we to make of the geometrical shapes and patterns scattered in between these creatures?
>
> Dr. David Whitehouse, *BBC News*

In this chapter "Ancient Astronomers" we look at some of the great open-air ancient monuments, pyramids, medicine wheels and myths that contain astronomical meaning. But what about doing astronomy underground, deep in the cold embrace of the encircling Earth?

Dr. Michael Rappenglueck, of the University of Munich, believes that was precisely what was going on in the great painted caves of western Europe which contain some of the oldest art known to humanity. He believes he has found evidence that 15,000 to 17,000 years ago, in the great cave at Lascaux in southern France, our ancient Cro-Magnon ancestors were in touch with heavenly muses and brought that contact to life deep beneath the earth on the walls of the cave.

"The secret of understanding these caves," he says, "is to understand the people who painted these walls."

Andrew Collins is one author who has tried to do just that. In his book, *The Cygnus Mystery*, he wonders if the ancient cave painters were in fact a Shamanic elite who deliberately crawled back into the depths of the earth on spiritual journeys, perhaps under the influence of hallucinogenic mushrooms, to engage unseen spirits who guided them into an understanding of who they were and how they fit into the overall community of the cosmos. Perhaps the artists were seeking their true origins, asking the great question, "Where did I come from?"

Maybe the answer was, "You came from the stars."

How else to explain the mythic memories contained in the stories about star children? How else to explain why so many cultures teach that the heavens are our true home?

And how else to explain the star charts that appear painted on the walls of the great caves? There we find representations of many of the animals that make up the zodiac. There we find pictured dots indicating the phases of the moon, with a blank where the new moon would be. There we find painted, in perfect form, a picture of the Seven Sisters, the Pleiades star cluster that fig-

Among the many drawings of animals and hands in France's Lascaux caves, one can find a representation of the Pleiades star cluster (circled).

ures so prominently in cross-cultural myths and legends, as well as a representation of Taurus the bull and many other totem animals the ancients saw in the heavens. There we find stick figures representing, perhaps, the shamans themselves. Some of them are obviously anatomically correct males. Although most theories postulate that these are a portrayal of sexual potency, it is a well-known fact that the condition the figures find themselves in occurs frequently, if sometimes inconveniently, to modern male users of hallucinogens.

Did our ancestors have a way of communing with inhabitants of other dimensions, parallel worlds, or even with extraterrestrial beings they called spirits? Was it a method that didn't require such cumbersome vehicles as nuts-and-bolts spaceships that, because of the immense size of the cosmos, are probably useless anyway?

It is certain that when these folks came out of their caves they had, for all practical purposes, invented religion. The evidence of their art, the first examples of what is called symbolic or religious representation, is there for all to see. They experienced something down there that had a profound influence on them. Perhaps it consisted of an experience that, for the most part, we have forgotten.

> **//The secret of understanding these caves ... is to understand the people who painted these walls."**

Or have we? The Old Ones entered their caves, ingested their drugs, and communed with what are now thought to be the first gods of humankind. Is that really any different from the millions of Christians today who enter the "caves" of cathedral and church, hold in their hands a cup of wine, and commune with God? After all, wine is alcohol, which is also known as spirits.

MEDICINE WHEELS OF THE AMERICAN WEST

The range of human intelligence was probably the same forty thousand years ago as now, including the rare genius. What have evolved are the tools and gadgets we make. We learn how to do a new thing, and forget how to do an old thing.

Gordon Freeman in *Hidden Stonehenge*

Mystery on the Prairie

As European settlers began to move west across the Mississippi River, vast prairies and remote mountain tops from Canada and the northern tier of

American states revealed curious concentrations of stones, set out to imitate, at least to white-cultured eyes, spokes on a wheel. When asked about what they were, the native people who had lived in these places for millennia answered, "We don't know. They were here when we got here."

Were they being serious, or were they just feigning ignorance to keep whites from snooping into sacred sites that they didn't understand and would probably plow under or otherwise mess up?

Whatever the case, somewhere in the late 1800s the new settlers started calling them medicine wheels, beginning with the Bighorn Medicine Wheel in Wyoming. It wasn't an Indian term, by any means. But their stone construction looked like wheels, and the Indians obviously considered them to be sacred (medicine in white parlance). So the name stuck. It's still in use by whites today. If you fly over them in an airplane they look like bicycle spokes, with rays emanating out from a central core.

Nobody knows how old they are. There's no way of dating them by archeological standards and if the Indians know, they're not telling. Some archeologists say the Bighorn Medicine Wheel might go back as far as four or

The Bighorn Medicine Wheel in Wyoming is still considered sacred by Indians, who continue to visit it and perform ceremonies there.

five thousand years. That would place its construction in roughly the same time span as the Egyptian pyramids. Others, of a more daring mindset, suggest dates that go back as far as a million years. Given the amount of glacial impact in these parts, though, that's probably stretching things.

Definitions

Archeologist John Brumley, known for his work with American Indian sites in the West, developed a definition for describing medicine wheels that is now the official standard. According to Brumley, a medicine wheel contains at least two of the following three features:

- A central stone cairn

- One or more rings of concentric stone circles

- Two or more lines, or rays, of stone radiating out from a central point, or hub

If we employ his criteria, there are at least one hundred, and maybe closer to two hundred, historic Native American medicine wheels still in existence today. The number varies because some of the smaller circles could very well be old tipi rings. Most of them are found in Alberta and Saskatchewan, but others are located in northern United States—North Dakota, Wyoming, Montana, and Colorado.

They are not big and imposing like Stonehenge. They didn't involve the transportation of immense, megaton boulders, but they are just as mystifying. It is precisely that aura of mystery that has made building medicine wheels so popular with everyone from so-called New Age spirituality types to modern Wiccans and pagans, many of whom have adopted their own spiritual interpretations of what medicine wheels mean.

Modern Sensibilities

Because of all this it is really important to emphasize a very basic point.

It would be difficult to overemphasize the disdain that modern Indian traditionalists have for a practice such as this. White culture has taken something very holy and sacred, given it a white name (medicine and wheel, both of which have nothing to do with Indian spirituality), defined it by a western criteria which separates an object into parts rather than acknowledging its wholeness, and then attempted to determine how it was used. Is it any wonder that even if any Indian (again—a white label) who honors the sacred traditions of the ancestors and knows the purpose of such a sacred space, will remain quiet about it? Even if a well-intentioned, white, New Age, armchair Indian sympathizer shows up on the scene and seems to display a sincere empathy, their superficial knowledge and attitude will be off-putting to those who were born and raised in the deep culture of the Old Ones.

That being said, we continue with fear and trepidation, knowing we are probably stepping all over holy ground. (Point of full disclosure here—my wife and I built a medicine wheel in the woods below our house in South Carolina. You can read all about it in my book, *The Dragon Awakes: Rediscovering Earth Energy in an Age of Science*, which you can find in Further Reading in the back of this book.)

The Majorville Medicine Wheel

The largest medicine wheel existing today is to be found near Majorville, in southern Alberta. Twenty-nine spokes radiate out from a central cairn, forming an outer ring almost ninety feet across. If the projectile points found at the site are any indication, and if precise radiocarbon dating of bones found nearby are accurate, the site was built some five thousand years ago, making it the oldest medicine wheel in existence today, and indicating that its construction coincides with the era of Egyptian pyramid building.

Gordon Freeman has done more work than anyone else here. In his technical but very readable book, *Hidden Stonehenge*, he concludes that the site is the remains of an ancient sun temple that predates both the pyramids and Stonehenge. His research indicates that the sacred hoop of the site is oriented toward the sunrise on the winter and summer solstices, the shortest and longest days of the year. This is similar to the Bighorn site with its twenty-eight spokes, which, with a diameter of eighty feet, is almost as big. He offers numerous site line calculations and mathematical data indicating a huge, complex, astronomical observatory.

Motivations

The big question, though, is still, "Why?" Oh, there are numerous theories, mostly delivered with more conviction than they merit. Take this one, for instance, from the Stanford Solar Center:

> In 1974, an archeo-astronomer named Jack Eddy visited the (Bighorn) Medicine Wheel and studied its alignments, that is, its arrangements of rocks, cairns, and spokes. He found the arrangements point to the rising and setting places of the Sun at summer solstice, as well as the rising places of Aldebaran in Taurus, Rigel in Orion, and Sirius in Canis Major—all bright, important stars associated with the Solstice. Later, another astronomer, Jack Robinson, found a cairn pair that marked the bright star Fomalhaut's rising point with the Sun 28 days before solstice.

There is nothing wrong with that description and it no doubt proves true upon scientific scrutiny. But it really doesn't address the central question.

Why are locating those particular stars important enough to expend the labor, time, and trouble of delineating them, especially during an era when so much effort was needed just to survive in a difficult environment?

Obviously, the builders of this site are members of a civilization that is lost to us. We simply don't know how they thought, what was important to them, and why they built such a masterpiece.

Maybe Sandra Laframboise and Karen Sherbina, writing in an article for the Dancing to Eagle Spirit Society, convey as much hidden truths as we are likely to ever discover:

> These ceremonies would make it correct to say that a Medicine Wheel is a physical manifestation of our Spiritual energy. In other words an outward expression of our internal dialogue with the Creator (God) and the spirit within.

Robin Wall Kimmerer, writing in her beautiful book *Braiding Sweetgrass*, opens a possible window on ancient spirituality while describing how to make a traditional Potawatomi black ash woven basket. Her instructor, after teaching a class to begin the process by laying out two ash strips at right angles, forming a symmetrical cross, says to them, "Now, take a look at what you've done. You've started with the four directions in front of you. It's the heart of your basket. Everything else is built around that."

From this simple instruction she concludes:

> Our people honor the four sacred directions and the power resident there. Where the two basket strips meet, at the intersection of those four directions, is right where we stand as human beings, trying to find balance among them.

Her instructor then completes her thought, "See there, everything we do in life is sacred. The four directions are what we build on. That's why we started like that."

Is it really the guiding impetus of the medicine wheel to point out the four cardinal directions, with an added intent to identify various points of interest in the mysterious heavens? Or is this simply a contemporary teaching superimposed on a reality that obviously meant a lot to a lost civilization, but now remains hidden from our view? After all, it seems kind of silly to drag hundreds of rocks all over the landscape if you can teach the same lesson with two strips of black ash.

The simple truth is, we just don't know.

MYSTERY HILL AND THE STONE STRUCTURES OF NEW ENGLAND

> Through Manitou we see our landscape anew. Now when we go
> to the woods, where before we saw just low walls, we have
> learned to see stone mounds and marked trees, vigil places,
> pointer, marker and god stones. Walking there has come to be an
> honoring of a time when all life was holy.

> Nancy Jack Todd in *Annals of the Earth*

America's Stonehenge

On a granite hilltop in Salem, New Hampshire, sits, in the words of
Winston Churchill (although he was admittedly speaking of Russia in 1939),
"a riddle, wrapped in a mystery, inside an enigma." For marketing reasons it's
often called America's Stonehenge, but for many years it was known as Mystery Hill. As far as can be determined through radiocarbon analysis and astrological alignment sightings, it was built about four thousand years ago.

The popular connection to Stonehenge was an obvious one, but has
now been confirmed at a higher level than anyone could have predicted even a
few years ago. Now that GPS has brought new technology to the desktop of
anyone with a computer, Dennis Stone, who inherited the responsibility of running the place from his father, Robert, recently discovered site lines that would
have been impossible to spot previous to our time. While checking out a key
astronomical sighting at the site, he discovered that if he projected the line
along a great circle route on Google Earth, it would continue across the ocean
and proceed exactly through the central alignment at Stonehenge in England,
coming to rest on the central altar there. Continuing on, it would then connect
with modern-day Beirut, the ancient Phoenician capital from where many have
postulated that sailors of old once set out to discover a new world in what is
now New England, long before the time of Christopher Columbus.

The present-day owner now runs a museum and hosts events ranging
from academic and popular tours to New Age festivals based on the Wiccan calendar, for if the structure stood anywhere in England, Scotland, Ireland, Wales,
or even western France, there would be no doubt as to who built it. It seems to
be, most definitely, a megalithic structure right out of the golden age of stone
building. It features stone walls and chambers lined up with standing stones that
mark both lunar and solar events such as sunrises at the equinox and solstice.

The highest structures don't tower overhead as at Turkey's Göbekli
Tepe or England's Stonehenge. They are only about eight feet tall. But the

presence of an Oracle Chamber, complete with speaking tube, and an altar, which some imagine was used for sacrifice, seems to belie any interpretation that suggests the edifice was built to be an early colonial root cellar, which is the usual description of any stone chamber found in New England.

Located near Salem, New Hampshire, America's Stonehenge (Mystery Hill) appears to have been constructed about four thousand years ago.

The obvious site patterns from the central complex out to standing stones placed in strategic positions that mark contemporary solstice and equinox dates didn't quite line up with any significant astronomical events today, so careful measurements were sent to the Harvard-Smithsonian Center for Astrophysics. There they determined that because of the slight wobble of Earth's orbit, they would line up exactly if they had been built in 1800 B.C.E., plus or minus a century or two. The oldest site radiocarbon dating of 2000 B.C.E., or four thousand years ago, seems to be a pretty good estimate of when the place was built.

In England this would all be quite run-of-the-mill megalithic stuff. But the Indians of New England never built anything else like this, let alone at just the time when similar structures were being built across the Atlantic.

Like many historical sites around the world, this one has been plundered through the years. Early colonists "borrowed" some of the rocks to build their homes. Others decided they needed granite for construction companies and found this a convenient source. Evidence seems to indicate that still others tore down some of the structures just because they feared pagan rituals might be enacted there. (The "work of the devil" was a common theme in early New England Puritan sermons!)

The wonder of the whole edifice is that so much of it still exists, and the reason for that is probably because the stone used in its construction is so massive that it was simply too much trouble for modern workers to mess with it.

Forgotten Architects

Which begs the inevitable question: Who built it and why?

Native Americans were in New England soon after the retreat of the glaciers 12,000 years ago. But there is no evidence of this type of construction being part of their architectural tradition. True, there are numerous stone beehive huts, or monks' caves, that exist from Maine to New York State. But these structures, too, are amazingly similar, and in many cases identical, to their counterparts in Western Europe and Great Britain's outer islands.

The obvious conclusion—that these structures were built by an ancient people who were working in Europe at the same time—flies in the face of history books. But while it admittedly contradicts history as it has been documented thus far, let's consider the timing, using Stonehenge as an example.

> **I**t wasn't until Stone-henge III, sometime around 2600 to 2400 B.C.E., that the famous outside ring of Sarsen stones was constructed.

The first post holes marking that well-known structure were sunk during the Mesolithic period, sometime around 8000 B.C.E. About 3100 B.C.E., the so-called Stonehenge II circular bank and ditch construction still employed earth and wood for its building materials. It wasn't until Stonehenge III, sometime around 2600 to 2400 B.C.E., that the famous outside ring of Sarsen stones was constructed. Then came Stonehenge IV, around 2280 to 1930 B.C.E. This is the same time period when America's Stonehenge was constructed. In England, the stone masters were putting the final touches, consisting of the well-known trilithons and a few other minor modifications, on their edifice as late as 1066 B.C.E. This would have been almost 1,000 years after the American structure had been built!

Could complex stone building societies have arisen independently on both sides of the Atlantic? Certainly! But doesn't it seem a bit of a stretch when all you need to connect two such similar cultures is a boat? And there is no question that humans had been sailing from Africa, Asia, and Europe to places like Australia, Greenland, and many other islands around the world much before then. Most of the evidence of a seafaring culture, however, has been lost.

The First Americans?

What does all this mean? If it is true that the folks who formed megalithic culture crossed the Atlantic, and probably more bodies of water besides, they were way out in front of Columbus or the Vikings, and maybe even the Celts, the Phoenicians, the Libyans or … whoever. Rising sea levels following the late glacial maximum (about 13,000 to 10,000 years ago) and the possibility of a post-megalithic dark age consisting of a few generations, during whose time the technology of sea travel was eventually lost, may have resulted in marooning people in America. But the evidence surely raises a suspicion that late fifteenth-century mariners were *re*-discovering, not discovering, America. And when people arrived with a written language to describe their new surroundings, they found evidence that they were not the first to wonder at what they found. Even the Native Americans apparently didn't know who the people were who built with stone, and who used stone to worship, study, or otherwise honor the heavens. Those people were here long before even the Indians arrived on the scene.

Places such as Mystery Hill are linked to other New England sites as well. James Mavor and Byron Dix were the first to popularize New England astronomical sites in their informative book *Manitou*, which describes their findings in Vermont at the now-famous Calendar One site. Here they found, built into the very landscape, an immense astrological calendar and observatory. This, coupled with the miles of stone walls throughout New England, many of which they determined predated the first European settlers, offered more than a suggestion that the work of an entire lost civilization had been hiding in plain sight throughout the familiar landscape.

A preserved sailing vessel at the Viking Ship Museum in Oslo, Norway. The Vikings are known to have traveled as far as North America.

This line of questioning can't help but make us think about the first people who had been drawn to America's shores. Who were the very first folks to step foot on the continent, and when did they arrive?

Because many speak disparagingly, sometimes even insultingly, of this and other riddles, it makes us pause, for one of the most common debate techniques of the fundamentalist, be he or she religious, scientific, academic, or political, is to simply denigrate the opponent instead of first examining or contemplating their arguments. Mystery Hill, America's Stonehenge, is here. It's real. It's puzzling. The enigmatic stone structures of New England exist, and no amount of labeling them root cellars is going to stand up to scrutiny for long, now that people are beginning to ask about them. The stone alignments at the Calendar One site that portray an ancient New England civilization that valued astronomy is real. It still exists. All these things deserve our study.

NEWGRANGE

When the sunbeam reached the edge of the chamber, its yellow-orange light began to glow upward into the gathering, gilding the

Elder's faces. The ray seemed to hesitate for a moment. And then it surged forward until it splashed into the great stone bowl. It began to fill the dish—and it filled it exactly. Not a drop of sunshine slipped over an edge—not here, not anywhere. The final resting place of the sun for that brief moment was precisely within the full circumference of the bowl, leaving no area of the bowl's stone surface dark or cold. It lay there like a golden sphere.

Frank Delaney in *Ireland: A Novel*

Capturing the Sun

On the day of the equinox, Kukulkan, the plumed serpent, is seen descending sinuously down the steps of the pyramid at Chichen Itza, Mexico. The mystery of sun and shade perfectly captures the image of the god descending from the heavens to Earth.

At the summer solstice, high atop a butte in Chaco Canyon, New Mexico, a vertical dagger of light pierces a spiral petroglyph pecked into a cliff face behind three giant slabs of sandstone. Six months later, on the morning of the winter solstice, two shafts of light perfectly bracket the same spiral.

And in Ireland, on a clear morning of the winter solstice, light from the rising sun floods a shaft in an ancient passage tomb called Newgrange. It races down a carefully constructed corridor to exactly fill, for seventeen minutes, a sandstone bowl, shaped just for this purpose, for reasons only guessed at today, but that might have had something to do with warming the bones of the ancestors of the builders of this earthly temple.

From Mexico to the American southwest to far-off Ireland, the sun is captured on special days of the year and made to do the bidding of the architects of these wondrous artifacts of a forgotten civilization.

It begs the question: What were they thinking? Why was it so important to build structures that, from an astronomical perspective, still work perfectly in our day, long after the mystery of their construction has faded into the mists of time?

More Pitfalls of Archeology

In "Ancient Ancestors" we pointed out some of the pitfalls of archeology. Here is another. When we dig things up, we really have no idea what they meant to early civilizations. Consider, for instance, what might happen if an archeologist who lives 10,000 years in the future, in an era long after Christianity has been forgotten, discovers a magnificent cathedral from the time of the Middle Ages. He might notice that it is built along an east/west orientation and so deduce that it represented a religion that was astronomical in nature. He might unearth a cruci-fix and determine that it was a religion that practiced torture and human sacri-fice. If he finds an old text of holy day instructions and discovers a central celebration whose name suggests the ancient goddess Ishtar (we call it Easter), held on a mountain top on the first Sunday after the first full moon following the spring equinox, he would probably decide the cathedral is a pagan temple.

We could go on, but that is certainly sufficient to remind us that some-times what we leave behind may give a completely false impression to some-one who doesn't know anything about who we are.

Constructed 5,200 years ago, Newgrange is six hundred years older than the Pyramids of Giza and a thousand years older than Stonehenge. Because of damage done by road builders and looters, we may never know exactly what it looked like originally, but thanks to preservation laws passed in 1993, we still can trace its central function of capturing the sun on the solstice. The monu-ment still works, and a limited number of people are selected by lottery every year to observe and appreciate the genius behind its construction.

Although legend invests the surrounding area with all sorts of impor-tance, from the final resting place of kings to the coming of Christianity to Ire-land, it is the solstice miracle that gives Newgrange its celebrity.

Like so many of its ancient counterparts around the world, the question that it raises is "What were they thinking?" Because it was built in an age

Newgrange is a megalithic tomb located in Ireland's Boyne Valley. It is approximately 5,200 years old and is older than Stonehenge and the Great Pyramids.

before people wrote down their innermost thoughts and dreams, we are forced to guess. Only a powerful concept, probably religious, could have motivated people to go to such trouble and produce such intriguing enigmas.

Were they so motivated? Obviously!

Were they brilliant? That, too!

Were they in touch with ideas and forces we have completely forgotten? Sadly, yes. They have become testaments in stone to our cultural amnesia.

One can only suspect that we are the poorer for it.

ORION, CYGNUS, AND MYSTERIES OF THE NORTH SKY

'As above, so below.' It was a simple axiom, voiced in the hermetic writings of Graeco-Roman Egypt.

Andrew Collins in *The Cygnus Mystery*

Forgotten (and Ignored) Wisdom

Of all the mysteries and forgotten wisdom of lost civilizations, perhaps the most profound examples are to be found in their study of the heavens. It's not that we lack information about the cosmos today. Because of computer analysis and radio telescopes that the ancients never even dreamed about, we know far more about the universe than they did. But what we don't understand is why and how they built some of the most magnificent, astronomically precise, and enigmatic stone structures ever conceived of. Was it to study the night skies, presumably hoping to bring the magic down to earth? Why was that so important to them?

> Orion seems to have been the guiding light for the construction of the Giza Pyramids ... and Cygnus seems to have been of paramount importance to the builders of Göbekli Tepe....

Of all the star, moon, and sun alignments, angles and precession movements the Old Ones studied, the position of two constellations, Orion and Cygnus, appear to have been particularly important. As we shall see, Orion seems to have been the guiding light for the construction of the Giza Pyramids (although that is now a point of contention) and Cygnus seems to have been of paramount importance to the builders of Göbekli Tepe (although that is a debatable point as well).

We cannot hope, in a short entry such as this, to condense all the books and scholarly articles written about the astronomical alignments built into these two monuments. For a more detailed study in this book, see "Ancient Mysteries: Pyramids and the Sphinx" and "Ancient Civilizations: Göbekli Tepe." But we can raise some questions as to why our forgotten ancestors put so much time and work into them. Maybe, by doing so, we can come to understand a little more about what type of folks we come from. Let's take them one at a time.

A relief from Egypt showing Osiris, god of the underworld, bestowing immortality upon Ramses II.

Orion and the Giza Pyramids

When Robert Bauval and Adrian Gilbert wrote *The Orion Mystery* in 1995, it popularized a theory which had been percolating in various circles since the 1960s that the Pyramids of Giza were built to mimic on Earth the position of the stars in the belt of the constellation Orion, the Hunter.

Orion is one of the easiest constellations in the night sky to identify. The three stars of his belt are quickly spotted and it's the first constellation many beginning star gazers learn to recognize.

The belt stars seem to be straight until you look closely and see that they are just a little out of line. One is offset. If you fly over the pyramids, or study a map of Egypt in a format such as Google Earth, you quickly see that the three pyramids are offset in identical fashion.

In Egyptian mythology, one of the chief gods is Osiris. An Osiris cult ruled in Egypt for centuries, and since he has traditionally been identified with Orion, the relationship makes perfect sense. This identification was further buttressed when it was discovered that a southern shaft running upward from the King's Chamber of the Great Pyramid would have formed, during the age traditionally attributed to the building of the pyramids, a straight shot, similar to the barrel of a gun aimed at the belt of Orion.

In Bauval's words, as recalled by Graham Hancock in his book *Fingerprints of the Gods*:

> What I found was that the shaft had been precisely targeted on Al Nitak, the lowest of the three belt stars, which crossed the meridian at altitude 45 degrees around the year 2475 B.C.... If you look carefully on a clear night you'll see that the smallest of the three stars, the one at the top which the Arabs call Mintaka,

is slightly offset to the east of the principle diagonal formed by the other two. This pattern is mimicked on the ground where we see the Pyramid of Menkaure is offset by exactly the right amount to the east of the principal diagonal formed by the Pyramid of Khafre (which represents the middle star, Al Nilam) and the Great Pyramid, which represents Al Nitak. It's really quite obvious that all these monuments were laid out according to a unified site plan that was modeled with extraordinary precision on those three stars…. What they did at Giza was to build Orion's Belt on the ground.

What more satisfying a theory could there be? It included traditional Egyptian mythology while placing the building of the pyramids within traditional time spans taught by traditional Egyptologists. Everyone was happy.

According to conventional wisdom, it simply couldn't be! Paleolithic humans just couldn't have done it!

Alas, it was not to remain that way. Bauval couldn't leave well enough alone. After carefully calculating everything, measuring to scale and superimposing a map of the ground over a map of the heavens, he determined that although the general consensus of his theory could be seen in all eras, there was only one era when the stars were in an exact position to line up perfectly with his theory, and that was in 10450 B.C.E.

That was way too far back in time to satisfy traditionalists. This was, of course, before the discovery of Göbekli Tepe, which preceded the pyramids by five thousand years, so no one was ready to say that any human civilization existed way back then that was remotely capable of building such a structure. According to conventional wisdom, it simply couldn't be! Paleolithic humans just couldn't have done it!

So two groups developed. One group took the 2475 B.C.E. date as gospel, the other jumped on board the 10450 B.C.E. ancient-civilization bandwagon. And that's where things stood for a while, until more information threw another monkey wrench into the works.

The Sphinx

Standing right next to the pyramids is an even more enigmatic structure. It's called the Sphinx, and has traditionally been cloaked in the enfolding blankets of the conspiracy of silence as well as the shifting desert sands of the Giza Plateau. Nothing about this structure quite fits traditional parameters.

For one thing, it is a form carved right out of the native bedrock to represent the body of a lion with the head of a man. That makes no sense at all unless you offer some purely speculative motives for the project.

And that leads to a second point. The image has absolutely nothing to do with pyramids. It seems totally out of context. Because it is carved into bedrock, it sits in a deep well of sorts. The well is constantly filling up with drifting sand, to the point where for many thousands of years only the head has been sticking up out of the desert. No one even knew about the lion body until it was excavated.

Without adding to the tremendous amount of literature written about the riddle of the Sphinx, suffice it to say that the traditional position of most Egyptologists is that the whole complex, pyramids and Sphinx together, were built at roughly the same time—about 2575 to 2467 B.C.E.—by three pharaohs of the Fourth Dynasty, Khufu, Khafre, and Menkaure (or, if you prefer their Greek names, Cheops, Chephren, and Mycerinus.) According to accepted doctrine, the pyramids were built as tombs, and that's it. Nothing more esoteric was involved. There are no great mysteries here.

The theory became known as "Tombs and Tombs Only," and that's the way it stands to this day with those who prefer to invoke the conspiracy of silence when it comes to discussing ancient aliens, lost civilizations, or any

The famous Spinx of Egypt bears evidence of water erosion, meaning it was built when water was more plentiful on the Giza Plateau, but this would place its construction over eleven thousand years ago.

other such New Age nonsense. Giza is a necropolis, period! It's a home for the dead. Or so the story goes.

But if that's the case, how to explain the Sphinx? It doesn't seem to have much to do with burying somebody. There are no tombs inside.

"Well," the traditionalists reply, "that's easy. The Sphinx bears the head of Pharaoh Khafre, who had it built as a monument to his glory."

But that doesn't explain two problems related to it.

1. After careful inspection, years of arguing and hundreds, if not more, carefully worded and peer-reviewed papers, the consensus now seems to be that the head of the Sphinx is a modified addition to the original work. In other words, the head was originally that of a lion, just like the rest of the structure. Pharaoh Khafre, if he had anything at all to do with it, probably had it re-sculpted to look like him. This, of course, implies that the Sphinx does, indeed, bear his likeness. It could just as easily be someone else.

What this means is that the Sphinx was originally crafted before Khafre's time and is, therefore, older than the accepted dates of the pyramids. How much older? That leads to the second point.

2. The Sphinx has spent much of its time, thousands of years, buried in the drifting sands of the Giza Plateau. It's only when someone takes the time and spends the effort to dig it out that it is exposed to erosion and wear. But the body, the oldest original portion of the figure, shows unmistakable signs of water erosion. How could this be? It stands, or rather reclines, in a desert! It doesn't rain in the Sinai, at least not enough to cause the kind of visible wear evidenced here. What's going on?

Well, as it turns out, the Sinai is a young desert. It wasn't always dry. Eleven thousand to fifteen thousand years ago the Giza Plateau was a well-watered, palm-covered paradise. While it would have made no sense to build such a great edifice in a way that was guaranteed to cover it up with drifting sand, it would have made perfect sense to build it back when it was surrounded by lush forests and grass.

But that makes the Sphinx at least eleven thousand years old—way too old for traditional Egyptologists.

Back Home Again

Now we return to our original theme—astronomy. More to the point, astrology. Let's assume that the experts are correct when they say the Sphinx was originally a lion in both head and body. Can its position reveal anything about its age?

Indeed it can! The lion on the Giza faces due east. Every spring equinox, the day when night and day are equal in length, it is positioned to watch the sunrise. But behind that sunrise he sees the house or compartment of stars out of which the sun appears. In the introduction to this book we learned about the animal signs of the zodiac. One of those animals is the heavenly counterpart to the earthly Sphinx—Leo the Lion.

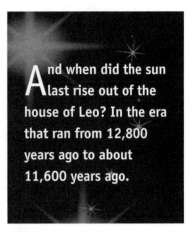

And when did the sun last rise out of the house of Leo? In the era that ran from 12,800 years ago to about 11,600 years ago. This was the epic geologists call the Younger Dryas. When was the Giza Plateau last favored with a rainy climate? You guessed it! Precisely at this time. And when do Egyptologists place the Zep Tepi, the "First Time," the age when the original ancient gods of Egypt began the Egyptian civilization? Right again!

Graham Hancock explains it concisely in his book, *Magicians of the Gods*:

> The essence of the argument is that there was an ancient globally-distributed doctrine—"as above, so below"—that set out quite deliberately to create monuments on the ground that copied the patterns of certain significant constellations in the sky. Moreover, since the position of all stars change slowly but continuously as a result of the precession, it is possible to use particular configurations of astronomically aligned monuments to deduce the dates they represent—i.e. the dates when the stars were last in the position depicted by the monuments on the ground.... The heart of the matter involves two constellations—the constellation Leo, rising due east above the sun at dawn on the spring equinox in the epoch of 10500 B.C.E., and the constellation of Orion, which the Ancient Egyptians visualized as the celestial figure of the god Osiris, the deceased god-king who ruled over the afterlife.

Does everyone agree with this theory? Of course not! It's met with ridicule and scorn by traditional Egyptologists who just wish the whole thing would go away and hide beneath the covers of the conspiracy of silence.

Squabbles in the Camp

As a matter of fact, even non-traditionalists have trouble with it. Andrew Collins, for instance, whom Egyptologists usually place in the same heretical camp as Graham Hancock, argues that the Giza complex does not mimic Orion. It mimics Cygnus the Swan, the great Northern Cross, the backbone of the Milky Way. In ancient times, Cygnus was known simply as the bird constellation. When you look at Cygnus on a clear night, you can see behind it the luminescent band of stars that make up the plane of our galaxy, the Milky Way. Cygnus highlights this sight.

His argument is that throughout the world, many religions fix the location of heaven, both the source of life and the destination of death, in the same segment of the northern sky covered by Cygnus. His question is, why?

In Collins's words:

> In December 2005, an American scientific think tank called the Meinel Institute of Las Vegas, founded by former consultants to the NASA-linked JPL (Jet Propulsion Laboratory), came forward and announced that it now believed that cosmic rays from a galactic binary system producing relativistic jets was responsible for a rapid acceleration in animal and human evolution around 40,000 years ago. It was at this time that great changes occurred in human advancement, most obviously the appearance of anatomically modern human beings in Europe and Asia and the emergence of cave art.

In other words, humankind took a giant leap of creativity forward some forty thousand years ago when cosmic rays out of Cygnus, in the north sky, bathed our planet with energy. This was precisely when modern humans began to produce symbolic (religious) art deep in the caves of western Europe. Could this step have been a heavenly boost, a divine intervention, remembered in myth and legend? It would certainly explain why heaven is seen as being in the north.

Again in Collins's words:

> It becomes clear that the memory of this cosmic influence, seen as divine, was behind the emergence of religion, art and intellect. This was abstractly recognized and preserved, eventually becoming the basis for the ancient cosmology behind the symbolism found even today among various world religions, including Christianity, Islam, Judaism and Hinduism.

After arriving at this theory, Collins set out to find earthly proof for his heavenly concept. In structures such as the newly discovered Göbekli Tepe he found evidence that pointed to a Cygnus connection. The structure seemed to be oriented toward Deneb, the brightest star in the constellation of Cygnus the celestial bird. The plot thickens when we discover that 17,000 years ago, Deneb was in position to be the polar star, the "fixed" star that stands above the earth's North Pole around which the rest of the heavens appear to rotate.

His full argument, which is quite technical, is put forth in his book *Göbekli Tepe: Genesis of the Gods*, but to summarize—the twin pillars of Enclosure D at Göbekli Tepe feature a drilled sighting hole and seem to be oriented in such a way that a priest or shaman:

> ... would have been able to look through the stone's sighting hole to see Deneb setting on the north-north-western horizon, a quite magnificent sight that cannot have happened by chance alone. Clearly, this is powerful evidence that the enclosure really was directed toward this star during the epoch of its construction.

Another one of the places he looked to confirm his theory was Giza. He wasn't happy with the Orion belt-star theory. According to his calculations, the pyramids on the ground didn't quite fit with the celestial measurements above.

But in stars forming the wings of Cygnus, he claimed to have found an exact fit. And not only here in Giza. Eventually he ...

Cygnus, the constellation of the swan, was a source of cosmic rays that affected Earth some forty thousand years ago, about the same time humans began creating religious art.

> ... uncovered an astronomy that is about 17,000 years old, with standing stones, temples, and monuments across the globe oriented towards Cygnus' stars. He also found that the use of deep caves by Paleolithic man led to the rise of religious thought and the belief in life's stellar origins.

This, of course, caused a stir in the non-traditionalist camp.

One thing is clear, however: Lest we relegate these arguments and theories to the field of irrelevant interests, no longer important to modern society, remember that our very language preserves the memory of these concepts. If Cygnus the Swan, for instance, suggested to our ancestors that a heavenly bird brings us into earthly existence from out of the north, we need to remember that we retell that myth whenever we tell our children that they were born when a stork deposited them in our homes. And when we die, just before we make the final trip to our heavenly home, we sing our metaphorically operatic swan song.

The Challenge Ahead

Out of such ideas come new insights and questions. Maybe, in the end, it doesn't matter who is right and who is wrong. Maybe the purpose of such battles is to break open the conspiracy of silence and challenge the institution-

> **A**fter all, the question is not so much what Orion and Cygnus represented to our ancient ancestors. The question is why they were so intrigued in the first place.

al status quo, entrenched in doctrines that refuse to acknowledge the march of time and new information.

After all, the question is not so much what Orion and Cygnus represented to our ancient ancestors. The question is why they were so intrigued in the first place.

What were they thinking? What answers were they seeking? What was in their hearts and minds when they gazed upward at the north sky? Were they searching for something new, or remembering something old that they had forgotten—a memory that shimmered in the recesses of their minds, recalling a civilization that once was and could be again?

PYRAMIDS AROUND THE WORLD

Diffusion may be simply defined as the spread of a cultural item from its place of origin to other places. A more expanded definition depicts diffusion as the process by which discrete culture traits are transferred from one society to another, through migration, trade, war, or other contact.

Michael Goldstein and Gail King
and Meghan Wright in "Diffusionism and Acculturation"

The Pyramid Band

In a band around the earth, situated between twenty and thirty-two degrees north latitude, in countries as far apart as Egypt, Peru, Mexico, Guatemala, the Sudan, Mesopotamia, and China, there exists a series of pyramids that are both breathtakingly similar and intriguingly unique. Because this band also includes such popular mystifying areas as the Bermuda Triangle in the Atlantic and the Devil's Sea in the Pacific, all sorts of theories exist about it, ranging from indications of a worldwide electromagnetic grid to beacons or ports signaling aliens from other worlds.

Spectacular theories aside, however, the pyramids exist. There's no denying them. They stand there, steeped in mystery, despite matter-of-fact attempts to describe them as commonplace artifacts of known civilizations.

But they are not commonplace. Of course mystery surrounds them. How could it not? The questions hang in the air and there is no escaping them. Why pyramids? Why in that narrow band and nowhere else? What do they mean?

Even the most down-to-earth archeologist is forced to cringe when confronted by such inquiries, and scientific platitudes addressing the who and when questions don't suffice. It may be uncomfortable to say, "We don't know!" but that's the only answer they can give at this point.

Questions about physical construction and era of building? Sure! Those are scientific questions and yield to scientific scrutiny. But philosophical and metaphysical questions? Those they defer to others.

The conspiracy of science settles in by default, and since nature abhors a vacuum, rampant speculation rushes in to fill the void.

Either indigenous people came up with the idea themselves, or the idea came up somewhere and then spread outward from culture to culture.

There are only two ways of approaching the problem. Either indigenous people came up, with the idea themselves, or the idea came up somewhere and then spread outward from culture to culture. Surveys suggest that people who study such things are followers of one theory or the other and seldom change their minds.

And therein lies the problem. Human nature being what it is, when our minds are made up it is very difficult to remain open to arguments from the other side. And once we start looking to find facts supporting our argument, we tend to find what we are looking for, while ignoring that ugly little fact which might destroy a beautiful theory. Thus the conspiracy of silence, even though it may be self-imposed, triumphs again.

What does this mean in a practical sense as it relates to pyramid building? There is no dispute that indigenous cultures built pyramids within what we have called the Pyramid Band. After all, they are there and they stand within that particular latitude. That's not the point. The questions remain: "Why?" and "Why there?"

Let's approach the problem though the back door of analogy and survey another discipline—the practice of religion.

Diffusionism

Religions develop denominations. "Isms" develop around a central belief which is then taken to extremes. Christianity, for instance, split into Catholicism and Protestantism. Then Protestantism developed its own plethora of isms—Lutheran*ism*, Calvin*ism*, Presbyterian*ism*, etc.

Sad to say, in this sense of the word, archeology is a religion. Archeologists used to believe in Diffusionism. This is the belief that if two cultures developed similar ideas (concerning, for instance, pyramid building), chances are that they had had contact at some time in the past. One culture passed on its wisdom to the other. Ideas spread through contact. If a certain type of pottery was made here, and then it appeared there, chances are the people here had been in contact with the people there. It's as simple as that.

Lately, however, what has become known in some circles as New Archeology has questioned that belief. Their arguments run along these lines:

- Diffusionism doesn't give credit to indigenous peoples. It doesn't think them capable of coming up with ideas on their own.

- Diffusionism overlooks the thrust of human evolution, which influences people to do similar things at similar points of development.

- Diffusionism calls for ancient peoples being able to cross oceans and trek great distances when there is no evidence of things like boats or overland migration.

Pretty soon the Diffusionists began to respond. It wasn't long before they themselves began to split into denominations. Hyper-Diffusionists separated from Moderate-Diffusionists and Cultural-Diffusionists. All three elected to maintain at least some form of contact between peoples while making room for human evolution of cultural ideas. Pretty soon Diffusionist Fundamentalists began arguing with the Indigenous Liberals who refused to recognize Diffusionism at all. On and on it went, each group preaching to their respective choirs in assemblies, universities, and conferences across the land.

Pyramidal structures across the world's ancient cultures, such as this Mayan pyramid near Uxmal, Mexico, look remarkably the same. Is this merely coincidence, or something more?

In the matter of pyramids, it came to a heated argument. Ardent Diffusionists believe pyramid building began in Egypt and spread throughout the world. Moderate Diffusionists believe there may have been some contact by small groups of travelers but not necessarily full-scale exchange of ideas. The New Archeologists, in the absence of any evidence of boats and other means of transportation, preach that when humans reach a certain point of cultural growth, they build pyramids. That's just what you do if you're a human.

"But why the similarities? And why at this latitude?" scream the conservatives.

"Why not?" answer the liberals. "Maybe it has to do with how weather affects our evolution. People who are cold don't go to the effort or have the raw materials at hand."

Meanwhile, lay people outside the fray, looking in, offer their own ideas. "It must have been ancient aliens. It must have to do with electromagnetic power points around the earth grid. It must have been a lost civilization of teachers. It must have been...." Well, add your own idea here.

Ardent Diffusionists believe pyramid building began in Egypt and spread throughout the world.

There is more dry theory taught in university departments about this subject than is possible to recount. There is also more nonsense in the popular media than can be ever assimilated.

But the questions remain. The pyramids are there. Why?

Is there a lost wisdom behind their construction and a reason for their location? Because of all the work that went into them and the fact that they stand where they do, it seems there must be.

But we just don't know.

✳ ✳ ✳

STONEHENGE

After the end of the grand construction phase of Stonehenge, around 2400 B.C.E., the monument was altered, but the era of mega-monument building was over. "That's basically when their world changed," Dr. Parker Pearson said. New people crossed the channel from Europe, bringing bronze and metal making to the stone age culture. "It's a very interesting shift," he said. "In a way, Stonehenge is a swan song."

Kenneth Chang in the *New York Times*: November 9, 2015

Thinking and Feeling

It's been said that there have been more books written about Atlantis than any other single subject. Without the slightest bit of evidence to back me up, I politely disagree. I think Stonehenge holds that honor. For thousands of years it has stood silent and alone on the Salisbury Plain in southern England, refusing to yield its ultimate secrets. It has become the darling of the New Age, a pilgrimage destination for contemporary Druid and Wiccan societies, a tourist bonanza to local businesses and an archeologist's nightmare when it comes time to obtain permits needed to dig. It is attributed in legend to a fraternity of mystics whose numbers include Merlin the Magician, giants of old, ancient architects with varying motivations, astronomers of equally mixed intentions, aliens, hunters, farmers, Druids, and various warring factions. According to fanciful accounts, it was raised either by using music, simple log rollers, alien technologies, or some forgotten wisdom of the Old Ones. It is said to be magical, practical, mystical, spiritual, and religious, or some combination of all of the above.

There are probably as many explanations for it as there are people who have seen it.

But what do we really know about it?

Dr. Mike Parker Pearson, an English archeologist, has done most of the latest research. He and his teams of volunteers have discovered a lot of new information.

- They have found Stonehenge to be part of a much larger complex than previously considered, spread out over a huge landscape, indicating it was part of a megalithic, complex center of great importance.

- They have discovered buried and forgotten villages for people who, at various times, built it. They can tell you what the workers had for supper and how they lived.

There have been many theories as to why ancient Druids constructed the now-famous Stonehenge, which is about 80 miles (129 kilometers) southwest of London, England.

- They, and archeologists who dug here before, have discovered a rich history extending out over thousands of years, beginning with a simple ditch and mound, continuing through eras of wood posts and ending with mega-ton dressed stones, some of which were dragged a hundred miles and more over the landscape.

- They have seen evidence of sophisticated mortise and tenon stonework that seems very advanced for the time of construction.

- They have discovered avenues and approaches that seem to indicate seasonal, ceremonial processionals.

But what does all this mean? It took a tremendous amount of work over thousands of years. That is evident, to be sure. But why?

A Personal Pilgrimage

Rather than duplicate the wealth of historical material, identify the scores of astronomical sight lines, and restate the complex figures of star placements, moon sightings, and solstice sun rises that have been the subject of more books than anyone can possibly read, I'd like to interject a personal point of view here.

Throughout this chapter about ancient astronomers I've wondered about the fact that our ancestors were fascinated by the night sky and proved their interest by building complex ways to study it. But sometimes the intellectual approach just doesn't cut it. Yes, Stonehenge is a monument to ancient astrologers. That goes without saying. But what does the average person feel when he or she visits Stonehenge? What is it like to visit an ancient memorial to a group of astrologers who, let's be frank, saw the world through different eyes than we do? Can we get inside their heads, or maybe even more important, their hearts?

I recently visited, over the course of two days, two cathedrals that were built many centuries apart on the Salisbury Plain—Stonehenge and Salisbury Cathedral. Both are magnificent works of art. Both were built by teams of real live human workers who demonstrated great talent and superb craftsmanship. Both show evidence of advanced religious thought. Neither required alien technology or magic.

What follows are my recollections—my feelings, if you will—of the experience. My hope is that by approaching the subject on the feeling level, rather than the thinking level, we might enter into the experience of ancient

> I've wondered about the fact that our ancestors were fascinated by the night sky and proved their interest by building complex ways to study it.

> **S**tonehenge and Salisbury Cathedral .... are magnificent works of art. Both were built by teams of real live human workers who demonstrated great talent and superb craftsmanship.

astronomers more profoundly than is possible by a simple reiteration of facts that are written elsewhere in so many books, as important as they are.

This is not an attempt to channel a divine entity to arrive at any sort of archeological conclusion of import. I'm not trying to negate the tremendous archeological work that has been done here. It isn't at all a scientific endeavor. It is, instead, a very human endeavor.

Recollections: June 2015

Stonehenge is worth the trouble of traveling to it. It really is as spectacular as the pictures make it seem. Sitting, as it does, out on the Salisbury Plain, the views are wonderful. Of course, the first question that comes to mind is, "How?" But the second is like unto it. "Why?"

The "How?" question is addressed in the small Stonehenge village built at the Visitor's Center. There stand replicated huts and sledges that attempt to transport you back into the epoch of long ago.

Moving closer, and knowing that the hundred or so people scattered well across and around the monument would be replaced by some thirty thousand this weekend at the time of the Summer Solstice, I decided to sit and meditate at the monument itself. I wanted to try to get down underneath the hype and try to connect with the builders.

Alas, to my great sorrow, I couldn't get anywhere. I sensed something way down deep, some depth of heartfelt wisdom and spirituality, but I couldn't reach it. There were too many people, too much commercialism, and, truth be known, too much jetlagged fatigue that stood in the way. But that didn't detract from the beauty. Or the sense of wonder.

Next day, after an English breakfast, I stashed my luggage, hired a cab, rode in comfort down to the front door of Salisbury Cathedral, arranged to be picked up in a few hours, and entered the magnificent, classic cathedral that took thirty-five years to build 750 years ago. It has England's tallest spire and is still an active church.

It's magnificent, there's no doubt about that. But something was wrong. Just as I had experienced at Stonehenge, I couldn't find the holiness I expected. Again, there were too many layers of commercialism. They didn't charge for anything, but they constantly directed your attention to the fact that they needed money. Donations for this, donations for that, contributions for causes, and over it all hung the unstated opinion that you were a lesser human being if you didn't comply. Rich and important people were buried everywhere. Everybody who was anybody rested there for eternity. Most of them have names that sound as if they should have been portrayed on the screen by Peter O'Toole. The place was just so darned big and self-satisfied. Beautiful? Yes! Awe inspiring? Certainly! Sacred? Dripping with it! But I couldn't find a single place to quietly meditate.

As I followed my guidebook, I finally decided I needed to find a quiet chapel somewhere. Suddenly, right before me, I found one dedicated to Thomas Becket. Maybe I could find some peace and quiet there.

Sure enough, there was nobody in the chapel at the time and I could sit in meditation for a few moments.

But once again, nothing. Just as it was at Stonehenge, I couldn't penetrate the human ego that saturated the place. There was no "there" there. Once again, I sensed something very profound buried deep. Probably it was just me, but the layers of human busy-ness, power struggles, ego and self-satisfaction, the encrustation of tradition that clings to Christianity like a shroud, was simply too powerful. I couldn't penetrate it.

Perhaps it was no coincidence that what I sensed at Stonehenge felt so similar to what I sensed at Salisbury Cathedral. Both were part of a mystical tradition that had, by the time of their construction, been covered over by layers of human tradition. Both, at the core, were built to encode a message.

At Stonehenge the original energy probably came from the cosmos itself. It took thousands of years of trial and error to reach the monument stage that it exhibits today. There was a complex mathematical code and a sophisticated astronomy built into its very architecture. But I wonder if, by the time Stonehenge reached its final form, it might have already been a relic to a forgotten spirituality. I wonder if the stones themselves, and the monumental effort required to move them into place, were by then simply a tribute to a forgotten mystery, remembered by an elite who had long since lost the experience of the heavens that inspired the original builders, and retained only memories and traditions of it.

Salisbury Cathedral in England was built about 750 years ago and is still an active place of worship.

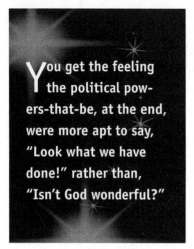

You get the feeling the political pow-ers-that-be, at the end, were more apt to say, "Look what we have done!" rather than, "Isn't God wonderful?"

I sensed the same thing at Salisbury Cathedral. Christianity had once, for better or for worse, turned a world upside down. Many of those memories were built into the very architecture of the Cathedral in code, using what is called Gematria, a calculation of the numerical equivalence of letters, words, or phrases that, when understood by the initiated, reveal insight into the interrelation of different concepts between words and ideas. Did the Cathedral, with all its complex symbols, represent the power of that mystery? Or was it only a monument to it?

We humans have a unique tendency to take that which is insightful and holy and imbue it with traditions and rules that too often corrupt the original meaning of the founders who were there at the beginning. There isn't a religion in the world today that would be understood or recognized by the founder who began it. The humble carpenter of Galilee would be shocked at the Salisbury monument built to honor his name. It was said, for instance, that he was immensely angered at what the Temple of Solomon had become by his day. I wonder if at Salisbury Cathedral he would have seen the ropes cordoning off great sections of the altar as good material with which to make a whip of cords to drive out the moneychangers?

It's quite a thought, isn't it? I'm sure the builders of the Cathedral, like those of Stonehenge, were religious men, at least in their outward lives. I'm sure they were at least somewhat aware of the significance of the ritualistic symbolism they were building into a magnificent monument. But I wonder if at the time of final construction of both Stonehenge and the Salisbury Cathedral, their original institutions had solidified and proven themselves to be a two-sided coin with both dark and light housed within their calcified walls. What they were building was, even before it was finished (and there is evidence that in the case of the Cathedral they rushed it at the end in order to meet some kind of deadline), a relic to a different kind of power—an earthly, ego-driven power—rather than a spiritual force. You get the feeling the political powers-that-be, at the end, were more apt to say, "Look what we have done!" rather than, "Isn't God wonderful?"

In short, I wonder if the Stonehenge we see today is something akin to Salisbury Cathedral—a monument to what once was, rather than a statement of what is.

Perhaps Qoheleth, the preacher of the Old Testament book of Ecclesiastes, was right: "There is nothing new under the sun." If so, then what we see on the Salisbury plain today are two cathedrals, built to illustrate the reality of two spiritual traditions, both of which had experienced their day in the sun, but by the time of the construction of their greatest monuments, existed only in encrusted memory. Today they are visited by people who have to ask, "Why?" because they have moved so very far away, in both time and spirituality, from the source that originally inspired them.

Final Thoughts

What I have just written is intensely personal, of course. It doesn't stand up to any test of objectivity and no archeologist worth his or her salt would pay any attention to it. Instead, it is an attempt to get inside the heads of the ancients. What were they thinking, what were they feeling, when they built these great megalithic monuments to astronomy and religion? After all, in many ways they were just like us. They had thoughts and feelings about family, friends, dinner, entertainment, religion, and spirituality.

In the end, it is these feelings that we are trying to understand when we view the works of their hands … and wonder. Perhaps we will never really understand those who came before us until we stand in their sandals, turn off our electric lights, gaze up at the night sky, and contemplate eternity.

The Web of Knowledge

The original root of the word "disaster" meant to be out of touch with the stars. ("Aster" means star.) It may be that at least part of the solution to the many disasters dotting the transitional landscape of the [twenty-first] century would be to reclaim our astronomical heritage and get back in touch with the stars.

L. Robert Keck in *Sacred Eyes*

In the first chapter, we explored the questions, "Who are we? Where did we come from? Who are our ancestors?"

In this second chapter we tried to understand a little about who they were by examining what they did.

In short, they felt drawn to explore the heavens. There was something about the stars, expressed through the zodiac they envisioned on the horizon, that excited them enough to compose mythic stories such as Arth Vawr and the Pendragon. They built stone structures around the world such as those at Karahunj, the medicine wheels of the American West, Mystery Hill and the stone structures of New England, and Newgrange in Ireland. They went deep underground into the caves of Lascaux to spiritually explore the consciousness of the cosmos.

In Orion, Cygnus, and the mysteries of the north sky they searched for that which was beyond their understanding but seemed to touch the edges of a distant memory, a time when their evolutionary growth took a giant step forward.

They seemed moved to export their knowledge of the mysteries of the heavens when they built, maybe without realizing what they were doing except in a deep, Freudian sense, pyramids around the world.

In megastructures such as Stonehenge they contemplated the eternal and strove to build a solid structure to house what had become their religions.

But was there more than a search for spirituality in their quest? Could it be that they were not only looking inward, but remembering something real, perhaps even terrifying....

But was there more than a search for spirituality in their quest? Could it be that they were not only looking inward, but remembering something real, perhaps even terrifying, that had come from the skies and changed their lives forever?

To put it plainly, in the obsession our ancient ancestors had with the skies, can we see echoes of a physical encounter with the cosmos, something they did not understand, such as a deadly visitor from outer space in the form of a comet, for instance, colliding with the earth, utterly destroying what had been, up to then at least, a promising civilization? Could it be that their study of the night skies was an attempt to understand what they believed to be catastrophic divine intervention with life on Earth?

If so, it would explain a lot about how even modern-day religions concern themselves with a heaven that is somehow up there in the clouds, and a hell where fires and misery reign forever. That whole concept could be a vestigial memorial of a fiery cataclysm. It must have felt something like that.

A Walk on the Wild Side

That's why I ended this chapter with a personal account of what it felt like to be at Stonehenge and try to connect with the ancient people who built it. I thought it important, despite the fact that many might read those words, chalk it up to one man's opinion, and write the whole experience off.

Even though I was unsuccessful in my attempt to mind-meld with them, I still think we should try. I live in the woods of South Carolina, far from any city and its lights. I watch the stars every night and every early morning. I must confess that I'm not as rugged as the old timers. If it's cold in the winter, when the stars are at their brightest, I watch them from a hot tub. I am very familiar with constellations, shooting stars, and precession. I have raised standing stones to mark the solstice and equinox. I sometimes hold celebrations on those special days, although they are not nearly as elaborate as the ones held by the ancients. Mine are much simpler and probably more fun.

I am very familiar with the heavens and have a quite profound spiritual life, as my book *The Dragon Awakes: Rediscovering Earth Energy in the Age of Science* makes clear. In short, I have tried, over the years, to walk the paths of the Old Ones.

So my question is this: Why is the opinion of any honest and real seeker of truth less important than that of an astronomer whose knowledge comes out of a sterile telescope, a computer simulation, or a laboratory? We are accustomed, in this scientific age, to worship at the altar of the measurable. Instruments designed to do just that have the final say in scientific research. The ancients had none of those things. Their experience was firsthand, up close, naked-eye, and personal. Just like yours if you devote time to the process. If their experience was such that they needed to construct megaton monuments to the heavens, something you and I would probably never be moved to do even though we might be totally sympathetic and starry-eyed, they must have had a reason—something that happened to them that is outside the experience of those who only measure what the old-timers built.

Thus we move beyond asking how. The archeologists can tell us that. We want to know why.

The work of a scientist is important. But if we want to know more about the "whys," we have to resort to different means. We, as citizens of the twenty-first century, have to put ourselves in the position of the Old Ones. They had the same bodily organs, the same size brain, the same needs and desires we have. In every way that is important, they were just like us. By turning inward we can begin to walk in their footsteps. It's an authentic way for modern humans to bridge the gap of time.

"But," we are told, "that's not scientific."

Well, no. It's not. But it's important. If people today can put themselves in the position of the people of yesterday, maybe we can develop theories that the scientists can then confirm or disprove. It's a new way of thinking. It won't pass muster without a lot of argument and ridicule. But perhaps it's a way we can break the present impasse when it comes to determining the real reasons behind the megaliths that sought to unveil the great mystery called life. It doesn't mean we have to entertain wacky ideas and flighty theories. It means we have to try to put ourselves in the position of being human beings, living in a different time of history, and ask, "What would we have done?"

Only in this way can we really honor the Old Ones and give them the respect they deserve.

> **W**hy is the opinion of any honest and real seeker of truth less important than that of an astronomer whose knowledge comes out of a sterile telescope, a computer simulation, or a laboratory?

Author Graham Hancock became upset that a wooden roof was built on top of Göbekli Tepe to provide modern people with shade.

Connecting or Cutting Off?

Here's a case in point. Graham Hancock, writing in his book *Magicians of the Gods*, reports with moving simplicity and not a little anger that the temples at Göbekli Tepe now feature an ugly wooden roof over the whole area. The purpose, we are told, is to protect the complex from the elements and give the volunteers some shade while they work.

Fine and good. The archeologists decided to spend a great deal of money that could have gone into research to construct a roof that, although we are told is temporary, will probably, considering the expense, be there for a long while.

But it raises a question. How can a site that might very well be dedicated to celestial observation possibly be understood if it is shut off from the skies? The archeologists decided, in advance, that they were not willing to even consider the fact that the heavens had any importance to the original builders. They look down at their feet while the message of the monument is to focus on the heavens. The objective of the archeologists is practical, but it cuts them off from the very humanness that they are searching for. You can't find what you are looking for if you're looking in the wrong place. It's as simple as that. Perhaps it's time to let some subjective humanity enter the stuffy walls of science.

In the next chapter we will try to do just that. We will explore the possibility that something from the heavens once dramatically changed life on Earth. If so, it must have left evidence. That leaves room for the work of science and the work of people who seek the "whys," as well as the "hows." By searching for that evidence, and make no mistake, many reputable scientists are doing just that, we may finally discover the truth of why our ancient ancestors were so interested in the skies above them. As we shall see, we may even discover a warning for our time.

ANCIENT CATASTROPHES

Near the end of the last Ice Age 12,800 years ago, a giant comet that had entered the solar system from deep space thousands of years earlier, broke into multiple fragments. Some of these struck the Earth causing a global cataclysm on a scale unseen since the extinction of the dinosaurs. At least eight of the fragments hit the North American ice cap, while further fragments hit the northern European ice cap. The impacts, from comet fragments a mile wide approaching at more than 60,000 miles an hour, generated huge amounts of heat which instantly liquidized millions of square kilometers of ice, destabilizing the Earth's crust and causing the global Deluge that is remembered in myths all around the world.

But there were survivors—known to later cultures by names such as "the Sages," "the Magicians," "the Shining Ones," and "the Mystery Teachers of Heaven." They travelled the world in their great ships doing all in their power to keep the spark of civilization burning. They settled at key locations—Göbekli Tepe in Turkey, Baalbek in the Lebanon, Giza in Egypt, ancient Sumer, Mexico, Peru and across the Pacific where a huge pyramid has recently been discovered in Indonesia. Everywhere they went these 'magicians of the Gods' brought with them the memory of a time when mankind had fallen out of harmony with the universe and paid a heavy price.

A memory and a warning to the future…. For the comet that wrought such destruction between 12,800 and 11,600 years ago may not be done with us yet. Astronomers believe that a 20-mile wide "dark" fragment of the original giant comet remains hidden within its debris stream and threatens the Earth. An astronomical message encoded at Göbekli Tepe, and in the Sphinx and the pyramids of Egypt, warns that the "Great Return" will occur in our time …

Graham Hancock, introducing Magicians of the Gods

A series of impacts … occurred 11,600 years ago, the exact date that Plato gives for the destruction and submergence of Atlantis…. An advanced civilization that flourished during the Ice Age was destroyed in the global cataclysms between 12,800 and 11,600 years ago.

Graham Hancock, in Magicians of the Gods

Responding to Loss

In 586 B.C.E., the Jewish civilization in Israel suffered a catastrophic loss. Nebuchadnezzar and the armies of Babylon surrounded Jerusalem, laid siege to it and eventually sacked the city, burned it to the ground and enslaved the cream of Jewish society. They deported the population back to Babylon. Jewish civilization was, for all practical purposes, ended. If it was going to grow again, it would have to be built on the ruins of what had come before.

The Jews, now encamped by the rivers of Babylon, responded by writing a number of books now known as the Hebrew Scriptures. In Christian circles, it is called the Old Testament. Others know it simply as the Bible. It asked searching questions: "What happened?"—"Why?"—"How could God do this or allow such a thing to happen?"—"Where did we go wrong?"

It was written both to remember what once was and to guide future generations who might someday build on the ruins of what was destroyed back in the old country. Eventually, under leaders named Ezra and Nehemiah, they did just that.

When any civilization falls, whatever the reason for the loss, the human response is to first try and understand why. The second response is usually to record what once was so as to leave a testament for the future. When people have the written word to fall back on, the testament is usually left in notations, either in the pages of a book or pecked in stone. In the absence of writing, either legends and myths or monuments in stone must suffice. The third is to rebuild.

Expand that historical analogy for a moment. Picture the loss not of one particular civilization through the ravages of war or internal conflict, but a

The Younger Dryas comet impact radically changed the landscape of the world where humans were getting a tentative foothold. Northern Europe was tundra, and really only areas around present-day Spain, Turkey, Italy, and Greece were comfortable environments.

worldwide devastation of epic proportions. Imagine a comet, for instance, exploding in the atmosphere, releasing thousands or even millions of times more energy than the entire combined nuclear arsenal of every country on Earth. Think about worldwide fires, floods, darkened skies, and volcanic winters. Picture a world in which the continued existence of whole species stands in the balance.

It is not idle speculation. It has happened before. About 12,800 years ago, for instance, many species faced their demise. Some of them, now known as mega-fauna such as mammoths, mastodons, saber-tooth cats, dire wolves, and many more, went extinct. They couldn't adapt and rebound.

But one species, our own human species, is nothing if not adaptable. Evidence from around the world indicates that some of us made it through the devastation and came out on the other side of a major extinction event. But we were changed forever.

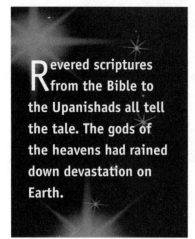

Revered scriptures from the Bible to the Upanishads all tell the tale. The gods of the heavens had rained down devastation on Earth.

How did we respond? The way humans do. If universal mythology and historical legends serve as a reliable guide, we first asked questions. "Why did this happen?" We gazed up at the heavens, the home of the object of devastation, and wondered if it had divine implications. Had we done something to deserve this? Is God punishing us? Where did we go wrong?

In that moment of time we developed a new world view, the results of which are recorded in almost every existing organized religion. Revered scriptures from the Bible to the Upanishads all tell the tale. The gods of the heavens had rained down devastation on Earth. We had somehow failed to live up to their expectations. The myths of the Hopi, the stories about Atlantis, the tales of a divinely ordained worldwide flood, and the morality tales of a Golden Age all have one thing in common: They remind us that we are descended from a civilization that was thought to have grown too smug, too conceited, too puffed up with vanity, and too full of pride. We planted the seeds of our own self-inflated egotism and reaped the whirlwind of destruction. But a few chosen folk, having "found grace in the eyes of the Lord," passed through the devastation.

What did we do next? According to the myths and legends, and, as we shall see, perhaps even the archeological record, we built edifices that shout, "We were here!" They were monuments with many purposes. Obviously one was to preserve a record that would last through the ages. For that reason the structures are massive and substantial. But they were also built to study the heavens from whence came our destruction. Would it happen again? What if we could prepare next time?

But we also set about recording in stone, myth, and expressions of art the knowledge of who we were so that future generations could learn from our mistakes and build on the ruins of our destruction.

We did all this because we are, after all, human. That's how humans respond to adversity. That's how cultures perpetuate their values.

Devastation

That the world has been devastated by flaming invaders from space is not a fanciful supposition coming from New Age philosophers. Look around you. Do you see any dinosaurs? Of course not. They were destroyed in a fiery devastation that came from outer space some 65 million years ago. An asteroid landed in the Yucatan peninsula. You can even Google the crater it left and see the ground zero impact for yourself.

That it will happen again in the future is no longer conjecture either. Scientists don't say "if," they say "when." They have backed up their theories by spending a lot of money on programs to track comets and asteroids which might endanger us. The idea is that if we have enough advanced warning, we might be able to do something about staving off the collision.

As long as we keep the time of the impacts cordoned off in our minds, placing them far in the past or far in the future, we don't tend to worry very much. "It won't happen to me," we say. "I have more immediate things to think about."

Evidence seems to be mounting that we are doing exactly that when it comes to acknowledging the human-created weapon of mass destruction called climate change. We are affecting the very future of humanity on the planet, but as long as things are going to come to a head a generation or two in the future, we don't care. We need to drive to work in the morning to work at a fossil-fueled, climate-controlled office building. Why should we worry about our carbon footprint? You can't ask us to give up our standard

This structure in Norway might not look like much, but it is the entrance to the Svalbard Global Seed Vault, where all the seeds of the world are being stored in case of a global disaster.

of living just to satisfy the whims of a few alarmists. "You say we're heading for trouble? Then do something about it! But don't ask me to change my lifestyle!"

Meanwhile, a group of concerned naturalists are quietly gathering seeds of every plant in the world and storing them in the Svalbard Global Seed Vault on the Norwegian Island of Spitsbergen, some eight hundred miles from the North Pole. It's kind of a horticultural Noah's Ark. "Not that there's any real concern, of course," is their response when questioned about it. "But just in case." And the underground Hutchinson Vault, also known as the Forever Vault, in Kansas is fast filling up with precious mementos we want to be remembered by if future civilizations want to know about us—such as the first Walt Disney *Steamboat Willie* cartoons and the entire *Star Wars* series of movies.

Are they acknowledging something obvious that we are ignoring, perhaps to our peril?

Gathering the Evidence

"Where's the evidence of mass destruction?" you ask. "Is there any proof this kind of disaster has occurred when the human race was alive and flourishing on the planet?"

Yes, there is. It's in the stories people have passed down through the generations. We call them myths. It's in the historical record they preserved after they had developed the art of writing. We call them scriptures. And it's in the massive stone structures they built to study, observe, and reflect on the heavens, searching for that next visitor or, at the very least, drawing our attention to the heavens, the abode of the divine. We call them megaliths.

We need not ask where the evidence is that our civilization is built on the ashes of what came before. It is all around us, written in myth, in legend, and in stone. All we have to do is open our eyes and look. That's what we'll do in this chapter.

THE ATLANTIS TRADITION

In those days the Atlantic was navigable; and there was an island situated in front of the straits which are by you called the Pillars of Heracles; the island was the way to other islands, and from these you might pass to the whole of the opposite continent which surrounded the true ocean; for this sea which is within the Straits of Heracles is only a harbor, having a narrow entrance, but that other is a real sea, and the surrounding land may be most truly called a boundless continent. Now in this island of Atlantis there was a great and wonderful empire which had rule over the whole island and several others, and over parts of the continent as far as Egypt, and of Europe. This vast power shone forth in the excellence of her virtue and strength, among all mankind. She was pre-eminent in courage and military skill. But afterwards there occurred violent earthquakes and floods; and in a single day and night of misfortune all her warlike men in a body sank into the earth, and the island of Atlantis in like manner disappeared in the depths of the sea. For which reason the sea in those parts is impassable and impenetrable, because there is a shoal of mud in the way; and this was caused by the subsidence of the island.

Condensed version of Plato's account of Atlantis,
as translated by Benjamin Jowett

Plato

Some 2,400 years ago there lived in Greece one of the most profound thinkers the world has ever known. Plato was a philosopher and mathematician whose most famous teacher was Socrates and whose most famous student was Aristotle. Pythagoras influenced him as well. He was the founder of the Academy of Athens, the first great university in the Western world. His work, still studied today, is considered to be the foundation of Western philosophy and science. Alfred North Whitehead once offered the now-famous opinion that all of Western philosophy is "merely footnotes to Plato." Because Augustine of Hippo, a major figure who shaped Christian systematic theology, had such a reverence for Plato, Friedrich Nietzsche once called Christianity "Platonism for the people."

It was the Greek philosopher Plato who first recorded the tragic story of the lost civilization of Atlantis.

Plato invented a whole new method of teaching and writing called the dialogue. He would record a scenario in which a teacher would confront a pupil, engaging him in conversation. Hence—dialogue. The teacher would begin by asking a pertinent question and then proceed to tie the student up in knots, trapping him in his own arguments. He would prove his point with devastating and overwhelming logic.

In two of these dialogues, the *Timaeus* and the *Critias*, Plato described a long-lost, technologically sophisticated, sea-faring civilization that once existed on an island in the ocean outside the Pillars of Hercules, that is, the Strait of Gibraltar. It was called Atlantis. Although this civilization had the capacity to conquer the world, it developed, as human civilizations tend to do, arrogance. Plato implied that it grew too sophisticated for its own good, delving into knowledge that it ultimately couldn't control. For this reason it was destroyed "in a single terrible day and night," sinking into oblivion below the waves.

According to Plato, this information came from a distant relative of his named Solon, who had traveled and studied in Egypt, where he was taught the tradition that had been passed down for nine thousand years.

Never has so little been written that generated so much discussion, books, thesis, hyperbole, exaggeration, flights of fancy, and accusations. If Plato had written nothing else but these few pages, he would still be immortalized by the many arguments that followed concerning the long-lost island of Atlantis.

Myth or Madness?

Those who hear the "A" word (Atlantis) tend to gravitate quickly into one of two camps. The vast majority of academic scholars, probably pretty

Ⓘf Atlantis is a fig-
ment of the imagina-
tion, why is Plato so
insistent about giving
its demise such a spe-
cific date?

close to 100% of them, believe Plato made up the whole story to make an allegorical point and that the dialogues were teaching devices, not history lessons. They are brilliant pieces of fiction, and certainly deserve to be studied for philosophical reasons, but Atlantis existed only in the mind of Plato, seen through the literary device of having his former teacher, Socrates, engage in a dialogue with a student in order to prove a point. All we know about Atlantis comes from the lips of Socrates, placed there by Plato, the author.

If that is, indeed, the case, no more needs to be said here. But, obviously, there is another side of the story. There are those, and their number is legion, who ask two very pertinent questions:

1. If Atlantis is a figment of the imagination, why does Plato give it such a specific location and describe it in so much detail? There is far more information here than is needed just to prove a literary point.

That leads to the second question.

2. If Atlantis is a figment of the imagination, why is Plato so insistent about giving its demise such a specific date? According to him it happened in exactly 9600 B.C.E. That was precisely the time when global floods, signaling the end of the Younger Dryas Ice Age 11,600 years ago, caused the oceans to rise quickly, and in some cases, catastrophically, inundating shore-based cities and developed regions. They are not figments of the imagination. They exist and have been explored by underwater archeologists. That was also the time when many of the worldwide flood legends, such as Noah's flood and the stories in *The Epic of Gilgamesh*, claim "God" destroyed humankind. It was when Göbekli Tepe was first built by an early megalithic people who had, seemingly, no former experience with this kind of building. Plato certainly could not have had access to glacial core samples from Greenland, which prove this was exactly when the Ice Age came to a sudden and catastrophic conclusion.

Let's consider these questions.

Where Was Atlantis?

According to Plato, Atlantis was an island in the Atlantic west of Gibraltar, a stopover on the way to *the whole of the opposite continent which surrounded the true ocean*. The words in italics seem to be an accurate description of the Americas, thought to be unknown to the Greeks of this time. He describes a flourishing agricultural society, a fairly high technology which seems to include some kind of central lighting system, a great fleet of ships involved in maritime trade and other activities, and a superb construction

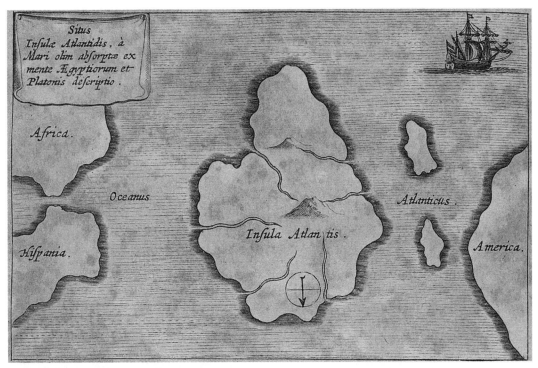

Situs
Insulæ Atlantidis, à
Mari olim absorptæ ex
mente Ægyptiorum et
Platonis descriptio.

Africa.

Oceanus

Hispania.

Insula Atlantis.

Atlanticus.

America.

A 1678 Dutch map speculated the size and location of the lost continent of Atlantis (note that the North Pole is toward the bottom of this map).

technology that included the building of great temples and public buildings. He even throws in a description of elephants and other domesticated animals.

If Plato intended Atlantis to be only a teaching device, elephants certainly seem to be a bit of overkill.

But here's the problem. According to a lot of sophisticated search methods, utilizing all the modern bells and whistles developed by modern oceanographers, there is no sunken island in the Atlantic where Plato says it used to be, and there never was one. So what's a poor Atlantis booster to do?

Theories

Well, one thing is to say that Plato got everything right except the location. This has led to some interesting theories.

One of the most prominent is that Atlantis was in the Mediterranean, not the Atlantic. The best guess from a geological standpoint seems to be the sunken island of Santorini, where there is evidence of a catastrophic disaster caused by an immense volcano exploding and producing a measurable tidal wave that destroyed the island very quickly.

That doesn't satisfy true believers, though. Why would Plato get everything else right but miss the correct location? The Mediterranean, even in Plato's time, was certainly not anything like the Atlantic.

Back to the Atlantic, then. Or more specifically, the Bahamas. There the submerged, so-called Bimini Road that seems human-built offers a tantalizing clue that the whole area was once above sea level, consisting of a single land mass. Granted, it's a little far west to exactly fit Plato's description, but it's in the right direction. The underwater paved structure, if it is, indeed, a road leading to a harbor, appears to be constructed by humans. Even Edgar Cayce, America's Sleeping Prophet, thought this was the place and predicted it would rise again. Does the Bimini Road lead to Atlantis?

> **If this second impact was violent enough ... it could have instigated some massive shifts of the plates upon which ride the earth's continents.**

Many are not convinced. Graham Hancock, in his book, *Fingerprints of the Gods*, put forth a pretty convincing argument that plate tectonics were involved in the destruction of Atlantis. Researching ancient maps and following clues left by Charles Hapgood of Keene State College in New Hampshire, he discovered descriptions of a continent that was amazingly similar to Antarctica. But traditional theory says that as long as there have been humans on the earth, Antarctica has been hidden beneath great ice sheets. How could ancient cartographers have ever seen the shoreline in order to describe and map it so accurately?

The answer is that maybe Antarctica might have been in a more northerly latitude before the comet impact of 11,600 years ago—the very impact involved at the end of the Younger Dryas Event described in a later entry of this section. This presupposes, of course, two hits from the same comet stream—one at the beginning of the Younger Dryas and another encounter 1,500 years later that ended it. If this second impact was violent enough, and it certainly seems to have been, it could have instigated some massive shifts of the plates upon which ride the earth's continents. This could have pushed a tropical Antarctica suddenly into a southern polar location, beginning a sudden freeze. Riding this circular wave, so to speak, the shift would have moved southerly locations to the west further north. Globally, this would have the effect of not only destroying mega fauna such as mammoths, but it would also explain why many of them found in what are now northern latitudes were flash frozen. One day the poor beast would have been dining on plants and flowers in a relatively balmy land. The next it would be frozen solid, the contents of his last dinner still in his stomach, so that archeologists could discover it thousands of years later.

There's a lot going for this theory. It explains some interesting phenomena. Of course, most oceanographers and geologists who study such things aren't buying it, even though none other than Albert Einstein was quite interested when he first read the theory as it was put forth by Professor Hapgood. Another person who jumped on this idea was Clive Cussler. He made it the central theme of his book *Atlantis Found*, featuring his famous fictional character, Dirk Pitt.

Putting together similar streams of information stemming from Egypt, Turkey, Greece, Peru, Mexico, Siberia, the Arctic, and many other places around the globe, the gist of Hancock's argument in *Fingerprints of the Gods* is this:

> An advanced civilization had been wiped out at the end of the last ice age. There were survivors who settled at various locations around the world and attempted to pass on their superior knowledge, including knowledge of agriculture and architecture, to hunter-gatherer peoples who had survived the cataclysm. Indeed even today we have populations of hunter-gatherers in the Kalahari Desert, for instance, and in the Amazon jungles, who coexist with our advanced technology culture—so we should not be surprised that equally disparate levels of civilization might have co-existed in the past.

He envisioned a great Ice Age civilization coming to a catastrophic end. The survivors then made their way by boat around the world, landing in places that would someday cradle what we call our civilization, helping the indigenous people climb their way up the ladder of cultural success that we enjoy today.

If Hancock is correct, we are the recipients of a forgotten civilization—an Atlantis tradition—who were the brains behind the Zep Tepi, when ancient Egyptians believed the gods walked the earth and began Egyptian history. They were the instructors who taught a bunch of hunter-gatherers in Turkey how to forsake their wandering ways, settle down and build the world's first temple— Göbekli Tepe—while instigating what we now call the agricultural revolution. They were the inspiration behind the great Mesoamerican cultures of Mexico and South America, whose descendants included the ancient Olmec, Mayan, Incan, and, later, Aztec civilizations.

> They were the inspiration behind the great Mesoamerican cultures of Mexico and South America whose descendants included the ancient Olmec, Mayan, Incan, and, later, Aztec civilizations.

Skeptics, of course, want proof. They want a single, incontrovertible fact that removes all doubt. Believers, however, make the claim that a whole pile of circumstantial evidence is probably all we're going to get. In a court of law, that is often the case. Until the verdict is rendered, however, the Atlantis tradition is an engaging one. It's not going away any time soon.

K-T BOUNDARY, BLACK MATS, AND NANODIAMONDS

Over the course of a few brilliant summer nights in 1994, scientists watched with awe as the comet Shoemaker-Levy 9 broke apart and slammed into the planet Jupiter. Pictures that flashed around the world showing the July 16–22 event were both spectacular and unnerving. In cosmic terms, Jupiter isn't that far away. What if Earth had been the target?

Jim and Barbara Willis in
Armageddon Now: The End of the World, A to Z

Knowing Our Boundaries

Sixty-five million years ago, at the end of the Cretaceous Period, almost every animal on Earth that weighed over fifty-five pounds suddenly died. Whole species, including most of the dinosaurs, went extinct. The grave of the culprit that caused the extinction can be found today at the tip of Mexico's Yucatan Peninsula. It's called the Chicxulub Crater, and it marks the spot where an asteroid between four and nine miles wide hit the ground, penetrated the earth's crust, threw unknown billions of pounds of dust and debris up into the atmosphere, blocking out the sun for months and maybe years, sparked worldwide fires, severe storms, seismic and even volcanic activity, acid rain, and incineration of everything burnable at extremely high temperatures, including every life form caught in its path.

Meanwhile, on the other side of the planet, either coincidental with or shortly before or after this catastrophe, another asteroid left its mark in what geologists call the Shiva Crater. It's located under the Arabian Sea off the coast of India, near Bombay, and marks ground zero for an asteroid that must have been some twenty-five miles in diameter.

Aside from that, it had been just another quiet day on planet Earth. But after this one-two punch from the skies, things were never again the same. The great dinosaurs of the past were gone.

In the aftermath, however, some small, insignificant mammals peeked their timid heads out from their burrows, saw the devastation, instinctively understood that their time had come, offered a quick prayer of thanksgiving to whatever mammalian god they served, and went forth to populate the earth. To these little creatures, who quickly learned to take advantage of the landscape now that their competition was gone, we owe our very existence. Without an invasion from the heavens, it would have been left up to the dinosaurs to invent cell phones and iPods.

The asteroid left its mark all over the earth in other, more subtle ways. It announced its presence when geologists discovered a thin layer of material called iridium that is found much more abundantly in asteroids and meteors than in naturally occurring deposits on Earth. Spread out in a uniform layer around the world, it marks what is called the K–T Boundary, the boundary layer that separates the Cretaceous and the Tertiary epochs of history. (The "K" comes from the German word *Kreide,* or chalk, which describes the chalky sediment found during this time in Earth's history. "T," of course, stands for Tertiary.) Below this layer we find dinosaur bones. Above, nothing. The age of the dinosaurs was over.

Perhaps geologists were prophetic when they labeled the crater in India after Shiva, however. Shiva is the god of destruction and renewal. It took a while, but the earth recovered.

There were no humans back then to remember the event. There would be no gathering around the campfire to tell tales of how great-granddad and great-grandma survived the bleak day of destruction.

But 12,800 years ago something very similar happened. This time there were human witnesses. And they remembered. Their stories are still told.

Strangely, however, most people didn't start to believe the tales until 2007. That's when evidence of the "smoking gun" was discovered. We talk about this evidence in more detail in the entry about the Topper Site of South Carolina and the Younger Dryas Event, so we won't go into detail here. Suffice it to say that the burning biomass following a segmented comet hitting the earth at that time laid down what is called a black mat from Chesapeake Bay to the Andes. It consists of soot and ash from fires that burned across the North American continent and around the world. It was not as dev-astating as the double punch from sixty-five million years ago, but it must have seemed like it to the Clovis people who were alive at the time. It led to the extinction of their principal food supply. Mastodon and mam-moth steaks gave way to elk, deer, and buffa-lo. Below the black mat lay artifacts and evidence of a thriving Clovis culture. Above it, a totally new civilization appears. It was a new age for new people. Humans had sur-vived to begin again.

Associated with this boundary level, however, was proof that the devastation hadn't simply been caused by wildfires burn-ing out of control. At every Clovis site

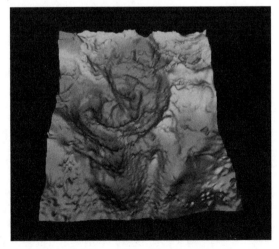

A gravity map of a section of Mexico's Yucatan Peninsula clearly indicates a large impact crater.

It was not as devastating as the double punch from sixty-five million years ago, but it must have seemed like it to the Clovis people who were alive at the time.

across North America were found nanodiamonds, formed when visitors from outer space generate intense heat upon entry into the Earth's atmosphere.

When the discovery was announced in 2007 it was, of course, greeted with a profound yawn generated by the conspiracy of silence. But it could not be denied. Although the idea of such a catastrophe that occurred within the time-span of humans on the planet was new and exciting, it was also outside the academic box. But it had two areas of convincing arguments going for it.

The first was geological. The black mat and nanodiamonds were there. They could not be denied. And they were found at the right historical levels so as to explain the end of the Clovis culture and the disappearance of the great mega fauna.

The second was anthropological. Every culture found around the world has a mythology and tribal legends that tell about a great catastrophe that ended a way of life, from which a few survivors ventured forth to begin again. When you read the biblical account of Noah and the flood, when you listen to Hopi legends about previous worlds, when you hear stories about the Golden Age of Atlantis, you are hearing handed-down versions of the stories told about those who were alive on Earth when the comet hit.

Boundaries exist on the earth in the form of both geological and anthropological evidence. Usually, experts in the two different areas of study don't talk much to each other. Maybe it's time they did.

LEMURIA, THE MU RUINS, AND FRINGE HISTORY

There is a body of markedly non-mainstream work regarding an ancient civilization and language known as Naacal, allegedly carried to Mesopotamia, Egypt, India etc. in very remote ages by Mayan adepts. The first recorded use of the term is by the maverick archeologist Augustus Le Plongeon. Le Plongeon believed in a late-pre-historic world civilization centered on a Pacific continent known as "mu" or "Lemuria" (later submerged, giving rise to pre-Polynesian cultures in places such as New Zealand) and massive early diffusion more generally.

Skeptical Humanities: http://skepticalhumanities.com/

The "Religion" of History

From time to time in this book we have talked about both the positive and negative aspects of archeology. The field has certainly produced a continuing body of science that has gone a long way toward furthering our understanding of who we are, where we came from, and where we might be headed. On the other hand, it has acquired, over the years, a reputation for chewing up and spitting out its own when even respected archeologists bring in data that contradicts the traditional tenants of the field's *textus receptus,* or "received text."

In a different field of study, religion has proved to be a great blessing to countless billions of people down through time in terms of bringing comfort, understanding, and meaning. Over the course of centuries, however, religion has divided itself into conservative and liberal groups who often will have nothing to do with each other. People may worship the same God, believe many of the same things, read the same Bible, sing the same songs, and pray the same prayers, but their differences have caused untold conflict, heartache, and sometimes outright war.

What do these two seemingly unrelated subjects have in common? Sad to say, historians, archeologists, geologists, anthropologists, and others who study the roots of humanity have arranged themselves along a line that, just like religionists, runs from conservative to liberal. Each group has its holy scriptures from accepted writers. Each group believes it is sound. Each group has its evangelists. And each group speaks, sometimes in extremely hurtful language, disparagingly of the others.

French-American photographer Augustus Le Plongeon was also an amateur archeologist who specialized in the Mayan culture; he was controversial for ideas about Lemuria.

The Fundamentalists

The fundamentalists of the history religion are the traditionalists. At the extreme right of the spectrum are those who simply won't budge when it comes to considering evidence contrary to their position. Fifty years ago it was anathema to even consider that any European but Columbus discovered America earlier than 1492. Indigenous Americans arrived by walking across a Siberian land bridge some 12,000 years ago. Indigenous populations built the megaliths found in the Egyptian deserts and Central American forests. Any opposing claims are called revisionist history. That's it, plain and simple. We know the truth and the truth has set us free. Stop trying to muddy the waters!

The Liberals

Way over on the other side of the field are the liberals. They very much want to muddy the waters! According to the fundamentalists, they preach fringe history. It goes by many names ranging from pseudohistory to pseudoscience. They are called maverick archeologists, wackos, and many names less polite. Those in this camp have the annoying habit of latching on to and advertising to the world the embarrassing problems that fundamentalists want to keep cloaked in the conspiracy of silence.

- "If Columbus was the first European to have discovered America in 1492, how is it that he had a map?"

- "If the first people of America came here 12,000 years ago, how come we can date some pre-Clovis sites thousands of year earlier than that?"

- "If indigenous people built the pyramids of Egypt and Central America, where did they obtain the needed technology?"

The Battle is Waged

All across the spectrum, of course, there are camps and what might be called religious denominations who, to varying degrees, disagree with each other. The fundamentalists pretty much control the academic world. They issue the degrees, write the textbooks, and strictly control who is to be considered sound. Through the bestowing of degrees from accepted institutions, they ordain the next generation of their number.

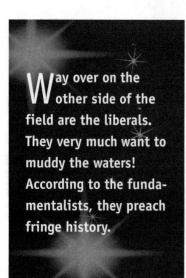

Way over on the other side of the field are the liberals. They very much want to muddy the waters! According to the fundamentalists, they preach fringe history.

This has led to difficult confrontations. Al Goodyear, a much-respected archeologist from the University of South Carolina, has been quoted in print saying he knew he would be risking his career if he discovered pre-Clovis material at one of his digs. Before Dennis Stanford and Bruce Bradley brought out their controversial book, *Across Atlantic Ice*, they had to think seriously about jeopardizing their reputations. Such is the power of traditionalists, be they archeological or religious. They can command allegiance because they control the establishment's infrastructure.

The liberals, however, have all the good TV shows, what with *Ancient Aliens, America Unearthed,* and the many History Channel offerings. They also tend to be more interesting at parties and conventions. They have run an end-around the establishment and gone straight to the public without restraints. You don't need a degree to be famous, although you do need to quote some traditionalists from time to time to keep yourself honest. Sometimes it even helps not to be formally trained. You can approach a problem with an open mind rather than with preprogrammed training. Even though the liberals are fond of quoting establishment authorities when it suits them, which adds a certain credibility to their arguments, they really don't need them. A good TV series and a bestselling book pay better and bring more recognition, anyway.

> **Y**ou don't need a degree to be famous, although you do need to quote some traditionalists from time to time to keep yourself honest.

And so the battle is waged. Liberal vs. Conservative. Us against Them. Traditional academics (a phrase uttered in disparaging tones) vs. pseudo-historians" (muttered with dripping sarcasm).

Thus it is that if even established and accepted archeologists dare to challenge the status quo by discovering inconvenient facts that don't fit the received parameters, they are in danger of being ostracized to the fringe.

Of course, there are stages along the way. Some "fringers" are more conservative than others. And a few traditionalists are sometimes a little "fringy."

Enter the Buzz Words

What does all this have to do with Lemuria and the Mu Ruins? Just this. If you are ever at a party of traditional archeologists, for heaven's sake, don't mention the word Lemuria. And if you are a grad student looking for a dissertation topic, don't even consider looking for the lost continent of Mu. Either one will get you kicked out of the club so fast you won't even hear the door being closed behind you. It would be like going up to Billy Graham and asking him what his astrological sign is. It just isn't done! Of all the theories concerning lost civilizations and ancient humans, these two are the most loaded with portent. Lemuria and Mu exist way out there on the fringe, to the left of everything, including Atlantis. Even some popular "fringers" don't want to be identified with them. You will find the terms conveniently missing from the indexes of their popular books. They are terms loaded with dynamite and dangerous to use in public.

So, what do these terms mean and why are they so explosive?

Lemuria / Mu

Sometimes the terms are used interchangeably, referring to the same legends. Others tend to separate them, describing Lemuria as a sunken conti-

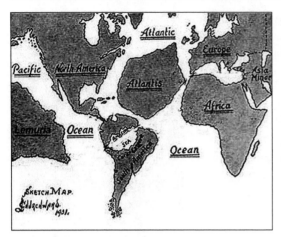

A 1931 map showing Lemuria (at left), as well as Atlantis.

nent in the Pacific and Mu as a lost landmass off the coast of India. But both are generally said, by those who speak of them in public and write about them in popular books (often called books of fiction by the traditionalists), to be the real cradle of civilization. It was from the survivors of a civilization that arose on one of these lost continents, destroyed by an ancient catastrophe, that modern humans descended.

Why is this any different from the Atlantis tradition? Well, here the story takes a dark turn. Besides the fact that the subject became the darling of the theosophy set when Helena Petrovna Blavatsky wrote about it back in 1888 in her book, *The Secret Doctrine*, there are new forces at work to keep the information out on the radical fringe and away from serious science.

Dark Side of Human Thought

The man who presently is the foremost spokesman on this topic is probably Frank Joseph. His book *Before Atlantis: 20 Million Years of Human and Pre-Human Cultures*, written in 2013, is a well-written page-turner of an up-to-date synthesis outlining the current fringe history position on the subject. Joseph believes, along with many traditionalists, that 75,000 years ago the predecessors of modern humans had reached a sort of evolutionary bottleneck. Then came the event that determined our next course of evolution. Mt. Toba erupted in Indonesia. The results, described more fully in a later entry on this subject, were catastrophic in the short term but beneficial in the big picture. In Joseph's words:

> It signified a line drawn in the sand, after which *Homo sapiens'* diversity terminated and his racial diversity began, as mass migrations in search of better living conditions moved northward out of Africa. It was there, in Europe, that the so-called Great Leap Forward much later took place, as preserved in the magnificent cave paintings and stone sculptures of Paleolithic art. For all its near-genocidal fury, Toba made possible the advent of modern man.

After the eruption, the human race, in a very short period of time, was reduced from "approximately 2 million individuals to as few as 1,000 breeding couples."

Why was this a good thing? Because, according to Joseph, it was "the most beneficial occurrence our kind had so far experienced. Until then, there was little to distinguish man from any other mammal."

After quoting quite a few myths from Middle Eastern, Southeast Asian, Melanesian, Micronesian, and Polynesian sources, Joseph continues:

> These and numerous other traditions seem inescapably paralleled with the Old Testament's (Adam and) Eve and indigenous accounts of a sunken island-kingdom more famously known as Mu or Lemuria, described in a series of early twentieth-century books by the British Army colonel and engineer, James Churchward. While directing Indian famine relief during the 1870s, he assisted in the translation of secret Hindu monastery tablets inscribed with the history of an early paradise in the Pacific, where humankind supposedly originated and eventually prospered for many centuries. After its inhabitants raised the world's first civilization, an unspecified natural calamity—about twelve thousand years ago—obliterated the Motherland. Some of its inhabitants allegedly perished, but enough survivors migrated to influence the subsequent development of high cultures as far removed from each other as India, Tibet, Southeast Asia, China, Japan, Polynesia, British Columbia, Mexico, and South America.

So far, so good. There's nothing here much different than other theories involving ancient catastrophes and lost civilizations. Even the dates match up. The "12,000 years ago" matches well with the comet that either began or ended the Younger Dryas Event. The "lost continent" in the Pacific is similar to Plato's Atlantis in the Atlantic. Why all the vitriol against Lemuria/Mu?

After the eruption, the human race, in a very short period of time, was reduced from "approximately 2 million individuals to as few as 1,000 breeding couples."

Attacking the Messenger

Go back and read Joseph's words again. Did you notice his use of "racial diversity," his emphasis on the European basis for humankind's "Great Leap Forward" in art and his use of the word "Motherland?"

Others did. They wondered if these phrases and ideas had a familiar ring to them. A little checking revealed that Frank Joseph was really Frank Joseph Collin, a former leader of the National Socialist Party of America who was instrumental in planning the Neo-Nazi rally and march on Skokie, Illinois, that resulted in the Supreme Court's controversial decision that the party had a right to express itself under the First Amendment even if it meant displaying a swastika.

Frank Joseph Collin was actually a leader of the Neo-Nazis and helped organize the party's rally in Skokie, Illinois.

Later, allegations that Joseph's (then Collin's) father was Jewish, along with his conviction for child molestation, got him kicked out of the party and earned him some jail time. When he got out of prison, Collin dropped his last name, changed it officially to Joseph and began a new career in writing, while editing a prominent magazine, *The Ancient American*, that featured articles about fringe history. He became famous for his hyper-diffusionist theories supporting his hypothesis that the populating of America happened first from Europe. In other words, white people got here first. According to his views, the Indians, or red people, came later and took it away. He never said in print that he believed the white race was superior and was following a manifest destiny to inhabit the earth, but he did mention that the white Asians had a better "brain-food" diet of seafood than their "African counterparts" and thus advanced up the evolutionary ladder more quickly. Charges of racism dog him to this day. It doesn't help any that he now seems to have become a Wiccan.

Soon others jumped on the racist bandwagon. There were those who embraced the purely academic Solutrean hypothesis, for instance, because it justified how the U.S. government treated the Native American Indians. "After all," they reasoned, "white Europeans were here first. The Indians took it away from 'us.' We're just taking back what is rightfully ours by way of discovery!"

Joseph claims to have put his past behind him, but, as is the case in today's cyberspace environment, that is a difficult thing to do. (See R. D. Flavin's article, "Frank Collin: From Neo-Nazi to Hyper-Diffusionist and Witch" at http://www.flavinscorner.com/collin.htm)

Back to Mu and Lemuria

Aside from this subplot, however, can we separate the ideas from the controversy? Is it proper, or even helpful, to dismiss otherwise interesting facts because of a man's personal life? In other words, can we dismiss Mu and Lemuria just because a former neo-Nazi with a questionable past wrote about them? If we attack the theory because it lacks geological and anthropological evidence, that's one thing. But to attempt to destroy an idea simply by denigrating the messenger is neither scientific nor ethical. Sad to say, that's exactly what has happened.

There are questions to be answered about the ancient history of Easter Island, for instance, a prime suspect that enters into the Lemuria legends that traditional archeology simply has not answered. Thor Heyerdahl tried to do so in 1958, with his book *Aku Aku: The Secret of Easter Island*. Although it enjoyed a modicum of success, his ideas were quietly put aside after the invention of DNA research even though much of his evidence for diffusion has never been refuted. But at least his ideas were seriously considered until something better came along.

People have carried out underwater expeditions while diving off the coast of India and come back with pictures of ruins that certainly look man-made, right where legends of Mu claim they should be. But woe to the archeologist who uses the dreaded M word. All someone has to do is mention Lemuria/Mu and he will no doubt become the object of a slanderous online

Thor Heyerdahl was one of a number of people who thought there might be a connection to Easter Island and the legend of Lemuria. The stone statues there are still a mystery.

attack that runs something like this: "So-and-so brought up the old, outdated myth of Lemuria, proving he is nothing more than a fringe historian like the hyper-diffusionist Frank Joseph who has a questionable past." It's not scientific but, sad to say, that's the way it often works. So people tend to remain quiet rather than risk their reputation. And the conspiracy of silence again shrouds legitimate questions.

Speaker of the House Paul Ryan once said, in a *60 Minutes* television interview, "It used to be that when you disagreed with someone you argued with their ideas. Nowadays, it seems, you attack their character!"

It appears that is the way humans operate, whether in the field of religion, science, archeology, anthropology, politics, or any other public forum. We can only hope that brave women and men in every field will continue to press on. We need them if we are to discover lost histories and hidden truths.

MOUNT TOBA ERUPTION AND VOLCANIC WINTERS

The largest super volcano eruption of the past 2.5 million years was a series of explosions of Mount Toba on the Indonesian island of Sumatra about 75,000 years ago. Researchers say Toba spewed out a staggering 700 cubic miles (2,800 cubic kilometers) of magma, equivalent in mass to more than 19 million Empire State Buildings. By comparison, the infamous blast from the volcanic Indonesian island of Krakatau in 1883, one of the largest eruptions in recorded history, released about 3 cubic miles (12 cubic km) of magma.

Charles Q. Choi in *Live Science*

The super-volcano Mount Toba erupted 75,000 years ago. Although Vesuvius and Santorini both destroyed civilizations that lay buried for thousands of years, Toba was the single most violent eruption that ever occurred within the span of human history on the planet. It exploded with a released energy similar to the effect of an asteroid at least a mile wide colliding with the earth, sending so much dust and ash into the sky that it blotted out the sun, reflected its rays back out into space, and introduced a phenomenon called volcanic winter that lasted for perhaps as long as ten years. At least a dozen of these super-volcanoes still exist today, awaiting a day of reckoning. Some of them lie at the bottom of the sea. There is simply no way to know what kind of tidal waves they will unleash if they become active.

At the precise time in history that Toba erupted, humankind had reached what scientists call a genetic bottleneck. According to this theory, supported by genetic evidence, the human population decreased sharply, reducing population levels worldwide to between three and five thousand surviving individuals. DNA research suggests that every human alive on the planet today is descended from this small group of survivors. Food supplies disappeared. Temperatures fell sharply. The sun refused to shine. It must have been absolutely terrifying to the scattered few who managed to last it out.

If this theory is true, genetic differentiation in the human species didn't develop over millions of years, as has been the previously accepted supposition, but only in the last 70,000 years. This would have staggering repercussions both on what might have been and what was lost in terms of millions of years of human evolutionary thought and development. What was destroyed? Were there human populations that had progressed a lot further than we will ever know? Who was left? If only widespread, less advanced members of the species who lived on far-off islands or high in mountainous terrain, whose lifestyle consisted of subsistence gathering, survived, civilization would have had to start all over again from the least developed of our species. We would have had to start, quite literally, from the beginning. A few million years of our development would have been wiped out.

Recently, however, a new theory suggests the eruption might not have caused as much devastation as we think. In April 2013, Charles Q. Choi, writing for *Live Science*, reported that even though the number of humans dropped

Lake Toba in Indonesia marks the remains of the eruption of Mount Toba some 75,000 years ago.

precipitously, the giant plume of ash that stretched from the South China Sea to the Arabian Sea might not have been as significant as we first thought. The reason is that prehistoric artifacts discovered in India which date from the time of the eruption seemed to indicate that people coped fairly well with the aftereffects. Furthermore, layers of dust appearing in the geologic record seem to prove that the land rebounded fairly quickly after the eruption.

How do we explain the genetic bottleneck, the sudden drop-off of human population? Well, perhaps modern humans descended from small groups of people that left Africa at different times and were better equipped to survive than their predecessors, who died off for reasons unknown.

The whole question is very much undecided at this point. As is usually the case, there are people on both sides of the issue who speak with great urgency. Those who propose a theory of ancient human development lost in catastrophic conditions tend to go with the eruption/extinction conclusions. Those who are heavily invested in Uniformitarianism guiding human evolution are more apt to conclude that Mount Toba wasn't as big a deal as has been previously thought.

On the other hand, those who believe that the past offers lessons for the future only have look to the volcano now slumbering beneath Yellowstone National Park. It has the potential to outdo Toba's devastation by a substantial margin. Experts say it's only a matter of time. Is the United States about to become ground zero for another extinction event?

Only time will tell.

TOPPER SITE OF SOUTH CAROLINA

"This independent study is yet another example of how the Topper site with its various interdisciplinary studies has connected ancient human archaeology with significant studies of the Pleistocene," said [Dr. Al] Goodyear, who began excavating Clovis artifacts in 1984 at the Topper site in Allendale, S.C. "It's both exciting and gratifying."

Peggy Binette, University of South Carolina

The First Americans

Who were the very first folks to step foot on the American continent, and when did they arrive? And then, what happened to them?

Forty years ago, if you took a class in history and anthropology, you would have been told the answer. The textbooks had it down pat. They informed you that the most modern, up-to-date geological studies proved that glaciers covered the northern poles and had crawled down as far as what is now the central part of the United States, effectively sealing off what we now call North America from any human contact at all. The human race had by this time spread out from its genesis in Africa (a theory that had only relatively recently replaced our beginnings in the Fertile Crescent's Garden of Eden) and inhabited land from Africa in the south to Asia in the east and Europe in the west. With the glaciers locking up so much of the earth's water, sea levels were much lower than they are now. There was a land bridge, now called Beringia, a thousand miles wide, connecting Siberia to Alaska. When the ice started to melt, however, a brief corridor opened up for a time, allowing humans to follow migrating herds of mammoths and other now-extinct species right into the heart of the virgin American continent. The hunting was so good that human predation, coupled with a series of climate fluctuations and resultant habitat changes, caused the extinction of many of these great species. We've known for a long time that humans were efficient hunters because we found a sample of their primary weapon near Clovis, New Mexico, in the same site as an ancient mammoth kill. The weapon consisted of a highly efficient fluted spear point named after the location of the find—the famous Clovis Point, whose technical name is the Paleo-Indian Projectile Point. The mammoth bones were carbon dated and found to be about eight thousand years old. That coincides with the time of the most recent ice-free corridor between Asia and the Americas only a short time before the mammoths went extinct. Because this was the earliest clear indication of human activity in America, it was assumed that these were the first people to enter the North American continent.

It was an elegant, simple theory that tied together an accepted archeological find with a certified ice-free corridor and a positive extinction of

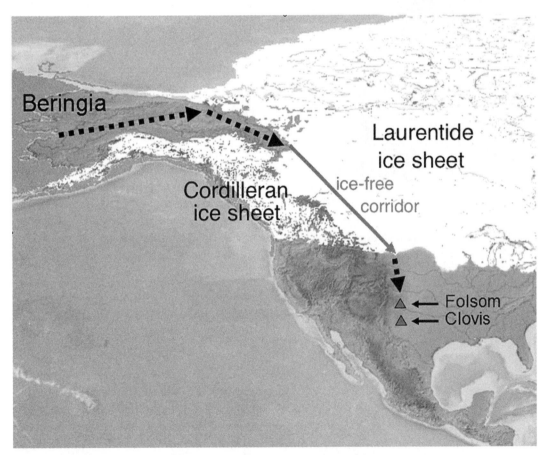

A popular theory about the arrival of humans in North America is that they crossed a land bridge—Beringia—during a time when sea levels were lower.

ancient animal species. What's not to love about a theory like that? Clovis First became the archeological gospel and woe to the student who tried to publish anything different! Disputing Clovis First was a surefire way to get laughed out of the next symposium. Eight to thirteen thousand years, give or take a century or two, was when the first humans migrated to America and began the first American culture. That's the end of that! Case closed!

Clovis First?

But fundamentalism, whether religious, political, scientific, or even archeological, is fraught with pitfalls. A few sites, notably in Chile, Pennsylvania, Oklahoma, Virginia, and most recently in South Carolina, refused to conform to fundamentalist guidelines. Reputable archeologists at those sites and others seemed pretty confident that they were dealing with material much older than a mere 8,000 to 13,000 years. They were ridiculed and laughed at, but they persevered. Doubts began to arise about Clovis First. Despite the evidence of antiquity, archeologists couldn't answer a few important questions.

> Doubts began to arise about Clovis First. Despite the evidence of antiquity, archeologists couldn't answer a few important questions.

First and foremost, if people were in America before the glaciers melted, how did they get here? The Ice Age is a given. They couldn't have migrated on foot. There's plenty of geology to back that up, and the dates are fairly well set in stone. So how did these people, assuming the archeological dates are correct, wind up in a Chilean cave, a Pennsylvanian overhang, or a site overlooking the Savannah River in South Carolina? It didn't seem possible that they could have gotten here; it was tempting to assume that they didn't get here. It was the archeologist's old stand-by: "That artifact can't be here because it's not supposed to be here!" Better to ridicule the messenger than rewrite the textbooks. So the issue became cloaked in a conspiracy of silence.

The Topper Site

The South Carolina dig that is causing such a chink in the armor of traditional thinking is called the Topper Site. Dr. Albert Goodyear, a much respected archeologist affiliated with the University of South Carolina, had been uncovering lots of Clovis tools and artifacts there, so in 1998, moved by discoveries in Pennsylvania and Virginia, he decided to risk his reputation and dig a little deeper. What he found shook the world of archeology to the very core. He had, until now, been a Clovis First guy himself. But in strata undeniably dated to at least 35,000, and perhaps even 50,000 years ago, by no less an authoritative laboratory than the distinguished University of California at

Irvine, he discovered what appeared to be human-made stone artifacts and Paleolithic debitage—the chips left over from the making of stone tools. As reported in *Science Daily* on November 18, 2004, Topper instantly became "the oldest radiocarbon dated site in North America." There are sites equally as old in Brazil and Chile. Perhaps a site in Oklahoma suggests that humans were present in the Western Hemisphere as early as 30,000 to 60,000 years ago. But Topper is garnering most of the ink because so many archeologists and institutions have traveled there to check it out. The Stafford Research Laboratories in Lafayette, Colorado, double-checked the evidence by collecting burnt plant remains from the same levels as the early artifacts. Carbon from this kind of material can be dated with standard, accepted, scientifically verified techniques.

There are more than four hundred Clovis sites found within a hundred miles of Washington, D.C., and only a few dozen in all of the Rocky Mountain West.

Their verdict? It is 50,300 to 51,700 years old.

The Big Problem

So how and when did humans get to North America? Where did they come from? And what happened to them?

Sherlock Homes used to say that when you have eliminated everything else, whatever is left over, no matter how farfetched, must be the truth. Using this philosophy, one answer stands out: by boat from Europe.

Once you dare put forth a theory so outlandish, you simply have to go looking for proof.

The search led to the European culture now called Solutrean, whom we looked at in the first chapter of this book. They lived in northern Spain and southern France. The art and the remnants these people left behind in fire pits indicate that they were hunting and eating deep-sea fish and mammals. For that kind of activity they needed boats. Recent studies of glacial activity indicate that with lower sea levels caused by an almost unimaginable amount of water tied up in frozen glaciers, it would have been entirely possible for them to make the trip right along the face of a broken glacier from their home in southern France to North America, ending up roughly where Chesapeake Bay is today. Evidence on this side of the pond corroborates this because they seem to have brought their pre-Clovis technology with them. There are more than four hundred Clovis sites found within a hundred miles of Washington, D.C., and only a few dozen in all of the Rocky Mountain West. Clearly the capital of Clovis culture was in the east, not the west.

But what happened to the evidence of boats? Why haven't we found any? The answer is simple, when you think about it. At that time in history the Grand Banks, now two hundred miles off the coast of Labrador, marked the edge of the continent. When the people landed, they certainly didn't go to the trouble of dragging their boats two hundred miles inland just to satisfy future archeologists. They left them on the shore where, as sea levels quickly rose at the end of the Younger Dryas, they were eventually drowned under hundreds of feet of water.

Made in the U.S.A.

These first immigrants were pre-Clovis people. The underlying technology from which the Clovis culture evolved cannot be traced back to Siberia. Siberians used a completely different technology involving tiny stone chips attached to grooved bone blades. The ancestral technology to the Clovis can only be found in the European Solutrean culture. There on the west coast of northern Spain and southern France, stone artifacts have been collected and classified for generations. Although they don't look exactly like Clovis Points, the method of manufacturing them, a technique called bifacial knapping, is identical. So the art of the Clovis Points, featuring elongated flutes along each side of the point, seems to have originated in the American southeast. Perhaps the Clovis Point was the very first American invention. The development of Clovis Points from Solutrean technology can be traced, if you have a good eye and a lot of academically trained imagination, in projectile points from France and Spain compared to points found in Pennsylvania, Virginia, North Carolina, and other places.

What happened to these people after they had settled in southeastern America for a few thousand years and developed such a rich, big-game hunting way of life? Did they just hunker down and evolve along normal social developmental lines, eventually becoming Cherokee Indians?

Alas, it was not to be. The latest evidence points to a massive visitor from outer space ending what was a promising future, wiping out the Clovis culture, marooning the survivors in North America, and allowing the descendants of the original Solutreans to become those who helped give birth to what is now called the Folsom culture, the ancestors of many American Indian peoples.

Is it possible the Clovis people survived, eventually becoming the Cherokee?

The End of the Beginning

Remember the glacier that still existed up north? The water that melted from its massive bulk every summer probably flowed down through the Mississippi River system, eventually out to the Gulf of Mexico. Normal ocean currents in the Atlantic carried cold water from the north first east to Europe and then south, where it was warmed in the lower, equatorial latitudes before traveling north again, up the coast of North America, where it was cooled in the northern latitudes, thus keeping the great Atlantic conveyor system moving. But according to geophysicist Dr. Allen West, that all changed rather drastically one day when what was probably a giant, segmented comet plummeted down to Earth, huge portions of it landing on the glacier itself somewhere up in Canada, north of the Great Lakes. Dr. West has found, at every Clovis site he examined from the U.S.–Mexican border way up into Canada and from California to South Carolina, the answer to three great questions that have puzzled archeologists for years:

- What happened to the Clovis culture? Why did it end so abruptly?

- Why did North American mega-fauna, such as mammoths and mastodons, saber-toothed cats, camels, and giant sloths, along with many more species, suddenly go extinct?

- What caused the sudden, great climate change called the Younger Dryas, a cold, dry, and extremely disruptive event that lasted for more than a thousand years?

What did he find that answered these questions? Something called nanodiamonds. We looked briefly at them earlier in this chapter.

This subject is fraught with controversy and is highly technical. There are many traditional archeologists who dispute and refute the evidence. But the academic field of archeology sometimes changes more slowly than theological propositions in the Catholic Church. It will probably take years for this theory to be accepted. So suffice it to say that what Dr. West found—nanodiamonds— at similarly dated sites across the continent, was something that can only come from outer space and is associated with a comet event similar to the one that wiped out the dinosaurs millions of years ago. That event left a huge asteroid crater in the Yucatan Peninsula. Dr. West proposes that a comet, probably segmented as was the case with the famous Comet Shoemaker–Levy 9 that crashed into Jupiter in July of 1994, slammed into the earth only 12,800 years ago.

Where are the craters left over from that collision? Simple. This was, you will remember, the height of the Ice Age. Much of the Earth's northern hemisphere was covered with ice a mile or more thick. If comet pieces hit in

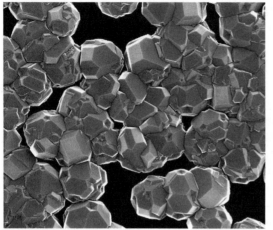

A look at nanodiamond crystals under a microscope; these tiny stones are evidence of a powerful impact from space.

places such as the Laurentide glacier, the crater melted away long ago when the Ice Age ended.

Imagine the catastrophic conditions! The explosion alone must have killed all the animals within range of the event. Fires, dust storms, winds, and smoke would have devastated much of the continent. Chances are good that it also broke off the ice dam that kept glacial melt from flowing east, out the St. Lawrence River into the North Atlantic.

Do you remember that Atlantic oceanic conveyor-belt current we discussed a moment ago? When cold, heavy, glacial water was able to flow east into the Atlantic as well as south into the Gulf of Mexico, the earth suddenly entered into another glacial age that lasted for more than a thousand years. Worldwide climate change occurred suddenly, almost overnight.

The burning bio-mass left what is called a black mat visible today on the shores of the Chesapeake Bay, among many other places. Below that black mat are found Clovis Points and artifacts. Then—nothing. Just a foot or so of dust and grit. No human artifacts at all until, after more than a thousand years had passed, new people came back to the now-habitable region. These late arrivals are, for the most part, the ancestors of today's Eastern Indian tribes.

A New Start

Remember, now, that all this happened only 12,800 years ago, after people had been living in what is now the United States for perhaps as long as 25,000 years or so, if these new theories prove to be correct. The cultures that had arisen in that vast period of time could have been very sophisticated for their era, but devastated and obliterated by the destructive results of such an impact. Evidence of their existence that survived the catastrophe had some 1,500 years to decay and rot away before any people returned to the scene of the disaster, and another 10,000 years or so to disappear before the first European explorers with a written language appeared on the scene. Only people such as the Hopi remembered, recalling the lost worlds of their ancestors in story and myth.

It might have happened something like this:

- 25,000 to 35,000 years ago, or maybe long before that—Solutrean people from northern Spain and southern France arrive by boat in the vicinity of Chesapeake Bay via the Georges Bank and, over many thousands of years, spread out over the entire continent. Eventually, building on the Solutrean technology, they develop, probably first in America's southeast, the famous Clovis Point, the crown jewel of the Paleolithic tool kit.

- 12,800 years ago—What up to now has been a good life is interrupted when a visitor from outer space (probably a comet) smashes into the ice sheet a thousand miles north. These people have never seen that particular glacier and probably wouldn't have understood its importance even if they had. But for a few nights they may see the fiery tail of the comet lighting up the night sky and wonder what it means. This would explain pictographs found from Arizona to China that seem to portray a flaming or exploding starburst. It also seems to be the source of many Native American myths about a star with a flaming tail. The devastation will eventually ruin their climate and drastically change their environment.

- Very probably, those in the southeast who survive manage to migrate west, there to eventually meet up with a new group of folks who had made the journey on foot across the Siberian land bridge and are pushing slowly eastward. When they discover each other, do they make love or war? There is a good chance the Clovis people, descendants of the Solutrean stone crafters, influenced the newcomers from Siberia and created a new civilization we now call the Folsom culture. Perhaps they took advantage of a chance to mix cultural history, share their stories and marriageable young people, and evolve into a new group.

- After 1,500 years or so, with the extinct mega-fauna now the stuff of tribal legends and myths, this new Folsom culture migrates back into the now-habitable Eastern Woodlands, there to become the ancestors of those who lived here when the Spaniards invaded 8,000 years later.

By now, the Old Ones, the Solutreans, were long forgotten. But their cultural influence lingered on. We recognize it whenever we reach down in the soil along some eroded river bank and pick up a bifacial projectile point—an arrowhead.

YOUNGER DRYAS EVENT

A cataclysm rocked our planet 12,800 years ago, causing the mass extinctions of large animals such as the mammoth and sloth bears, and all but wiping out our own race. An entire episode in the human story was rubbed out, a chapter not of unsophisticated hunter-gatherers but of advanced technology,... Within the next 20 years, Earth [again] faces a collision with the remnants of a comet big enough to end all life as we know it....

Graham Hancock in *Magicians of the Gods*

The Past

From all over the world, from culture to culture, in tales and legends familiar to all who study mythology, read the Bible, or peruse other sacred texts of world religions, come stories that tell of a former human civilization being destroyed by fire or flood.

Up until the first years of the twenty-first century, that's all they were—tales, legends, and myths. But beginning in 2007, evidence began to reach the popular press that there may be a whole lot more to the story. Words such as nanodiamonds and microspherules entered the popular lexicon.

According to a study published on September 17, 2007, in *Proceedings of the National Academy of Sciences*:

In 2007, archeologists led by Dr. Richard Firestone of the Lawrence Berkeley National Laboratory found spherules of metals and nano-sized diamonds in a layer of sediment dating 12,900 years ago at 10 of 12 archeological sites. The mix of particles is thought to be the result of an extraterrestrial object, such as a comet or meteorite, exploding in the Earth's atmosphere. Among the sites examined was the Topper, one of the most pristine sites in the United States for research on Clovis, one of the earliest ancient peoples.

Consider some relevant myths from people around the world. The following are only a few that have been gathered and compiled by Graham Hancock in his book, *Magicians of the Gods*.

From the Brule people of the Lakota nation:

A fiery blast shook the entire world, toppling mountain ranges and setting

Among the animals likely brought to the edge of extinction by the Younger Dryas impact were woolly mammoths.

forests and prairies ablaze.… Even the rocks glowed red-hot, and the giant animals and evil people burned up where they stood. Then the rivers overflowed their banks and surged across the landscape. Finally the Creator stamped the Earth, and with a great quake the Earth split open, sending torrents … across the entire world until only a few mountain peaks stood above the flood.

Similar stories are told by the Cowichan of British Columbia, the Pima of Arizona, the Inuit of Alaska, and the Luiseno of California.

From the Ojibwa people of the Canadian grasslands, who:

… remember a comet called Long-Tailed Heavenly Climbing Star which swept low through the skies, scorching the Earth and leaving behind a different world. After that, survival was hard work. The weather was colder than before. And then came … a fiery blast that shook the entire world, unleashing a tsunami.

And what about these familiar words from the biblical book of Genesis?

I will send rain on the earth for forty days and forty nights, and I will wipe from the face of the earth every living creature I have made.

These words are repeated in other ancient Sumerian texts and Babylonian inscriptions.

We could go on and on. Hancock estimates that there are more than two hundred ancient myths that tell of a human civilization that "was brought to an end by flood and fire."

We know these things have happened in the distant past. The geological evidence is beyond dispute. That it could happen again is also beyond dispute. Government agencies such as NASA are constantly searching the not-so-friendly skies for just such as event.

The Future

During the summer and fall of 2015 a letter allegedly sent from John Casey, president of the Space and Science Research Center (SSRC) to the Federal Emergency Management Agency (FEMA) went viral on the Internet:

… we are about to enter a potentially catastrophic period of record earthquakes and volcanic eruptions throughout the United States.… Our research, to be published in our June 10, 2015, Global Climate Status Report (GCSR), suggests the high probability for catastrophic earthquakes or volcanic eruptions in all the major seismic and volcano regions of the United States has increased significantly. We believe the USA and the world has now entered the most dangerous period for catastrophic earthquakes and volcanic eruptions in over two hundred years. In fact, a new trend of increased number and intensity of earthquakes and volcanoes globally has already started and is generating serious concern in the geology field.

Of course, the usual back and forth ensued, denials were issued, conspiracy fanatics entered the fray and a good time was had by all. But the fact that such a situation cannot be flat out denied by those who are considered to be the foremost experts on the geology of the planet should give everyone pause to consider.

Similar catastrophes have happened. No one denies it. The evidence is obvious. The question is, have they happened during the era of human development and were there actual eyewitnesses who lived to tell the tale?

Graham Hancock's research leads him to think that there were, and that they were not primitive hunter gatherers but a sophisticated civilization with advanced technology:

Geysers and hot springs at popular Yellowstone National Park exist because the land sits atop a giant reservoir of molten lava with the potential to erupt as a supervolcano. Geologists have noted that the land at Yellowstone is rising, indicating this could happen in the not-too-distant future.

All the signs are that the remnants of this civilization struggled on, sustained by a few individuals who knew the secrets of the former age. To their primitive contemporaries, it appeared that they possessed magical, holy powers—they were what I call the Magicians of the Gods.

Graham Hancock, *Magicians of the Gods*

If that isn't enough, he is convinced that they left us an urgent warning. They believed that what happened to them could also happen to us. The comet that hit them could have had a twin that will hit us after traveling its long, 12,000-year orbital path. Built into the very architecture of structures such as Göbekli Tepe and the Giza pyramids, Hancock believes he has found mathematical codes that point to a day of reckoning that might occur on planet Earth, perhaps as early as the year 2030.

Signs in Stone

When asked why such codes can be found in the language of mathematics rather than written texts, Hancock's answer is simple. Ancient languages evolve and often die out. Formulas in mathematics, especially those that point to dates decipherable through the science of astronomy and physics, never do. The ancients were very familiar with those sciences and could leave a message in a bottle, so to speak, that points to an era when the stars and constellations align in a precise way. He believes that era is now.

To that end, Hancock believes we need to pay urgent attention to enigmatic structures such as the Sphinx, ancient temples, Göbekli Tepe, the pyramids, Stonehenge, and other monumental edifices of the ancient past. More than curiosities, they might contain information we need to decipher in time to think about ways to survive another such cataclysm.

What happened 12,800 years ago? What exactly is the period we call the Younger Dryas Event?

The National Climatic Data Center of the National Oceanic and Atmospheric Administration (NOAA) describes it this way:

> The Younger Dryas is one of the most well-known examples of abrupt (climate) change. About 14,500 years ago, the Earth's climate began to shift from a cold glacial world to a warmer interglacial state. Partway through this transition, (12,800 years ago) temperatures in the Northern Hemisphere suddenly

The ancients were very familiar with those sciences and could leave a message in a bottle ... that points to an era when the stars and constellations align in a precise way.

returned to near-glacial conditions This near-glacial period is called the Younger Dryas, named after a flower (Dryas Octopetala) that grows in cold conditions and became common in Europe during this time. The end of the Younger Dryas, about 11,500 years ago, was particularly abrupt. In Greenland, temperatures rose 10° C (18° F) in a decade.

Clearly this was a tumultuous time for humans then living and even thriving on the planet. Imagine the following scenario, having first read again the Hopi legend discussed in the prologue of this book.

Toward what would naturally have been the end of the last Ice Age, a fiery comet breaks apart above the skies of Earth, many of the segments exploding within the atmosphere of the planet. At least four of them, and perhaps as many as nine, each more than a mile across, strike the glacial surface of the Laurentide and Cordilleran ice sheets in central and western Canada in North America. The effect is thousands of times more devastating than any nuclear blast the earth has ever witnessed. The heat alone would have melted vast amounts of ice, but the worst was yet to come. Almost unimaginable amounts of dust and soot would have been thrown into the upper atmosphere, blotting out the sun for months, if not years. Temperatures dropped almost overnight, plunging the earth into what amounts to another Ice Age—the Younger Dryas—that lasts for some 1,500 years.

In the Near East, tales from the Zoroastrian religion remember "a fierce, foul frost" and a "fatal winter." The Maya of Guatemala describe it as "black rain and mist, and indescribably cold." Mammoths and mastodons are flash frozen, with undigested food still in their stomachs.

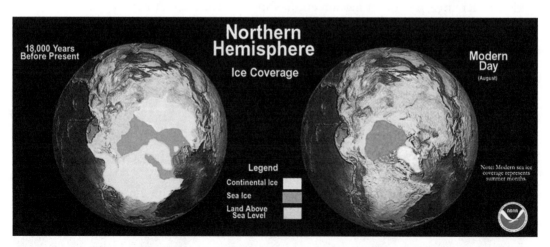

This maps shows the extent of ice sheets over the Northern Hemisphere during the last big Ice Age.

Perhaps the Hopi describe it best. The first world was destroyed by fire. It was followed by a world that was destroyed by ice—the ice sheets of the Younger Dryas. But with the sudden melting of all that ice a thousand or more years later, as the earth rebounded back into what we call normalcy and the great ice dams that held back vast lakes of ice water disintegrated, perhaps the worst was yet to come. The Hopi say the earth was then destroyed by water. Jewish and Babylonian myths speak of a great flood, a story which is echoed by virtually every other culture in the world.

Fire—ice—water. A deadly combination that ravaged the earth for 1,500 years. The stories also tell of humans who lived through it, managed to survive and record their tales in what we have, until recently, written off only as myth and legend. Such stories cannot be dug up and analyzed under a microscope. They are not hard facts. But the conspiracy of silence enveloping the near universality of these stories is now being broken. Christian preachers can no longer tell their congregations that Noah's flood is unique in the annals of religious mythology, and then hope no one reads the tales of Gilgamesh or the legends of the Algonquians. It is everywhere. It is out in the open. And even geologists are finally beginning to admit it.

But the myths go even further. Turning again to the tales of the Ojibwa, we are told that "the star with the long, wide tail is going to destroy the world someday when it comes low again."

In sites as separated as Turkey, Central America, and Mexico, wise men who survived to tell the tale appeared on the scene, usually being described as bearded gods who brought much wisdom with them.

How would the primitive people of that day have reacted? What questions would they ask themselves?

"Did we somehow cause this by angering the gods? What can we do to assuage their anger?"

Or perhaps their questions would be of a more pragmatic nature.

"Is this a reoccurring phenomenon? How can we prepare for such a catastrophe if it happens again?

Maybe their questions were even more altruistic.

"How can we prepare future generations? What can we teach them?"

Civilization quickly advanced wherever these wise men of old appeared to give the local culture a kick-start toward a new future. Megastructures were built, appearing full-blown and suddenly on the scene with no evidence of practice sites.

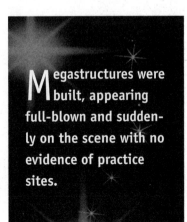

Megastructures were built, appearing full-blown and suddenly on the scene with no evidence of practice sites.

The Old Ones knew what they were doing. They had done it before, and passed on the wisdom from one generation to the next. And as our civilization rose out of the ruins of the Younger Dryas, we thought it was happening for the first time. We spoke of it as being "in the beginning."

The question remains, however. If it happened before, can it happen again?

Out of the Ashes

We are preceded by innumerable species no longer among the living. Our destruction, while everything to us, would be just another extinction event in the many thousands that make up Earth's history. Human die-off means nothing to an eternal process perpetually renewing itself with fresh life, remorselessly discarding flawed examples for improved performers. Flying in the face of this stark reality is to court Nature's wrath, which has already begun to show in more than disturbed weather patterns, however ultimately symbolic they may be. Our own evolutionary track record is filled with a rich variety of hominids that no longer exist, although they lasted longer than we have so far, leaving us the only human type left standing.

Frank Joseph in *Before Atlantis*

What does all this mean? How does it all fit together in a human tapestry that paints a vivid picture of our place in the grand scheme of things? Who are we?

In the first chapter, we began by asking that exact question. We looked at a few of the many theories that explain how humankind began and took the place it now holds at the top of the food chain. We discovered the answer isn't as easy to arrive at as one might think. So in the "Ancient Astronomers" chapter we took another tack. Instead of looking back at who our earliest ancestors were, we surveyed some of the things that they did. In short, the first members of our civilization showed a marked propensity to look at the sky. They talked about it in myths and legends. They wrote stories about it. They considered it, in many cases, to be the home of the gods. They built great monuments and observatories. They seemed fascinated at what was up there.

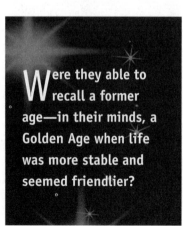

Were they able to recall a former age—in their minds, a Golden Age when life was more stable and seemed friendlier?

Why? Could it be that they remembered a day when something of great import, perhaps terrifying, rained down upon them from the heavens? Were they able to recall a former age—in their minds, a Golden Age when life was more stable and seemed friendlier?

That seems to be the message of the perennial Atlantis tradition that will not go away. It's backed up in a geological record consisting of the K-T boundary, nanodiamonds, and other records of catastrophe. In stories about Lemuria and the Mu ruins, humans keep alive the stories of a mythic past, even if it is labeled "fringe" history by most experts. The fact remains, however, that cataclysms don't have to come from the skies. They lie sleeping beneath our feet as well, as is shown by the catastrophic Mount Toba eruption and the volcanic winter that followed in its wake. In the Topper Site of South Carolina we see evidence for a destruction that once leveled a whole continent, ushering in the 1,500-year-long Younger Dryas event that ended the Clovis culture.

Modern human beings have been on Earth for a mere 200,000 years. What we call "our" civilization began only about six thousand years ago. The industrial age that is the hallmark of that civilization didn't start until the 1800s. The whole Age of Flight, from the Wright brothers to the Apollo Missions, is only a hundred years old.

But remember—and please let this sink in because it's very important— our ancestors have been around for at least six million years! That's a lot of

A diver explores the ruins of a Roman port off the coast of Italy that is now underwater. Older ruins of even earlier civilizations have apparently been lost beneath the waves, as well.

time. We could drop any number of experiments-in-civilization into that immense time period and never find evidence of them, buried as they are in the sands of time. Like drowned islands in the sea, sometimes only their tops stick up for us to see. The vast bulk of their lands lie below the surface. In the same way, once in a while we catch a glimpse of a curiosity, an artifact, a misplaced remnant, either in the archeological record or the subtle turn of a phrase in a forgotten myth or legend. Because it doesn't fit what we think we know, we ignore it, shrouding it in a conspiracy of silence. We hope it will go away.

But a stubborn few refuse to let it go. The history we were taught in school, much of what we were told and even tested on to prove we were educated young people, has now fallen by the wayside, buried under the logic of those who keep gnawing at the bone of historical evidence that doesn't fit the traditional pattern. Before 2007, anyone who even suggested a comet once destroyed a continent within the life span of humankind was drummed out of the club. Before 1950, anyone who suggested Viking ships, let alone a whole host of others going back thousands of years, could brave the North Atlantic and sail here from Europe was thought to be a dreamer. Indigenous people could never have raised the standing stones of Europe or Mesoamerica. American Indians weren't smart enough to have built a civilization. On and on it goes. And that's just the field of archeology. Let's not even mention scientific breakthroughs in cosmology. Tradition dies hard. But, as we have seen, it is dying. It's a slow and painful death, to be sure. But it's starting to change.

In every single year since 2007 dedicated teams of scientists have published peer-reviewed papers proving, almost beyond doubt, that a segmented comet, now officially dubbed the Clovis Comet, was responsible for the destruction of North America and much of what was living on it at the time. That included the Clovis culture of human beings, wherever they might have come from. Furthermore, the destruction was not limited to North America. Evidence from around the world indicates it was a worldwide event, similar in scope to the asteroid impact of 64 million years ago that wiped out the dinosaurs.

Caution

This next point is so important, we're going to highlight it:

Proof of a comet impact, even proof of worldwide destruction, is not proof that it destroyed an advanced civilization. Instead, what it gives us is a mechanism that would have destroyed that civilization if, indeed, it really existed!

In other words, we know that a comet impact 12,800 years ago destroyed the Clovis culture. We just don't know how advanced that culture was. What that tells us is that if pockets of a developed culture, one that was highly advanced, did indeed exist, evidence for it probably would have been destroyed in the explosion, high winds, continent-wide fires, and subsequent flooding from the sudden release of almost unimaginable amounts of ice-cap water. Such evidence would have been incinerated, drowned, blown away, or covered under sediment. It would have, for all practical purposes, disappeared forever, leaving only fragments here and there. Those fragments now can only be found by luck, coupled with careful, open-minded analyses, if we're looking for material, solid evidence.

But there are other lines of evidence. People were alive then, some of whom survived to tell the tale. They left evidence of another kind. We call them myths, stories, scriptures, and legends. They are the evidence of eye-witness accounts.

When police are investigating a traffic accident, the first thing they do is interview the witnesses. Sure, they collect material evidence for analyzing in the laboratory later on. But eyewitness accounts are very important. Not from just one witness, mind you, but from as many as possible. If all the witnesses say the same thing, that will stand up in a court of law.

Myths, especially myths from all over the world, told by people who could never have met to corroborate their stories, are extremely important. They are the eyewitness accounts of a disaster so vast it shaped the mythology of an entire planet. For too long, scientists have been preoccupied with only material evidence. It's time to listen to the myths as well. And if the myths agree as to the severity of the catastrophe, perhaps what came before is just as important. Eyewitnesses who saw the cataclysm also saw the society that existed before it struck. They remember. They were there. We need to listen to them and begin to believe they knew what they were talking about. It means listening carefully and piecing together what might have been. It's hard work. But it is important to do if we are ever to know where we came from, let alone learn from those who preceded us.

In the next chapter, we will finish laying the groundwork. Having seen where we came from, what our predecessors might have been remembering when they gazed upward at the night sky and what could have caused them to do so, it's time to start looking at the early civilizations that might have once existed, many of them only to be obliterated in a moment of time. Mystery abounds. But by the end of the next chapter, after having surveyed a few of those forgotten, lost civilizations, we will have built a solid foundation upon which to look at the mysteries surrounding them, the mythologies that memorialize them, the religions that sustained them, and the technologies that built them. Perhaps by then we will have discovered some of their lost histories and hidden truths.

ANCIENT CIVILIZATIONS

To try to figure out what these people believed, how they worshipped, if they worshipped, and what they were thinking when they did so—well, that means going out on a limb and using techniques not accepted by modern, academic archeologists. This by no means says we're not going to do just that. But let the buyer beware.

Jim Willis in *The Dragon Awakes*

In the way of linear time, you might hear Nanabozho's ('first man') stories as mythic lore or history, a recounting of the long-ago past and how things came to be. But in circular time, these stories are both history and prophecy, stories for a time yet to come. If time is a turning circle, there is a place where history and prophecy converge—the footprints of First Man lie on the path behind us and on the path ahead.

Robin Wall Kimmerer in *Braiding Sweetgrass*

Civilization Reincarnated

Civilizations, even advanced civilizations, have disappeared in the past, leaving only ruins in their wake. It doesn't take a catastrophe from space or a volcanic eruption, a flood or fire, to bring about their destruction. Sometimes the cause can be as simple as a population surge that outstrips its food supply, a religion no longer strong enough to inspire its supplicants, or an evolutionary track that merges a better new idea with an outdated old one. Whatever the case, even in relatively modern times within the last thousand years or so, we have seen the demise of enigmatic civilizations that leave little traces of their existence beyond archeological ruins. Sometimes even those are questionable. A civilization doesn't have to build skyscrapers, launch mass communication systems such as the Internet or manufacture miles of wire to qualify as advanced. Farmers in the Midwest plowed under a good many natural hills before they realized they were dealing with human-made mounds built of soil gathered one small basketful at a time. Equatorial rain forests have smothered pyramids in South America to the point at which people actually climbed them before realizing they were mounting the steps of an ancient temple. Recently a satellite image from space discovered a previously unknown temple site in Russia that people have been crossing and re-crossing for centuries without recognizing what was right under their feet.

If these things happen regularly by what we might call natural causes occurring in relatively modern times, how much more difficult is it to find hidden evidence of civilizations that existed in very ancient times, especially if the main export of that civilization was something ephemeral, like wisdom or spirituality?

Graham Hancock asked this question in his book, *Magicians of the Gods*:

The notion of a global disaster more than 11,000 years ago, and particularly the heretical idea that it could have wiped out a high civilization of that epoch, is strenuously resisted and indeed ridiculed by the archeological establishment because, of course, archeologists claim to "know" that there was not, and never

Evidence of past civilizations is sometimes lost for centuries, buried under foliage within deep jungles before being rediscovered.

under any circumstances could have been, a high civilization at that time. They "know" this not because of any hard evidence which absolutely rules out the existence of an Atlantis-type civilization in the Upper Paleolithic, but rather on the general principle that the result of less than two hundred years of "scientific" archeology is an agreed timeline for civilization that sees our ancestors moving smoothly out of the Upper Paleolithic, into the Neolithic (both, by definition, Stone Age cultures) at around 9600 B.C.E., and thence onward through the development and perfection of agriculture in the millennia that followed....

It is absolutely beyond question that the science of archeology has found evidence of Stone Age people who existed at the time "our" civilization began to progress in the well-choreographed dance that led to the present-day world we know today. Stone Age people still exist, as a matter of fact. If, a few thousand years in the future, two archeologists dig in strata that dates to the early twenty-first century, but one works in the rain forests of Bolivia while the other digs on Manhattan Island, they will get completely different results as to what the world of our time was like.

Twelve thousand years ago there were, no doubt, vast areas of Earth populated by Stone Age people. But were there also pockets of sophisticated cultures now lost to history, the evidence of their existence ignored because it doesn't fit into our preconceived timelines? Given how fast we are pushing back the dates on fully formed megalithic structures, arising with no previous history of trial-and-error development but requiring advanced and complicated construction techniques, it seems a virtual certainty. When we couple that with the fact that we also seem to be discovering earlier and earlier dates concerning human origins, thus greatly expanding our time on Earth, it raises more than a few eyebrows.

If civilizations, even relatively recent ones that perished for reasons unknown, were sophisticated enough to leave evidence behind, what hidden truths died with them? What could they teach us? How did they organize themselves? Are we heading in the same direction they did, perhaps at our own peril? Might we someday follow them into oblivion, perhaps for the same reasons? Does history repeat itself? Are we on the way to the same ruin that brought them down? Can we learn from them?

There is evidence, for instance, that both the Anasazi of the American West and the inhabitants of Easter Island in the Pacific perished because of overpopulation and subsequent overexploitation of natural resources. Is that any different from the path we are following today?

> What could they teach us? How did they organize themselves? Are we heading in the same direction they did, perhaps at our own peril?

Or how about this observation from Edward Gibbon? In his analysis of *The Decline and Fall of the Roman Empire*, written in 1783, he listed these five reasons for the demise of the world power of the Caesars:

1. Sports and entertainment received more and more money while the plight of the poor was neglected.
2. Money went to the military rather than to public works.
3. Violence became more accepted and prevalent.
4. People's faith in government was undermined, and justly so.
5. Religious roots fragmented and became a cause for dissension.

That echoes this morning's newspaper headlines, doesn't it?

In the chapter that follows we cannot hope to examine all the lost civilizations that now lay hidden beneath the sands of time. Instead we will consider a few very relevant ones, chosen because they have left a special mark on

Sporting events such as football have become a priority in modern societies, so much so that they receive far more money than social programs and education. Is this one sign of a civilization in decline?

human curiosity. We will try to discover what they have to teach us. Some that we have already discussed, like the Atlantis tradition and the Clovis culture, are associated with a catastrophic ending. Others have simply disappeared. All are associated with ancient gods. All are examples of lost histories and can teach us hidden truths. Most are enveloped in a conspiracy of silence.

They all have a story to tell.

Adena, Hopewell, and the Mississippian Mound Builders

Let the mighty mounds that overlook the rivers, or that rise
In the dim forest crowded with old oaks answer.
A race that long has passed away built them; a disciplined and
    populace race
Heaped, with long toil, the earth, while yet the Greek
Was hewing the Penteleicus of symmetry, and rearing on its rock
The glittering Parthenon. These ample fields
Nourished their harvests, here their herds were fed,
When haply by their stalls the bison lowed
And bowed his maned shoulder to the yoke.
All day this desert murmured with their toils,
Till twilight blushed, and lovers walked, and wooed in a forgot-
    ten language,
And old tunes, from instruments of unremembered form,
Gave the soft winds a voice. The red man came—
The roaming hunter tribes, warlike and fierce,
And the mound-builders vanished from the earth.

From *The Prairies*, by William Cullen Bryant

Six thousand five hundred years ago, plus or minus 140 years, a person living near what is now Baton Rouge, Louisiana, had an idea. For reasons that are assumed to be associated with either religious purposes, ceremonial celebrations, or upper class residential neighborhoods, he somehow convinced his neighbors to spend endless days carrying basketfuls of dirt, one at a time, in order to build a pyramid shaped, flat-topped mound.

Thus, the Mound Builder civilization was born, and no one really knows why. For the next five thousand years or so, the culture would go through at least three separate phases called the Adena, Hopewell, and Mississippian periods. The idea certainly caught on. It spread up the Mississippi River to the Great Lakes and all the way to the East Coast.

Ever since the 1800s most scholars have assumed they were built by the indigenous people who lived there, but guesses have been an intriguing part of their history. In 1787 a man by the name of Benjamin Smith Barton thought

Benjamin Smith Barton (1766–1815) was an American physician and botanist who speculated that mounds found in Louisiana might have been constructed by Vikings.

that they might have been built by Vikings. Others put forth the idea of early Greeks, Africans, Chinese, or various categories of Europeans. A variation of the popular suggestion that the ten lost tribes of Israel built them is still believed by many members of the Church of Jesus Christ of Latter Day Saints (Mormons). Many Mormons believe that the builders were a group of Israelites consisting of the Nephites, Laminites and Mulekites. These folks, they conclude, were not what are commonly called the ten lost tribes of Israel, but rather descendants of known tribes who migrated here in 590 B.C.E. But some Mormon scholars believe that the descriptions of the early mound builders fit better in a Mesoamerican setting.

There are, of course, some who believe the builders were migrants fleeing destruction from the lost continent of Atlantis or Mu. That probably goes without saying when dealing with any mysterious lost civilization.

When Hernando de Soto led the first European expedition through the southeast, eventually circling back to the Mississippi, he came across mounds built near present-day Augusta, Georgia. The leader of the indigenous people there was a person he thought to be, in his words, a queen. Her name was Cofitachequi. He asked her who built the mounds. She said she didn't know, but her people were using them as burial places for nobles.

Within the mounds are to be found a few oddities called animal effigies, the most famous of which is the Great Serpent Mound in Ohio. Although theories abound as to why this was built and what it means, the truth is that no one knows. Animal effigy mounds are found throughout the eastern United States and south as far as Peru.

There is no question that Native American people built these mounds in their final form. But carbon dating suggests that the tradition was six thousand years old when first discovered by Europeans. We know where it started in Louisiana, but really have no idea who started it, why they started it, what they were trying to accomplish, or how the mounds were used. It must have taken an incredible amount of work at the beginning. The social coordination required boggles the mind. What was their motivation? What moved people to drop what they were doing and go to so much trouble? And then, at the height of the Mississippian period, right when the civilization was at its peak, they suddenly stopped. Everyone seems to have up and quit what was then a five-thousand-year-old tradition. Why? Did the population outstrip the food supply? Did the darker aspects of the religion turn people away? Did disease rear its ugly head? Did intertribal warfare doom them to destruction?

Back to the Fringe

We just don't know. But, as always, when traditional archeology fails to answer the questions we deem most important, folks arise who think outside the box. One of the most intriguing of these is Frank Joseph. We talked about his Lemuria theories earlier when we looked at what is commonly called fringe history. But, in his position as editor in chief of *Ancient American* magazine, one would suspect that he has devoted considerable thought to the early American Mound Builders. And as it turns out, one would be correct.

According to Joseph, about three thousand years ago a people known as the Kelts, or Celts, migrated into what is now known as the British Isles. There they learned about the existence of the Americas, which had been the destination of the indigenous people of western Europe for at least twenty thousand years. Groups of Kelts made their journeys, arriving on the eastern shores of America at precisely the same time the mysterious Adena arose, who, coincidentally, introduced agriculture, astronomy, ironworking, road building, and the technology needed to construct monumental mound architecture.

Were the European Kelts, then, the same as the Adena, the first Mound Builders? Joseph thinks so. He also believes that somewhere around 300 B.C.E.,

The Great Serpent Mound is located in Adams County, Ohio. It does not appear to be a burial mound but, rather, an effigy in honor of the snake.

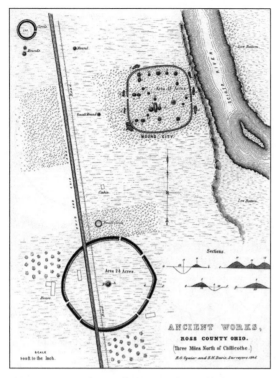

An 1848 map of Mound City in Ohio, which was part of the Hopewell civilization that was largely destroyed in that area by Indians around 400 C.E.

Japanese seafarers known as the Yayoi, also a mound building culture, and a group we will look at in more detail when we talk about the Jomon people of Japan, arrived on the west coast of America. Slowly working their way inland they soon found much in common with the Adena people, the former Kelts from Europe. Merging, as is the way of all peoples everywhere, into one civilization, they became known to the modern world as the Hopewell people. Somewhere around 400 C.E., this Hopewell culture was finally killed off by attacks from Native American tribes who had the overwhelming advantages of numbers and ferocity. Centuries of intertribal warfare ensued, until the last of the Adena were destroyed in a great and final battle that took place at the falls of the Ohio River near Louisville, Kentucky.

But that wasn't the end of the Mound Builders. As luck would have it, somewhere around 900 C.E. the Maya, from the Yucatan and Central America, arrived at a point in their sacred calendar that indicated it was time for them to move north. They relocated to west-central Illinois and eastern Missouri where, building on the Adena and Hopewell ruins found there, they eventually built the great Mississippian capital of Cahokia. Aztalan, their most northern outpost in southern Wisconsin, was built about 1240 C.E. By this time, what Joseph calls the neo-Mayas, having spread out to cover the whole southeastern seaboard and much of the Midwest, were once again forced to move, following the dictates of their sacred, prophetic calendar. They evacuated the Mississippi Valley and migrated south toward the Valley of Mexico.

Do traditional archeologists accept this theory? Of course not. But isn't it fun? And, when you stop to think about it, why not?

ANASAZI

Toward the end of the 13th century, some cataclysmic event forced the Anasazi to flee their cliff houses and their homeland

and to move south and east toward the Rio Grande and the Little Colorado River. Just what happened has been the greatest puzzle facing archeologists who study the ancient culture.

From *Riddles of the Anasazi,* Smithsonian.com

A Familiar Tale

Not so long ago, at least as archeologists measure such things, a group of immigrants moved into a vast and varied land that seemed to offer great potential. They settled down and began to find ways to channel the abundant resources surrounding them. They invented brand new methods of dryland farming and soon began to grow more food than they could ever eat themselves. So they pioneered a vast trading infrastructure that covered thousands of miles. It wasn't long before yesterday's luxuries became today's necessities. Soon a housing boom developed, providing jobs for all in a burgeoning market. They built multistory condominiums, many of which featured wonderful views and open-air vistas. Specialized labor freed up people to explore their personal gifts and abilities. Religion flourished and a centralized class of priests developed new insights and traditions. It seemed as though a never-ending string of tomorrows would stretch out into a future that looked better and better in every way. This was high civilization!

But eventually a few far-seeing people in power began to notice something troubling. Each year the crops yielded a little less than the year before. The earth seemed a touch more barren. Their warnings fell on deaf ears, of course. People involved in urban planning depend on growth going on forever. Priests need to assure their congregations that they have everything under control and God is looking after His chosen people.

There was always an excuse for a poor harvest. "It didn't rain enough last year, that's all. These things go in cycles. Don't worry. Wait 'til next year! Things will soon be back to normal. It's always been like this!"

But the day came, inevitably, when the use of natural resources reached a tipping point. Fuel was harder to come by. Each year seemed to set new records for warmth. Weather patterns changed. Instead of helpful rain, there came storms and floods. The rivers seemed to be either too high or to disappear altogether. Old-timers were heard to say that it wasn't like this when they were younger. But they were ignored, of course. What did they know? Old-timers are always complaining!

The social planners assured the people that they could make up their deficits by extending trade with for-

> They built multistory condominiums, many of which featured wonderful views and open-air vistas. Specialized labor freed up people to explore their personal gifts and abilities.

eign countries. But prices, controlled as always by supply and demand, continued to rise. The standard of living began to drop. Young people left home to look elsewhere for a better future and a place to make a living. The crime rate rose as people who had less looked with envy upon people who had an abundance. Those "haves" began to look askance at the "have nots" and began to demand protection from the lower classes. A type of police state developed as class warfare threatened to destroy the culture.

As always, in times of confusion such as these, people turned to fundamentalist religion. They wanted to get back to the good old days. The priests responded the way priests always respond. The people had forsaken old-time religion. What did they expect? Of course, God was punishing them. But God would heal their land if they just got back to practicing traditional values. The young people were out of hand! Discipline! Order! Time-tested wisdom! That was what they needed.

Oh, and they needed to donate more money to the priests in order to build new, improved places of worship that would pacify the gods.

It didn't take long for the crisis to reach epidemic proportions. Resources dwindled exponentially. Those in power were starting to feel the pinch. So God ordered the people, at least according to the politicians and

Ruins of the Escalante Pueblo bear evidence of the once-thriving Anasazi civilization that existed in Colorado, Utah, New Mexico, and Arizona.

priests, to go to war with those who had more resources, especially fuel and expensive items now considered mandatory. The only place to get such things was from foreign countries, so war was justified.

Of course, as in all wars, the ones who ordered the charge stayed home. The young, the poor, and the innocent were the ones who died.

When the smoke of battle finally drifted away, a good and once prosperous civilization had disappeared from the face of the earth. They all moved away, died in battle, died from disease or died in the poverty of old age with no one to help out.

The Dust of History

This may sound like a modern tale, but it all took place a thousand years ago in the Four Corners area where Arizona, Colorado, Utah, and New Mexico come together. We don't know what the people called themselves. In the nineteenth century we called them Cliff Dwellers. In the twentieth century we began to call them Anasazi, a Navajo word meaning enemy ancestors. The Hopi and Zuni people of Arizona and New Mexico believe themselves to be the descendants of these people, so today we call them Ancestral Puebloans. But they were an industrious people who built to last. Their multifloored cliff dwellings still stand today. At the height of their culture there were more people living in southwestern Colorado than live there today. By the end of the thirteenth century Chaco Canyon was the largest city in America. It featured a structure that held the honor of being the largest building in North America—containing some six hundred rooms—until it was finally surpassed by a hotel in New York City in 1882. People there traded with California, Peru, the Mississippi River Valley, and Minnesota. They built four- and five-story buildings and far surpassed the level of astronomy held by many people today.

But by the fifteenth century they were gone, leaving only ghostly, empty megastructures and mystery.

To this day, no one is really sure why. There are many ideas and theories, but we really don't know for sure what happened. It was probably due to many causes which came together to provide a perfect storm. A drought certainly would have made it impossible to practice dryland farming. Every tree for miles around was harvested to fuel the endless fires needed for cooking and firing pottery. Tree-ring analysis seems to indicate the people simply used up their resources, exploiting their environment beyond what it could produce. As much as people hate to admit it, the earth is not forever. It never was. It never will be. Wisdom demands seeing what is plain for all to see. But all don't want to see it.

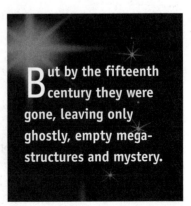

But by the fifteenth century they were gone, leaving only ghostly, empty mega-structures and mystery.

The process that brought about Anasazi Armageddon probably followed a familiar track. It began with population explosion. Too many people on the land led to planting more and more crops. Crops need water. Soon there was not enough. Agriculture failed them. That led to warfare and genocide. There is even some evidence of ritualistic cannibalism. Apparently the priests foisted a religious terrorism to keep folks in line. Eventually, the people simply walked away.

A Modern Experience

On a hot summer day some years ago, my wife, Barbara, and I were living in Arizona, researching and writing a book called *Armageddon Now: The End of the World A–Z.* We had interviewed Hopi elders and clambered up and down a lot of Ancestral Puebloan ruins searching for the reason behind the Anasazi Armageddon and one day found ourselves on a mesa top, standing on the half-finished walls of what was thought to be an ancient temple—a megachurch, if you will. Work on the edifice had begun at the very end of the mysterious people's time in that region. The people had simply stopped working. The walls were left unfinished. No one knew why. No guide book or expert we could find had an answer. What had happened here, some seven hundred years ago?

Without any corroborating evidence, we have a theory. It seemed to us as though the builders, tired, discouraged, and desperate for food, had simply heard one too many commands issued by the priestly elite who had ordered this building. They probably just looked at each other, nodded their heads, put down their tools and said, "This is no fun. We're going home." And they left. The ruling class had no one left to rule. They probably couldn't understand how, in one moment of time, a hierarchical civilization could simply cease to exist. It had seemed so real, so permanent, so much a part of life that they couldn't imagine anything else. But now it was finished. There was no one left to boss around. Just like that, it was over.

Life works that way, sometimes.

EGYPTIANS

The (Egyptian) Edfu texts invite us to consider the possibility that the survivors of a lost civilization, thought of as "gods" but manifestly human—albeit with mysterious "powers"—set about "wandering" the world after the flood. By happenstance it was only hunter-gatherer populations, the peoples of the mountains and the deserts—the "unlettered and the uncultured," as Plato so eloquently put it in his *Timaeus*—who had been "spared the scourge of the deluge." But the civilizers entertained the desperate hope, if their mission would succeed, that mankind might not have to "begin again like children, in complete ignorance of what happened in early times."

Graham Hancock in *Magicians of the Gods*

Celestial Calendars

If you visit the Hoover Dam someday, make sure to look at the great Monument of Dedication. This impressive sculpture, consisting of two huge winged figures, can't help but catch your eye. But look closely at the base. There you will find an inscribed star chart. Its purpose is described by a pamphlet issued by the United States Department of the Interior:

> The chart preserves for future generations the date on which President Franklin D. Roosevelt dedicated Hoover Dam, September 30, 1935. In this celestial map, the bodies of the solar system are placed so exactly that those versed in astronomy could calculate the precession (progressively earlier occurrence) of the Pole Star for approximately the next 14,000 years. Conversely, future generations could look upon this monument and determine, if no other means were available, the exact date on which Hoover Dam was dedicated.

If the idea of building astronomical calendars into monuments sounds like a good idea, it's important to note that Oskar Hansen, the sculptor who built the monument, didn't think of it first. It goes all the way back to the Egyptians. Maybe even further. And when the pamphlet assures us that "future generations could look upon this monument and determine, if no other means were available, the exact date on which Hoover Dam was dedicated," they

One of two winged figures on Hoover Dam that sit atop a chart showing a celestial map to indicate the date the dam was dedicated.

are being entirely accurate. The system works. And it has worked for the last 12,000 years.

The Egyptian Zep Tepi

I once spent an entire day at the Museum of Egyptian Antiquities in Cairo. Something happened that day that I did not think possible. I actually got bored. Not that there wasn't anything to see. Precisely the opposite happened. I got saturated to the point at which I simply couldn't take any more in.

Before it was unified, Egypt was divided into a Lower kingdom, which had its center in Memphis, and an Upper kingdom to the south, which had its capital in Thebes.

There used to be considerable debate about whether civilization got started in Sumer or in Egypt. A consensus now seems to have agreed that the answer is—"Yes!" Civilization began in both, somewhere around 3200 B.C.E. If that is the case, Egypt sure seems to have the advantage when it comes to marketing image. So much has been written about Egyptian history that it would be silly to attempt any kind of summary here. There is just too huge a file to choose from. But we will pause for a moment to look at the very beginning, the time of the gods, the First Time, the time Egyptologists call the Zep Tepi. The story is a fascinating one, though much disputed.

Generally speaking, traditional theory says that hunter-gatherer tribes moved into the Nile region by 6000 B.C.E. By that time the Sahara was beginning to dry up. Until then it had been a well-watered and flourishing place. The rest of the world was just exiting the perils of the Younger Dryas Ice Age, but in Egypt the weather was balmy in comparison and well suited to early experiments in agriculture.

By 3100 B.C.E. various communities had developed. When these communities were united, the first Egyptian dynasty formed. When Upper and Lower Egypt were finally brought together as one kingdom, the first Egyptian civilization began.

So far, so good. But there are loose ends to this argument.

Let's begin by reviewing Plato again. Earlier we read what he had to say about Atlantis in his *Timaeus* and *Critias*. Now we will turn to his *Laws*, and read a short but fascinating quote about the origins of Egypt as reported by Graham Hancock in *Magicians of the Gods*. Here's Plato speaking:

> If you examine their art on the spot, you will find that ten thousand years ago (and I'm not speaking loosely; I mean literally ten thousand), paintings and reliefs were produced that are no better and no worse than those of today.

Plato was born somewhere around 428 B.C.E. If we go back ten thousand years, as Hancock insists we should ("I'm not speaking loosely; I mean literally ten thousand"), that places an early civilization in Egypt around 10,428 B.C.E. Add another two thousand or so to get to our date on this side of the B.C.E./C.E. calendar boundary and we arrive at 12,500. Even if we give or take as much as a century from that date, it places his understanding of the beginnings of Egyptian civilization in exactly the same time frame as the comet that began the Younger Dryas Ice Age. Traditional archeologists, of course, don't believe there was any civilization until after the ice age ended. But, as we have seen over and over again throughout this book, it might be that what traditional archeologists call the beginning could very possibly have been only a new beginning—a cultural human "do over."

It isn't enough, of course, to simply take Plato at his word. He was as prone to mistakes as any of us. So we need to search for other evidence—evidence that might very well be cloaked behind the conspiracy of silence because it doesn't fit the traditional mold. As it turns out, the Egyptians themselves have something to say about the topic.

As Above, So Below

The first hint comes from astrology. The Younger Dryas Ice Age corresponds exactly to the time frame of the astrological age of Leo the Lion. During those centuries, as the vernal equinox sun rose in the east every year, it was back-dropped by the constellation Leo. In other words, the Sphinx, the lion with the head of a man who faces due east, would have been staring right at his heavenly counterpart. And the belt of Orion, if the three principal pyramids indeed represent those three stars, would have been in alignment directly to the south, precisely as they appear on Earth.

If there was a doctrine held by the priests of an early Egyptian religion, it was exactly this: As Above, So Below. Almost all religions preach the same concept. Christianity says it this way: Thy will be done on Earth as it is in heaven. What the ancients saw in the heavens, they sought to reproduce on the earth.

Were these people the ancient gods, existing at the time of the Zep Tepi, that united the hunter-gatherers of the Nile region and began what we now call civilization?

Of course, this raises a lot of issues. There is no question, according to the latest scientific research, that the Sphinx and the pyramids were finished some eight thousand years later, around 2500 B.C.E. The latest evidence done by a technique called surface luminescence dating indicates a probable date well within traditional theory. But other evidence, astrological as well as textual, seems to indicate a much older date.

So which is correct?

How about both? Might it be possible that an older civilization, existing during the Younger Dryas Ice Age and Atlantian in nature if not in name, came to the Nile area to both escape the rigors of the weather and to start a civilization that might mimic what they had known before the comet wreaked havoc upon them? Were these people the ancient gods, existing at the time of the Zep Tepi, that united the hunter-gatherers of the Nile region and began what we now call civilization?

Did they lay down the earthly blueprint for what was completed some 8,000 years later by their descendants? Was there a long-lasting Egyptian cult of civilizers, a kind of priesthood, responsible for what we now call Egyptian civilization? In other words, could we consider that the floorplan of Giza was designed some 8,000 years before it was finally completed? This gives us two dates that bracket what we find at Giza in the pyramids and Sphinx. The earliest work was begun around 10,500 B.C.E., indicating ancient dates. The final work was completed round 2500 B.C.E., yielding traditional dates.

Egyptian Texts

Egyptian texts seem to indicate that is the case. The Edfu texts, for instance, reveal that:

… the gods left their lands (after a great cataclysm had destroyed their island kingdom) and sailed to another part of the primeval world. They journeyed through the lands of the primeval age. In any place they settled they founded new kingdoms.

The texts go on to describe these ancient gods. They were:

Builder gods who fashioned, in the primeval time, the Lords of the Light, the Ghosts, the Ancestors who raised the seed for gods and men, the Senior Ones who came into being at the beginning, who illuminated this land when they came forth united.

These are just a few of the texts illuminated by Graham Hancock in his books, most of which are detailed in this book's bibliography. He dares to raise some real questions which are mostly ignored by traditional archeologists.

One can only ask why. It would certainly be inconvenient to have to revisit many of the facts traditional experts feel they have already addressed. But science ought to be inconvenient. The search for truth ought to take us wherever the facts may lead. If Egypt is one of the cradles of our civilization, we need to know why, when, and how it came about. It is, after all, our legacy.

GÖBEKLI TEPE

We used to think agriculture gave rise to cities and later to writing, art, and religion. Now the world's oldest temple suggests the urge to worship sparked civilization.

Charles C. Mann

Uncloaking the Conspiracy of Silence

We may very well be living in the decade that once and for all turned a pet archeological theory completely on its head, thanks to a discovery near, of all places, the town where the biblical patriarch of monotheism, Abraham, is purported to have been born. Before we can even begin to look into this find, though, we need to provide some background.

The generally accepted version of how civilization came to be is that we humans took a giant stride up from our primitive, hunter-gatherer ancestral culture during a period known as the Neolithic Revolution. This theory, put forth in the 1920s by V. Gordon Childe, a flamboyant Australian-British thinker with a gift for synthesis, went something like this:

About six thousand years ago, in an area called Sumer, some clever humans, probably women, since they were the ones who presumably gathered plants and seeds while the men hunted, discovered that because of warming weather patterns in the

Archeologist and philologist V. Gordon Childe (1892–1957) was a proponent of culture-historical archeology, which analyzes the material artifacts to distinguish societies by culture and ethnicity.

wake of the last ice age they could now plant wild grains, take care of them for a while, water them when the weather refused to cooperate, pull a few weeds, and then, after a reasonable wait, harvest them. The advantage was that this provided a predictable, reliable food source. The disadvantage was that they had to stick around while the crop matured. Before this time, for thousands upon thousands of years, humans had survived by following wild game and gathering what food crops they found while living in whatever shelter nature happened to provide. These were the cavemen we learned about in grade school.

Domesticating crops, however, changed everything. It sparked what has since been called the Agricultural Revolution and marked the beginning of civilization. A stable, local food supply led to the birth of settled towns, which soon exploded into cities. Populations flourished. People began to adapt special occupations. A cobbler, for instance, could practice his trade and get paid for it in consumer goods. He didn't need to go out and hunt anymore. Eventually, money was invented to represent commodities such as food, thus making transactions easier to handle. Writing was developed to keep track of who got what and how much was paid. Economy was born. One city might grow barley while another grew wheat. Trade flourished. A merchant class grew to oversee caravans. You can see where this leads.

And, so the theory goes, there was yet another byproduct. Trade between regions led to an immense social upheaval in the field of religion. Prior to agriculture, gods took the form of animals. After, gods were needed to oversee grain production by sending rain in due season. A priestly class arose. Because they lived in one settled place and now had the manpower to build, temples were constructed.

Here the story takes a dark turn. Inevitably, one town's fields began to encroach on another's. Resources had to be protected. "This is our field, not yours!" To enforce that claim, armies developed. But armies need strong male gods. The goddess can't intimidate people as well as the god. Mother Earth is gentle. Yahweh, Baal, and Zeus are not.

The Bible tells the story in myth and poetry that stems from this very region of the world. Cain, the agriculturist, kills Abel, the pastoralist. He immediately goes out and builds a city. Genesis 4 lists some of the specialized occupations that developed: builders, agriculturists, musicians, industrialists, soldiers, priests, lawyers. No wonder the final verse of the chapter says, "At that time, men began to call on the name of the Lord."

Shortly after, a man named Abraham left Ur of the Chaldees, which, by the way, is right downstream from Göbekli Tepe, taking with him his own family army, and traveled across the Fertile Crescent to Israel. (The biblical writers used the name Canaan.) He went forth armed with an idea: "My God is better than your God!" (Later Hebrew composers would say it much more poetically in their psalms: "Our God is a great God, above all other gods.") From this journey evolved the concept of monotheism. Abraham emigrated because God told him to. Judaism, Christianity, and Islam followed.

From these simple beginnings in the Fertile Crescent sprang specialized tools, pottery, writing, cities, trains and buses, wars, stress, high blood pressure, obesity, Facebook, Twitter, and all the other benefits of modern civilization.

This is the accepted story. It has been poked and prodded, shaped a little differently and molded into academic shape, but it remains basically the same since Childe first called it the Neolithic Revolution, the Agricultural Revolution that took place in the New Stone (*Neo-Lithic*) Age, a radical change, fraught with revolutionary consequences for the whole species. He declared it to be "the greatest event in human history after the mastery of fire!"

A New Paradigm

That's the way things stood until 1995, when a researcher named Klaus Schmidt, then with the German Archeological Institute but since deceased, began to dig at a place in Turkey called, by the locals, Potbelly Hill, or Göbekli Tepe. What Schmidt found there caused him to report, "In 10 or 15 years, Göbekli Tepe will be more famous than Stonehenge. And for good reason!"

Göbekli Tepe is a temple built of immense stone pillars arranged in sets of rings. The tallest are eighteen feet high and weigh sixteen tons. Carved into their surfaces are bas relief totemic animals of prey—a whole menagerie. The hillside in which all this was built is littered with flint tools from Neolithic times—knives, projectile points, choppers, scrapers, and files. The T-shaped pillars themselves are immense, and they appear to form a very complex structure.

But what makes the discovery so fantastic is this: Göbekli Tepe was built 11,600 years ago! That's seven thousand years older than the Great Pyramid of Giza and thousands of years before even the beginnings of Stonehenge. And, so far at least, there is no evidence whatsoever of existing agriculture in the surrounding area. The temple seems to have been built, impossibly, by hunter-gatherers with no communal support structure except for hunting teams that would fan out, kill what game they could, and bring it back to the workers. The bones of their evening meals consist mostly of auks and gazelles.

How did a hunter-gatherer culture supply the manpower to carve and move sixteen-ton rocks? It must have taken thousands of laborers. What motivated them? Religious temples supposedly didn't come into play until generations after the Agricultural Revolution, but here was a huge religious temple found springing up from the landscape thousands of years before religion was thought to have been organized enough to even attempt such a thing! As far as we knew, when Göbekli Tepe was discovered, it was by far the largest building

Excavated structures of the Göbekli Tepe in southern Turkey date back about 11,600 years!

project ever attempted by humankind up to that point in history and there seem to be no precursors—no trial and error, no history of evolving concepts, no evidence of any practice sites as is evidenced, for instance, by the pyramid-building tradition in Egypt or the standing-stone tradition culminating at Stonehenge. And it didn't precede those traditions by a few hundred years. It was built almost seven thousand years earlier! If anything, the tradition seems to devolve rather than evolve. The most sophisticated building happened first, at the bottom of the dig. It appears that later generations built on top of it. But their work exhibits less and less skill with each succeeding layer. It seems as though Göbekli Tepe illustrates the unraveling of a tradition rather than the building of one. And, in the end, it was completely and deliberately buried like a time capsule, preserving it intact so that it could be dug up and studied in 1995.

The "Birth of Religion"

What was the motivating force that gave birth to this amazing temple? In a word—religion. In an article written for *National Geographic* magazine

(June 2011), Charles C. Mann calls this temple site the birth of religion. The presence of so many carved shamanic totem animals, the lack of any contemporary nearby towns or support villages, and the almost certain conclusion that this temple marked a religious site seems to cry out that these people were in touch with something so big, so meaningful, so stupendously important in their lives that they had to build a monument to it. The result is Göbekli Tepe.

It seems as though Göbekli Tepe illustrates the unraveling of a tradition rather than the building of one.

We can never know what specific beliefs inspire and motivate someone. Most often, we don't even know what our own personal belief system consists of, and it's apt to change many times over the course of a single lifetime. We may have a basic ideology. We may use a catch-all identifier like Christian. We may narrow that down to Methodist. But even two Methodist Christians probably disagree about much of what their faith proposes. What stands out, however, and what we can measure, is depth of commitment. To paraphrase the Gospel of Matthew 7:20, "By their deeds, ye shall know them." In other words, if someone does something big and obvious in the name of faith, they probably have a big, obvious faith. Their faith has either inspired them or caused them to fear their God in a big, obvious way.

These folks at Göbekli Tepe had a big, obvious, motivating religion. What could it have been? At this stage in human development it apparently had something to do with Animism. This is the belief that spirit animates everything in nature—that animals, trees, rocks, landscape, and humans meet in Mother Earth's protective embrace. But it is just as obvious that astrology figured in somehow. In other words, the very structure of Göbekli Tepe marries the earth to the sky. There are too many star, sun, and moon sightlines to ignore.

Göbekli Tepe isn't an easy place to get to. The builders were motivated by what they saw and felt on the landscape, not by where they found it convenient to work. There is no nearby water source. There were no towns, villages, or fields because these hadn't been developed yet.

No, they built where they did because they felt called to a particular spot of ground in order to manifest a very powerful religion that ties an earthly landscape securely to a heavenly perspective.

Archeologists are beginning to suspect that Childe's theory about the Agricultural Revolution leading to, among other things, religion, may have to be revised. Now it appears that there is good evidence to support the fact that religion came first, and agriculture, leading to what we call civilization, arose to support those who lived around these sacred places. Such places exist all over the planet. They may not be as spectacular as Göbekli Tepe, but they draw thousands of seekers each year. And it is intriguing to know that as spectacular as Göbekli Tepe is, only a small portion has been uncovered so far. What else lies beneath the sands and stones of this wonderful place?

How and Why?

By far the biggest riddle is this: How did a primitive, hunter-gatherer society suddenly learn to build this way and express their religion in such a manner? Could they suddenly have learned such things on their own? Or were they taught?

The answer may well be suggested in the date of Göbekli Tepe's construction. It appears to have been built in the waning years of the Younger Dryas Ice Age epoch. Could it be that sophisticated builders, well-versed in such construction methods, arrived on the scene having witnessed a heavenly event, such as a comet impact, that reaped devastating havoc on Earth? If so, they might well have inspired a religion that married heaven and Earth into one theological construct. Göbekli Tepe might very well be the first temple of that new religion.

The gods called the Anunnaki appeared in Assyrian and Babylonian mythology in which they are credited with building great cities.

Babylonian religious texts such as the *Enuma Elish*, written just a little south of Göbekli Tepe, speak of ancient gods called Anunnaki, who suddenly appeared on the scene at this time of history to organize, some say mate with or even genetically manipulate, the ancestors of this very people. In Genesis 6:2 the Bible makes a pointed reference to the fact that "the sons of God saw that the daughters of men were beautiful, and they married any of them they chose." The puzzling passage is set in this very geographical location and speaks as if it were relating historical fact rather than religious mythology. The products of these unions resulted in a mysterious race called the Nephilim, "heroes of old, men of renown" (Genesis 6:4).

Scholars such as Andrew Collins trace the origins of this ruling class back to the Swiderians, descendants of the Solutreans, recognizing them as the mythical "sons of God." Are these texts more than ancient stories and academic speculation? Are they based on historical facts?

Testament or Prophecy?

There is another riddle at Göbekli Tepe that might be even more important and relevant to our time in history. It ties in with another mystery inherent in the Mayan calendar, the Egyptian complex at Giza, and perhaps a few more important places scattered around the globe. It has to do with the future of humankind on the planet.

To begin to explore this subject, we need to start with the Mayan calendar. As we will see when we turn our attention to Olmecs, Aztecs, Inca, and the Maya, in December 2012 there was a great deal of interest in what is called the Mayan Long Count Calendar. Many people mistakenly believed it to be a prediction that the world was going to end on December 21st that year, because the calendar appeared to end on that date. Obviously, they were mistaken. But that calendar, like all calendars, didn't signify an end as much as a new beginning. Every calendar, even the ones we use today, have to end somewhere. But they always imply that the next January 1st brings with it a new year, a new beginning.

The Mayan Long Count Calendar was no different. It marked the end of the 26,000-year circle of precession (earlier we called it Earth wobble) that marks the time between the conjunction of the winter solstice sunrise with the center of the flat plain of the *Milky Way* galaxy as it appears on Earth. As we discovered when we looked at ancient astronomers, this event occurs every 26,000 years. In our time, on December 21, 2012, the solstice took place and appeared the same in the sky as it did to our 26,000-year-old ancestors.

But precession is much too imprecise to our earthbound eyes to narrow such an event down to one day. Indeed, the best we can do is to estimate a period that lasts for some 80 years. So we might just as well say that the winter solstice sun is rising in conjunction with the visible plain of the Milky Way now, just as it has since 1960 and as it will continue to do until 2040. The Mayan calendar was well within that time frame, but doesn't pinpoint an exact day.

What does this have to do with Göbekli Tepe? Just this: In Graham Hancock's *Magicians of the Gods*, he describes the jolt he felt while reading a paper presented by Paul Burley in June of 2011, called *Göbekli Tepe: Temples Communicating Ancient Cos-*

The Mayan calendar caused some panic in 2012, when some people misinterpreted it to believe the ancient people were predicting the end of the world that year.

mic Geography. For an in-depth study of the topic, I refer you to Hancock's book, but the bottom line is that on Pillar 43 at Göbekli Tepe the builders had carved an exact relief of what the sky would look like at the time of the winter solstice during our time of history, the same time that marked the end of the Mayan Long Count Calendar.

In Burley's words:

> What's important here is that for some unknown reason the builders of Göbekli Tepe constructed a temple apparently high-lighting a time 11,600 years in their future. Yet this time is intentional. The symbolism is clear and in keeping with many mythologies describing this very same event occurring at the very same time we live in today!

To understand how this might have come to pass, we need to cast our eyes on the heavens for a minute.

The Taurid Meteor Stream

Thirty thousand years ago an immense comet entered our inner solar system and was captured by the sun's gravitational field. It was locked into a large orbit around the sun. Twenty thousand years ago, because of both internal and external stresses, it broke apart and spread its debris in a huge arc, still orbiting around the sun. Picture it now as a large doughnut consisting of fragments both large and small, with the sun in the middle.

Twice a year, every June and October, the earth crosses that debris field and encounters some of the fragments. Most of them are tiny objects that burn up, harmlessly if not spectacularly, in our atmosphere. We are usually alerted

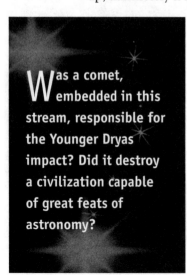

Was a comet, embedded in this stream, responsible for the Younger Dryas impact? Did it destroy a civilization capable of great feats of astronomy?

to their presence and told by meteorologists on the Weather Channel to rush outside and view the Taurid meteor shower. What we see are called shooting stars. We see other examples throughout the year called the Leonids, the Perseids, and the Andromedids. John Denver immortalized such demonstrations when he and some friends spent the night viewing a similar display in Colorado. That night he wrote the song "Rocky Mountain High" and sang about seeing it "raining fire in the sky."

Not all the fragments, however, are harmless. There are some big ones out there, embedded in the stream. They come around every 12,000 years or so. We're scheduled to meet up with them sometime between 2035 and 2040.

When we tie all this together, it raises interesting questions. Was a comet, embedded in this stream, responsible for the Younger Dryas impact? Did it destroy a civilization capable of great feats of astronomy? Were the survivors capable of realizing that it would happen again? And could they figure out when? Did they encode this message that would someday be recovered by the civilization that existed when the comet would return? Did they do all this at Göbekli Tepe and then bury the whole site so it would become, for all practical purposes, a time capsule?

Was this the same message embedded in the Mayan Long Count Calendar and in myths from around the world? Do the Ojibwa and ancestral Hopi legends bear the same message when they talk about the long-tailed star returning some day?

Is some day going to happen in our time? Can we expect a return of the Younger Dryas comet before 2040?

Listen to the words of Professor Emilio Spedicato of the University of Bergamo, who believes he has discovered evidence of an object embedded in the heart of the Taurid meteor stream that might be as large as thirty kilometers in diameter, again referenced by Graham Hancock in *Magicians of the Gods*:

> Tentative orbital parameters which could lead to its observation are estimated. It is predicted that in the near future (around the year 2030) the earth will cross again that part of the torus (the debris stream) that contains the fragments, an encounter that in the past has dramatically affected mankind.

Have we in fact discovered, with the aid of our advanced scientific instruments, what the ancients were warning us about when they built Göbekli Tepe, encoded a warning for the future, and then buried their work so it would serve as a message in a bottle meant for a future generation?

Work Still to Be Done

There are far more riddles yet to be unearthed at Göbekli Tepe. The work there has just begun. But if an enlightened, technological group of engineers/astronomers survived the cataclysmic Younger Dryas epoch, inspired and instructed a new, emerging civilization, and cleared the way for the beginning of what we now call our culture, this may very well have been one of the places where they first began their work. If so, they were there at what we call the beginning. Did they also prophecy the end?

GUNUNG PADANG

The archeological establishment is scrambling to find some reason to reject and pour scorn on the extraordinary consequences of the excavations now taking place at Gunung Padang in Indonesia. Since its first exploration by archeologists in 1914 the site was thought to be a natural hill with 2500 year-old megalithic structures on top of it. But in 2010 geologist Dr Danny Hilman Natawidjaja (who earned his doctorate at Cal Tech) recognized this "hill" as a possible man-made pyramid and began to explore it using ground penetrating radar, seismic tomography, resistivity survey, and other remote sensing techniques, as well as some direct excavations and deep core drilling. The results were immediately intriguing....

Graham Hancock:
https://grahamhancock.com/gunung-padang-latest-hancock/

The Mountain of Enlightenment

If you have been reading this book from front to back rather than dipping in here or there to study specific topics that interest you, you have just read the previous entry about Göbekli Tepe. It caused a furor when news of its discovery percolated down to the public. In one fell swoop it pushed the birth of civilization back some five thousand years and overturned a well-thought-out and accepted view of our early beginnings in the Fertile Crescent.

If you found that exciting, hang on to your hat. You ain't seen nothin' yet! We turn now to an Indonesian site called Gunung Padang, and if the archeological dates hold up, as they certainly seem to be doing so far, they make Göbekli Tepe seem almost modern.

We've already talked some about Indonesia. In the first chapter we saw that it's the home of the brand new discovery of a human species called *Homo floresiensis*, quickly dubbed the Hobbit because of its small stature. Members of this species seem to have survived for thousands of years after Neanderthal and Denisovan either became extinct or were absorbed by our species. *Homo floresiensis* became extinct about 12,000 years ago. Remember that date. It corresponds almost exactly to the catastrophe at the very end of the Younger Dryas Ice Age. That was the event that caused rapid, worldwide flooding and turned Indonesia into islands rather than a single land mass.

Indonesia made the headlines in 2014. The October issue of *Nature* magazine featured an article about the discovery of sophisticated cave paintings on the island of Sulawesi. They appear to be close to 40,000 years old. That's at least as old as, and possibly even older than, the famous cave paintings of Europe. Such art is referred to as symbolic representation. When we look at mythology and religion in later chapters, that will become very important.

On December 3, 2014, the Smithsonian announced the discovery on the Indonesian island of Java of the "bones of what appeared to be an ancient

The Gunung Padang site in Indonesia includes chambers that have been dated back to approximately 26,000 years ago.

human, surrounded by animal remains and shells decorated with geometric engravings" generally interpreted as indicative of modern cognition and behavior. The engravings represent the earliest evidence of such decorative marks and also the first known use of shells to make tools. But these engravings were dated to 500,000 years ago! That's at least 300,000 years before modern humans were supposed to have evolved.

With this as a backdrop, we now turn to the dig that is rewriting the history books. In 2011, Dr. Danny Hilman Natawidjaja was the first to notice something special about a mountain called the Mountain of Enlightenment, or Gunung Padang. Up until then it was thought to be a natural mountain with some interesting 2,500-year-old ruins on the top. But Dr. Natawidjaja suspected that it was, in fact, a human-built pyramid. Subsequent archeological work uncovered evidence of chambers buried deep within the structure that carbon-date back 26,000 years! If those dates are substantiated, as they so far have been every time they have been tested, this is by far the oldest human-built structure ever discovered on Earth, pushing the dates of such accomplishments far back into the last Ice Age.

It is arguably the single most astounding find ever recorded by an archeologist and will force the complete rethinking of everything we know about human history and civilization. Nothing else comes close. It is older by 14,500 years than even Göbekli Tepe. It had stood for more than 20,000 years when Stonehenge was built. It predates the traditional date for the pyramids by more than 21,500 years.

Such a discovery should have been welcomed with open arms. But of course, it wasn't. Infighting has caused the delay of funds, time, publicity, and resources needed to get to the bottom of the dig, although there now seem to be indications that tourist dollars will finally prevail and the project will get the attention it deserves.

> Dr. Natawidjaja's claims have stood up to some very rigorous checks and balances. He's standing by his claims and has received some very impressive support.

Obviously mainstream archeology isn't at all happy with the findings. They are simply too radical for the traditionalists. This is sad, but if the history of science teaches us anything, it is that radical ideas are never accepted right away.

Indeed, there is a team of Indonesian archeologists who are already on record making the claim that Gunung Padang is simply a naturally occurring, extinct volcano. The so-called chambers located by underground radar are simply hollow lava tubes. Ancient carbon-dating dates are the result of old lava flows.

So far, however, Dr. Natawidjaja's claims have stood up to some very rigorous checks and balances. He's standing by his claims and has received some very impressive support.

The central claim of archeology is that civilization didn't begin until after the last Ice Age, about 11,600 years ago at the very earliest, and even this date was reluctantly accepted only a few years ago. If Göbekli Tepe took a while to be accepted, Gunung Padang will probably have to pay its dues. It sounds too much like Atlantis. It simply couldn't be! Human beings back then were uncultured, primitive hunter-gatherers. They could never have built something this sophisticated!

But as it turns out, each new day brings more surprises. We now enter the halls of complete and utter wonder. Early humans may not have simply been great builders. They may have even generated electricity.

Ancient Power Source?

We can't close off this discussion without mentioning what might be the single most unbelievable discovery in the history of archeology. According to the article:

Dr. Danny Hilman (Natawidjaja) is responsible for the archeological team conducting research on the site and they have recently announced the discovery of an oddly shaped metal device that is presumed to be the world's oldest electrical device. According to researchers, this object is made out of gold and copper and seems to resemble a primitive electrical capacitor. According to some researchers, this newly found device seems very similar in structure to the biblical descriptions of the Ark of the Covenant. Carbon dating confirms the device to be 2,500 years older than the Ark of the Covenant....

The discovery of the electrical device at Gunung Padang is getting a lot of attention. Even President Susilo Bambang Yudhoyono of Indonesia visited the site, congratulating the researchers on their discovery and declaring that he has great interest in the results of the research.

Was the Ark of the Covenant actually an advanced electronic device left behind in Egypt by the Old Ones?

"The findings on the Gunung Padang site will shock the world," said the president's special staffer for social aid and natural disasters, Andi Arief.

Obviously, if this find passes muster, it will be front page news everywhere. For those who believe in Atlantis or other lost civilizations, it seems too good to be true. This wouldn't have been built by the survivors of the Younger Dryas comet catastrophe. It would have built 13,000 years before the event itself!

The whole situation lends itself to conspiracy theories galore. One can imagine such a device making its way into Egypt, thereby resolving one of the most intriguing questions about the building of the pyramids: "Given the absence of any kind of soot on the ceilings of interior passages, how did they provide light for the workers?"

Biblical writers would love this as well. When Moses stood before Pharaoh and uttered his famous catchphrase, "Let my people go!" the Pharaoh was, at first, only too glad to oblige. Later, for no given reason in the *Exodus* account, he changes his mind and pursues with his whole cavalry.

What happened to cause such an abrupt turnabout? Could it be that Pharaoh learned that Moses was escaping with a technological device that the Egyptians had inherited from the Old Ones but, after the passage of centuries, had forgotten how to manufacture on their own? In other words, was he stealing the only prototype? And was that device the Ark of the Covenant? Given Moses's privileged status during the forty years he was raised in the very household of the Pharaoh, he probably would have learned of such a valuable treasure. It would certainly go a long way toward explaining all the weird power surges and special effects linked to the ancient, mysterious object that so confounded Indiana Jones and the *Raiders of the Lost Ark*.

Of course such speculations are, at this point, merely a lot of fun. There is obviously a lot of work to be done.

Proving an Outlandish Theory

Dean Radin, in his book *The Conscious Universe*, points out that every uniquely new idea in any science has to pass through four stages before it becomes accepted:

Stage 1: The idea is flat out impossible! (And the one who produced it is an idiot!)

Stage 2: The idea is possible, but weak and uninteresting. (Here the idea is usually consigned to the conspiracy of silence.)

Stage 3: The idea is important, but further study is advised. (Wait to see if the experts come around.)

Stage 4: Of course the idea is correct! (We all knew it all along!)

At this point everyone conveniently forgets how contentious the whole affair really was.

If this pattern holds true as regards Gunung Padang, we're somewhere in the middle of Stage 2 at this point. But thank goodness for the Internet! It makes it very difficult to bury interesting theories that rock the boat.

Probably George Washington thought to himself, more than once, "A little revolution from time to time is a good thing!" This may be such a time.

JOMON PEOPLE OF JAPAN

Experts have followed the trail of mitochondrial DNA pattern even further back in time, and deep into Siberia. Experts now conclude that the prehistoric Japanese people and ancestors of the Jomon people originated from somewhere around Lake Baikal area in Russia. Back then during the ice ages, only small tribes of paleo-asiatic stone tool-using hunters had been able to survive the harsh climate of the glacial ages up to 25,000 years ago by living in warm pockets along Lake Baikal in Siberia. When the global climate started to warm up some of these hunters started moving south in pursuit of large animals such as mammoths, while others may have crossed the Bering strait to reach the North American continent.

Condensed from *Heritage of Japan* at
https://heritageofjapan.wordpress.com

The Hidden Truth of Enough

When we think of a lost civilization, or, for that matter, any civilization, most of us form our ideas from a position of unexamined assumptions.

Try this thought experiment. Close your eyes and say the words "lost civilization." If you are like most people, the words probably bring to mind buildings hidden in the jungle or lost beneath ocean waves. We may picture flying machines or people wearing foreign clothing such as white robes. If you play video games you may even see ancient battles and exotic methods of warfare or advanced technologies.

Let me suggest something else. Think, instead, about the word "wisdom."

An exhibit at the National Museum of Nature and Science in Tokyo, Japan, depicts a daily scene of life among the Jomon people.

A lost civilization can teach us something totally divorced from technologies couched in the language of architecture and cities, death rays or crystals. A lost civilization might even contain within its store of wisdom something that we desperately need to understand if we are to avoid becoming a lost civilization ourselves.

After studying the Jomon people of Japan, I wonder if such is not the case. Is it possible that they can teach us a hidden truth about the wisdom of enough? It is a truth we have forgotten in today's consumer society that describes economic security and comfort only by employing the word growth. When the economy is growing, when new construction starts determine whether or not we are economically healthy, when people are happy only when wages are up, when politicians are elected at least in part because of their promises to get the economy booming, and when towns adopt the policy that they must grow or die, it is obvious that the word "enough" doesn't even enter our mindset when it comes to determining our level of happiness.

Perhaps we can learn something, a hidden truth, from an ancient Japanese people who might be more involved in the formation of our civilization than we have ever been taught. If a conspiracy of silence has shrouded anyone from public view, it is these folks.

Reading between the Lines of History

At first glance they don't seem very interesting. The history books tell us that they were an old hunter-gatherer culture that inhabited the islands south of Japan on the way to Taiwan. Because they lived during the height of the Ice Age, the ocean levels were much lower because so much of the world's water was tied up in glacial ice farther north. Their homeland, now consisting of islands, was then a much bigger land mass and allowed them to walk across areas now covered by water. Beringia, the land bridge from Siberia to Alaska, was fully exposed, as well. They never discovered agriculture, never progressed past a subsistence life, made only a few stone tools and spent their days grubbing about trying to stay alive. They lived some 17,000 years ago and only achieved a level of success when they were conquered or absorbed by the much more aggressive Yayoi people about 2,500 years ago, from whom the modern Japanese descended.

What do people like this have to teach us in the modern civilization of the twenty-first century?

Let's read between the lines a little.

First off, it is acknowledged by accepted, traditional archeological methods that these people existed with very little change over a period that lasted for some 16,500 years. That's a long time! Think about it. They spoke the same language, acted in the same ways, went about their daily life and suffered very little social turmoil for more than sixteen millennia! The record shows no evidence of warfare or social upheaval until the Yayoi arrived on the scene. It is only then that archeological evidence indicates that the Jomon people disappeared from the scene. Whatever caused their demise came from without, not within, their culture.

How do we know all this? From pottery shards. That's right. The Jomon invented the world's first pottery. That's something often left out of the equation. As a matter of fact, some archeologists insist the discovery of pottery must be attributed to the Yayoi. But Jomon corded pottery, named after the distinctive cord marks embedded in their clay pots, has been excavated that unequivocally dates back to 16,500 years ago and is found continuously throughout the archeological record for the next 14,000 years.

Some of it even shows up in ancient layers in archeological digs from Fiji to—wait for it!—Valdivia in South America! When the discovery of thousands of Jomon pottery shards in Valdivia was reported in *Smithsonian Contributions to Anthropology* in 1965, it set off a major battle in the field of anthropology that is still being fought today. How could ancient Ice Age Japanese pottery show up in South America?

Because it didn't seem possible, it was declared to not be possible. And a curtain of silence descended across Act One of this particular pageant being enacted on the archeological stage.

But then other problems arose. It seems as though kernels of rice were discovered baked into really old Jomon pots. Rice? Impossible! Rice is a culti-vated crop. Were they saying the Jomon people invented agriculture thousands of years before anyone else? Never! Lower the curtain on Act Two as well.

Now the plot thickens. DNA research came into play in the American West. It seems as though the ancestors of many American Indian tribes carried DNA from Asia. That was to be expected because the folks who crossed the Siberian land bridge, after spending countless generations around the shores of Lake Baikal, were probably of Asian descent. But here is where it gets even more interesting. As it turns out, skeletons unearthed in the Lake Baikal region share similar DNA with the ancient Jomon people. It now seems that as the Ice Age was beginning to work its magic on the ancient landscape, the folks who would soon become Jomon set out on foot to migrate both east and south, some of them to eventually become the ancestors of the American Indi-an peoples, others to become the ancestors of the Japanese.

Were they saying the Japanese might be related to the first Americans, thus giving them a claim of first possession in North America? Heaven forbid! Ring down the curtain on Act Three!

But the story wouldn't go away. Other evidence seemed to indicate that Jomon sailors followed the so-called Black Current that sweeps north up the Pacific, swings east below the Aleutians and then south down the American west coast all the way to South America. They may have left a record of their passage behind in the form of stone anchors found off the coast of California.

An example of Jomon pottery is on display at the British Museum. Pottery of this sort has been found at digs from Fiji to South America.

First they walk over to America via Beringia. Then they sail over to visit their long-lost cousins in prehistoric boats? These were uncivilized, uncouth, and unlettered proto-Japanese! It simply couldn't be!

At this point, many archeologists not only ring down the curtain on the whole the-ory, they get up and walk out of the theater!

A Non-Expert Opinion

We could go on and on about the Jomon, including how they might even have built megalithic structures that now rest beneath Pacific waves off the coast of Japan, but this is enough to let us ask a few ques-tions. We know for sure that they are old. We are pretty sure they invented pottery. We suspect that they were great travelers and seem to be the ancestors of at least some American Indian tribes as well as modern Japanese. They could very well have been accomplished sailors.

All this, and they did it against the backdrop of a culture that lasted for 16,500 years without a great deal of outward change. When you think of how we have gone to war, polluted and paved our own country in a period of only a few centuries, it makes you wonder. How did they do it without breaking apart? All civilizations eventually die. Just ask Greece and Rome about that. But the Jomon had a pretty good run, accomplishing a lot along the way. It might even be said that they changed the course of the entire human species on the planet. If pottery was made 16,000 years ago, they invented the process. If plants could be made to grow for the benefit of humankind, they discovered the agricultural techniques. If there was a collision with a comet 12,800 years ago, they saw it. If there was a sudden meltdown following the Younger Dryas 11,600 years ago, they experienced it. If there was a Siberian land bridge, they walked it. If boats sailed down the coast of California to South America, they navigated them. They were a prolific people with an impressive resume. Yet they didn't change all that much. That's the one thing anthropologists agree on.

Might it be possible, without one shred of archeological evidence except common sense to make such a claim, that they didn't change very much because they didn't see the need to do so? Had they discovered, probably by accident rather than philosophical pursuit, that life could be enjoyed and bring accomplishment without increasing its speed? Did they survive for so long because they never felt the need to overexploit their environment? Did they discover the wisdom of enough?

We'll never know, of course. When they were finally absorbed by a much more aggressive people, the Yayoi, they began their quick descent into modernism. The doors swung open on aspects of civilization more familiar to us—war, consumerism, overexploitation, abundance, and all the rest.

But for a long time, before the antecedents of modernism discovered and eventually overwhelmed them, they must have had a pretty good life.

OLMECS, AZTECS, INCA, AND THE MAYA

The Olmec, Mayan, Incan, and Aztec civilizations are some of the greatest ancient civilizations in history, and yet we know very little about them compared to other parts of the world. The Olmecs are frequently forgotten entirely, and the rest are often lumped together or confused, but they were all completely distinct. In short, the Maya came first, and settled in modern-day Mexico. Next came the Olmecs, who also settled Mexico. They didn't build any major cities, but they were widespread and prosperous. They were followed by the Inca in modern-day Peru, and finally the Aztecs, also in modern-day Mexico.

Simon Griffin in
The Difference Between the Aztec, Maya, Inca and Olmec:
http://knowledgenuts.com/?s=Aztec%2C+Maya%2C+Inca.

Sorting Out What We Thought We Knew

When it comes to early American history, the best we can say is that our knowledge is in a constant state of flux. Take Mexico, for instance. Who was the Mother Culture, the Olmecs or the Mayans? It used to be a matter of dogmatic doctrine that the advanced civilizations that settled in South America, Central America, and Mexico followed a definite pattern. First came the Olmecs of Mexico, who gave birth to the Maya. The Incas arose independently in Peru, followed by the Aztecs, who inherited the Olmec/Maya traditions and were in power when Cortés landed.

In Belize at the Lamanai site where there was a Mayan city, the decoration on this wall of a face is clearly inspired by the Olmec. Archeologists are arguing which civilization came first, or did they parallel each other?

Now, as reported in an article titled "New Evidence Unearthed for the Origins of the Maya" by Nicholas Mott in the April 2013 edition of *National Geographic News*, this doesn't appear to be the case at all. Once again, confirmed, doctrinal archeology has been turned on its head. And once again we find ourselves pushing dates back further into the remote past:

> The Maya culture began differently than previously thought. Experts have traditionally believed that when the Olmec were busy building their civilization at large sites such as La Venta, near the Gulf Coast in modern Mexico, the people who would become the Maya were living in loosely associated nomadic groups in the jungles to the east and southeast. This theory holds that the Maya derived their entire society—including their architecture and social structure—directly from the Olmec. But [Takeshi] Inomata's work has revealed that the Olmec is not an older civilization. In fact, Ceibal pre-dates La Venta by as long as two centuries. And although some Olmec cities are indeed older than both La Venta and Ceibal, they likely did not interact with the Maya.

Notice the phrasing: "Experts have traditionally believed....," "This theory holds that....," "... Inomata's work has revealed....," "... Ceibal pre-dates La Venta....," "Olmec cities are indeed older." It sounds very precise. Now we know.... As if the matter is now settled once and for all. But it's not. Not by a long shot!

Whenever the archeological dust settles over the whole Olmec, Maya, Inca, Aztec debate, including who came first, who influenced whom, how they built the amazing structures they are famous for, and what kind of people they must have been, one thing will be certain: They were amazing cultures, shrouded in mystery and overflowing with an abundance of enigma. And it may turn out that over the whole picture looms another shadow of a culture that was a parent to them all.

Wisdom Lost

Nazca, Cuzco, Coricancha, Sacsayhuaman, Machu Picchu, Tiahuanaco, Kalasasaya: The words flow off the tongue like liquid magic. The Inca peoples of what is now Peru and Bolivia remember how it all began. Their mythology, written down years later by Spanish priests whose predecessors had burned all the original documents, speaks of a "white man of large stature and authoritative demeanor. He was past his prime, with grey hair ... but he spoke to them with love." He brought to them the blessings of civilization. Before he came, say the legends, the land was full of chaos. When he departed across the Pacific—some say he walked on the water, others say he used rafts—he left order and a better life in his wake. His name, they say, was Viracocha, the Foam of the Sea. In

Machu Picchu is the site of an ancient citadel in Peru's Andes Mountains. Many archeologists believe it was constructed for the Incan Emperor Pachacuti back in the fifteenth century.

other versions of the tale, especially the one made famous by Thor Heyerdahl, he was called Kon-Tiki.

In Mexico and Central America a similar tale is told. The words carry the same sense of magic: Kukulkan, Tikal, Puma Punku, Chichen Itza, Cholula, La Venta, Tres Zapotes and San Lorenzo. Here the bringer of civilization had a different name. He was Quetzalcoatl, "a large white man, '*era Hombre blanco*,' with a flowing beard." Like Viracocha to the west and south he wore a long, white robe, condemned the sacrifices that polluted the people, taught them how to use proper cooking fires, and showed them how to "live together as husband and wife." He arrived from the sea "in a boat that moved without paddles," and "taught the people how to live in peace." When he was eventually rebuffed by a local group who felt threatened by his message, he left, sailing away "toward the rising sun."

The final message of both peacekeepers was the same, however: "I'll be back."

Perhaps they never should have made that promise. The people remembered and waited. Much later, perhaps thousands of years later, when other white men with flowing beards stepped ashore for quite a different purpose, the people welcomed them with open arms, thinking the heroes of old had returned. When Francisco Pizarro found himself being feted in the Inca capital, he calmly locked the doors and ordered the slaughter by the thousands of unarmed, rejoicing people. In Mexico and Central America, the conquistadors under Hernán Cortés did the same.

The nation of Spain and the Catholic Church have a lot to answer for, not the least of which is the loss of centuries, perhaps even millennia, of wisdom they attributed to the forces of evil. Were they really destroying the work of the devil? Or were they doing the devil's work? History will be the judge.

The Written Word

One thing that is especially fascinating about all these cultures is that, like the Egyptian and Sumerian cultures of old, they were people who had a rich mythology that eventually made it into print. We have more than archi-

An 1846 painting by John Everett Millais depicts the Spanish Conquistador Francisco Pizarro capturing the Inca people. The Inca at first might have thought the Europeans were godlike people come to help them, but they were betrayed.

tectural wonders to help us in our quest to understand them, even though the vast bulk of evidence we might have had was destroyed by the Spanish, who considered it all to be pagan scriptures and works of the devil. Who knows what hidden truths they burned in the fires of conquest?

But portions of some texts survived, thanks to the few farsighted priests who translated them and thought them important enough to be preserved. One such prime example is the famous Quiché Mayan *Popol Vuh*. It is undated, but seems to have been copied down in its final form between 1554 and 1558 C.E. The legends it records, of course, are far more ancient. This is similar to the way the Bible came to be. Although written down after 1000 B.C.E., the Old Testament tells stories that date much further back in time. Indeed, the *Popol Vuh* almost echoes the familiar words of the book of Genesis when it recalls the creation of the world. What follows is a condensation of a translation by Allen J. Christenson:

The Popol Vuh

This is the beginning of the ancient people of this place called Quiché. Here we shall write. We shall begin to tell the ancient stories of the beginning, the origin of all that was done in the citadel of Quiché, among the people of the Quiché nation.

First the earth was created, the mountains and the valleys. The waterways were divided, their branches coursing among the mountains. Thus the waters were divided, revealing the great mountains. For thus was the creation of the earth, created then by Heart of Sky and Heart of Earth, as they are called. They were the first to conceive it. The sky was set apart. The earth also was set apart within the waters. Thus was conceived the successful completion of the work when they thought and when they pondered. Then were conceived the animals of the mountains, the guardians of the forest, and all that populate the mountains—the deer and the birds, the puma and the jaguar, the serpent and the rattlesnake, the pit viper and the guardian of the bushes. She Who Has Borne Children and He Who Has Begotten Sons then asked: "Shall it be merely solitary, merely silent beneath the trees and the bushes? It is well that there shall be guardians for them," they said. Thus they considered and spoke together, and immediately were created the deer and the birds. Having done this, they then provided homes for the deer and the birds.

Those who have read the first two chapters of the Bible will immediately find themselves on familiar ground. But the *Popol Vuh* isn't nearly finished yet. The similarities continue. It goes on to describe the creation of the first humans:

These are the names of the first people who were framed and shaped: the first person was Balam Quitze, the second was Balam Acab, the third was Mahucutah and the fourth was Iqui Balam. These, then, were the names of our first mothers and fathers.

These first people, however, seem to be endowed with some rather miraculous powers.

Their frame and shape were merely brought about by the miraculous power and the spirit essence of the Framer and the Shaper, of She Who Has Borne Children and He Who Has Begotten Sons, of Sovereign and Quetzal Serpent.... They were able to speak and converse. They were able to look and listen.... Perfect was their sight, and perfect was their knowledge of everything beneath the sky. If they gazed about them, looking intently, they beheld (everything) that was in the sky and that which was upon the earth. Instantly they were able to behold everything. They did not have to walk to see all that existed beneath the sky. They merely saw it from wherever they were.

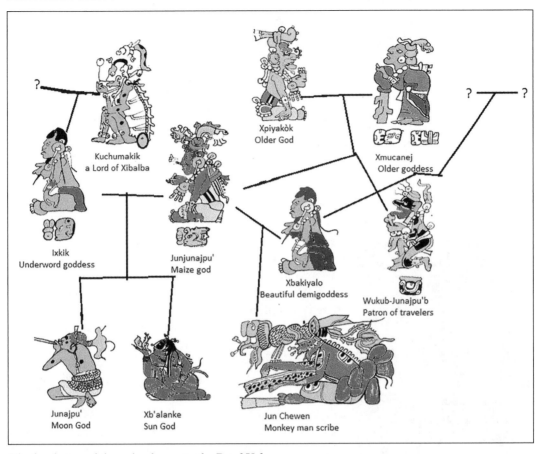

The family tree of the gods who are in the *Popol Vuh.*

Thus their knowledge became full. Their vision passed beyond the trees and the rocks, beyond the lakes and the seas, beyond the mountains and the valleys.

Anyone who watches television today can mimic their special powers of instantly being "able to behold everything. They did not have to walk to see all that existed beneath the sky." Well, neither does a modern couch potato armed with a remote.

But, just like their biblical counterparts, these first people had ambitions of being like their god. And, just like Adam and Eve, they got into trouble because of it when they said:

We have learned everything, great and small.

The gods heard. Gods don't like it when humans try to emulate them too much. Their powers brought on their downfall:

Thus their knowledge was taken back by She Who Has Borne Children and He Who Has Begotten Sons: "What now can be done to them so that their vision reaches only nearby, so that only a little of the face of the earth can be seen by them? For it is not good what they say.... It is a mistake that they have become like gods." Thus their eyes were blinded. They could (now) see only nearby; things were clear to them only where they were. Thus their knowledge was lost.

Myth or History

Reading between the lines, what we seem to have here is a mythical account describing an early era sparked by a mysterious third-party people who, by the time of the writing, had made the jump from history to myth and legend. In the chapter "Ancient Religions," we're going to see the same thing happen over and over again in cultures around the world. But if we dare to ask if there is more than just fiction at work here, we are left with some very interesting questions. Who were these mysterious first people? What sort of technology did they have that allowed them to see the whole world without moving from where they were? We aren't suggesting they had televisions or an ancient equivalent. But were the ancestors anatomically as modern as we are, in touch with parts of their minds that have since atrophied in modern times because of misuse? Did such mysterious people appear to be gods simply because they were psychically advanced in comparison to the early Olmec or Mayan hunter-gatherers? Were these folks responsible for jumpstarting the first great American civilization, as they seem to have done in Egypt and Göbekli Tepe as well? Is it time to start listening to the ancient myths with an open mind?

> Who were these mysterious first people? What sort of technology did they have that allowed them to see the whole world without moving from where they were?

The Olmec Heads

There's more than the written word that points to these ancient gods. We may know what they looked like.

As we pointed out earlier, not everyone is in agreement about the Maya coming before the Olmecs. Many believe the Olmecs came first and were some of the greatest builders of their age. But what is even more fascinating are the magnificent sculpted heads attributed to them that are undoubtedly of ancient origin. What makes them remarkable is that they seem to display African features.

The question of whoever built them is not as important as what they represent. They are ancient, they are African, and they exist. How do African heads show up at an ancient site in Mexico? When we look at these sculptures, are we seeing ancient Olmecs? Are we viewing the folks who first inspired the Olmecs to great construction projects? Or are we gazing into the eyes of a people who came before the Maya and inspired them, if indeed the Maya were the first? If so, were these founding fathers African?

Black and White?

The issue gets more intriguing when you consider the famous figure carved on Stela 3 at La Venta. When the picture of a bearded, obviously white man was discovered in 1946, the likeness was so familiar and striking that the archeologists who uncovered it immediately christened it Uncle Sam.

An example of one of the many carved stone heads left behind by the Olmec.

Do these stone sculptures picture an ancient people who perhaps arrived at their destination in Mexico trying to jumpstart a civilization made in the image of the one that was destroyed in the great cataclysm of the Younger Dryas?

If so, they failed, because thousands of years went by before the Mesoamerican experiment finally took off. By that time these statues would have been old beyond the imagination of the early Maya or Olmecs, whoever came first. But they still would have been inspiring. They must have been strung 'round with the mystery of legend and myth. And perhaps those myths were still being passed down from one generation to the next.

There is a much deeper story here than has so far been told.

SUMERIANS

Mesopotamians generally, and the Sumerians specifically, believed that civilization was the result of the gods' triumph of order over chaos.

Joshua J. Mark in *Ancient History Encyclopedia*

The Cradle of Civilization

The official story of how our civilization got started goes something like this. Somewhere around 4000 B.C.E. people began to group together, reap the benefits of agriculture, develop a modified sedentary lifestyle and then, about 3000 B.C.E., the first official civilizations sprang into existence simultaneously in Egypt and Sumer. Somehow, somewhere in China, it happened again. A few thousand years later the same thing occurred independently in the Americas. Since then we have steadily evolved to the point where we are today. Woe to the official academic who dares venture far from this scenario!

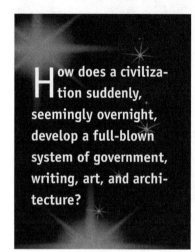

How does a civilization suddenly, seemingly overnight, develop a full-blown system of government, writing, art, and architecture?

What this means is that civilization arose at the rivers. In Egypt it was the Nile. In Sumer it was the land between the Tigris and the Euphrates. This kept the biblical scholars happy. The Garden of Eden was thought to have been nearby, in the land we now call Iran and Iraq. Mount Ararat rose right up north. It all worked.

But in the last few years there have been enough certified archeological discoveries to question this whole story. For one thing, how does a civilization suddenly, seemingly overnight, develop a full-blown system of government, writing, art, and architecture?

Imagine discovering a brand new Ferrari buried somewhere in the sand. Until you discover a Model T Ford and a 1958 Chevy, it's kind of hard to imagine how the Ferrari came to be. But that's precisely the problem with ancient civilizations. When they appear full-blown on the scene, with no windup, no earlier models, it tends to raise questions.

Listen to the words of the late Walter Emery, an Egyptian scholar from the University of London, as related by Graham Hancock in *Magicians of the Gods*:

> At a period approximately 3,400 years before Christ, a great change took place in Egypt, and the country passed from a state of Neolithic culture with a complex tribal character to one of well-organized monarchy ... writing, monumental architecture and arts and crafts develop to an astonishing degree.

Sumer and Egypt seem to share a lot in common in terms of architecture and building techniques. But the professor is puzzled by that as well, because the countries don't seem to be sharing techniques as much as receiving instruction from a third party.

> The impression we get is of an indirect connection, and perhaps the existence of a third party, whose influence spread to both the Euphrates and the Nile.

We've already looked at Egypt. We've hypothesized who the elusive third party might be. Let's examine Sumer.

A Sumer Tutorial

The name Sumer means something like "Land of the Civilized Kings," when you translate it into English. It's an appropriate title because Sumer is considered to be one of the cradles of civilization. Other such cradles include Egypt, Turkey, China, and, later in time, Mesoamerica.

One of the hallmarks of civilization is said to be the invention of writing. Indeed, what we call history is the time that followed the first use of the written word. Anything that happened before that is considered prehistory. Sumerians were probably the first to invent writing. Their ancient texts, preserved in what is known as cuneiform script, contain some of the most famous stories of old. *The Epic of Gilgamesh,* which we examined in the first chapter, is the best-known example. These ancient texts refer to Sumer as the land of the black-headed people. The biblical book of Genesis refers to this land as Shinar.

For a long time the traditional wisdom of academia taught that Sumer was settled about 4500 B.C.E., but that notion, like so much of what was once thought to be wisdom set in stone, is now up for grabs. As is so often the case, the date is currently being pushed way back.

The first inhabits of Sumer are presently thought to be a previously unknown people called Ubaid. Artifacts from this civilization go back to at least 5000 B.C.E. and possibly even earlier. They include some pretty advanced things for a supposedly stone age culture: pottery shards, hoes, knives, bricks, and even finely sculpted figurines. Obviously these were not simple hunter-gatherers who moved from place to place. By 3600 B.C.E. they had invented the wheel, produced the first written language that we know about, mastered sail boats, and developed agriculture aided by advanced irrigation systems. They had even built what some consider to be the first city, although that claim is disputed by folks in India and China. The oldest city in Sumer was probably Uruk, but its capital was Eridu, said to have been the place where the gods first gave humans the gifts necessary to establish the first civilization. This, it is said, was where real civilization first started and marks the location where the journey to the modern world began. It is worthy of note that this was also the location of another Sumerian city, called Ur of the Chaldees in the Bible. It was supposedly home to Abraham, the Jewish patriarch.

The Gods of Sumer

Now things get interesting. Sumer was located in the river valley between the Tigris and the Euphrates. The Sumerians believed their civilization was founded by gods.

Who were these gods and, assuming they didn't come from some Sumerian heaven, where did they come from?

Let's begin with the who.

The principal civilization-bringing god of Sumeria was a being called Uan in Sumerian, often called Oannes in Greek. You'll remember Oannes

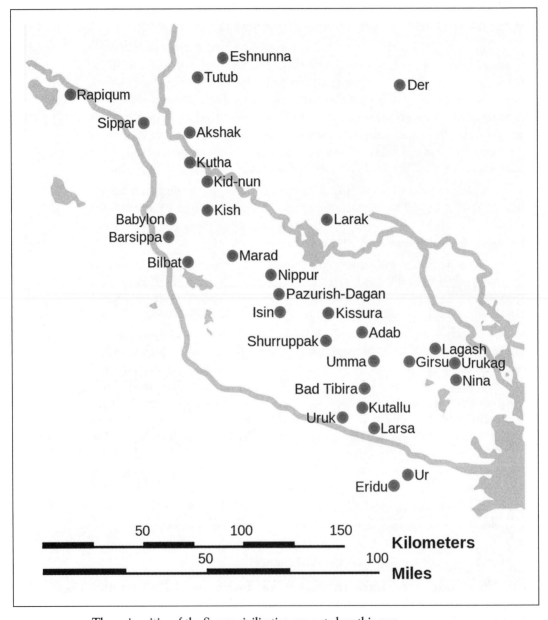

The major cities of the Sumer civilization are noted on this map.

from an earlier chapter when we looked at the *Homo aquaticus* theory. There we learned that:

> [His] whole body was like a fish; and had under a fish's head another head, and also feet below, similar to those of a man, sub-joined to the fish's tail. His voice, too, was articulate and human; and a representation of him is preserved even to this day.... When the sun set, it was the custom of this Being to plunge into the sea, and abide all night in the deep; for he was amphibious.

Ancient Babylonian texts written by a scribe named Berosus say that Oannes:

> ... gave them insight into letters and sciences, and every kind of art. He taught them to construct houses, to found temples, to compile laws, and explained to them the principles of geometrical knowledge. He made them distinguish the seed of the earth, and showed them how to collect fruits; in short he instructed them in everything which could tend to soften manners and to humanize mankind.
>
> *Myths from Mesopotamia*, translated and edited
> by Stephanie Dalley, Oxford University Press, 1990.

This is precisely the kind of myth that experts tend to ignore, but that demands to come out into the open, defying the conspiracy of silence. The Sumerians were brilliant people. They came up with all the hallmarks of what we call civilization—the three r's of readin' 'ritin' and 'rithmetic. So when they say they were given these gifts in the beginning by someone they called by name and described in great detail, maybe we ought to take them at their word.

Where might these gods have come from? Again, if we take the myths seriously, all we have to do is head upriver from Sumer. If we follow the Tigris and Euphrates upstream, we come to Göbekli Tepe, where, as we already saw, the first temple was built. Nearby stands the traditional location of the Garden of Eden, where, according to Genesis, after the biblical agriculturist Cain killed his pastoral-minded brother, Abel, he went out and built a city. Was that city named Uruk, by any chance? Upstream also is home to Mount Ararat, where Noah was supposed to have grounded the ark. It's not far from there to Karahunj, which, as we've already seen, is another candidate for the cradle of civilization.

Putting Flesh on Ancient Bones

If you put all this together it begins to form a perfect picture. The myths, ignored by most archeologists because they are not scientific, meaning

> **T**hey were survivors from a worldwide catastrophe that concluded with the meltdown following the end of the Younger Dryas Ice Age. The dates match perfectly.

they are not something you can dig up, date, and put in a museum, seem to say that a group of gods, who might very well have been remnant members of a civilization advanced enough to appear well beyond the capabilities of a hunter-gatherer society existing between the Tigris and Euphrates rivers, suddenly arrive on the scene, jumpstart the locals, start a civilization that would endure while keeping alive the memories of the founders, and begin a work that continues to this day. In Sumer and Egypt they succeeded. It took a while to catch on in Mesoamerica.

Who were these people? Where did they come from? Why did they offer their services so freely?

We simply don't know. An explanation might be one that we've already considered. They were survivors from a worldwide catastrophe that concluded with the meltdown following the end of the Younger Dryas Ice Age. The dates match perfectly. Göbekli Tepe suddenly sprang up from the ground then, with no record of a practice history in building techniques. Sumer and Egypt soon followed, again seemingly overnight with no previous trial-and-error learning curve.

Is there any archeological record of all this? Well, yes and no.

If you consider straightforward dig-and-discover methods, the answer is up in the air because those methods cannot uncover motive and inspiration.

But if you read the myths and dare to take them seriously, the answer starts to swing toward "Yes."

What we do know is this. If the gods who taught the ancient Sumerians the arts of civilization were really folks from a forgotten past, we owe them the very world we inherited. They were our mothers and fathers. They conceived our civilization and midwifed its birth. We are who we are today because of them.

WATCHERS OF THE *BOOK OF ENOCH*

When Jared had lived 162 years, he became the father of Enoch…. When Enoch had lived 65 years, he became the father of Methuselah. And after he became the father of Methuselah, Enoch walked with God 300 years and had other sons and daughters. Altogether Enoch lived 350 years. Enoch walked with God; then he was no more, for God took him away.

Genesis 5:18–24

This one employs a pretty wide breadth of biblical and mythological knowledge, so hang in there. It's well worth the effort.

The Mysterious Enoch

When we discussed the Anunnaki, back in the first chapter of this book, we briefly talked about a mysterious group of giants called the Nephilim and another enigmatic fellowship called the Watchers. It's now time to cover them in a bit more depth and in a new context.

We need to begin with a Hebrew patriarch called Enoch. All we know about him from the received text of the Bible is the brief verse quoted above. There we learn that he is the son of Jared and the father of Methuselah, the oldest man in the Bible who died during the year of Noah's flood. According to the Bible, Enoch never died. Instead, he was taken before the flood began. Evangelical Christians often see this as a symbol of what they call the Rapture.

That is, just before the flood, Enoch was taken bodily up to Heaven, thereby saving him from the coming judgment.

"As it was in the days of Noah," says Jesus in Matthew 24:37, "so will it be at the coming of the Son of man." Thus, according to Evangelical theology, Enoch was a type or symbol of what will happen at the return of Jesus Christ. Christians will be taken—raptured, to make a verb out of a noun—before the final judgment, just as Enoch was.

If that were the only allusion to Enoch in ancient literature, we would be left with a simple allegory. But the strange biblical verse didn't stay mysterious forever. In 1770 a man by the name of James Bruce of Kinnaird, in England, visited Ethiopia for three years. He returned to Britain with a copy of the *Book of Enoch*, long a mainstay of ancient Hebrew mystical theology, but only through references from other texts. It was thought to have been lost forever. It turns out that in Ethiopia the old book had been translated into Geez, the Ethiopic sacred language. Ethiopia, it must be remembered, is thought by some to have ancient ties with Israel going back to the

Very little is said about the Hebrew patriarch Enoch in the Bible, though his story is related in the *Book of Enoch* that is not included in the Old Testament.

time of King Solomon. Some even believe it to be the present location of the long-lost Ark of the Covenant.

To make a long story short, the *Book of Enoch* was not included in what Christians now call the Old Testament of the Bible, or what Jews call Tanakh—the official canon of the Hebrew scriptures. It wasn't considered worthy. But the original authors of Genesis must have known about it because they did include the short verses about Enoch quoted at the beginning of this entry.

The *Book of Enoch* has since been translated a number of times and it tells a strange and somehow compelling story.

For what follows I am in great debt to Graham Hancock, who meticulously pieced together the threads of the Watchers of Eden that we share with you now.

Ancient Scriptures

In the *Book of Enoch* we learn that Enoch was very probably an ancient shamanic figure. He had dreams. In his dreams he came into contact with spirit figures who presumably exist on other planes of existence. Or at least he said he did. But he was also a Hebrew patriarch who no doubt embodied some of the very same cultural prejudices of his descendants.

That's right, I'm talking about sex. The writers of the Old Testament didn't like sex very much. It was a practice very strongly regulated in the book of Leviticus and other books of the law and led many otherwise exemplary leaders to their downfall, King David among them, according to the book of Samuel.

One night Enoch had what sounds a lot like a shamanic dream. In it he was given advanced warning of the coming deluge that was going to destroy the earth. The reason for the coming flood is a familiar one to anyone who has ever read any other inundation epics:

> When human beings began to increase in number on the earth and daughters were born to them, the sons of God saw that the daughters of humans were beautiful, and they married any of them they chose. Then the Lord said, "My Spirit will not contend with humans forever, for they are mortal; their days will be a hundred and twenty years."

> The Nephilim were on the earth in those days—and also afterward—when the sons of God went to the daughters of humans and had children by them. They were the heroes of old, men of renown.

> The Lord saw how great the wickedness of the human race had become on the earth, and that every inclination of the thoughts

of the human heart was only evil all the time. The Lord regretted that he had made human beings on the earth, and his heart was deeply troubled. So the Lord said, "I will wipe from the face of the earth the human race I have created—and with them the animals, the birds and the creatures that move along the ground—for I regret that I have made them." But Noah found favor in the eyes of the Lord.

Genesis 6:1–9

So much is fairly well known. But there's a lot more. In the Quran, the name for Enoch is Idris. Islamic tradition also links Idris/Enoch with Hermes, the god of the Greek pantheon. According to the Persian philosopher Abu Ma'shar:

The name Hermes is a title. Its first bearer, who lived before the Flood, was he whom the Hebrews call Enoch, whose name in Arabic is Idris....

This Enoch/Idris/Hermes was apparently quite an astronomer:

He wrote many books, whose wisdom he preserved on the walls of Egyptian temples lest it be lost. It was he who constructed the pyramids.

Tamara Green in *The City of the Moon God*

Whoa! We've suddenly gone from Mesopotamia over to the pyramids. What's going on here?

Here is where things get complicated.

The Egyptian Connection

In the Temple of Horus at Edfu, on the west bank of the Nile, there exists to this day a series of inscriptions called the Edfu Building Texts. Although they are, for the most part, weathered away, they tell of a very remote time in the past called the Early Primeval Age of the Gods, or Zep Tepi. The gods, it appears, were not Egyptian. Instead, they came from somewhere called the Homeland of the Primeval Ones, which was a sacred island in the midst of the ocean. A long time prior, the island was destroyed in a great cataclysm in which the earliest mansions of the gods had once stood.

Some of them survived and, according to the Edfu texts, set forth in their great ships to wander the world in order to bring about the resurrection of the former world of the gods. Their mission, in other words, was to recreate their destroyed world.

Now, what does this have to do with Enoch?

One of the more well-preserved parts of the Edfu temple with legible writing. Deciphering the writing reveals stories of an Age of Gods.

Enoch, it turns out, was also said to be the inventor of writing. Besides that, he is said to have been afraid the secrets of the art of building were going to be destroyed in the great flood that was to come, so he wrote them down on a stone that he then buried in the bowels of the earth. For this reason, he figures prominently in Freemason tradition of ancient builders.

Those who carved the Edfu texts did not invent them. They specifically say they copied them. In other words, we are talking about a tradition that was passed down.

This raises a question. Was Enoch a carrier of the building tradition that was known in both Egypt and Mesopotamia, as well as other places around the world? Does his identification with Hermes tie the various locations together and reveal that they were all recipients of an ancient tradition? We saw when we studied Göbekli Tepe that as soon as this most ancient temple in the world was built, right after the global catastrophe of the flooding in the wake of the Younger Dryas and almost within sight of the traditional landing place of Noah's Ark, it was deliberately buried, recalling the stone that he (Enoch) then buried in the bowels of the earth. Was this the work of Enoch/Idris/ Hermes? Does Göbekli Tepe contain the secrets of the art of building tradition that was copied and retained in the Edfu texts?

The Watchers

Now we come to the most interesting part. It seems as though Enoch is most concerned about two things. First, that there is a great flood coming that is going to destroy a wisdom tradition that is thought to be the civilizing factor of humankind—that is, the secrets of building. But second, it seems that this flood is coming because of what Enoch considers to be sin.

The Bible says that:

The Lord saw how great the wickedness of the human race had become on the earth, and that every inclination of the thoughts of the human heart was only evil all the time. The Lord regretted that he had made human beings on the earth, and his heart was deeply troubled. So the Lord said, "I will wipe from the face of the earth the human race I have created."

But what had caused this wickedness? According to the *Book of Enoch*, the culprits were a group of bad angels called Watchers. Their mission, it seems, was to watch humans. He even provided their names—Azazel, Semjaza, Armen, Rumjal, Turel, Armaros, Danjal, and Kokabel.

In the Bible, according to Hancock's theory, they are called the sons of God. The problem is that these "sons of God saw that the daughters of men were beautiful, and they married them."

Now enters the part about sex that drives Enoch over the edge. Hancock believes that these Watchers were really human beings of an advanced civilization, possibly even in the Atlantis tradition, who had been sent out to observe, and only observe, the Stone Age peoples of the Middle East. But, like missionaries sometimes do, they had gone native and begun to marry the locals. Such a practice got under the skin of Enoch, who was a Jewish patriarch with typical Jewish Old Testament sensibilities. In Abraham's time, Jews were forbidden to mix with non-Jews. That might have been because four thousand years earlier the Watchers had set a bad example by mixing with the indigenous population.

> Hancock believes that these Watchers were really human beings of an advanced civilization, possibly even in the Atlantis tradition....

The offspring of these unions were pretty impressive specimens. They were called the Nephilim, and their offspring were even more famous. They were called "the heroes of old, the men of renown," in Genesis 6:4.

The term is used in only one other place in the Bible. In Numbers, when the Israelites were camped on the banks of the Jordan, ready to enter the Promised Land, they sent twelve spies into Israel to check out the situation. After the requisite forty days and forty nights, they came back, in true committee fashion, with a majority report and a minority report. The minority report was delivered by a man named Caleb and the future hero, Joshua. "Let's go," they said. "We can take 'em!"

But the majority report carried the day and sentenced the Israelites to forty years wandering in the desert.

What was their message? "There are giants in the land! Next to them, we look like grasshoppers!"

And what word did they use that is translated, in our Bibles, as giants? You guessed it. Nephilim. You can read it for yourself in Numbers 13.

There's one more thing to note in passing. Five hundred years later, when Israel needed a king, they got David. He rose to power after using his

The story of David versus Goliath is a well-known biblical tale, but could Goliath's stature have been real? Was he one of the Nephilim?

slingshot to slay a giant named Goliath. Kind of makes you wonder, doesn't it? To top it all off, in I Chronicles 20 we discover that Goliath even had four brothers! Whoever those Nephilim were, they were sure hard to dispose of!

Now, if the results of these marriages were so impressive (after all, they were called "the heroes of old, the men of renown"), why was it a bad thing? Simple. The world fell apart because of it. The Younger Dryas ended with a bang and a flood. The results were horrendous. The biblical writers called it Noah's flood and all the people in the world, or at least the world that was known to them, perished in the deluge. Enoch saw that as God's coming judgment on the whole situation.

Who is to say he was wrong?

The Good Guys

While all this was going on, according to the *Book of Enoch*, the Watchers were being watched. There was another group of angels with names like Uriel, Raphael, Michael, and Gabriel. Perhaps these were sent out from the homeland to reign in the ones who had got out of hand. Who knows? Enoch doesn't say. But there must have been quite a stir back at headquarters.

Whatever happened, there is no denying it had impressive results. Right after the deluge, Göbekli Tepe was built. People discovered the arts of agriculture. Somebody organized them into what we now call the Neolithic Revolution which marked the beginning of our civilization. This led to writing and all sorts of civilized stuff. The world has never been the same.

In Hancock's *Magicians of the Gods*, he envisions these Watchers as members of an advanced civilization which, after the drastic floods of the Younger Dryas Ice Age event destroyed their homeland, set out to rebuild. The Egyptian Edfu texts tell the story. They settled in places with which they were already familiar with because of the cultural missionary work of their previous encounters. They went to Egypt, to Turkey and Göbekli Tepe, to Lebanon at Baalbek, and eventually to Central and South America.

Because Göbekli Tepe is so central to the flood story, located as it is within shouting distance of the birthplace of Judaism, Abraham's hometown of Ur of the Chaldees, and because it sits on the outskirts of the traditional location of the Garden of Eden, it makes us wonder, when we read the old, familiar stories of the Bible, whether Enoch, the Jewish patriarch, encountered real men after all, not gods, and that the myths have some flesh on them. The tales of that encounter grew, no doubt, with the telling and retelling after thousands of years. But when we read them with this insight, at the very least it breathes life into them.

Cultural missionaries who sound like a kind of Peace Corps, development programs to assist urban planning, interracial sex, revolutions, agriculture, and even a little magic. All in all, it makes the past sound suspiciously like the present, doesn't it?

Lost Histories

By invoking civilization at such a tragic and dangerous time [9/11/2001], our political leaders tapped into a latent but powerful belief and showed how central it is to our sense of ourselves. Our civilization is a reflection of who we are and what we value, but we are not used to thinking about what civilization really means to us. Now that the idea of civilization has been hauled out into the light, it must inevitably be subjected to closer examination: if the war *against* terror is a war *for* civilization, then we need a strong sense of what civilization is.

Roger Osborne in *Civilization: A New History of the Western World*

Civilizations don't need to exhibit electrical, nuclear, or fossil fuel-generated power to demonstrate an advanced state. Indeed, most of these technologies are pretty new on the scene anyway. Wires don't necessarily mean technology. What a civilization needs to demonstrate success is a culture that is passed down from one generation to the next. Culture consists of ideas, traditions, and, hopefully, wisdom. These are things that often escape the archeologist's shovel.

We have now considered a few civilizations of the past that shed light on what a culture is, how it comes to be, and what happens after it has burned its flame brightly on history's stage for a while before succumbing to the vicissitudes of human frailty.

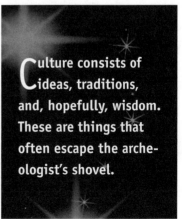

Culture consists of ideas, traditions, and, hopefully, wisdom. These are things that often escape the archeologist's shovel.

Think about what these civilizations, and many, many more that we could have considered, have to teach us. First, look at a few hard and fast facts:

- Fact: With the possible exception of the entry about the Watchers of the *Book of Enoch*, every one of the civilizations we have just studied were historical in the sense that they left behind unequivocal archeological evidence of their existence. And even the Watchers (if you use the term to refer to the architects of Göbekli Tepe, the Ubaid of Sumer, and the primeval gods of Egypt's First Time) have left behind historical evidence.

- Fact: In almost every case these civilizations seem to have arisen full-blown, as it were. One day there was nothing on the scene but a small group of hunter-gatherers making a subsistence living. The next day there appeared to be a fully organized society exhibiting all the trappings of civilization. This is illustrated especially in the cases of Egypt, Sumer, Göbekli Tepe, the Mesoamerican cultures of the Olmecs and the Maya, and the Mound Builders of the Mississippi region.

- Fact: In almost every case there exists a complex mythology remembering the roots of the society as being the product of gods who taught the people the arts of civilization.

- Fact: Religion played a great part in the founding, the day-to-day sustenance, and, eventually, the demise of each civilization.

- Fact: Every civilization had an inordinate interest in astronomy and demonstrated it in the structures they left behind.

- Fact: From the Anasazi to the Mound Builders and all the way to Egypt, Sumer, Japan, and Mesoamerica, every civilization built tremendous architectural wonders that utilized artful stone work, sometimes transporting and erecting megaton boulders in ways we still don't understand.

- Fact: Every civilization collapsed amid conflicting reports that somehow they had done something wrong or offended the gods in some way. They believed they had squandered their opportunity for abundant life and were paying the price for their shortcomings.

Revisiting the Radical Concept

In the Introduction to this book we began with what we called a radical concept:

This book proposes a rather radical concept for us to consider. We, the current ruling species on the planet, have indeed suffered a catastrophic accident. Maybe several. We are not the first civilization to come down the pike. We have developed cultural amnesia. What we call the beginning is really a new beginning, built on the ruins of what came before.

Could it be that our civilization is not the first? Could it be that other "worlds," just as in the Hopi myth that forms the Prologue of this book, have come before us? Could the Hopi-inspired legend about the destruction of former "worlds" by fire, ice and water be more than a tale told around an evening campfire? Could the myth be a poetic description of events that really took place? Were there people alive who were eyewitnesses? Did they survive to become the heroes of old, the "Ancient Gods" of renown? Did they pass on wisdom from a former time, thus shaping the future of the human race?

We have now looked at a few lost civilizations that have come and gone since the cataclysm that ended the Younger Dryas Ice Age. We have named some of the actors who have played their part in the great drama we call history. In the immortal words of William Shakespeare in *Macbeth*:

> Life's but a walking shadow, a poor player
> That struts and frets his hour upon the stage
> And then is heard no more.

For the most part, these civilizations from our past are Shakespeare's "poor player … heard no more." Even Egypt, still an active player on the stage, is a shadow of her former self. If this were a simple history lesson, the story would end right here.

But this is not just a history lesson. If these civilizations carried the legacy of their founders, remembered in myth and legend as ancient gods who were there when history changed forever, if their mysterious existence is now shrouded in lost histories, they were once physical expressions of a wise elite who survived a cataclysm and lived to tell the tale. In this regard they can teach us hidden truths. We need to listen to their stories. We cannot let them be shrouded in a conspiracy of silence.

Why? Because encoded into what they left behind is a message from long ago. It is meant for us. Nothing lasts forever. These past civilizations are themselves a written word, a sacred text, that bears a simple message:

> It has happened before.
> It will happen again.
> Nothing lasts forever.

We need to be ready. We need to prepare. We need to heed and learn from their errors lest we bring upon ourselves their fate and force humankind to begin all over again.

In the first part of this book we received a message in a bottle, written by lost civilizations of our past. It has drifted for centuries in the ocean of history.

Now that we've opened the bottle and named some of the players in the drama, in the next part, we will search out the clues needed to fully interpret the message. It may prove to be surprising. It may even show the way to salvation for a species who live in a dangerous, turbulent cosmos, but who, for better or for worse, seem to possess infinite promise.

SEARCHING
FOR CLUES

INTRODUCTION

How often have I said to you that when you have eliminated the impossible, whatever remains, however improbable, must be the truth?

Sherlock Holmes

Having searched for our ancient ancestors, having discovered their unifying passion for the night skies, a trait common to ancient astronomers across all cultures and eras, having pondered the possible ancient catastrophes that may have brought a few ancient civilizations to a close while ushering in our own, it is time to search for clues they may have left behind—mysteries that survive into the present day to tantalize our imaginations. They have much to teach us.

There exist too many ancient mysteries, too many ancient mythologies that reveal ancient religions, and hints of too many ancient technologies to ignore. Although we are culturally programmed to think we were the first, although we are rationally wired to the point at which we automatically reject anything outside of our own experience, Sherlock Holmes' wisdom quoted above applies in this case. The old mysteries, mythologies, religions, and technological necessities left their traces. They were real. The evidence is plain before us.

We don't know how the Old Ones performed their magic, but the results are right there for all to see, often in plain sight. The Nazca Lines, the statues of Easter Island, legends of gods and angels, the flood stories, mysterious temples, the practice of out-of-body travel that makes possible an expanded consciousness—all these subjects and many more, as we shall soon see, point to a past that is quite different from the safe and secure story we have been force-fed in the textbooks. It's time to raise the conspiracy of silence that for too long has been draped over that story. The lost histories and hidden truths we may discover can certainly change our perception. They may even reveal the nature of the universal search for ancient gods.

What we are doing is looking for truth. We are asking age-old questions: "Who am I?" "What is the meaning of life?" "Is there life after death?" That kind of thing. The only answer we are suggesting is this: Our ancestors felt and experienced something that is at the very root of our existence. They left clues along the path of their search. Some of them are tiny—information hidden away in myths and legends. Others are huge, standing in plain sight in the form of megalithic structures. Many are disguised in the landscape of a forgotten past. A few are found only within tantalizing hints buried in the dust of history. But the Old Ones seem to have, in many ways, experienced the very stuff of a universe from which we have, in many ways, cut ourselves off. They felt the vibrations of other planes of existence. With sacred eyes they pierced the veil of the Higgs Field long before we understood anything about particle accelerators.

They often made a religion out of it. They imagined unseen deities and spirit beings. They invented divine entities and named them. That doesn't mean we have to do the same. This is not a call to bring back any old-time religion. But it does give us plenty of food for thought.

> They left clues along the path of their search. Some of them are tiny—information hidden away in myths and legends. Others are huge, standing in plain sight in the form of megalithic structures.

In our day we have, in many ways, limited our search for life's meaning to the material world. That began when church and science came to an agreement centuries ago. One would study meaning, the other material existence. A line of demarcation was drawn in the sands of time, and neither was allowed over that line into the playground of the other. That was a shame.

But thanks to the work of many astute and courageous physicists, most notably one Albert Einstein, who with one elegant equation pushed the whole field of hidden reality into the popular consciousness, the old magic has come roaring to life out of mathematical equations and particle physics labs around the world. It hasn't been easy, but the public consciousness has been tweaked. The ideas of theoretical physicists are bubbling up to the surface of both scientific and popular thought and the universe has begun to be reborn out of the murky depths of nothingness.

As we shall soon discover, however, many of the findings of contemporary physics were foreshadowed by ancient scribes, priests, rishis, and shamanic practitioners. We are arriving at our modern conclusions through the primary use of the left hemisphere of our brain, the analytical side. They arrived at some of the same insights while employing the right hemisphere, the intuitive side.

How we arrive at our conclusions is not important. What matters is the final destination. It's time to unite our brains—right and left hemispheres, old and new wisdom.

What follows in this part of this book is a survey of the many mysteries, mythologies, religions, and possible technologies that point to a rich and deeply experienced human history far different from the one we have been taught. Our ancestors were not all brutish and dull folk. In important matters, such as self-satisfaction and contentment, they might even have a lot to teach us rootless and restless moderns. They may be able to reveal the hidden wisdom of spirituality to a material world.

The Horns of a Dilemma

Many of the topics soon to be raised will no doubt be hard for modern folks to absorb. It takes a great deal of effort and open-mindedness to throw off the shackles of modern cultural conditioning. We risk being impaled on two horns of a dilemma:

- On the one hand, we have to constantly check to make sure we don't reject something out of hand just because it is outside our personal experience. "I won't believe it until I see it with my own eyes!" is a common but telling affirmation. It is the protecting fence that skeptics build around their safe little world. It ensures that anything allowed within that fence is limited to the experience of the one making the affirmation. It's a safe way to live, but sad, for how could one person possibly experience enough in one lifetime to embrace every possibility in the universe?

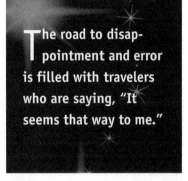

The road to disappointment and error is filled with travelers who are saying, "It seems that way to me."

- On the other hand, it's easy to give in to what many are now calling the "woo-woo" factor of modern metaphysical thought. Just because something is outside our experience, even if it comes from the Internet, doesn't mean it's true. Human imagination has led many a gullible practitioner down the proverbial primrose path. The road to disappointment and error is filled with travelers who are saying, "It seems that way to me."

How do we remain upright against the pull of these two strong but equally compelling forces?

I'm not sure. Let's just consider the information, file it away, and decide for ourselves.

A Word of Warning

We have to issue a word of warning here. You are no doubt familiar with the old story of Eve and the apple. God, it is said, placed our first parents in a garden that offered all the ease and contentment life had to offer. It was a safe and secure place to live. Eve and Adam were in good hands as long as they avoided the fruit of two trees. One of those was the tree of knowledge. But with so many good things to choose from, so what? Life was good. Why rock the boat by learning new things?

Then the famous serpent of Eden showed up. "God knows that if you eat the fruit of the tree [of knowledge], you will be as gods," he said.

We all know what happened next. Eve ate the apple.

In our time the tree of knowledge is shrouded over by a conspiracy of silence. With so much to do and so many things to keep us busy, why bother to go to the effort and take the time to pursue hidden truths from a lost history?

There are those who want to live their lives safe and secure in the garden of willful ignorance. It's comforting to simply take refuge in Facebook and the other forms of social media, to enjoy the fruits of an easy-to-use technology and close our eyes to the power of books that may contain information that is permanent, rather than expedient.

Wisdom cannot usually be formulated in a limited number of characters that fit into a specified box. Sometimes it takes more than a bumper sticker.

Maybe it's time to take a bite of the apple and see what happens.

ANCIENT MYSTERIES

It has often been said that in order to see the sunrise, we first have to experience a sunset. That may be true. But it is also true that if we are going to fully experience the sunrise, we first have to turn around and face in a new direction.

Jim Willis

By no means are all our mysteries solved, the wonders all discovered; tomorrow's headline can announce a newly discovered Maya tomb or a previously unknown Andean culture. Nor are all scholars and scientists agreed on the record of the past, for it is a field rife with conflicting evidence and passionate controversy.

Robert Dolezai, *Mysteries of the Ancient Americas*

The Lure of the Unknown

Almost everyone loves a good mystery story. The fun of engaging with one is found in gradually discovering the clues as they unfold. No one clue is sufficient. It takes a string of them to point us in the right direction. It's the step-by-step accumulation that eventually unlocks the key to the final answer.

We've laid out a real mystery so far in the first four chapters of this book. We've presented the picture of a victim of amnesia, struggling in the darkness to discover a forgotten identity. To quote the immortal Pogo from the old comic strip, "We have met the enemy, and he is us!"

Who are we? Were there civilizations, the survivors of which have been turned into ancient gods of myth and legend, who can provide us with a sense of our lost identity? Can they describe our lost histories and enlighten us with their hidden wisdom?

In any good mystery story, after setting up the plot and confronting us with the parameters of the mystery, the author begins to slowly reveal, step by step, the clues needed to solve the puzzle. That's what we are now going to do. We're going to look for clues. In this chapter we'll survey a number of them, snooping around in three areas.

The Mystery in the Written Word

The first area we're going to peruse is that of the written word. Stories, legends, and curious documents have been discovered that give us our first hints. We will look at clues found in ancient maps, scriptures, and stone carvings.

Since these are the kinds of clues most overlooked by archeologists, concerned as they are with evidence they can dig up and hold in their hands, we need to spend a little time explaining just what we mean. This is more important than you might first think.

Words reveal thoughts. The primary tool of the psychologist is to decipher words in order to discover what a patient is really thinking and feeling. Consider the following example. It's typical of many conversations that are common to the profession of psychology.

A patient walks into a talk therapy session for the first time. She is nervous. Does she really want to be here? Is she ready to reveal her innermost thoughts to a total stranger?

Doctor: "Good morning. My name is Dr. Wilson. Welcome to your first session."

Patient: "Good morning Dr. Wilson. I'm sad to meet you."

Doctor: "What?"

Patient: "I said I'm glad to meet you."

Doctor: "No, you didn't. You said you were *sad* to meet me."

Patient: "Oh, I'm sorry. It must have been a slip of the tongue."

What the doctor discovered is commonly called a Freudian slip. It's a word spoken supposedly by mistake but that actually reveals something hidden away in a person's subconscious. It happens a lot and has served as a source for both humor and insight ever since Sigmund Freud first brought the subject to light as a part of his therapeutic techniques.

Although we don't intend to imply that history is full of Freudian slips, we do hope to suggest that stories, myths, and legends reveal more than we might see at first glimpse. They are important artifacts.

Look at the clues embedded in the founding stories of the three great monotheistic religions, for example:

- Moses journeys to the wilderness where he hears the voice of God coming out of a burning bush. He is told to remove his sandals because he's standing on holy ground. The voice instructs him to take a message of hope and freedom to his people. It also reveals the name of God—I AM.

If this story wasn't found in what is considered to be a holy book of scripture, it would sound like a very typical shamanic journey. All the elements are there—a wilderness journey, a holy place, a fire, perhaps a suggestion of burning a wild-growing herbal hallucinogenic, a voice from an unseen dimension, a command to service, the identity of a supernatural being. This is a good description of a rather typical initiatory shamanic experience. But

The biblical story of Moses hearing the voice of God emanating from a burning bush sounds very reminiscent of a shamanic experience.

because it comes to us encrusted with 3,500 years of tradition, we rarely pause to consider that it might be a clue to something much more ancient. We just receive it as holy writ.

- Jesus, before embarking on his life's work of teaching, healing, and preaching, undergoes an experience in the wilderness designed to bring about a vision. For forty days he fasts and prays, engaging in a spiritual battle with a force of evil that threatens to derail his ministry. He is triumphant and returns from his ordeal with a new vision for his tribe, the Jews. Only later is his mission translated into a universal message.

This follows all the steps of a typical vision quest that was carried out by many American Indian tribes of the southwest. A young man needed to purify himself and commune with his god. He needed to receive a vision that would then accompany him throughout his life. It would give him meaning and a greater purpose. If successful, he was deemed worthy to begin his work. The story of Jesus in the wilderness would seem very familiar to a young American Indian boy.

- Muhammad sought an experience of God. He went alone out into a desert mountain cave where he prayed and prayed until finally Allah spoke to him. There in the cave he was given a message to deliver to all of humankind. Although Muhammad himself couldn't read or write, the message came in the form of a book of instructions which eventually found its way into print. Today we call it the Quran.

This experience was typical of the shamanic mystery caves found all the way from Indonesia to western Europe and across the Americas. Any shaman from 35,000 years ago would have recognized the story and identified with it.

These are examples of clues embedded in the stories of three religions. They were established over a period of two thousand years but exhibit an underlying similarity common to an ancient spiritual practice called shamanism that goes back at least 35,000 years. Together they point to an ancient mystery that might reveal lost histories and hidden truths behind religious practices that are common to more than a third of the modern world's population.

The Mystery in the Landscape

There is another place to search for clues and that is in the very landscape that surrounds us. The mystery lies right beneath our feet and we often don't recognize it. As we shall soon see, from invisible Ley Lines (see page 222) to very visible Nazca Lines, we are often unaware that we live on what amounts to holy ground. There is nowhere we can go on Earth that doesn't echo to the footsteps of those who have come before us.

Perhaps this was stated best in words attributed to Chief Seattle:

And when the last red man shall have perished from the earth and his memory among white men shall have become a myth, these shores shall swarm with the invisible dead of my tribe, and when your children's children shall think themselves alone in the field, the store, the shop, upon the highway or in the silence of the woods they will not be alone. In all the earth there is no place dedicated to solitude. At night, when the streets of your cities and villages shall be silent and you think them deserted, they will throng with the returning hosts that once filled and still love this beautiful land. The white man will never be alone. Let him be just and deal kindly with my people, for the dead are not altogether powerless.

If there is magic in the existence and residual spiritual experience of ancient ancestors, we live in a land of magic. All of us.

The Mystery in the Structures

The final place we will look for ancient mysteries has been hiding in plain sight for as long as anyone can remember. In great, enigmatic structures

The remains of the city of Izapa in Mexico may date back to 1500 B.C.E. The ruins are just one of many clues left behind by ancient people for us to decipher.

of places such as Izapa and Machu Picchu, in the less spectacular but just as mysterious rock piles that dot the fields and woods of the American southeast, there is ample mystery for all to see. Who built them and why? How did they do it? Is there a message in the structures themselves? If so, how do we read it?

The ancient mystery is now before us. Let's go searching for clues.

Ancient Maps

One of the most remarkable and mysterious technical advances in the history of the world is written on the hide of a 13th-century calf. Inked into the vellum is a chart of the Mediterranean so accurate that ships today could navigate with it. Most earlier maps that included the region were not intended for navigation and were so imprecise that they are virtually unrecognizable to the modern eye. With this map, it's as if some medieval mapmaker flew to the heavens and sketched what he saw—though in reality, he could never have traveled higher than a church tower.

"The Mystery of Extraordinarily Accurate Medieval Maps:" http://discovermagazine.com/2014/june/14-the-mapmakers-mystery

Renaissance Man

In 1971 I moved to a small town in central Massachusetts and stayed in that area for the next twenty-five years. It was there that I first heard about a professor who had taught at Keene State College for ten years during the '50s and '60s. If there is one man from his generation who best personifies the basic premise of this book, it is Charles Hapgood. He had a master's degree from Harvard, had served on what would eventually become the U.S. Central Intelligence Agency, and had once been a liaison officer between the White House and the Secretary of War. He was a brilliant man who lectured on topics as varied as American history, the history of science, anthropology, and economics. He had written a book about crustal displacement that featured a forward written by no less a luminary than Albert Einstein. Although I never met him personally before his tragic death after being hit by a car in the nearby town of Greenfield, Massachusetts, in 1982, it was hard to live in central Massachusetts, have an active interest in almost any academic or esoteric subject, and not be drawn to Hapgood's work.

Why don't we know more about him? Well, he had what academics might call a fatal flaw. He possessed an open, inquiring mind that led him afoul of the mainstream America of his day. It's probably no wonder that his

Wikipedia biography states that even though the great Einstein himself found him compelling, his ideas "were never accepted as valid competing scientific hypotheses, yet his ideas have found popularity *in alternative circles* (emphasis mine)." That's just another way of saying he was banished to the fringe and enveloped by the conspiracy of silence.

It probably didn't help his collegial relationships when he established a friendship with and professional interest in the work of Elwood Babbitt, who was often called the Medium of Massachusetts. Elwood was a psychic and medium who was New Age before the name had even been invented. This was, you'll remember, the heyday of what is now called, for better or for worse, American Values. If you followed either Billy Graham or Bishop Fulton Sheen (and back then it seemed as if almost everybody swore by one or the other of them), you were told that when Babbitt channeled spiritual entities he was, according to the narrow mindset of that day, doing the work of the Devil. Hapgood put Babbitt on the map by writing three books: *Voices of Spirit, The God Within: a Testament of Vishnu, a Handbook for the Spiritual Renaissance*, and *Talks with Christ*. Each of them was inspired by Babbitt's contact with a spiritual dimension that wouldn't raise an eyebrow today, but was pretty scandalous back then.

That in itself was probably enough to make Hapgood into an academic pariah, but he didn't stop there. During his tenure at Springfield College, one of his students asked a question concerning the lost continent of Mu (a subject we covered in an earlier entry). Most professors would have probably employed a little sarcasm and closed the subject while perhaps humiliating the student enough to forestall any other such fringe discussion in the classroom.

Not Charles Hapgood! He welcomed such inquires and used the question as a springboard to talk about Atlantis theory. The class came alive and launched into a serious attempt to search out possibilities of such an occurrence as a historical catastrophe that occurred within the span of human life on the planet. By 1958 Hapgood had amassed a book's worth of material and published *Earth's Shifting Crust: A Key to Some Basic Problems of Earth Science*, the work that caught the attention of Albert Einstein and prompted him to write the foreword. The book is still in print and available, although original editions have been known to sell for more than $1,000. In it Hapgood questioned the theory of continental drift and instead proposed that the entire skin of the earth's surface has at times shifted "just as the peel of an orange might shift around the orange itself."

This leads to the topic of ancient maps. One of the proofs he put forth concerned his intense study of ancient cartography. I've often thought that (if you'll excuse the pun) Charles Hapgood put ancient cartography on the map.

His work is summed up in his book published in 1966, *Maps of the Ancient Sea Kings: Evidence of Advanced Civilization in the Ice Age*, which he

In *Voices of Spirit: Through the Psychic Experience of Elwood Babbitt,* Hapgood claimed he had help from Albert Einstein from beyond the grave.

followed with *Path of the Pole*. That book has been through three printings and was last brought out by Adventures Unlimited Press in 1999. Clearly it sparked a lot of interest. And for good reason. In *Voices of Spirit: Through the Psychic Experience of Elwood Babbitt*, Hapgood claimed he had help from Albert Einstein from beyond the grave. On page 106 he recalls the first time he visited Elwood Babbitt at Babbitt's house. Elwood asked him to write down on a piece of paper the name of someone he knew who had passed into spirit and then fold up the paper so no one could see it. Hapgood wrote down the name Albert Einstein. Listen to his words:

> In later discussions we discussed the theories of my book 'Earth's Shifting Crust,' and he [Einstein, from the grave] suggested that one of them was wrong; as a result of this I revised my book, which subsequently was republished as 'the Path of the Pole'. My own further research confirmed the truth of his observation, which involved technicalities of geophysics.

The crux of Hapgood's argument is based on a series of maps he examined that, at the very least, raise some interesting questions. Let's consider a few of them.

The Piri Reis Map of 1513

Piri Reis was a Turkish admiral who, because of his rank, had access to the Imperial Library at Constantinople, one of the great centers of learning at that time. There he compiled what is recognized as one of the oldest maps now known to exist. He drew it on a gazelle skin in the year 1513 and wrote a series of notes in the margins in which he confessed that the map was a copy of a much older document, now lost. His map was filed away and not seen again until its discovery in 1929. It shows the western coast of Africa, the eastern coast of South America and—here comes the problem—the northern coastline of Antarctica.

Why is that a problem? First of all, Antarctica wasn't discovered until three hundred years after Reis drew his map. And that's the easy part. What's even more troubling is that, as far as geologists know, Antarctica has been covered by glaciers and the area around Queen Maud Land, shown in striking detail in Reis's map, could not possibly have been ice-free for at least six thousand years. How on earth could anyone then alive have charted a coast that is buried by a glacier, especially one that wasn't "discovered" until three hundred years after it was mapped? As for the rest of the continent, official science says that the area illustrated by the map has been covered with the polar ice cap for

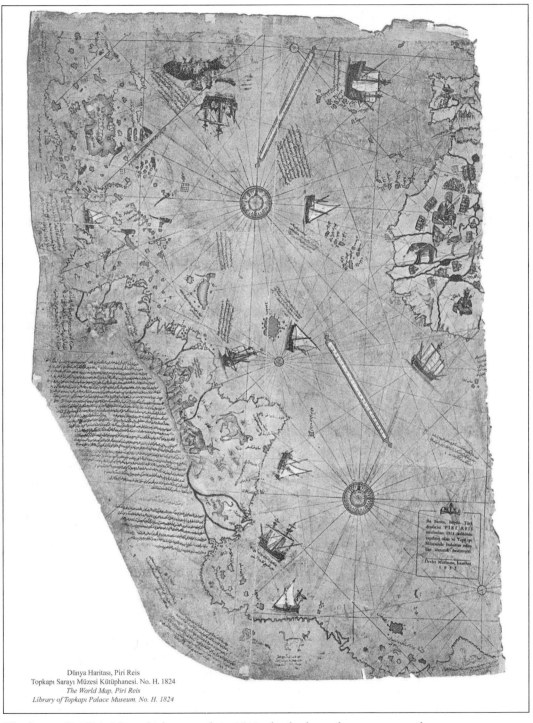

Dünya Haritası, Piri Reis
Topkapı Sarayı Müzesi Kütüphanesi. No. H. 1824
The World Map, Piri Reis
Library of Topkapı Palace Museum. No. H. 1824

The famous Piri Reis Map, which was made in 1513, clearly shows the eastern coastal
region of South America.

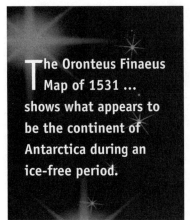

at least a few million years. But the Piri Reis Map shows topography in vivid detail which, in our era of high-tech instruments that can map a land surface even beneath a glacier, has now been mapped and shown to be exactly as Reis said it was.

If the first civilization arose in the Middle East some five thousand years ago, and the continent of Antarctica has been buried by an ice sheet for at least the last four thousand years, and probably much more, who could have possibly drawn the map that Reis copied in Constantinople in the year 1513?

Hapgood's solution was that Antarctica was mapped by an Ice Age civilization, now lost to history, when it stood some two thousand miles north of where it is now. Thus it was ice free. Then an earth-crust shift occurred, sending it very suddenly south into frigid latitudes where it developed the ice covering it to this day.

What might the continent have been called by its inhabitants, who one day thousands of years ago saw the destruction of its Atlantic-based homeland? We'll never know what they called it, of course, but Hapgood called it Atlantis.

The Oronce Finé (or Oronteus Finaeus) Map of 1531

What is today commonly called the Oronteus Finaeus Map of 1531 was another of Hapgood's proofs of an Ice Age civilization. It again shows what appears to be the continent of Antarctica during an ice-free period. In 1961, Hapgood sent the map to the U.S. Air Force cartography unit stationed at Westover Air Force Base. During off hours they looked it over and were baffled. They admitted that the map was accurate, but couldn't come up with any reason how it could be. In their words:

> The coastline had been mapped before it was covered by the ice-cap. The ice-cap in this region is now about a mile thick. We have no idea how the data on this map can be reconciled with the supposed state of geographical knowledge in 1531.

In short, they came to the conclusion that the map had been copied from an original source document, now lost. That document could only have been drawn up when Antarctica was ice free. How it could have been possibly created was a mystery. Hapgood's theory, put forth in his books, was that an advanced civilization, existing during or even prior to the last Ice Age but now lost to history, drew the original maps. It is so far the only theory offered. And no one seems to want to talk much about it.

The Ottoman Mappamondi Haci Ahmet: 1559

Another of Hapgood's ancient maps that deserves mention is the so-called Map of the World by Haci Ahmet (or Hadji Ahmed) of 1559. What makes this world map so unique is that it clearly shows a land bridge existing between Siberia and Alaska. This was the land bridge we now call Beringia and is considered to be a route by which early Americans entered the country. But no one knew about this area until relatively recently. How ancient must the source material that was used by Hadji Ahmed have been? And, since the map was printed in Venice, how did an old Turkish map wind up in a principal city of a European seafaring nation?

It was no doubt a political statement as well as a piece of cartography. The author meant to show how much Turkish scholarship could contribute to an understanding of the true nature of the world. He offered a nice sentiment in the margin:

> Whoever wishes to know the true shape of the world, their minds shall be filled with light and their breast with joy.

Other Maps

Hapgood considered a few more old maps, of course. Pictures of them are available on the Internet. There's the Philippe Buache Map of 1737, which was based on a long lost source map that is undated. It pictures the entire con-tinent of Antarctica with no ice at all, but is perfectly accurate and a match with a seismic survey done in 1958. Others include the Zeno Map of 1380, the Dulcert Portolano of 1339, and an intriguing map of the North done by Claudius Ptolemy, who was a custodian of the famous Alexandrian Library in Egypt before it burned to the ground, allegedly destroyed by Christians who considered the thousands of treasures there to be pagan relics.

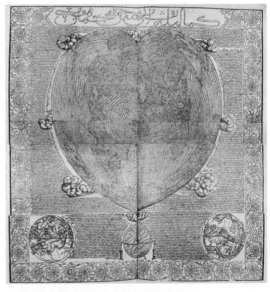

If all these maps were based on pre-Columbus voyages, and in some cases even pre-Ice Age times, who made them? According to traditional archeology there were no civilizations that far back in history. Yet the maps exist and can be seen today by anyone who owns a computer. They indicate that the history we were all taught in school is in need of some revision.

The map of the world created by Muslim cartographer Haci Ahmet in 1559. It has remarkable details of Siberia and Alaska.

BIBLE CODE

From ancient times, rabbis have passed on the tradition that the Torah, the first five books of the Bible, were given to Moses on Mount Sinai, written on stone tablets by the very finger of God. Tradition states that the books were written in Hebrew, with no breaks between the words. The entire Torah is some 304,805 Hebrew letters long. If the original text, or at least a close approximation, in the form in which it might have been given to Moses was then arranged in columns of forty rows, each row would contain some 7,551 letters. The letters would form a grid that could be read from right to left, as in Hebrew, or left to right, as in English. It could also be read up and down and corner to corner. In short, it would resemble a larger version of the find-the-words games that appear in many newspapers.

Jim and Barbara Willis in *Armageddon Now*

Hidden Messages

Does the Bible contain a hidden, coded message from an entity unknown? Is there more to the text than the obvious meaning of Scripture?

Michael Drosnin, author of *The Bible Code*, *Bible Code II: The Countdown*, and *Bible Code III: Saving the World*, thinks so. He has found, hidden in the grid of letters produced when the original Hebrew biblical text is arranged according to the method described above, that the assassinations of Yitzhak Rabin and John Kennedy were prophesied centuries before the birth of Jesus. He found a prediction concerning the infamous day of 9/11 and the Twin Towers plot. He has identified prophecies concerning World War II and the Holocaust, the atomic bomb blast at Hiroshima, the moon walk, and the Cold War.

He also found a prediction that the world would end in 2006.

Codes are tricky things. They are subject to interpretation. Take the following example. Eliyahu Rips, a Jewish mathematician who did the actual presentation of the code when it was announced, became a part of the code's history. Read the following sentence:

Rips explained that each
code is a case of adding
every fifth or tenth or fiftieth
letter to form a word.

Now read the sentence again, this time emphasizing every fifth letter:
Rips **e**xplained **t**hat **e**ach
Code **i**s a **c**ase **o**f **a**dding
every **f**ifth **o**r **t**enth **o**r **f**iftieth **l**etter **t**o form a word.

The message says: "Read the code."

Drosnin's detractors are legion, but he is undeterred. The strange thing about the whole situation is that he claims to be an atheist. He doesn't believe God placed the code in the Bible. Instead, he believes we were visited by aliens some six thousand years ago, at the birth of our civilization. The sudden spurt of human progress that led to reading and writing, great building projects, the birth of cities and all the trappings of civilization came from them, and they left a message for us in an obvious place—a holy book which they believed was destined to become a best seller and wind up in millions of homes. Warfare, according to Drosnin, is wrapped in religion. When the world stands on the brink of disaster such as an unthinkable Armageddon event, where else will people turn but to the holy book revered by the three great monotheistic religions of the world? And there they will find the message.

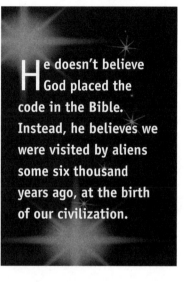

He doesn't believe God placed the code in the Bible. Instead, he believes we were visited by aliens some six thousand years ago, at the birth of our civilization.

But others wonder if there is another explanation. They wonder if there is indeed a spirit guiding humankind, one that reveals itself at various periods of our history again and again.

Why the Bible? The answer is, why not? And what about the other great scriptures of the world? Do they also contain hidden messages? Who is to say there is not a *Bhagavad Gita* code as well? Or a *War and Peace* code? Or even a *Moby Dick* code?

That was the situation when Drosnin issued a challenge to Brendan McKay, his biggest detractor. McKay had declared that any book of sufficient length would produce a code when subjected to a broad enough study. In the June 9, 1967, issue of *Newsweek* magazine, Drosnin said, "When my critics find a message about the assassination of a prime minister encrypted in *Moby Dick*, I'll believe them!"

As we reported in *Armageddon Now*:

Using the same software and techniques with which Drosnin supposedly deciphered the Bible Code, McKay went to work on *Moby Dick*. There he found revealed the assassinations of, among others, Indira Gandhi, Martin Luther King, Jr., John F. and Robert Kennedy, Abraham Lincoln, and Yitzhak Rabin. He also discovered the exile of Leon Trotsky. Besides all that, he discov-

וְאֵלֶּה שְׁמוֹת בְּנֵי יִשְׂרָאֵל הַבָּאִים מִצְרָיְמָה אֵת יַעֲקֹב אִישׁ 1
וּבֵיתוֹ בָּאוּ: רְאוּבֵן שִׁמְעוֹן לֵוִי וִיהוּדָה: יִשָּׂשכָר זְבוּלֻן וּבִנְיָמִן: דָּן
וְנַפְתָּלִי גָּד וְאָשֵׁר: וַיְהִי כָּל-נֶפֶשׁ יֹצְאֵי יֶרֶךְ-יַעֲקֹב שִׁבְעִים נָפֶשׁ
וְיוֹסֵף הָיָה בְמִצְרָיִם: וַיָּמָת יוֹסֵף וְכָל-אֶחָיו וְכֹל הַדּוֹר הַהוּא:

An example of possible code in the Bible (in this example, in Hebrew). Taking a passage from Genesis and reading every fiftieth letter spells the word "Torah."

ered the name of Princess Diana and, in close proximity, the words MORTAL IN THESE JAWS OF DEATH.

If all that weren't enough, McKay discovered in *Moby Dick* a prediction of Michael Drosnin's death. The letters M. DROSNIN are crossed by the words HIM TO HAVE BEEN KILLED. With the other words scattered throughout the letter-picture, McKay deduced that Drosnin would be killed by someone DRIVING A NAIL INTO HIS HEART that SLICES OUT A CONSIDERABLE HOLE. The event will transpire in ATHENS or at least in GREECE (both words appear in the quote) and apparently happen on the FIRST DAY of Drosnin's visit there. Even the names of the murderers are revealed. They happen to be two famous code researchers. (Apparently all this information was predicted in Herman Melville's *Moby Dick*. McKay issued a disclaimer explaining that he was merely illustrating a principle, not suggesting that Melville was a prophet.)

What Does It All Mean?

What are we to make of all this? Why do such speculations even belong in a book of this nature? Think of it in this way: there are really only three possible ways to approach this subject.

- First—The Bible Code doesn't really exist. Language being what it is, if you take any book of sufficient size, set it up in blocks of words and analyze it, you will find "hidden" messages that are really simply coincidences. If you search hard enough, you can make any book say anything you want.

- Second—The Bible Code does exist and was placed in the Bible by entities, either spiritual or extraterrestrial, to speak to a specific people at a specific time in history, probably at that time when they would have developed sufficient technology to find it.

- Third—The Bible Code is real and can be found not just in the Bible but in any book of sufficient size, because the words serve as a kind of Freudian slip. In other words, as we saw in the beginning of this chapter, words bubble up from our subconscious and reveal deep things about ourselves of which we were not aware. Just as DNA quietly programs us to evolve in a certain way without our ever knowing how it operates, our words reveal a spiritual, for lack of a better word, component to humanity that, in effect, programs us to evolve toward higher consciousness. In effect, we have prewritten our own history and are now living it out in time.

Whatever the future holds for the Bible Code, there is no doubt that it has opened up a wealth of discussion and speculation. Could previous civilizations have discovered this source of wisdom long before us? Did they build into their very infrastructure some of the hidden wisdom they discovered deep in the vaults of human consciousness? Do the clues they left behind point us to the fount of their understanding, an understanding that may be resurfacing in our current civilization?

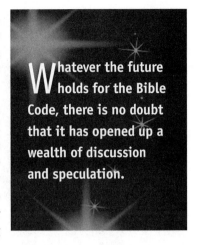

Whatever the future holds for the Bible Code, there is no doubt that it has opened up a wealth of discussion and speculation.

EASTER ISLAND

In what has been labeled a "wacky theory," Robert M. Schoch claimed in 2012 that the writing system of Easter Island is actually 10,000 years older than popularly believed. This also makes the island itself older than originally thought.

Estelle Thurtle: http://listverse.com

A Mystery in the Ocean

Easter Island is home to one of the world's most well-known mysteries. Almost every theory about its first inhabitants, its immense statues, and the demise of its culture is debated fiercely. Who built the huge Moai, the famous heads that gaze across its barren landscape? How did the builders maneuver such wonders into place? Why did they do it? What caused the sudden collapse of their social structure? What are the mysteries of their enigmatic birdman cult, if, indeed, it ever existed? Does the collapse of its ecology offer warnings that we need to heed today?

Every one of these topics has spawned books, articles, TV shows, and scholarly papers. Easter Island helped make Thor Heyerdahl a household name. But what makes it especially important to the topics covered in this book is its possible ancient antiquity, shrouded as it is in the infamous conspiracy of silence.

A professor of natural science, Dr. Robert Schoch put forth a theory that the Easter Island statues must be much older than previously thought.

The quote offered above is exhibit one in this regard. Robert Schoch is a respected, scholarly professional from Boston University, well-known for his work at the Sphinx of Giza and Gunung Padang in Indonesia. He is conservative in his approach to problems of geology and is usually found on the side of traditional research.

But when he studied the Moai of Easter Island he brought up a problem that most traditionalists simply want to ignore. For that, and that only, he is found guilty of harboring a "wacky theory." Sadly, this is often a sign of the conspiracy of silence at work: "If the facts don't agree with the traditional theory, disparage the messenger!"

Here's the problem. Traditional scholarship has put forth the doctrine that the first of Easter Island's statues were erected somewhere around 690 C.E., about four hundred years after the first humans arrived in 300 S.C. The last Moai was built about a a thousand years later. That would put the end of construction at about 1650 C.E. These dates are based primarily on carbon dating. So far, so good. We're on pretty safe ground.

But it was recently discovered that the great statutes are even bigger than first thought. In some cases, the heads are sitting on bodies that are buried some thirty feet below the surface. In this way they resemble ice burgs. Just the tip is visible with the great mass below ground.

Now, how does thirty feet of sediment build up in only three or four centuries? In order to reach that kind of depth, the statues have to be thousands, not hundreds, of years old.

This caused Schoch to look into some other evidence. It seems as though Easter Islanders did something unique of all small island nations in the world. They developed their own alphabet and their own written language, wrote down some mysterious engravings and then promptly forgot how to read them. All in a few hundred years!

That sounds suspicious and leads to another round of questions. Some of the statues are carved out of basalt. There is no basalt to be found on the island. There is, however, basalt located under the seas nearby in rather deep water. But the formations haven't been exposed on dry land since the Ice Age, thousands of years ago, when ocean levels were drastically lower than today.

Does that mean that Easter Island is an exposed top of what once was a much larger land mass during a period of time at least 12,000 years ago? And were there people living there who built the first of the great Moai, a tradition that was kept up until 1650 C.E., when the original people were long forgotten except in the myths that traditional archeologists refuse to believe contain history of any significant relevance?

No wonder the whole subject creates such debate. It sounds suspiciously like stories concerning the lost continent of Mu which was supposed to have existed in this area. Far easier to just call it a wacky theory! But you get the idea it's not going away anytime soon.

I Ching and the Binary Code

Row, row, row your boat gently down the stream.
Merrily, merrily, merrily, merrily, life is but a dream.

The Illusion of Digital Reality

Anyone who has played video games or watched movies for a number of years is familiar with the fact that they seem to be more and more real with each passing day. Technology has progressed to the point where it is sometimes difficult to tell if the figures on the screen are actors or digital representations.

It is important to remember, however, that the images which appear so real are actually computer-based representations that depend on two simple numbers. Every image is a series of ones and zeros—open or closed circuits. Two numbers, that's all. And yet those two numbers create illusions which make us feel as though we are out in space watching the Death Star explode. Two numbers allow a computer to create virtual reality that is gripping, to involve us emotionally, and to make images seem very, very real.

Now look at the eight "trigrams" above that form the basis for a system of exploring life that is at least five thousand years old, and maybe much older. They form the basis for the I Ching, or The Book of Changes. Its methods have been practiced first in China and then around the world ever since its legendary author, Fu Xi, first introduced it. You will notice that each character consists of a short line or a long line, or perhaps we might say a broken line and an unbroken line. The two lines, broken and unbroken, represent yin and yang, the polar principles of everything that exists. When arranged as above, the lines represent the eight principal forces of nature. Without going into

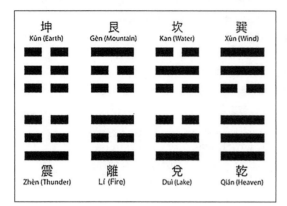

The eight trigrams of the I Ching.

more detail than we have room for in a book of this nature, by using coins (heads or tails) or, traditionally, yarrow stalks, the practitioner casts your future, comparing the results to an extensive commentary that indicates possible outcomes of paths to follow. It won't give an answer to questions such as, "Should I quit my job and move to another state?" But it will indicate favorable and non-favorable clues as to how to proceed in your life. In this sense, it is primarily a method of divination.

In the late 1600s, when Gottfried Wilhelm von Leibniz was looking for a simpler arithmetic than the commonly used decimal system, he discovered he could find nothing better than the ancient long-line/short-line system of the I Ching. With the advent of computers, it took on a life of its own. This simple binary system, now based on open and closed circuits on a printed board, is the basis for virtually every aspect of modern technology. We might say that the modern computer, with which I am writing this manuscript, is simply an extension of an ancient Chinese system for transcribing thoughts into words using two symbols, 1s and 0s.

It seems like magic, doesn't it? Sometimes, I must confess, when I sit down to a blank screen, I really have no idea what I'm going to say or how I'm going to express it. Then the yin and yang kick in, and I find words flowing from—where? Out of the blue, whether from my muse, my subconscious, or something beyond the material construction of life, words form which express ideas that generate something real in your mind so we can communicate and share an essential truth, even though we have never met. And we owe it all to 1s and 0s—open and closed circuits.

The same thing happens when we talk to someone on a cell phone, turn on the TV, or watch a movie. 1s and 0s. That's all. They represent the polar opposites, in other words, the totality, of every idea and symbol of an idea.

That brings up the important basis of I Ching and binary code. In the philosophy that undergirds them both, reality is not really real. It is an illusion, or perhaps it might be better expressed as a dream. The characters in a digitally produced movie are not real. They just act as if they are. The ancient Chinese would say that is true as well in what we call life. We are actors in a drama, and the basis of our existence, the ground of our being or perceived reality, is actually an illusion—a dream. The old campfire song has it right. "Life is but a dream." Yin and yang play out their infinite role through the material cosmos in which we live, but, at the base of it all, that material cosmos is expressed only through two figures—1s and 0s—dancing across an elaborate screen we call the universe which produce the movie of our lives.

Someday technology will advance to the point at which computers will produce a perfect illusion of reality. We won't be able to tell the difference between life and its virtual imitation.

The question is, have they already done so? Is there any difference between the pixels forming an image on a screen and the particles that form our bodies? Zoom in close enough and they both look the same. Are we already virtual players on a screen, unaware of the fact that we are taking part in a movie that is being played back from sometime in our distant future? Are we, in fact, a future someone's or something's virtual reality?

Down to Earth

Now let's tie all this into the subject at hand. Sometime long ago, an ancient genius recognized a truth that we are just beginning to understand. He came to believe that the core life every living thing leads can be expressed with a simple binary code that we have been able to implement but, as yet, have not been able to improve on.

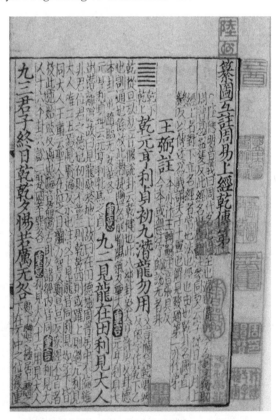

Earlier we speculated that one explanation of the Bible Code is that words, or symbols, might bubble up from our subconscious and inform us much as Freudian slips reveal things about us that we never knew were there. Did the ancient genius who composed the I Ching stumble across a lost wisdom that revealed hidden truths about the very nature of life itself? Did he catch a glimpse of the source?

Think about it. We're going deeper into this when we consider the God Particle, but through the modern-day magic of super colliders we have discovered that everything that exists on our side of the Higgs Field, everything that we recognize as having mass, is expressed to our senses through the 1s and 0s of a binary system-based computer, shown on a flat screen. We see virtual particles, collapsed bits of energy, and recognize more about how the universe

A page from the I Ching printed during the Song Dynasty about nine hundred years ago. The philosophical work poses that reality is not real.

works because of the open/closed, yin/yang binary system first told in an ancient Chinese system that expressed a philosophical methodology that informed the practitioner about reality and how to live in it.

Has that wisdom remained dormant down through the ages, finally to peek out through the complicated mathematical formulas that form the basis of our computer-generated world? Is life really a dream from which we will someday awake?

If an ancient genius figured all this out, or even if he or she just glimpsed a formula that might reveal the true nature of life itself, what else might that ancient genius be able to teach us?

Ley Lines

As I was going to Widdecomb Fair / All along, out along, down along the lea...."

Traditional Devonshire folk song

Set thee up waymarks, make thee high heaps: set thine heart toward the highway, even the way which thou wentest....

Jeremiah 31:21

The word 'ley' was first used by Alfred Watkins, in his book *The Old Straight Track*, to describe what he considered to be straight-track roads created by early humans to help them find their way from place to place. He never used the term ley line, now much misused and not considered to be a proper, technical dowsing term. It is usually replaced by the term energy ley, but old habits are hard to break. Most people who are not dowsers are not used to the new term, so ley line is still the popular usage.

Alfred Watkins

Watkins was certainly one of Britain's most entertaining characters. Born in 1855, he was probably the least likely of candidates for becoming what amounts to a New Age hero and the champion of a severely debated theory. When he published his bestseller, *The Old Straight Track*, which is still in print, his admirers and supporters formed a Straight Track Club to seek out ley lines across the English countryside. Archeologists, however, derided his theory with words like "poppycock!" (one of the most printable).

Who was this controversial figure?

Until the age of sixty-six he was an upstanding member of British society—solid, dependable, and predictable. As a young man he rode the English countryside working for his father as a brewer's representative—kind of a traveling salesman. Those long working trips gave him a wonderful familiarity with the countryside, which would later stand him in good stead. Although he seems to have built a whole storehouse of knowledge of local legends and folklore, he was, on the outside at least, a respected member of society. He was a safe, solid, local dignitary, the sort of man who anchored the Britain of his day. He was also an inventor and a manufacturer of photographic material. His exposure meter was widely used. Eventually he became a senior partner in a flour milling company, an administrator in the local school system, a justice of the peace, and a county councilor. In his spare time he was a fellow of The Royal Photographic Society, and some of his photographs have been featured in places like the Hereford Museum in Wales.

Francis Hitching, who wrote about him in the 1970s, does reveal a few oddities. He was a beekeeper and delighted in performing magic tricks. But, in Hitching's words, these "were no more than affectionate oddities that lightened his otherwise conventional rural respectability."

Beneath this solid British exterior, however, lurked the soul of a rebel. Although it wasn't fashionable to bandy such things about, Alfred Watkins was psychic. He kept it to himself, of course. In his Edwardian circles at that time, "such things just weren't done!" But besides the social repercussions, Watkins, being a product of his time and religion, was afraid that visions, predictions, and early childhood experiments with mind reading might lead him inexorably into the occult. So he kept his tendencies to himself. Even his family had only slight inklings about whom they harbored under their roof. But at the ripe old age of sixty-six, an age when some elders and mystics often just get started with their true purpose in life, Watkins had a vision.

> Watkins, being a product of his time and religion, was afraid that visions, predictions, and early childhood experiments with mind reading might lead him inexorably into the occult.

On June 30, 1921, he sat in his car on the outskirts of Blackwardine on a warm summer afternoon staring at a map he had opened on his lap. A landscape that had been hidden for thousands of years suddenly appeared to transpose itself over the familiar geography over which he had been riding all his life. A web of what he would later call "old straight tracks" appeared to transfix his map, connecting places and structures that once shook to the sound of ancient chants and prehistoric rituals.

His son Allen, who heard the story about the vision only years later, said that in that instant his father learned everything he ever needed to know about ley lines. The rest of Alfred's life consisted merely of doing the field research needed to prove their existence. He later wrote, "I knew nothing on June 30th last of what I now communicate, and had no theories. I followed up the clue of sighting from hilltop, unhampered by theories, and found it yielding astounding results in all districts, the straight lines to my amazement passing over and over again through the same class of objects, which I soon found to be (or to have been) practical sighting points."

In his book *The Old Straight Track*, which he wrote three years later, he waxed poetic about what he had discovered:

> Imagine a fairy chain stretched from mountain peak to mountain peak, as far as the eye could reach, and paid out until it touched the "high places" of the earth at a number of ridges, banks, and knowls. Then visualize a mound, circular earth work, or clump of trees, planted on these high points, and in low points in the valley other mounds ringed around with water to be seen from a distance. The great standing stones brought to mark the way at intervals, and on a bank leading up to a mountain ridge or down to a ford the track cut deep so as to form a guiding notch on the skyline as you come up. In a bwlch or mountain pass the road cut deeply at the highest place straight through the ridge so as to show as a notch afar off. Here and there, at two ends of the way, a beacon fire used to lay out the track. With ponds dug on the line, or streams banked up into "flashes" to form reflecting points on the beacon track so that it might be checked when at least once a year the beacon was fired on the traditional day. All these works exactly on the sighting line. The wayfarer's instructions are still deeply rooted in the peasant mind today, when he tells you—quite wrongly now—"You just keep straight on."

Ley Hunting

This is precisely where many modern ley hunters part company with Alfred Watkins. He believed the system of old straight tracks was a human invention, an infrastructure created by early humans to get from one place to the next, much as a modern highway system in any industrialized nation today. He called these tracks leys, choosing from the many Anglo-Saxon variants such as lay, lee, lea, or leigh, and believed they could often be followed just by following place names on a map—Wemb*ley*, Oak*ley*, Brad*ley*, for instance, or *Ley* Rock in Cornwall. But when he got into the field, he discovered that his tracks often passed through ancient structures, standing stones, circles, and even churches.

He decided to ascertain in a mathematical, statistical fashion whether it was possible that these structures were the ancient equivalent of mile markers

The Malvern Hills in England included what Alfred Watkins considered ley lines, spiritual alignments of land features.

or wayside stopovers, so he obtained a copy of Ordinance Survey Sheet #283 in the Andover District. He then circled every one of the fifty-one churches on the map and proceeded to draw straight lines through as many as he could. He discovered eight lines in which four churches could be linked in this fashion, and one instance where five of them lined up.

Then he took a similar-sized piece of paper, drew, at random, fifty-one crosses on it, and proceeded to try the experiment again. Only one straight line could be drawn that linked four crosses, and none could be produced that linked five. This experiment provided the modern definition of ley line. A ley line is a straight line that connects at least four sacred sites. To be positive, five or more is preferred.

He was, of course, roundly denounced by professional archeologists. But Watkins insisted, to his dying day, that he was onto something special. His legion of devoted ley hunters continued to follow his instructions. He taught them to employ careful drafting techniques. Using large-scale ordnance maps, they would make a 3/8th-inch circle around any of these criteria:

1. Ancient mounds, barrows, or cairns

2. Ancient, un-worked stones, either found in connecting patterns or standing alone

3. Moats and islands found in ponds and lakes

4. Wells accompanied by legends or tales of sacredness

5. Beacon points (high hills and rises in the landscape, visible from afar)

6. Crossroads with place names

7. Churches with ancient foundations

8. Old castles or palaces that contained ancient castle names

Once these were circled, the ley hunter needed to do field research, searching for signs of ancient tracks connecting them. Given modern agricultural practices, this was no easy task. Also, because even a pencil mark on a map is too wide to accurately mimic a ley line, only field research, preferably with a good dowsing tool, was adequate for precise measuring.

With the publication of these instructions, a cottage industry was born. Amateurs from all walks of life arose to drive professional archeologists batty. A veritable army of folk began to prowl the English countryside every weekend. Whether or not they accepted everything Watkins wrote or said in the talks he had begun to give to every nature club that invited him, it became a wonderful way to spend a productive, relaxing day.

The disclaimers, of course, were legion:

• What does a modern church have to do with an ancient ley line?

Well, a modern church, especially in Great Britain, is very probably built on an ancient holy site. After all, the Church appropriated many pagan practices. Christmas trees, Yule logs, Easter eggs, even the date of its two principal holy days, Christmas and Easter, came directly from the ancient religions of our ancestors. It is well known that the great Chartres Cathedral in France, for instance, is built on the exact spot where ancient Druids held court in their sacred grove before the armies of Julius Caesar destroyed it. And why did the Romans burn down the grove? Just because it was the center of religion for the people they were trying to conquer.

• But if you draw lines on a map and extend them far enough, you're bound to connect enough dots eventually!

That's why you have to do the field research, preferably with dowsing rods, so as to measure the energies present.

• What about stones that just stand alone, without any other structures or sacred spots for miles around?

Many of our traditions behind Christian holidays, such as Easter, are steeped in pagan beliefs.

That's why we need more research!

• I'd believe in a minute if you'd just show me some evidence.

Good grief, man, open your eyes! The evidence is everywhere you look, standing upright in farmers' fields, snaking out across the countryside, staring at you from the top of Glastonbury Tor to the utmost islands of the Hebrides. What more do you need?

The argument continues to this day, but the issue has been complicated by the fact that many people have come to believe that ley lines were not, as Watkins proposed, a simple human invention.

Earth Energy

In short, they say that although the old straight tracks were probably used to connect holy places, there is more at work here than simple convenience. If a group of travelers, for instance, wanted to get from point A to point B, why would they decide to trek up and over a mountain when it would be much easier to go around?

This point of view was championed recently when a system of straight lines across the deserts of America's southwest was discovered by NASA satel-

Were the ancients in America mimicking their cousins in Europe? Or were they building according to specifications built into the very fabric of the earth?

lite pictures. Straight roads, thirty feet across, from Mexico almost to Colorado, made by people who had not yet even imagined a wheeled vehicle. Why exactly thirty feet across when the builders knew only foot travel? When explored by archeologists on the ground, it was discovered that rather than bypass a canyon or mountain, the Old Ones had chosen to go the hard way. Often they even carved handholds in precarious cliffs where no one in their right mind would normally choose to go, especially if carrying a load on their back. A short detour would have made the way much, much easier. But no. Right over the top and down again into the valley! What were they thinking? And archeologists began to find signs of a stop-over—a motel, so to speak—made by the Old Ones at the end of each day's travel. What's up with that? Were the ancients in America mimicking their cousins in Europe? Or were they building according to specifications built into the very fabric of the earth? Were they following unseen energies and listening to music we have forgotten how to hear?

Other countries across the pond from England yielded enigmatic treasures as well. Bolivia and Peru in South America, and the countries of Central America, especially when seen from the air, appeared to be part of a worldwide network. China and Japan joined the club. Also added were North Africa, Australia, and the lands of southwest Asia that once were called Persia. Everywhere people looked, the old straight tracks were there.

In the words of Francis Hitching, who wrote *Earth Magic* back in 1976:

Expressed simply, the theory is this ... that the whole of [megalithic man's] civilization [was] locked together by a mysterious cobweb of interlocking straight lines, the evidence for which still exists on maps and in the scenery today.

Watkins concluded, in *The Old Straight Track*:

I feel that ley-man, astronomer-priest, druid, bard, witch, palmer, and hermit, were all more or less linked by one thread of ancient knowledge and power, however degenerate it became in the end.

Evidence in Our Backyards

And what is the evidence? Watkins believed that early peoples were more in touch with their landscape than we are today. They felt, perhaps could even see, that the earth pulsated with living energy. Just as blood vessels carry life-giving nutrients throughout our bodies, lines of energy are carried throughout the earth, which is, in realty, a living thing. Early people felt this energy, especially when lines crossed. There they built monuments, often of stone. When later people came along, they built their holy places on these spots, superimposing their own spiritual perspective upon that of a previous generation.

It might have gone something like this, to cite only one example:

- Ancient people worshipped in a magnificent clearing in a French wood.

- Druids later declared this a sacred grove and made it the center of their religious experience.

- Christians recognized this as a holy spot of ground and built Chartres Cathedral, where it stands to this day.

Over and over, we see this pattern repeated. First there was a magical place where ancient people built a monument to amplify its sacredness. Later peoples, following a different religion, built their own sacred temples, churches, or whatever on this spot of ground because they recognized, or rather felt, the power of a holy place.

In other words, all around the world, if you can locate the standing stones, churches, or sacred places, regardless of the religion responsible for

The ruins of Knowlton Church in Dorset, England, are surrounded by Neolithic earthworks, for the land was sacred to early peoples before the arrival of Christians in the twelfth century. It is a good example of Christians constructing religious buildings strategically to try to replace what were considered pagan beliefs.

building the monuments or when the particular edifice was raised, you will see a place with an ancient religious heritage.

In the words of John Michell, in his book *The New View Over Atlantis*:

We appear today to have lost touch with some source of inspiration known in former times, whose departure has left the churches as if under some malign enchantment. Empty, cold and shunned, their shelter denied to travelers, often locked up, the sensations they invoke are those of guilt and embarrassment. Moralistic vicars drove out the musicians, banned plays and processions, washed the colors off the walls. Now the incumbent, hopelessly bewildered, often appears to see himself as a custodian of an ancient ruin, endlessly worried by details of the rotting fabric, his thermometer sign at the gate pointing out the sum required to prevent the whole edifice from crashing about his ears.

It's sad, but here's the point. When such spots are plotted on a map, they often follow a straight line across the landscape, indicating a ley line, or Earth energy line, flowing through the landscape. Watkins's rule of thumb is still the standard. Whenever you find four or more such spots that fall on a straight line across the map, you may well be dealing with a ley line which denotes Earth energy.

When dowsers began to check it out, what they discovered confirmed the hypothesis. Sure enough, over and over again, dowsing rods, held in the hands of those who were adept at the age-old practice, indicated the presence of such lines. It seemed that just as any living animal has arteries and capillaries that carry blood throughout the body, the earth is connected by a huge grid of energy lines. What are they? Are they caused by underground water or electrical energy currents? Are they quantum grids? Can the old idea of Gaia, Mother Earth, be true? Is the earth a living organism?

Theories Abound

Today the field of energy leys is populated by a mixed bag of specialists, scientists, ley hunters, metaphysical practitioners, ecologists, social science engineers, quacks, and charlatans. An Internet search can provide hours and hours of delightful, maddening, thought-provoking, laugh-inducing, enlightening, and instructive entertainment. But the theories fall into a few constructive categories. Here is a systematic treatment for the most common, listed in order, perhaps, of the most accepted to the most esoteric.

Roads of an Ancient Time

Alfred Watkins, although he did demonstrate some doubts, died believing that ley lines were ancient trade routes, built upon the principle of line-of-sight. Pick a prominent spot on the horizon, lay out a path and go. This theory has a lot going for it, especially if you consider the routes laid out in other parts of the world. But as we have already pointed out, there are problems with it. Why go straight, for instance, if there is an obstacle like a hill or swamp that would be easier to circumnavigate? And, in the case of the American southwest, for example, why make it thirty feet wide if the only traffic your road needs to accommodate is foot travel?

Nevertheless, once you admit that ley lines exist, you need an explanation. And this one seems fairly conservative and safe.

There is even some good, old-fashioned religious backing for it, found right in the pages of the Bible. This story, for instance, begins with Scripture. In I Samuel 5, the Philistines (just a generation before their champion, Goliath, had his famous confrontation with David, the shepherd boy) had the misfortune of capturing the Ark of the Covenant, the famous gold box that contained the Ten Commandments, among other important artifacts. They recognized that it was a holy object, even though it belonged to the enemy, so they decided to put it on display in the temple of their god, Dagon. One would suppose that it was a "My god can beat up your god!" kind of thing.

But that's when the trouble started. Every morning, when the priests of Dagon went in to do whatever it was they did each day, they found that their statue of Dagon had "fallen on his face on the ground before the ark of the Lord!" (I Samuel 5:4).

What to do? Well, following the age-old political ploy of passing the buck, they decided to move the ark to a different village. But those folks didn't want it either. After seven months of enduring this kind of religious version of musical chairs, the Philistines finally sent for their priests, who were, you guessed it, diviners, another word for dowsers. They decided to put the ark in a cart, along with a guilt offering (kind of a "sorry about that" present), hitch the cart to some oxen and send it home to Israel.

But when they sent it off, the oxen, on their own, with no guidance, "went straight up toward Beth Shemish, keeping on the road and lowing [the Hebrew commentaries usually say singing or humming instead of lowing] all the way; they did not turn to the right or to the left."

In other words, they were following a straight track.

This story wouldn't really demand a place here were it not for a curious incident that happened much later. Fast forward a few thousand years now, for a story about how the Christian brothers of a much later age decided where to

A lfred Watkins, although he did demonstrate some doubts, died believing that ley lines were ancient trade routes, built upon the principle of line-of-sight.

build Waltham Abbey in Essex. It seems that in the time of King Canute, a holy man had a dream in which he found a treasure at the top of Saint Michael's hill in Somerset. (This is the very hill that now anchors one of the most famous ley lines in all of Great Britain.) When he told folks about the dream, people started digging, of course. Eventually they found a large flint cross of ancient lineage. Obviously it was too holy a relic to stash in a closet somewhere, so the people decided to trust it to the Lord to decide where the cross should be displayed. They placed it in a cart, hitched up some oxen, just like in the Bible story, and then sat back to await developments.

The oxen wouldn't move. They were prodded toward Glastonbury and then toward Westminster, but they wouldn't go. Finally, left to their own devices, they did the same thing their biblical counterparts did. They headed out, straight across the countryside, and "they did not turn to the right or to the left." Presumably they even "lowed" (or sang or hummed) as they went. Eventually they wound up at the site of Waltham Cross in Essex, and the rest, as they say, is history.

Old straight tracks thus have a bit of a lineage. But they are found in more than just folk tales. In Australia, for instance, their function today seems to be serving as sacred roads.

In 1960, Charles Mountford spent time in the outback with a group of Australian Aborigines who were on a seasonal journey to restore various

Waltham Abbey in Essex, England, was built there, legend has it, because a holy cross was destined to be stored there in a place that is also a famous ley line.

sacred centers that were found along straight tracks through the desert. Singing as they went, the elders would perform rituals that were to be found in their epic creation myths, creating, in their words, "a line of songs."

He later wrote a book about this experience, *Winbaraku and the Myth of Jarapiri*, in which he explained:

> It is an aboriginal belief that every food, plant and animal has an increase centre where a performance of the proper rituals will release the life essence or *karumba* of that particular plant or animal, and thereby bring about its increase.

The places where the rituals were performed were all marked by natural features that had been covered with paintings or etchings of serpents and various other mythological representations, and they were connected by what sounds very much like ley lines, or, as they are known in Australia, lines of songs.

History itself, however, has conspired to use ley lines for more sinister purposes.

When the Roman legions set out to conquer the world, they soon became known, among other things, for their infrastructure. All roads, as they say, led to Rome. The world was connected as never before by a set of highways. Dwight Eisenhower, the U.S. president who conceived and pushed through legislation for the building of the great transcontinental highway system of the 1940s and 1950s, would have felt right at home talking to Julius Caesar. *Pax Romana*, the "Peace of Rome," even though it was a peace enforced by the sword, gave the world a system of roads, a common language, a continental trade network, a common culture, and an educational system that united countries from Great Britain to Asia. Later on, it even gave the world a religion. Early Christian missionaries such as Saul of Tarsus used Roman citizenship as a passport to evangelism. Traveling over the safe highways of a united kingdom, the church became so strong that it was able to hold much of the crumbling world together during the Dark Ages that fell upon Europe when Rome had decayed into dust.

The efficient roads that Rome built in order to move her armies about and secure the way for her far-flung trade networks didn't happen by accident. Archeology has revealed time and time again that Roman engineers made use of an existing network of roads that already seamed the landscape. Rome may get the credit, but the original plan was laid down thousands of years before Julius Caesar was even a gleam in his daddy's eye. It seems as though Roman roads often followed megalithic ley lines.

And this created a historical precedent that is also a supremely ironic metaphor—a sad commentary on the historical process. When Roman legions marched down those roads, laid down thousands of years earlier by megalithic

The Via Appia (Appian Way) is a famous road system built by the Romans that is still usable today. It is said they constructed the roads on existing paths made by even more ancient peoples.

engineers, straight into the heart of a country they intended to conquer, they crunched into rubble that which was originally intended for religious purposes. In Persia, in Europe, in England, and later under Cortés and the Conquistadors, roads originally built for peaceful trade, or perhaps even for spiritual reasons yet unknown, knew the crush of chariot wheels where earlier they had known only the soft pad of a runner's feet. Beacons built on far-off hilltops—once used, perhaps, to signal the coming of spring—were now used to send messages of war. Everywhere they went, the Romans stamped out the wisdom of the very culture that had helped make their victory possible.

It's a sad commentary on the modern age. As we now stand in the early years of the twenty-first century, facing catastrophic pollution, wars, and rumors of wars, technology run amok, and an ever-increasing sense of futility with modern life, we are reminded by historical precedent that we are a people of war, built upon the ashes of the wisdom that might have been our salvation.

Heavenly Sight Lines

This illustrates, however, another possible explanation for the old straight tracks. For good or for ill, they might have been built by humans for the purpose of communication.

According to this theory—that ley lines were sight lines pointing to a greater reality in the heavens—we can stand on a mountaintop (in our minds, at least) on the day of new beginnings—the solstice, perhaps—and view a horizon that seems to expand forever. Suddenly, on a far distant hilltop, a signal fire blazes through the dark. It is a feeble light, though, and can only point the way into the new year. It is not strong enough to bring it to fruition. The best it can do is to show us where to look. Then, in a moment of triumph, the real light appears. Blazing from a distant mountaintop, it engulfs the feeble work of humans. Filling the horizon with warmth, it rises exactly where it is supposed to be, sparkling down a long, cleared avenue, reflecting off ponds that mirror and flash forth its light, and finally reaches a gathering of people who need nourishment and hope to face an uncertain future. Once again, all is well. Life can continue.

Terminal Moraine from a Mystic Age

John Michell, author of many, many books and articles about megalithic humanity and history as viewed from an unorthodox perspective, is, when it comes to numbers, facts, and detailed knowledge, so far ahead of his critics that they sometimes appear foolish, and often pompous, trying to catch up. His take on the ley line network, discussed in his book *The New View Over Atlantis*, is that it is a visible remnant of a culture that was once worldwide, mystic, highly inventive, and supremely intelligent.

As to the purpose behind the ley system, that still remains the deepest of ancient mysteries; but it is commonly agreed by most experienced researchers that it was connected with a former code of mystical science which acknowledged the existence of energy streams across the earth and the part they play in the renewal of all life on this planet. It was a science whose principles were numerically expressed, it unified all the individual arts and sciences and it has left traces of its mythology, folklore, customs, monuments, and cultures universally…. The memory of that archaic world-order was preserved into historical times by groups or castes of priestly initiates, such as the keepers of the Egyptian temples from whom indirectly Plato received it. His name for the lost world (was) Atlantis.

According to this view, ley lines are the remnants of an infrastructure left behind by a civilization long forgotten….

According to this view, ley lines are the remnants of an infrastructure left behind by a civilization long forgotten, but far different in scientific advancement from that of the primitive savages of yesteryear that fill our history texts today.

Much of what they accomplished has yet to be discovered, but one theory of ley lines is that, just as in modern America, if you follow the roads, they will lead you to places where people did things—sometimes, we might add, incredible things.

Gaia's Arteries

In the 1970s, the chemist James Lovelock and microbiologist Lynn Margulis proposed that the planet Earth contained so many interlocking systems that depended upon each other, and were so closely integrated, that they formed a single, complex, self-regulating system that maintained the conditions for life. Resurrecting an ancient name for Mother Earth, they called their idea the Gaia Hypothesis, following the suggestion of the novelist William Golding. The hypothesis suggested that the best way to study life as we know it is to face the fact that, in terms of function, the earth exhibits all the elements that we recognize as a single, interlocking organism. The biosphere and the evolution of life-forms contribute to the stability of global temperature, ocean salinity, oxygen in the atmosphere, and other factors that figure in to an explanation and understanding of such things as habitability and the sustainability of life itself.

Although it was initially criticized and ridiculed, it has now been proven so conclusively that their proposition is currently studied by geophysicists, Earth system scientists, biochemists, ecologists, and philosophers.

In layman's terms, the Gaia Hypothesis says that the earth is a living, breathing entity much like the human body, with its various systems and organs, and needs to be treated as such if humans are going to survive.

No multicelled organism can exist without its circulatory system—the blood vessels and arteries that carry life-giving energy throughout its body in the form of oxygenated blood. This, say many ley line enthusiasts, is what energy leys are all about. They are Gaia's arteries. Accompanied by lesser, but equally important "blood vessels" of energy lines that entwine their way around the arteries and continue to all extremities, energy leys carry the life-giving energy of electromagnetism, or quantum energy, or something that we really can't comprehend right now, throughout the earth.

It's a wonderfully comforting theory because it makes science become much more holistic than it usually proves to be. It unites disciplines after centuries of division. It fits in with the truly spectacular pictures we have of the earth as viewed from space. In those wonderful images, our planet is not divided by lines on a map, check points, barbed wire, or political ideologies. It is

Lynn Margulis (left) and James Lovelock proposed the Gaia Hypothesis, which basically views Earth, as a whole, as a living single being.

one living, blue, splendidly shining whole. We see land and ocean, continents and ice caps, mountains and rivers, rain forests and deserts, clouds and rainbows. We see every element contributing to the whole. It is unimaginable to leave any piece out and still have a whole.

Those who picture the earth just as a provider of resources obviously object to this hypothesis. After all, if humans want cheap gas, they certainly don't want to be stopped from having their way with Earth, and to hell with any Arctic caribou that may stand in the way!

But to those who view life from a broader perspective, it makes perfect sense. When you stub your toe, your whole body hurts. When part of the body suffers, you hurt all over. In the same way, when people destroy part of our habitat, even if they, personally, never go there, they are destroying part of a living, breathing organism called Gaia.

It makes a difference in your thinking when you go to throw that trash out of your car window. In the words of James Lovelock himself:

It may be that one role we play is as the senses and nervous system for Gaia. Through our eyes she has, for the first time, seen her fair face and in our minds become aware of herself. We do indeed belong here. The earth is more than just a home, it's a living system and we are part of it.

Electromagnetic Beacons

In our examination of the theories behind the ley line system, we've moved from early trade routes to sight lines, examining their physical appearance, their utilitarian possibilities, and their mythological-poetical meaning. We've considered that they may point backward in time to an earlier age not yet understood or appreciated. We then moved farther into the realm of the metaphysical, speculating about the possibility that they might carry the very lifeblood of our planet, conveying an energy that we do not fully comprehend. Now it's time to take another leap into the darkness of paranormal speculation. Remember as we do so, however, that once, before we understood it, electricity would have been considered magic.

In 1959 the great Swiss psychiatrist Carl Jung published a book about flying saucers. In this landmark book he didn't talk about aliens. Instead he studied the fact that more and more people were lifting their eyes to the heavens and reporting objects that he associated with what he called the collective unconscious. He believed flying saucers to be archetypes of gods, the product of a collective change taking place in the human psyche. To simplify his understanding—perhaps too easily—Jung taught that the collective human mind undergoes changes from time to time. People begin to view the world differently. This change takes place roughly every 2,160 years, coinciding with the astrological signs of the zodiac. The Christian era that began two thousand years ago is identified with the constellation *Pisces*, the sign of the fish. According to Jung, it was no accident that early Christians chose a fish symbol for their new faith, just as it was no accident that the Christian story identifies the first followers of the Christ as fishermen, and that Jesus bid them follow him in order to become "fishers of men."

[Carl Jung] believed flying saucers to be archetypes of gods, the product of a collective change taking place in the human psyche.

But that was then. This is now. As the groundbreaking, so-called hippie musical *Hair* pointed out in 1967, "this is the dawning of the Age of Aquarius!" As any astrologer worth his or her salt knows, Aquarians, under the sign of the water bearer, often go about accomplishing their goals in ways that are quite unorthodox. They are said to be prone to philosophical thought, and although they can become victims to sloth and laziness, they are also artistic, poetic and generous to a fault, traits often attributed to the hippies back in the sixties and seventies.

The great mythologist Joseph Campbell pointed out that in many of the ancient myths of the hero's journey, the hero would pass through water into an enchanted land, where his or her adventure would begin to unfold. Water was the dividing line, whether it was represented by Alice going through the looking glass or Arthur confronting the Lady of the Lake. Once you passed through the water, you were entering enchanted realms. Your worldview was about to be drastically changed. This is one of the many mythical motifs co-opted by the Christian Church in its practice of baptism.

Using the Greek letters that spell Iesous Christos Theos HUios Sotor (ICTHUS—Jesus Christ God Son Savior), the Greek word for "fish" is indicated, which is one reason the fish is a symbol for Christianity. But, too, in astrology, the Christian Era began in the Age of Pisces, the Fish.

According to Jung, during the Age of Aquarius people would move up out of the "water" that was the home of Pisces, the fish. The water bearer would begin the work of lifting people up to new heights.

So it was that after the explosion of the first atomic bomb taught everyone the futility of the path technology was following, after two thousand years of wars and rumors of wars, after the Christian age began to deteriorate into denominational bickering and institutional persecution, humankind began the journey into a new realm. Looking up from the mud and sludge that they had suddenly noticed was pulling them down into the earth, they raised their sights to the skies. And what did they discover? Flying saucers! Chariots of gods from a different realm. Hope from the skies!

This was also the time in history when the fundamentalist, which soon evolved into the evangelical, wing of the Christian church adopted the idea of the Rapture. Although many believers today assume this doctrine goes back to the very beginning of Church history, the term "rapture" was introduced in the United States only in the early 1800s. John Nelson Darby, a nineteenth-century Irish evangelist, discovered through his study of the Bible that passages in the New Testament seemed to indicate that Jesus would return at the end of an age that he called a dispensation. Further study revealed that human history consisted of seven of these dispensations, the sixth of which he called the Church Age. This, he said, is the age in which we currently live. It began with the birthday of the Church at Pentecost, following Jesus's return to heaven. It would end just before the seventh dispensation, called the thousand-year reign of Christ, or the Millennium. Because Jesus would return before the Millennium, this doctrine was called Premillennialism. The return itself would take

> The rapture theory continued to grow in popularity among evangelicals, largely because of a p reacher named William Eugene Blackstone.

place in two stages. The first was called the Rapture, from the Latin *raptura*. Jesus would snatch up, or rapture, his faithful followers before he would physically return to Earth, either immediately, three years later, or seven years later, depending on the interpretations of the different Christian sects. The Rapture theory continued to grow in popularity among evangelicals, largely because of a preacher named William Eugene Blackstone. His book *Jesus Is Coming*, first published in 1878, sold more than one million copies before 1940. All in all, the phenomenon illustrated Jung's "hope from the skies" theory, and it continues to this day.

It is no accident that many of the same people who now study ley lines come from a background of interest in UFOs and alien contact. The *War of the Worlds* (both the book by H. G. Wells and the radio broadcast read by Orson Welles), *Star Trek*, and *Star Wars* didn't become blockbusters by accident. This was the world prophesied by Jules Verne and H. G. Wells. Arthur C. Clarke was its publicist, Carl Sagan and Erich von Däniken, from two different "denominations," its theologians.

And the age is just beginning. It's difficult to turn to the Discovery Channel, or even the History Channel, without seeing shows about alien encounters. The famous actor and narrator Morgan Freeman regularly takes us *Through the Wormhole*. Quantum physics has revealed a world much stranger than fiction.

Is it any wonder that the discovery of an infrastructure such as that created by ley lines would eventually be depicted as a beacon of some sort—an electromagnetic or even quantum guidepost, perhaps put in place by the earth itself and maybe even created by an intelligent extraterrestrial race, but a beacon nonetheless—whose purpose is unknown but certainly capable of provoking speculation?

Worldwide Grid

This brings us to the final theory. This theory says that ley lines somehow involve focusing and increasing Earth's energy. Possibly they even harnessed an energy so great and allowed ancient people to perform works of such impact that they brought about their extinction.

The relatively new idea called string theory, whether it ever proves to be true or not, started scientists thinking along the paths of extra dimensions and possible movement from one to another. The mathematics of quantum physics allows for such things, and even serious scientists are talking about ideas like multiverses (many universes instead of just one) and universes whose boundaries consist of membranes (branes) that might be only a fraction of an inch away but separated from us by an impenetrable barrier of complex physics involving both time and space. Can such things be? Serious scientists seem to think so.

This prompts a question, of course. Could it be possible that ley lines carry energy not just out of and into space, but out of or into other dimensions as well?

First we have to ask what kind of energy we're talking about.

The sun constantly ejects immense quantities of charged particles from its corona. These consist of extremely high-energy electrons, protons, and who knows what other kinds of particles. Together they are called solar wind. To a certain extent, this is what we see during the phenomena called northern lights and southern lights (Aurora Borealis and Aurora Australis). Sometimes solar wind can be damaging. In the spring of 2012, for instance, scientists warned that a particularly violent outbreak could damage satellites and power grids on the earth. The warning proved to be a false alarm, but it was reported in detail on news programs just in case.

The Earth's core, you see, is composed of mostly molten iron. It produces the traditional magnetic north/south orientation that is familiar to anyone who has ever held a compass in their hand. Although there is evidence to support the theory that this orientation has flipped quite often in the past, it hasn't happened for hundreds of thousands of years, so its effect is unknown to humanity.

Nevertheless, magnetic currents continuously flow over the surface of Earth. They are known as Earth energy or telluric currents and consist of extremely low frequency (ELF) electromagnetic waves. Over the millions of years this energy has been doing its thing, this theory of ley lines proposes that the electrical lines have stabilized into a coherent grid of electrical waves. They have established what is known as a worldwide grid, a pattern of magnetic fields.

Picture for a moment a stream rushing down a mountainside. On the surface, the waves produced by rocks and shoals in its wake appear to be quite stable. But what you are actually seeing is a lot of water, constantly moving and rushing in an inexorable race toward the sea.

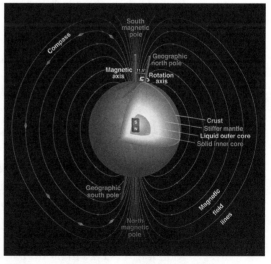

The center of Earth is composed of molten iron, which is also rotating; as it does so, it generates a magnetic current, which serves to protect the planet from radioactive solar winds.

Here's the point. Life on Earth evolved under the influence of this grid. We respond to it whether we are aware of it or not. Fluctuating on a twelve-hour period, two periods per day, we are controlled in ways we cannot readily feel anymore, except as we experience sleep cycles, periods of energy and relaxation, and other bodily responses, either daily or monthly.

Proponents of this theory believe that it might be entirely possible that our ancestors, living much closer to natural rhythms, never having heard of an alarm clock, were able to tap into this worldwide grid, which is marked, of course, by ley lines. By erecting rocks and monuments at places which especially demonstrated its force, they were able to amplify it.

Why else, they claim, would rocks be placed at such specific locations, even when they stand alone? Why else would the pattern be found worldwide, rather than at specific localities? Why else would Neolithic humans, concerned about the necessities of food and sustenance, expend so much time and energy doing something as energetic as moving megaton boulders across the landscape? Why was it so important to have certain stones, made of certain kinds of rock, in certain places, even if it meant moving them, in some cases, hundreds of miles?

We are made, it is claimed, from the dust of the earth, the very material structure of Earth itself. Could it be that we are affected by these currents of telluric energy far more than we know? Are our moods and feelings a product of the very essence of Earth's energy?

Women have often noted that when they are in close contact with each other for periods of time, their monthly menstrual cycles will adjust and begin to coincide with each other's. Clearly biology itself is influenced by forces we really don't understand.

But to explore a little further, think about the vibratory nature of energy itself. Try this experiment. Take a tuning fork and strike it in a quiet room. If you have other tuning forks available, they will all begin to resonate at the same time, even though you don't touch them. It has been said that music soothes a savage breast. Music does affect us, as Dobie Gray used to remind us: "Give me the beat, boys, to free my soul. I want to get lost in your rock and roll and drift away." And music, like light, is vibratory energy.

There is a distinct connection between light and music. Our very language reveals that we know this to be true. Did you ever tell someone, for instance, that he was wearing a loud shirt? You meant that the colors stood out. So why did you use an auditory adjective to describe a visible color? The body maintains a resonant relationship with Earth energy. Music is more than sound. It is energy in motion.

Dowsers who are sensitive to Earth energy often claim to be able to discern this energy through their dowsing implements, and some have claimed to be able to detect a pattern that is unmistakable. It might even explain why singing is so intertwined with the folk remembrances of how standing stones got to be where they are. Some tales, for instance, talk about stones that were moved long distances by priests who sang them there. Maidens were singing in a circle when they were turned to stone. Stones levitated into position by a singing congregation. Merlin raised Stonehenge with music. That sort of thing.

That is the point behind this last theory of ley lines that we have been discussing. Those who follow this theory believe that the vibratory grid covering the whole world is a powerful source of Earth energy, generated both from the earth and from its relationship with the sun and the universe. Did early humans feel the presence of this grid, learn to amplify it by building stone monuments at key locations, and use it to their advantage, perhaps even leading to, in some cases, their destruction when things got out of control—when the song, the vibratory energy, got too intense?

There are many apocryphal stories about the soprano who could sing so high and so strong she could break a glass with her voice. Are they based on more than legend? It's an interesting theory that contains just enough science to promote lots of speculation.

The End of the Matter

So the question goes on, seemingly forever. What are ley lines? Who or what laid them out to begin with? Did ancient engineers follow a pattern laid down by Gaia herself? Did human intention lead to the energy that might, or might not, surge through their telluric courses? Are they messages from the gods, or God, or aliens, or ancient mystics, or a prehistoric civilization now crumbling beneath the march of time?

We may never know. Even the man who is credited with their modern discovery wasn't really sure. But when Alfred Watkins died on April 15, 1935, his followers in the Straight Track Club were presented with a poem written in his honor by a Mr. H. Hudson. The final lines of that poem will bring a tear to the eye of any ley hunter:

He only knew how to climb
Amid forgotten way-marks on the old straight track
To where there gleamed for him the beacons of a world sublime.

NAZCA LINES, THE BAND OF HOLES, CARNAC STONES

What is prehistory, after all, if not a time forgotten—a time for which we have no records? What is prehistory if not an epoch of impenetrable obscurity through which our ancestors passed but about which we have no conscious remembrance? It is almost as though we have awakened into the daylight of history from a long and troubled sleep, and yet continue to be disturbed by the faint but haunting echoes of our dreams....

Graham Hancock in *Fingerprints of the Gods*

The Haunting Echoes of Our Dreams

A few years ago, my wife and I decided to build a Lakota medicine wheel in the valley below our house. It took quite a few days and involved hauling a few hundred stones from various places on our property in order to form the circle and spokes of the outline. When we were finally finished we were very happy with the results and have spent many fulfilling hours there meditating, thinking, and simply being.

Sometime later a neighbor stopped over and looked at the finished product. Her comment was quite revealing. "Somebody has too much time on

A medicine wheel constructed by the author and his wife in South Carolina.

their hands!" She couldn't understand why we considered a project such as this worthy of the time and effort needed to build it. We couldn't explain it to her. She simply wouldn't have understood. Our motives were spiritual, not practical, and we had built features into it that were personally very meaningful. To us it was an important, worthwhile endeavor. To our friend it served no real purpose.

Her response was another form of the question we have asked throughout this book: "Why?" Why build a Stonehenge or a pyramid? Of what purpose is a Göbekli Tepe or a Sphinx? What motivated our ancient ancestors to construct projects that we would be hard-pressed to build today? What were they thinking? To most moderns, surrounded since birth by a material, objective-oriented society, such undertakings seem foreign. But to the people who invested hundreds of hours in their construction, there was obviously a very real purpose.

We are told that the people who built such things were primitives, forced to hunt, forage, or grow their daily sustenance.

> What motivated our ancient ancestors to construct projects that we would be hard-pressed to build today? What were they thinking?

Perhaps we have been told wrong.

Around the world stand monuments to an idea that we have forgotten. To our ancestors it was an important idea, perhaps a spiritual conviction similar to what motivated Barb and me to build our medicine wheel. We don't know for sure what it was, but we can plainly see that it meant something to those who built the mysterious structures. They must have had good reason.

Although we don't know what that reason was, let's consider three enigmatic construction projects that didn't involve transporting massive boulders. Any small group of ordinary people, if sufficiently motivated and given enough time, could have accomplished the finished product. The question is not "How?" The question now is "Why?"

The Nazca Lines

In the March 2010 *National Geographic* magazine, Stephen S. Hall wrote an article about the Nazca Lines of Peru titled "Spirits in the Sand." In it he attempted to respond to that question. His first paragraph began by describing the mysterious lines themselves:

> Since they became widely known in the late 1920s, when commercial air travel was introduced between Lima and the southern Peruvian city of Arequipa, the mysterious desert drawings known as the Nazca lines have puzzled archeologists, anthropologists,

and anyone fascinated by ancient cultures in the Americas. For just as long, waves of scientists—and amateurs—have inflicted various interpretations on the lines, as if they were the world's largest set of Rorschach inkblots. At one time or another, they have been explained as Inca roads, irrigation plans, images to be appreciated from primitive hot-air balloons, and, most laughably, landing strips for alien spacecraft.

Notice a few things right off the bat.

First, the lines depicting various animals, birds, human beings, and various other figures were really not noticed by anyone until the advent of air transportation. In other words, they were meant to be seen from the air. Indeed, it is only from the air that they can really be made out at all. There are no towers you can climb or nearby mountaintop refuges where a person can stand and take in the whole panorama. You have to fly over it, as Erich von Däniken did when he first introduced the Nazca Lines to the general public with the publication of his now famous, or infamous, depending on your point of view, *Chariots of the Gods*.

Second, Hall notes that the lines are puzzling, even to the professionals.

Third, he disparages such puzzlement by introducing the idea of Rorschach inkblots. Those are always good for a laugh.

Fourth, although he admits they were built by a very earthbound people to be seen from the sky, he dismisses any thoughts of ancient air transport, especially of the alien variety, as laughable.

As he continues, he does appreciate a possible spiritual component to the product:

> The parched desert and hillsides made an inviting canvas: By simply removing a layer of dark stones cluttering the ground, exposing the lighter sand beneath, the Nazca created markings that have endured for centuries in the dry climate. Archaeologists believe both the construction and maintenance of the lines were communal activities—"like building a cathedral."

He then proceeds to offer his own conclusions. They are practical, of course. He sees the whole Nazca project as an elaborate way to provide water to a parched, desert land, and the effigies as a way to placate various animistic deities who might be called on to help.

At the very end of the article, however, he returns to the mystical component:

> As my footsteps continued around the curves of the spiral, it occurred to me that one of the most important functions of the "mysterious" Nazca lines is no mystery at all. The geoglyphs sure-

The mysterious Nazca Lines only make sense when seen from high above, such as in this case when the lines clearly depict a monkey.

ly provided a kinetic, ritualistic reminder to the Nazca people that their fate was tied to their environment—its natural beauty, its ephemeral abundance, and its life-threatening austerity. You can read their reverence for nature, in times of plenty and in times of desperate want, in every line and curve they scratched onto the desert floor. When your feet inhabit their sacred space, even for a brief and humbling moment, you can feel it.

It is precisely here that I find myself most drawn to Hall's beautiful prose. He felt the wonder. That is obvious. As should we all. The Nazca Lines are a captivating mystery. They imply a lost history and hidden truths from a mysterious people whose motivation is now, and perhaps forever, lost in the mists of a forgotten time.

Why did they do it? We just don't know.

The Band of Holes

Near the Nazca Lines, on the very same plateau, some 6,900 holes have been carved into rock. They form a band about eight to ten holes wide and about a mile long across some of the most rugged terrain you would ever want to cross on foot. Each hole is about three feet wide and three to six feet deep. Sometimes they line up very precisely, but they often appear staggered, with seemingly no pattern at all.

When asked why they were first built and who made them, the current inhabitants of the area say they don't have the faintest idea. It was obviously a long, backbreaking job that, in some instances, seems to be unfinished.

Why did they do it? We just don't know.

The Carnac Stones

Halfway around the world from Peru, in Brittany, near the French village of Carnac, stand the famous Carnac Stones. There are more than three thousand of them. They have been marching across the countryside for at least four thousand years, and maybe much more. They are the largest collection of megalithic standing stones in the world, probably put there by pre-Celtic people, but no one has any idea at all why.

There are single stones and clusters. Geometric figures tantalize but are never quite obvious enough to form recognizable patterns. They begin and end with a stone circle but you could place eleven football fields between them. The largest stones would dwarf an average-sized person but the smaller ones could probably be moved by two or three people.

Why are they there? What was their purpose? Why did they do it? We just don't know.

Conclusions

The purpose of describing these mysterious building projects is this: They offer tantalizing hints into our forgotten past. Our ancestors were complex people. They were moved by forces and ideas that we have, to put it mildly, forgotten. We are a culture suffering from amnesia. We don't know who we are. As long as we keep busy playing with our latest handheld techno-gizmos we think we are at the pinnacle of the evolutionary ladder of success and all who came before us were primitive and uncivilized. But as we move forward into the twenty-first century, it is slowly beginning to dawn on us that everything may not be rosy up ahead. We are playing with dangerous toys. It wouldn't take much to wipe out our electrical infrastructure and cyber network. If that happens, our civilization, existing as it does in the pampered hothouse of assumed ecological independence, could fail in a very short time. The only ones who would be left are those who know how to exist independently of modern conveniences. We may be at the top of the food chain, but we are still a biological species like every other biological species, many of which have gone extinct because they couldn't learn how to cope.

The Carnac Stones in Brittany, France, are a collection of some three thousand megaliths placed in rows or in other formations by, most likely, the Celts.

People have come before us who have done amazing things. They had big ideas, built mysterious lines across the desert, dug enigmatic holes for who knows what purpose, and raised standing stones for reasons only they understood.

They are all gone, lost in the mists of time. When we're gone, will there be survivors who, thousands of years from now, wonder why we built the structures we did and how we went about our daily lives? Will they wonder what motivated us?

Let's not get too cocky. Maybe we need to learn from our past, rather than simply wrap it up in a conspiracy of silence.

The Problem of Rock Piles

Some of the Pharisees in the crowd said to Jesus, "Teacher, rebuke your disciples!" "I tell you," he replied, "If they keep quiet, the stones will cry out."

Luke 19:39, 40

Throughout the Southeast there exist, in just about every state, piles of stones that may or may not be considered mysterious, depending on your frame

Some Native American traditions speak of honoring warriors who died in battle by burying them beneath piles of stone and continuing the honor by throwing a new rock on a pile every time you passed one.

of mind. Even now, if I look up from my computer and glance out the window, I can see two of them in one direction, five in another, and rest secure in the knowledge that I can walk to a dozen more in less than five minutes. The traditional way of explaining them is to view them simply as mounds that early farmers made when they cleared their fields for agriculture. No doubt that explains many, if not most, of the piles. But it doesn't explain them all. That's the problem.

The earliest European people, who came into this country carrying with them the written word, wrote diaries. And they wrote about finding rock piles all over the place. When they asked the Native Americans about them, they got a curious reply. In some cases, it was a tribal tradition to pick up a small rock and toss it on a pile whenever you came to one, as a way of saying something that was beyond the ability of words to express. It might mean, "I was here."

It could be seen as an offering to some god or spirit who might be in a position to grant traveling mercies. Some Native American traditions speak of honoring warriors who died in battle by burying them beneath piles of stone and continuing the honor by throwing a new rock on a pile every time you passed one. Maybe it was just a superstition or habit. No one knew why, exactly. It was just something you did. A similar practice is often followed by hikers today.

But when Europeans asked who originally started the tradition, the Indians didn't know. In some cases, the piles were said to have been started by the Old Ones, long before people then alive came along.

This prompted some archeological digs in Georgia, one of which resulted in an article featured in the 1990 issue of *Early Georgia* (Volume 18), called "Historic Patterns of Rock Piling and the Rock Pile Problems," by Thomas H. Gresham. Gresham's excavation, it seems, turned up some ambiguous results. Some piles were considered modern. Others were deemed to be much older. But a few turned up artifacts that went back much further in time than was expected. Hence, the problem of rock piles. They refuse to be pigeon-holed and neatly filed away.

Digging to the Bottom

Although extensive archeology has yet to be done, a number of piles yield similar results when examined by amateur diggers—such as my wife and I. Because we live in an area that features quite a few mysterious rock piles, some of which certainly cannot be attributed to agriculture, we decided to look for ourselves to see if we could solve the problem. Without a lot of fanfare, we simply started to dig.

The first layer often seems to consist of large rocks, piled on top of one another roughly in the shape of a circle. Many are above ground. That might have been done by farmers clearing their land for grazing or even growing cotton. In some cases, these rocks might also be explained by reading local records about German prisoners during World War II, who were brought to the South and made to work for the U.S. Forest Service. They would clear rocks from fields and woods, piling them up for later use in construction projects or simply to get them out of the way, although in our area the old-timers tell us that didn't happen near where we live.

In the second layer, things start to get interesting. The deeper you go, the smaller the rocks become. One would think that rock piles for agricultural use would show just the opposite tendency. I've piled plenty of rocks in my time, and my custom usually involved starting with the big ones and gradually adding smaller stones as the pile grew taller. As a matter of fact, the location of the biggest rocks in the field would tend to mark where the piles would be in the first place. Why move the biggest rocks when you can just build around them?

This brings up another point—location. Many of the rock piles are found near the top of a hill, usually facing east toward the rising sun. Now, this might be because it doesn't make a lot of sense to roll rocks all the way down a hill if you're planning to use them later. You would probably want to just clear the part you might later be plowing. That's usually the top. But one can't help but notice that it can be very pleasant just to sit and admire the view from many rock piles. They can offer a very nice place to work.

Where the questions really begin is when you approach the bottom of a typical rock pile. Often the stones get smaller and smaller, until you begin to find a floor of rock chips that had obviously been worked by human crafters. Lithic debitage is the proper name. Stone debris. The implication seems to be that the Old Ones who made stone tools came to convenient places such as these in order to excavate their raw material, choosing a nice, comfortable place to work while they sliced, diced, and chipped the blanks into serviceable items.

There are a couple of reasons people create rock piles. One is to honor the dead; another, which is the case for this pile in Mongolia, is to mark a site for rituals by shamans.

A Theory of Rock Piles

From all this develops our admittedly unproven theory of rock piles, as it were. It begins thousands of years ago when the Ancient Ones found a source of good stone from which to quarry blanks for making the tools they depended on. It just seems to make sense that an ancient crafter would sit at a place with a nice view as his apprentices brought him raw material to work up. After many years and lots of trips back to the quarry, he would have built up quite a pile of rock chips. Later on, when one of his descendants, removed by perhaps thousands of years, came back to this traditional place, he might have developed the habit of throwing another rock on the growing pile, perhaps saying to himself something like, "same time next season," or "next year in Jerusalem," or something to that effect. After a while, it would become tradition, and later maybe even superstition. Layers of history would have been piled on, similar to customs carried out every Sunday in every church in America.

Then along came Europeans, completely ignorant of native traditions. All they saw was a pile of rocks. They wanted to clear this land to make it easier to work, but it was covered with stones.

"Let's clean them up."

"Sure, but where do you want to pile them?"

"How about over on this pile that's someone's already started?"

And so it went. Thousands of years later, we are faced with the problem of rock piles. Of such mysteries, archeological arguments are born and continue to fascinate.

A Heavenly Theory

But now the story takes quite a different turn. Recently we invited a surveyor friend of ours to use his high-tech gizmos to plot some of the enigmatic, ancient stone piles we have found in the course of our walks through the woods around our home. We were interested to see if there might be any lines or connections between them. After plotting them on a topographical map, they looked like the picture shown on the following page.

Of course, we were immediately intrigued. They formed a familiar icon. Although I've been an ordained minister all my adult life, I did not associate this pattern only with the Christian church. Every night at sundown we have been stepping outside to look at another cross, the Northern Cross—sometimes called the Christmas Cross—that stands high in the northwest sky in December. We were so taken with the similarity between our rock piles and what we observed in the heavens that we called up a constellation chart on our computer and printed out the results. When we overlaid them, one on top of the other, we were amazed!

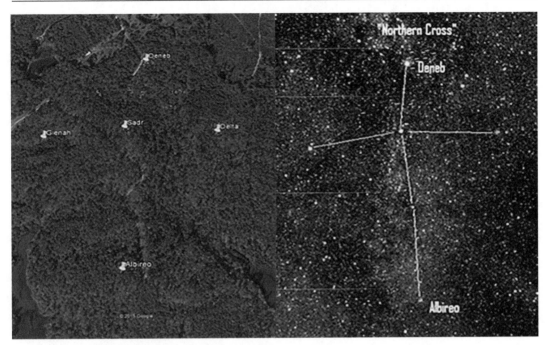

Comparing the location of five stone piles to the Northern Cross constellation reveals a striking similarity in the patterns.

The cross is an ancient symbol, predating the Roman/Christian connection. Its roots go back to the beginning of symbolic thought, picturing the marriage of heaven/Earth and male/female, all coming together at the heart. Could the Old Ones who used to live here have had this same thought and replicated the great mystery here in our back yard? If so, they predated in stone the meaning of the familiar prayer: Thy will be done on earth as it is in heaven. They also were in complete harmony with the ancient doctrine found from Egypt to Mesoamerica: As above, so below.

In the "Ancient Astronomers" chapter, when we discussed Cygnus and the Mysteries of the North Sky, we talked about the significance of the Northern Cross, which forms the basis of the constellation Cygnus, often referred to as the backbone of the Milky Way, the galaxy that contains our solar system. This was intriguing, to say the least. But when we thought about the fact that an obvious bird cult existed right across the Savannah River from us, as evidenced by the Eagle and Hawk Effigy Mounds found in nearby Georgia, we were excited, to say the least. In some cultures Cygnus is pictured as a swan. In others it is a hawk, eagle, or condor.

When we contacted Andrew Collins, a man who has done more work than anyone on the Cygnus mystery, we were led to read some of his work, which seemed to echo what we had found.

All this is circumstantial, to say the least. But it raises some interesting thoughts on a moonlit night as we gaze at the sky and ponder people who once lived in what is now our backyard.

STONE STRUCTURES AND ANCIENT TRANSPORTATION TECHNOLOGY

Few have traveled to the pyramids of Egypt and not wondered how an ancient civilization without modern technology could have constructed structures so large they can be viewed from space. Some have theorized they were built inside out. On the flakier side, some say aliens did it. Perhaps the most confounding mystery of all involves how incredibly large stones made their way to the middle of the desert without massive mechanical assistance. No camel, even the Egyptian kind, is that strong.

Terrence McCoy in the *Washington Post*: May 2, 2014

"It Was Simple, Really. All They Had to Do Was...."

Sometimes, when you weigh all the evidence and carefully consider all the latest scientific theories about something, the smallest detail trips you up. When I first entered the underground passageway of the Great Pyramid of Giza, battling claustrophobia all the way, I noticed the yards upon yards of electric wires that provided the power that lit up the way ahead. I looked up at the ceiling and saw that there was no smudging, no soot that would have certainly marked the passage of millions of people over thousands of years, carrying torches in those pre-electric epochs.

"How did they ever light this for the workers?" I asked my guide.

He quickly looked away. His very body language, as he moved forward down the passage, spoke volumes. He didn't want to answer.

"They must have had some source of light," he said.

The conspiracy of silence enveloped us. And I have never since received an adequate answer to my question.

Since then I find that I am forced to take all the patronizing explanations of the Egyptologists with a grain of salt.

Did the early Egyptians build these great mysterious structures? Of course they did! But when? How did they develop the construction techniques, seemingly overnight? Who lit the way out of, or maybe into, their darkness? Those are the real questions, aren't they?

The same kind of thing happened when I visited Stonehenge. I had studied and studied in preparation for my trip, wanting to be thoroughly prepped for what I was going to see. As I stood there in awe, I heard a tourist next to me ask her companion the question that was also in the front of my mind.

"How did they do it?"

Having sat next to these two in the bus on the way up from the Visitor Centre and listened to their conversation about what lay before us, thus knowing that her companion had probably watched a lot of television, I cringed, waiting for the answer. He didn't disappoint.

"It was simple. All they did was...." And he then proceeded to parrot a theory of someone who had probably never been there.

The point is that there's nothing simple about ancient megalithic structures and no one, no one at all, really knows how the Old Ones built them. There are theories galore, of course. Some of them may even be true. But they don't explain everything. Not by a long shot!

Unless the ancients had a technology that is way beyond anything we can imagine, to move gigantic stones miles across the countryside was a momentous project. It must have required a huge work force.

Anthropologists can and often do work their magic to estimate what the population of a particular area was during any given epoch. They jot down figures that seem to point to a specific number big enough to do the job. But that doesn't answer the question. Even if a work force of sufficient size might have existed, it doesn't mean that everyone present at the time would have wanted to commit themselves to years and years of backbreaking labor.

It's not as though they needed a job. Their economy wasn't dependent on money-for-goods as ours is. Certainly quite a few people must have considered the whole project silly and gone off to hunt or gather or grow their own food rather than devote their health and welfare to constructing something of megalithic size, whatever their priests threatened them with.

> Since then I find that I am forced to take all the patronizing explanations of the Egyptologists with a grain of salt.

And what if a sufficient work force could be found and properly motivated? They were busy all day working. How did they get fed? What about disease in the camp? How did supplies get provided?

All these questions are answerable. Obviously the structures got built. They must have found a way. But it wasn't simple by any means.

A team of modern volunteers can get together for a week or two, cut out and transport a huge stone for a ways, and struggle it into position. Then

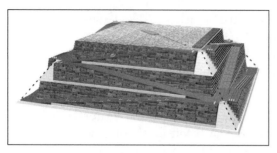

Archeologists have long debated how the pyramids were built. In this illustration, it is proposed that a series of ramps—and a lot of muscle—were used to move stone blocks weighing several tons each.

the leader of the team says, "There! That's how the old timers did it!" They all clap their hands and go home, thinking the problem solved. "We've proved it!"

But what have they done? They've raised one stone. Could they be convinced to spend their lives doing it again … and again … and again…. for a period of years, decades, or even centuries? I doubt it.

Here's where the mystery comes in. The Ancient Ones did it! Barring help from alien beings, they actually accomplished it. The proof stands before our very eyes. They placed megaton blocks of stone so closely together that even today, thousands of years later, we can't fit a playing card between them. They erected monoliths that we couldn't raise without a construction crane. They figured and engineered and plumbed and raised walls so exactly that their work continues to confound us. And they did it all over the world, on almost every continent, in a past so distant that we can't even tell exactly when it happened.

Despite all this, we continue to call them our primitive ancestors!

Rather than bluff our way through the mystery, rather than try to pretend to be smarter than we are, rather than attempt to protect our professional reputations with published nonsense, maybe it's better to give the only answer we know to be the correct one.

How did they do it? We just don't know!

The Mists of the Past

How can we know who we are if we don't know where we come from? It is clear from many fragments of evidence, traditions and lore that we have an incomplete picture of the earliest days of human civilization. It's possible that whole civilizations, some with advanced technology, have come and gone. At the very least, human culture reaches much further back in time than conventional history admits. There are many mysteries in our ancient past, but there may be clues to that past around the world in the form of sunken cities, ancient structures, cryptic hieroglyphics, artwork and more.

Stephen Wagner

The human story we have been taught suffers from a severe case of split personality. On the one hand, we are fed pictures of brutish-looking ancestors from whom we are descended. They grunt and stoop, are musclebound and hairy. They carry primitive clubs and spears and live in caves. On the other, we are shown pictures of indescribable stone monuments and sophisticated cities, proving that our ancestors accomplished mysterious and awe-inspiring feats of mental gymnastics while inventing and improving their lot every day.

We are told that the only thing separating one picture from the other is time. A long time ago we were primitive, then we learned to be sophisticated.

The trouble with that explanation, however, is that many of the breakthroughs and ingenious building projects of the past took place so long ago that they seem to overlap with the so-called primitive stage. There seems to be an insufficient amount of time in the story to make the prodigious leaps of evolution needed to move from one stage to the next.

At the beginning of this chapter we said we were going to look for clues. We were going to search through the written word, so we considered evidence in ancient maps, possibly the Bible code, and finally the I Ching and the binary code.

Our next search area led to the hidden landscape around us, both the things we could see and the things we could feel. We looked at Ley Lines, Nazca Lines, the Band of Holes, and the ancient and mysterious Carnac Stones of Brittany.

Finally, we turned to the obvious and unarguable structures left behind by the Ancient Ones at places such as Easter Island. We considered the possible cosmic implications of the problem of rock piles in America's southeast and considered the inherent problems associated with stone structures and ancient transportation technology of so-called primitive man.

When all is said and done, every one of these considerations gave us clues about the past but left unresolved the real questions we want to ask. The hows and whys hang in the air and leave us, ultimately, unsatisfied. Is there no way to delve more deeply into the areas we really want to answer? A carved rock offers proof of a carver, but what was he thinking when he carved it? A stone wall stands as testament to ancient builders, but why did they build it in the fashion they did?

Ultimately, if we want explanations, we need to talk to the Old Ones. Or at least listen. And in the stories they told, the myths and legends they passed down, we can do just that.

When we read ancient mythology, we are not just reading words. We are hearing oral stories that were passed down from generation to generation before they finally made it to paper or parchment. That's where we'll go next.

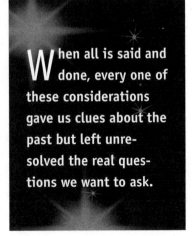

When all is said and done, every one of these considerations gave us clues about the past but left unresolved the real questions we want to ask.

But before we do, keep in mind some of the clues we've discovered. They stand like islands above the waves of the ocean of time. They tell us to look for something bigger underneath that is supporting the visible reality of stone and rock we view above ground. As big and mysterious as stone structures are, the myths and legends upon which they stand may be even bigger. That's where we might begin to find explanations.

The journey continues.

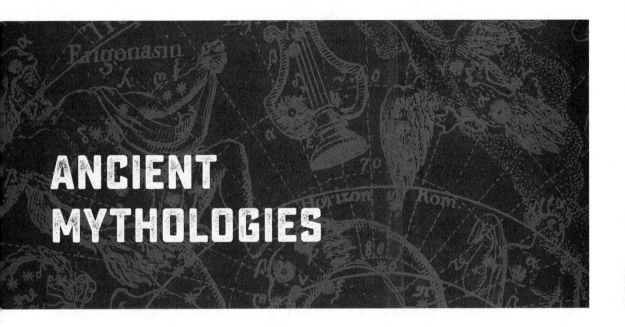

ANCIENT MYTHOLOGIES

Myths are clues to the spiritual potentialities of the human life.

Joseph Campbell

What we're learning in our schools is not the wisdom of life. We're learning technologies, we're getting information. There's a curious reluctance on the part of faculties to indicate the life values of their subjects. In our sciences today there is a tendency to specialization.... Specialization tends to limit the field of problems the specialist is concerned with.

Joseph Campbell in *The Power of Myth*

The Power of Myth

Quite a few years ago, I spent the better part of a year renovating a New England house that I knew was almost two hundred years old. I found evidence for antiquity in the main structure when I discovered hand-hewn timbers and cut nails. Then, as I took apart a wall in one added-on wing, I discovered a local newspaper somebody had tacked to the wall. It bore a date of 1942. I decided to play along so I tacked a modern newspaper right next to it before I covered it with insulation and wallboard.

All I could think of was the conclusions that would be drawn by some future archeologist who might excavate here someday. Depending on what he uncovered first he might place a construction date in the nineteenth century, the twentieth century or the twenty-first century.

I wondered if that's what happened in places like the pyramids of Giza. We find evidence of a construction crew working in the time of the fourth dynasty and determine that's when the original pyramid was built, when in reality it might have stood there for millennia before they started their renovation work.

I began to wonder as well if there was a better way to learn the secrets of the vintage house I was working on, so I decided to go to the trouble of calling on some of the old timers in town who had lived through a good part of this house's history. They had seen it unfold. As young people they, in turn, had heard stories themselves.

It led to some fascinating discussions. One wonderful old man, who died shortly after our talk, told me about secret meetings of the Ku Klux Klan that had been held in the basement of this very house. I was shocked. None of that was ever recorded in the town histories. Yet I believed every word he said. After all, history is often written, in part, by those who want to put a nice sheen on the past. No local historian would want to glorify in print an ugly chapter of the town's past. The man I talked to, on the other hand, was about to die. He had nothing to hide. He simply related to me what he had seen and heard firsthand.

A few years later, when I related this story to some local friends, they refused to believe it. "He was just an old codger who liked to hear himself talk!" was their response. "There's no proof that the KKK ever had a chapter in our town!"

They wouldn't even consider such a thing because it didn't fit in with their preconceptions about the past. It would have meant changing their entire mental picture of what their politically correct, liberal Massachusetts town had been like. They would have had to rewrite their mental history books.

Since then I have had a chance to talk to others who had heard the same things I had when I talked to the old-timers in town. Many times what they had heard was second- or even third-hand, but the stories concurred.

In the same way, a culture's myths may challenge our preconceptions about the past. But are myths simply stories told by "old codgers who like to hear themselves talk?" Maybe not. Maybe at least some of them are real stories passed along by those who were eyewitnesses to history.

Confirming the Stories

"But where is the material evidence?" you say. "How can you form a theory based on hearsay and old stories?"

Let me illustrate with this one example. In 1705 a Dutch tenant farmer discovered a five-pound mammoth tooth in the Hudson River Valley. He promptly traded it to a local politician for a glass of rum. The politician eventually sent it off on a long trip to London where it was tentatively identified as coming from an elephant. Up to then, no one had heard of mammoths. Even dinosaurs wouldn't be acknowledged for another hundred years. Any mammoth or mastodon bones found before then were said to be bones of giants because the book of Genesis said "there were giants in the earth" in the days before Noah's flood. No one believed an extinct species of such a giant animal could exist in America. If someone had suggested such a thing he would have been asked to show some evidence. "All you've got is one bone! Show me some proof!"

This despite the fact that the American Indian tribes in the area had myths galore that described elephant-like creatures with long noses and gigantic tusks. No one believed them, of course. "After all," went the thinking, "these were just stories told around the campfire by a bunch of heathens. What do they know?"

A fossilized mammoth tooth like this one was discovered in 1705 by a Dutch farmer in the Hudson Valley. At the time, no one knew these relatives of modern elephants had existed.

But the ancestors of these Indians were there when mammoths roamed the land. They hunted them. They had mammoth steaks for dinner. And they told their children, who told their children. If the white settlers of New York had simply listened to the myths they would have known right away what mammoth bones were. But they ignored the evidence. It took another hundred years before they started to believe the old Indians might know what they were talking about.

Insight and Historical Reality

When the themes of a myth are found universally in cultures spaced far and wide around the globe, could it be that they are valuable insights that should command our attention? Are they just as important as clues dug up, dusted off, and classified in a museum display?

In one sense they might be even more informative than museum displays. Myths are alive. They speak volumes about the storyteller. They contain flesh-and-blood insights and sometimes offer their own explanations and descriptions. They involve us in a personal way.

Take the mythology of Noah's flood, for instance. On any given weekend, someone, somewhere, delivers a sermon, homily, or classroom teaching about it. People constantly derive ethical or moral insights and draw conclusions from it concerning how to live in today's world. They even recently made a high budget movie about it.

Yet the story of Noah's flood is not just a Bible story. It is a myth that appears in virtually every culture that exists around the world. The insights derived from it are far more important than simply finding proof that a boat is stranded somewhere on Mt. Ararat. The story talks about good and evil, right and wrong. That's why it has survived. If a lost culture wanted to pass on its values to future generations who might have forgotten how to speak the language, it could not have invented a better method of communication than a good, gripping story such as the one about the world ending in a deluge.

> Yet the story of Noah's flood is not just a Bible story. It is a myth that appears in virtually every culture that exists around the world.

But those lessons, important as they are, could very well be grounded in someone's real experience. The story, it would seem, is based almost certainly in an historical event, a great catastrophe. One very real message from the myth has to be that if it happened once, it can happen again. If the original authors of the myth believed the catastrophe came about because of human endeavors, whether or not they were couched in sinful or bad behavior, the lesson was simple: "Shape up! It happened to us. It can happen to you!"

All this is to say that mythology is important on many levels. Yes, the old myths still teach us wisdom today, offering clues about how to live. In that sense, they are very important. But they may also speak about real history that was witnessed by someone who wanted his or her insights passed on for a reason.

"History repeats itself," we are often told. Maybe so. But that doesn't mean it has to. Maybe it only repeats itself when we fail to learn from it. And the best way to learn is to listen to the myths. Listen and learn!

A Change of Format

Up to now in this book we have proceeded, for the most part, alphabetically for the sake of convenience. In this chapter we're going to change that format.

First, let's remember the premise we proposed back in the Introduction. We called it a radical concept:

> This book proposes a rather radical concept for us to consider. We, the current ruling species on the planet, have indeed suf-

fered a catastrophic accident. Maybe several. We are not the first civilization to come down the pike. We have developed cultural amnesia. What we call the beginning is really a new beginning, built on the ruins of what came before.

What we're going to do next is divide those questions into their component parts and then examine some ancient myths to see if we can find, hidden in these wonderful stories of old, hints that reveal this theory, step by step. Beginning with the golden age of the gods, we will follow their history as they fall from grace, face the end of all they hold dear, and then become the architects of a new civilization. For these heroic efforts they were, long after they had passed from this earthly scene, awarded the title of ancient gods.

Although we will examine myths from many different cultures, we're going to use as our framework the most well-known myth of all found in the book of Genesis. The reason for this is that there are 3.8 billion Christians and Muslims, and another 14 million Jews, in the world today (almost half the world's population) who have studied, heard about, read about, or at least are generally aware of this story. All of them use the Bible as either their primary or secondary source when it comes to understanding their religion. If we can find evidence for our theory here, buried deep within one of the most revered books in the world, it will go a long way toward proving our point.

Shaping the Myth

Before we begin it might be a good idea to restate the theory as it stands in both historical research and myth.

The science of anthropology, in its study of the great painted caves of Europe, holds that modern humans are, at the very least, some 40,000 to 50,000 years old when it comes to their concept of symbolic, or religious, thought. Anatomically they go back almost 200,000 years. What that means is that our ancestors who lived within these timeframes had brains as big as ours and thought much the same way we do. The weather of planet Earth was gradually getting better as it emerged from a series of ice advances that were slow but steady. Thirteen thousand years ago temperatures were warmer and wetter than they are now. A number of identifiable cultures existed during this time, among them the Solutreans of southwestern Europe and the Clovis of America.

The sciences of astrology and geology hold that 12,800 years ago everything changed. The facts now seem to favor a segmented comet impact across North America and Europe that struck with deadly force, igniting continent-wide fires while throwing enough dust and debris into the atmosphere to block out the sun, causing an ecological winter. It suddenly brought about a return of Ice Age conditions that is called the Younger Dryas, which lasted for more than a thousand years. The entire world was plunged back into a severe Ice

Age that was dry, cold, and devastating both to the human survivors who witnessed it and the megafauna who filled the earth at that time. Most of them didn't make it and many species went extinct.

The Younger Dryas ended abruptly 11,600 years ago. No one really knows why, but its effect was nearly as catastrophic as the comet event that began it. The ice sheets melted rapidly and caused severe flooding all over the world.

All this is part of the scientific record. There is no speculation involved. We can read the story in the rocks and landscape, using tools acceptable to scientists everywhere. We can thus think of the Younger Dryas as one epoch, beginning and ending with catastrophic events—first fire, then ice, and finally flood.

The concluding floods of 11,600 years ago, along with the disappearance of the megafauna, is well documented in the myths of many cultures. There were people alive who witnessed it all and remembered. They passed on

The biblical flood recorded in Genesis is also part of the oral and written histories of cultures around the world (1845 illustration based on an artwork by Nicolas Poussin).

the history in myth and legend to their children. These myths were later recorded and we can read about them today.

What interests us now, however, is what else the stories record. There seems to be a universal memory of a people who were extraordinarily advanced for this time whose parent culture and homeland apparently were nearly destroyed by the events of 12,800 years ago and then rocked again 11,600 years ago. It was a one-two punch of devastating effect. But they seem to have built a great body of knowledge during the 1,200 years between the beginning and end of the Younger Dryas Ice Age. Most of this consisted of the civilized arts of astronomy, construction techniques, writing, ethics, and other forms of knowledge, the spread of which may have been directly related to the fact that they understood the nature of what had happened to them and wanted to pass on this information as a warning to future generations who might someday have to face the same thing.

Only this can explain how cultures such as those found at Göbekli Tepe, Egypt, Sumer, Lebanon, Peru, and Mexico could have so suddenly arrived on the scene fully mapped out, so to speak. There was no warmup, no practice. One day those areas were inhabited by stone age people, struggling to survive. The next those same people had seemingly developed fully-evolved cultures with sophisticated building techniques, written languages, agriculture, and complex mathematical systems capable of following such difficult subjects as details relating to astronomical precession.

It's important to reiterate this, however. Proof of a cataclysmic Younger Dryas extinction event does not constitute proof that an advanced culture existed. All it proves is that if such a culture did exist, it might have been the instrument of its destruction.

The myths seem to say such a civilization existed. Yes, there are also archeological clues in what they left behind. But as of now, this is simply a theory that proposes to reconcile mysterious ancient structures with the claims of mythology.

If all this is so, our civilization is not necessarily the first. Who might these Ice Age Old Ones have been? What did they know? What did they want to pass on to us? This is how our ancestors remembered them.

Stories of the Golden Age of the Gods

Hesiod had recorded a past Golden Age when life had been gracious in communal fraternity and joyful in peace, when human beings and animals spoke the same language, when death had followed on sleep, without old age or disease, and after death men had moved as good daimones or genii over the lands. Pindar, three hundred years after Hesiod, had confirmed the existence of the Islands of the Blest, where the good led a blameless, tearless, life. Plato the same, with further references to the fabled island of Atlantis; the Egyptians believed in a former golden age under the god Râ to which they looked back with regret and envy; the Persians had a garden of Eden similar to that of the Hebrews; the Greeks a garden of the Hesperides, in which dwelt the serpent whose head was ultimately crushed beneath the heel of Hercules; and so on. The references to a supposed far-back state of peace and happiness are indeed numerous.

Myths of the Golden Age:
http://www.sacred-texts.com/cla/pcc/pcc10.htm

Eden

God saw all that he had made, and it was very good.

Genesis 1:31

There seems to be a universal agreement among the ancient myths that things were better back in the old days. The really old days, that is. The Pima Indians have the Creator saying, "Thus I make the world. And lo! The world is good!" In the Hindu Upanishads God says, "I indeed, I am this Creation." The Sumerian *Dilmun* is an earthly paradise that was "virginal, pristine and pure." In the Vedic *Puranas* we are told that "with each breath, countless universes emanate from Vishnu in seed-like forms that expand. Then Vishnu … enters into each universe."

Curiously, a common feature found almost everywhere is that humans and animals could talk to one another, and that this is how the animals received their names. It seems that Dr. Dolittle wasn't the first to make this wish:

If I could talk to the animals, just imagine it….
What a neat achievement it would be…."

"Talk to the Animals" from *Dr. Dolittle*: Bricusse, Leslie

Bulfinch's Mythology, the classic go-to in all matters mythological, speculates that early people were:

… in close contact with Nature and in that degree of sympathy with and understanding of the Animals which led to the establishment of the Totem system.

In Genesis, God brings the animals to Adam one by one and he names them all.

The Bassari people of West Africa tell us that:

Unumbotte made an antelope, named Antelope … and a snake, named Snake.

And so on and so on.

What does all this mean?

We can speculate that the myths remember a time when human beings lived closer to nature—in other words, when they were hunter-gatherers, only about one half-step removed from the world of animals themselves.

In Eden, man and woman were one with each other, one with nature, and one with God. Isaiah had this in mind when he pictured a future day when:

The wolf will live with the lamb … the calf and lion and the yearling together, and a little child shall lead them. They will neither harm nor destroy.…

Isaiah 11:6–9

Do we need to read this literally? Did humans and animals once speak the same language?

Of course not. For one thing, they don't share the same vocal chords. But humans apparently felt closer to nature before they began to clear fields, build cities, and separate themselves.

When I read the myths of a Golden Age from around the world, it's helpful to remember my own Golden Age. When I was young, summers always featured beautiful weather. Every afternoon playing with my friends lasted about a week and a half. President Eisenhower was on duty to keep the greatest nation in the world free and prosperous. Politicians could be trusted. Rain was always soft, television programs were better than anything we have now, and no one was ever sick or in danger. Even snow was fun rather than dangerous.

In other words, myths always filter out the bad stuff, and the older they are, the thicker the filter.

In Genesis and other creation myths, humans are able to communicate with the animals.

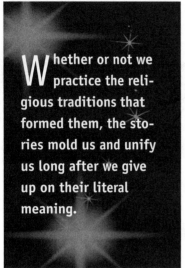

Whether or not we practice the religious traditions that formed them, the stories mold us and unify us long after we give up on their literal meaning.

As for talking to the animals, I'm sure that when people lived to follow the herds they hunted, they felt much closer to them and more comfortable in their surroundings. They probably even did communicate a little. American Indian myths tell of shamans calling or dreaming animals into the snares of the hunters.

Our dog, Rocky, is a valuable part of our family and we talk to him all the time. He goes everywhere with us and knows that when we reach for the car keys he's in for an adventure. On the rare occasions that he has to stay home, all it takes is a quiet "not this time" from us and he visibly droops, drops his head and tail, looks at us with a totally dejected face, and slumps his way beneath the porch. If that isn't "talking to the animals," I don't know what is. I'm sure our ancient ancestors felt the same kind of communication with the animals that gave them everything they needed to survive, shared companionship, provided the necessities of clothes and shelter, and offered themselves up for food.

All this is to say that the myths seem to remember a time before things changed. That is to be expected. What's fascinating, though, is what happened when times did change. Twelve thousand eight hundred years ago they changed drastically. The myths remember that time. They also tell us how the people felt about it. The world they shared with their animal envoys was devastated. Many of their loved ones perished. Many of the species they hunted went extinct. They felt it deeply.

In short, they felt it was somehow their fault. How had this terrible catastrophe come to pass?

And so they began to tell their stories.

The Serpent Myth

It began, you will perhaps remember from your earliest religious education, with a serpent. Eve and the apple is a classic, foundational myth of our culture. Not that we literally believe that humankind fell into sin because of a talking snake. Very few folks today believe that was a historical event.

It's just that we all know the story. That's the power of mythology! Whether or not we practice the religious traditions that formed them, the stories mold us and unify us long after we give up on their literal meaning. I doubt that there is a person in the western hemisphere, and, thanks to the *Harry Potter* movies, very few in the world, who do not recognize the fact that, according to western thought, serpents represent temptation and evil.

Where did this idea come from?

In Genesis a talking serpent, back in the days when people could presumably talk to the animals, seduced humans by telling them that if they disobeyed God then they, too, could be like gods.

When Eve ate the apple, it was the end of an era. Humankind lost Eden and all it represented. Unity between people, between people and nature, and between people and God, was lost. We started to till the soil by the sweat of our brow. We became agriculturists. The Neolithic revolution had begun. The first city was soon to be built. It's all told in just the first three chapters of the Bible.

And all because of a serpent. Is there more to this story than meets the eye?

THE FALL

One thing that comes out in myths is that at the bottom of the abyss comes the voice of salvation. The black moment is the moment when the real message of transformation is going to come. At the darkest moment comes the light.

Joseph Campbell in *The Power of Myth*

Out of Eden

God placed on the east side of Eden cherubim and a flaming sword flashing back and forth....

Genesis 3:24

According to the Bible, the eldest child of our first parents started a new culture, a new religion, and rejected the old ways. It happened like this.

Adam and Eve had two children, Cain and Abel. Abel was a humble follower of sheep. He was a pastoralist, following the herds from place to place. He was old school. He was free.

This didn't fit Cain's scheme. Cain symbolizes the beginning of the Agricultural Revolution. He was both a gardener and a builder of cities. He couldn't have Abel's ilk wandering around an open range better suited for crops and towns. So Cain killed Abel. The agriculturist killed the pastoralist. In doing so, he and his fellow farmers sent humankind off on a totally new route. Gone was the goddess, Mother Earth. Gone was the freedom of new

In the Bible, Cain kills his brother, Abel, out of jealousy; this might be interpreted as the defeat of the pastoralist by the agriculturist in human history.

horizons and wandering tribes. Instead, the female goddess morphed into the male God. Tribes settled down, planted crops, invented specialized occupations with unions, built walls and screened-in porches, moved indoors and invented computers with lovely, pastoral scenes as screen savers to remind them of an age gone by. It's all in Genesis, Chapter 4.

In a slightly different form, this story is repeated a few books of the Bible later. In the Old Testament book of Numbers 21, the people of Israel, having escaped from Egypt, are wandering around in the Sinai desert in the midst of their forty-year trek to the Promised Land. In the previous chapter, Aaron, the High Priest of the new religion, died. Obviously things must have been in a bit of religious upheaval. The people are complaining about their lot in life and looking for answers. "Why have you brought us up out of Egypt to die in the desert? There is no bread! There is no water!"

Once again we find them looking for an old religion to pull them back to the good old days.

The Lord is pretty upset about this whining, so He "sent venomous snakes among them; they bit the people and many Israelites died."

Moses, of course, has a real public relations problem on his hands, to say nothing of a community-wide epidemic. So he heads off up the mountain to talk to God and comes down with a rather radical idea. He tells the people to make an image. He has them make a bronze serpent and put it on a pole in the middle of the camp. From that time on, whenever anyone was bitten by a serpent he had only to look at the image and he lived.

(The story, though unknown and unread by most people, lives on. Next time you go to your doctor's office check out his diploma hanging on the wall. You'll find it stamped with an image of a serpent wound around a pole. If you don't find it, by the way, you'd better find a different doctor!)

So what's going on here? Is this the same God who commanded the people in the Ten Commandments, the very same carved stone tablets that they were presently carrying around with them in the Ark of the Covenant, not to make any graven images? If this is strictly a historical religious text, why would God urge the people to do the very thing he had just forbidden them to do a few pages earlier?

But what if this story, instead of being a document that describes actual history literally, is instead oral mythology, remembering a time when serpent imagery represented the religious hope of the people? What if it records a revival of the spirituality that nourished and supported people worldwide—that sustained them before the Agricultural Revolution that began at the end, the very end, of the Younger Dryas epoch? Indeed, what if the serpent myths are stories that describe the beginning of the Younger Dryas epoch itself? Then things begin to fall into place.

The Fiery Serpent

Myths from around the world feature the comet, the fiery "serpent" that changed everything so drastically 12,800 years ago.

In Genesis he is the "cherubim (with) a flaming sword, flashing back and forth...."

Earlier we looked at the Edfu texts of Egypt. They told the story of a wandering group of people from an advanced culture, or, in the words of the texts, ancient gods, who came to Egypt bringing the gift of civilization. Theirs, you will remember, had been wiped out by a cosmic catastrophe. Their homeland had been suddenly eradicated and they had considered it their obligation and quest to rebuild it on Earth. One of the places they had landed was Egypt.

What was their mission? In the words of the Edfu texts, it was to ...

... bring about the resurrection of the former world of the gods
... to recreate a destroyed world.

In their words, how did they describe what had happened to their homeland? It was destroyed, they claimed, by an enemy they identified as a serpent. They also called it the Great Leaping One. According to the pyramid myths, the attack by the serpent from above inundated their civilization, which had been located on an island, the location of which is a mystery. It killed almost all the inhabitants except for those lucky few who were off on business trips, sailing around the world. This all took place in an early age.

Serpent Religion

Let's assume the myths are garbled versions of a historical event, written down hundreds, probably even thousands, of years after it had occurred. The survivors of the attack by the serpent could very well have carried that

> If, as in Genesis, the serpent was identified with a punishment that humans deserved because of their hubris, they might have even formed a serpent cult.

image with them wherever they went. If, as in Genesis, the serpent was identified with a punishment that humans deserved because of their hubris, they might have even formed a serpent cult.

Cult, we recognize, is the root of the word culture. In other words, a religious culture formed around the cult. Its mythology, found all over the world today in monotheistic religions, is familiar:

- Humans once existed in harmony with nature.
- Humans, through their hubris, brought destruction upon themselves.
- This destruction was associated with the work of a serpent.
- The end came in the form of fire from above, or fire wielded by cherubim that prevented a return to paradise.

Was this the religion of the architects of civilization, the survivors of the comet strike 12,800 years ago? Did it inform the building of places such as Göbekli Tepe, Sumer, and the Pyramids of Giza, where serpent images abound? Were those places intended to be the centers of the rebuilt civilization?

It's possible that the religion flourished even as far away as Mexico. Earlier, in a discussion about capturing the sun at Newgrange, we noted:

> On the day of the equinox, Kukulkan, the plumed serpent, is seen descending sinuously down the steps of the pyramid at Chichen Itza [in Mexico]. The mystery of sun and shade perfectly captures the image of the god descending from the heavens to Earth.

This might very well be a picture of the descending serpent that once destroyed an advanced culture which, in what is now Mexico, sowed the seeds of civilization after its own destruction.

The Myths Continue

Apparently this old religion lived on for quite some time. In II Kings 18:4, the Bible tells us that long after Moses, Samuel, Saul, David, and Solomon had lived and died, the people were still worshipping the image of a serpent. The practice was so prevalent that during a Jewish revival under King Hezekiah:

> He [Hezekiah] removed the high places [where the people had erected standing stones for altars], smashed the sacred stones and cut down the Asherah [the name of the goddess] poles [these were the precursors to maypoles]. He broke into pieces the

bronze snake Moses had made, for up to that time the Israelites had been burning incense to it.

Thus, according to this account, the traditional Jewish scribes who wrote the Old Testament finally killed off the old religion that was prevalent before the fall.

Or did they? There is some evidence that later Christian writers had to deal with the same issue. They did it in the same way they dealt with other pagan rituals. They simply baptized the tradition. In the most revered text of Christendom, John 3:14, we read how they did it:

"You must be born again," says Jesus.

"What does that mean?" asks Nicodemus.

"As Moses lifted up the serpent in the wilderness," replies Jesus, "so the Son of man must be lifted up."

Do you see what just happened? The old religion from before the Fall was still being practiced by some of the common folks. It refused to die. So its central core was made to symbolize the new religion of Christianity. The ser-

pent on the pole became Christ on the cross. It was brilliant! It worked so well, the church made a practice of it.

And their M.O. continued well into the Christian era when the old religion, the religion of the serpent, was still fresh in the minds even of those who had found spirituality in the vibes of a new religion. The Gospel writers recognized the need to further drive out what had by now become pagan practices. One author, for instance, in the Gospel of Mark 16:18, foresaw the day when those who practiced the new religion of the resurrected Jesus wouldn't be able to resist the old ways. "They will pick up snakes with their hands," he declared.

And so it was that legends are born. For when Christianity entered the serpent's holy Celtic stronghold, the last holdout of the old ways, the old-timers were apt to say, "Sure and wasn't it the great Saint Patrick himself who drove out the snakes from the fair Emerald Isle, crushed the serpent's head and ushered in the new faith?"

The symbol of the serpent on the pole was transformed into the Savior on the Cross by Christianity.

STORIES OF THE END

> The Lord saw how great man's wickedness on the earth had become ... and was grieved.... So the Lord said, "I will wipe mankind ... from the face of the earth."
>
> Genesis 6:5–7

The End of an Epoch

Earlier we said that the Younger Dryas epoch needed to be seen as a whole. It began with a comet 12,800 years ago, catapulting the earth back into an extreme ice age. It came with fire, smoke, and ashes. It brought about the extinction of whole species of both flora and fauna. It almost destroyed humans, as well. But some survived.

At the Topper archeological site in South Carolina, Dr. Albert Goodyear, supervising archeologist at the dig, found evidence of the antecedents of the Clovis culture going back at least 35,000, and maybe even 50,000 years. But there came a definite break in the strata that marks the beginning of the Younger Dryas and the end of the Clovis culture. People suddenly disappear from the archeological record. They don't come back for more than a thousand years.

What happened?

His answer is that the Clovis Comet happened. It brought to an end a long and flourishing culture, either of Asian or Solutrean ancestry, and ushered in an age of ice, cold, and extinction. When the earth rebounded, people came back as well. After the calamity they had probably migrated west and south, there to merge with other cultures that had, in the interim, crossed into America on foot by way of the Beringia land bridge.

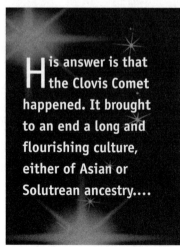

His answer is that the Clovis Comet happened. It brought to an end a long and flourishing culture, either of Asian or Solutrean ancestry....

But the Younger Dryas finished as spectacularly as it began. No one knows why, but it ended suddenly, accompanied by worldwide floods and inundations that are remembered today in thousands of flood myths. Perhaps the world simply rebounded from its abnormal conditions. Perhaps the planet reentered the comet stream and was again hit by fragments of the same comet, this time in Earth's oceans, where it threw up great plumes of warm water clouds into the atmosphere, bringing about drastic global warming and the accompanying sudden meltdown of the ice sheets.

We don't know why it happened, but it apparently made quite an impression on people, because flood myths form what might very well be the principle mythology found around the world.

We've already talked about Noah and Gilgamesh. We've quoted a few Hopi, Mexican, Peruvian, and indigenous American flood myths. There is no escaping it. Flood myths are universal.

We could list them all, but it would be far easier and more dramatic if you read them for yourself. Simply Google "flood myths" or "deluge myths." Beginning with the venerable Wikipedia listings (which everyone disparages but secretly go to first) you will find days' and days' worth of reading.

> The Younger Dryas Ice Age went out with a bang. And right after it ended, our civilization began at Göbekli Tepe about 11,600 years ago.

They will convince you of one thing. The Younger Dryas Ice Age went out with a bang. And right after it ended, our civilization began at Göbekli Tepe about 11,600 years ago. That's where we developed agriculture, megalithic building techniques, readin,' writin,' and 'rithmatic. It then moved southeast, between the Tigris and Euphrates, downstream to Sumer, and southwest to Egypt. It traveled to England and quite possibly across the Atlantic to the Americas. Five thousand years later it burst forth into the light almost everywhere we care to look.

Was it simply time for this to happen? Did human cultures everywhere, in a very short time span, all come up with the idea of civilization on their own? Or did they have help? That's the strategic question, isn't it?

In this book we've been operating under the assumption that they had help—that there was an ancient, forgotten civilization that managed to survive the one-two punch at the beginning and end of the Younger Dryas. If that's so, do we know anything about who this mysterious race was?

According to the myths, we do. We might even know some of their names.

ANCIENT GODS AND ANGELS: THE ARCHITECTS OF CIVILIZATION

As for you, be fruitful and increase in number; multiply on the earth and increase upon it.

Genesis 9:7

The Gods Set Forth

We are operating under the assumption that some myths tell real stories, however garbled they might have become over the centuries. The stories share some amazing similarities. The ancient gods are almost always associated with or identified as the ones who were the bringers of civilization.

Take Egypt, for instance. Osiris first introduced agriculture. Thoth brought the skills of writing. Hathor taught the arts of love, beautification with makeup and music. Ptah is remembered as the god of craftsmen and architects, and Maat the goddess of ethics—of truth and justice.

In Mayan culture Quetzalcoatl, sometimes known as Gukumatz, brought with him the philosophy of ethics and justice, but also the practical art of agriculture, fishing, and music.

Viracocha/Kon-Tiki came to Peru bearing similar gifts.

In Sumer we find a pantheon of gods—a committee, so to speak. Together they are called Anunnaki, Watchers, or Apkallu. They seem to be led by a committee chairman named Ea or Enki. But Oannes is the bringer of civilization. He is the one usually associated with the introduction of culture to Mesopotamia. Prior to his arrival, according to George Smith's *The Chaldean Account of Genesis*, the people there "lived in a lawless manner, like the beasts of the field."

Greek mythology remembers the Aloadae brothers, Otus and Ephialtes, the sons of Poseidon, who brought culture and the fine points of civilization to humanity.

As we shall soon see in the conclusion to this chapter, even Hebrew mythology from the book of Genesis provides a list of names associated with those who brought civilization to humankind.

Brother/Sister, Husband/Wife

There are other similarities as well. For some reason, the chief ancient gods were often identified as not only husband and wife, but also as brother and sister. Osiris/Isis are the principal deities of Egypt and are identified so strongly in this tradition that the ancient Pharaohs often married their sisters to produce legitimate heirs to the throne. The same practice was common in the South Pacific all the way to Hawaii.

The founding of the Inca capitol of Cuzco is associated with the first couple, Inca and his wife. Legend has it that the indigenous people of the area were living like wild beasts, with no religion, had built no houses or fields and produced no clothing. There are even hints that they were practicing cannibalism. The royal couple, who were also brother and sister, soon put an end to that.

Even the Bible hints at such a relationship between Adam and Eve. By the time the myth was written down, of course, no self-respecting Jewish scribe

Part of the ruins of Cuzco, the capital of the Inca Empire, which was, according to legend, founded by the god Inca and his wife.

was going to immortalize an incestuous relationship, especially concerning the first couple of humankind. But the fact remains that they did share the same father, even if that Father was God Himself. And there is the curious matter of Eve being formed of Adam's rib, whatever that means.

Real Names—Real People?

Are these the real names of real people who actually set forth during the Younger Dryas epoch to reestablish civilization among the Stone Age inhabitants of the earth who managed to survive the initial catastrophe of the Younger Dryas comet?

Who knows? But ask yourself this question. If the earth today were struck by such a comet, if we were immediately thrown into a chilling ice age, our infrastructure and principal cities destroyed, our way of life unalterably destroyed, isn't that what we would do?

We only have to look at preparations now in place in the event of a modern disaster. Continuity of government plans have been drafted by the United States Congress ever since the British invaded Washington during the War of 1812. Now, in the age of possible nuclear disasters, every government on Earth has contingency plans outlining what to do if catastrophe happens. If one place on Earth were to become incapacitated, wouldn't it make sense that we would want to continue our way of life somewhere else?

If that's what would happen today, why would the thinking have been any different for our ancestors who thought and acted much the same as we do?

Seen in these terms, it makes perfect sense. Our ancient ancestors, their homeland destroyed, moved the seat of government somewhere else. It happened a long time ago, but myths have a long shelf life. The Stone Age people affected by this new spurt of civilizing influence remembered. Their standard of living improved. Their comfort levels increased. It must have seemed like magic. They learned new things. Of course they remembered. And 12,000 years later, their stories live on.

What If?

Imagine the unthinkable. Suppose a huge disaster were to hit planet Earth? Civilization today is much more spread out and complex than it was 12,800 years ago, but ratchet up the size of the comet in comparison. This is, after all, just a thought experiment.

So suppose, as I write these words in the year 2016, a horrendous comet appears in the sky and blasts us, overnight, into another ice age. Both northern and southern poles are soon frozen solid well down into the inhabited areas that today feature great cities and power plants that provide energy to the world. It's all gone.

But before it hits, the president and his cabinet are whisked off in Air Force One. They see the devastation in much the same way the ancient sea farers saw what had happened to their homeland. What would they do?

Well, they would look for a place to land. They couldn't come home again, that's for sure. Washington, D.C., is now threatened by a glacier. So they would probably head for equatorial lands. There they would encounter survivors who, as is presently the case today, might be living with one foot still in the Stone Age. If that is the current situation, it certainly would have been the case back 12,800 years ago.

They would begin to slowly set about the task of rebuilding civilization. They would, whether they wanted to or not, form a cult that would eventually become a culture. The indigenous people would remember. They would pass on stories to their children. Civilization, like the mythical phoenix, would eventually rise from the ashes of the disaster.

And 12,000 years from now, maybe, just maybe, the one who will be remembered as the bringer of civilization will be the ancient god called Barack and his crew of helpers.

Disclaimers

Now faith is the assurance of things hoped for, the conviction of
things not seen. This is what the ancients were commended for.

Hebrews 11:1

Up to now in the course of this book, we have been gathering the pieces of the jigsaw puzzle together, spreading them out on the table before us, and examining each individual piece. That's important. We need to know what we're dealing with. But now it's time to put the puzzle together so it forms one, cohesive picture. We're going to dissect the prime Genesis myth and examine it side by side with historical, archeological, cosmological, and anthropological facts to see if the myth corresponds at all to what we know about our current understanding of material, scientific facts. Understand, of course, that the Genesis myth was written down thousands of years after the fact, so to speak. It's bound to have become embellished and garbled in that time. Besides that, it has, over the last few thousand years, become so entangled with religious and theological baggage that it takes real effort to unlearn all we have been

What if a world-altering disaster struck Earth today? What would the consequences be to our civilization, history, mythology?

taught by others and all we taught ourselves as we fought to get free from a typical, conservative interpretation. By that I mean that many people, as children, having been force-fed a theological story they just couldn't swallow, simple threw up their hands in frustration and refused to consider if there might be anything at all of importance in the early chapters of the Bible. In this way they may have thrown out the baby with the bath water.

Personal Confession Time (1)

To that end I now have a confession to make. I have been an ordained minister for more than forty years. Ever since 1971, I have stood before at least one congregation, and usually two, every Sunday morning and preached sermons based on the Bible. One would think, after all that time, I had the thing pretty much figured out.

One would be wrong.

I have never, until recently, been able to get a handle on the first four chapters of the Bible. They just never made sense to me.

On the one hand, there was a time when I read them as history. But that didn't last long. There are simply too many dumb mistakes in the text. First of all, every smart-aleck Sunday School kid (including me, of course),

//It says here that Adam and Eve had only two children, Cain and Abel. If Cain killed Abel and then went out and got married and built the first city, who did he marry?"

when asked to read aloud the story of Adam and Eve and the first family, figures he's the first genius in history to make a discovery that will thoroughly stump his teacher.

"It says here that Adam and Eve had only two children, Cain and Abel. If Cain killed Abel and then went out and got married and built the first city, who did he marry?"

Of such inquiring minds, future preachers are born.

The answer proffered by the teacher is usually some version of the following:

- "Who are you to argue with the word of God? The Bible says it happened! Sit down and shut up!"

- "Go ask the minister!"

- "The Bible says Adam and Eve had other children. He must have married his sister." (This one is usually used only as a last resort. First of all it implies incest and that's frowned upon in Christian circles. Second, it raises all kinds of questions about how many generations it would take to produce a population big enough to constitute a city, and whether Cain lived long enough to accomplish the feat.)

Any of these answers is blatantly unacceptable to the aforementioned smart-aleck kid. (Trust me. I'm speaking from experience!)

A better answer would have been: "I don't know." As it is, such roundabout, inauthentic answers only serve to introduce said smart-aleck kid to the conspiracy of silence.

What all this means is that if the original authors of this story (and they weren't dummies) meant to relate factual history in the form of myth, they slipped up pretty badly by introducing obvious contradictions that even a smart-aleck kid could spot right off the bat. I don't think they would have done that.

That eliminates a historical reading. It just doesn't work. So we're left with the second way to read the Bible—from a theological standpoint. It's what I did for years. But in the end, that doesn't work either, because if you're going to produce a myth designed to inspire religious, ethical, moral, or spiritual values, why include such red herrings as, "There were giants on the earth in those days," or having your one remaining child on Earth running off to build a city? That's too much information. It doesn't make sense to throw something like that into your mythical narrative with no context or relevance to the lesson you're trying to teach. It's simply unnecessary baggage for the reader to deal with if your object is to teach religion.

Personal Confession Time (2)

That leads to my second personal confession. I think I may have found a way to justify what the Bible says and why it says it the way it does. What follows is my reconstruction, based on almost seventy years of reading, research, rewriting and rehashing what amounts to a little short of ten thousand sermons, seminars, and classes and workshops. But I've often said that I've never had an original thought in my life. All my thinking is shaped by things I've read and studied. To that end I am much indebted to the work and writings of Graham Hancock. Most traditionalists put him out there on the fringe and refuse to take him seriously. But although I've never met the man, except through his books, he seems to have a zero tolerance level when it comes to the conspiracy of silence. He asks the questions I always wanted to ask but was so often ridiculed for asking. He inspired my own research into the possibility that ancient gods and lost civilizations might offer a new direction in understanding who we are and where we come from. To the extent that my ideas concur with his, I want to credit him here. If we disagree at any point, I strongly advise the reader to consider his work with an open mind. His books are listed in the back of this book. If you are at all intrigued with what follows, I encourage you to read them.

Fitting the Pieces Together

What follows is a reconstruction of the Genesis story. We won't quote every line and precept, but we'll include enough to make sense of the whole. This reconstruction covers the first four chapters of the Bible, from creation to Noah's flood. We're going to see if it ties in with what we know about Earth's history, including dates drawn from the geological record. I think it might change the way you understand the Bible. It presupposes that the Genesis account was written by scribes who were, for the first time in history, writing down stories that were, by their time, already ancient. They were recording, in other words, events from an ancient past.

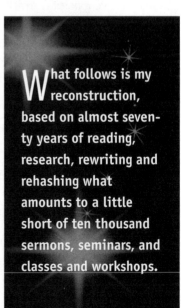

What follows is my reconstruction, based on almost seventy years of reading, research, rewriting and rehashing what amounts to a little short of ten thousand sermons, seminars, and classes and workshops.

But those events were still remembered. That's the important thing. And in the end, the scribes might have done exactly what those who lived through the actual times really wanted. They answered the central questions: Who are we? Where did we come from?

In their words, here is their story.

Out of Eden

Images of paradise are universal. It was always better back in the old days. The first two chapters of Genesis take us back to the beginning. We were one with nature. As we

Thousands of years ago, humans evolved the unique ability of symbolic thought, including writing, in which one thing represents another. A step that separated us from other animals.

read these verses, we are reading about an epoch that goes back some 200,000 years, to the emergence of anatomically modern humans and maybe even before that to our earliest ancestors. The Bible doesn't say how it happened in terms that would make a biologist happy. It just says God did it. The writers didn't understand the mechanics of spontaneous generation or evolution. But give them a break. Neither do we. Saying God did it is no weirder than seriously considering Panspermia or the Many Worlds theory. It happened, somehow. So let's move on. (We'll consider religious theories in the next chapter.)

What the writers do tell us is that for an unknown time we were one with the animals. We were one with nature. And, at least in memory, those times were good. "And the Lord God formed man from the dust of the earth and breathed into him the breath of life, and man became a living soul" (Genesis 2:7). Let the good times roll!

In those remote, ancient, and memory-shrouded times our human ancestors achieved something that no other animal did. They developed the capacity to think and reason. That goes without saying. But many other animal species can do that. Humans developed the ability to work together in community. But other species do that, too.

No, what we developed was the capacity to think in symbolic thought.

"This stands for that."

"This means that."

"I can paint a picture of something and you know what I'm saying."

"I am aware of that which is beyond myself."

"I believe in worlds that exist beyond my senses."

"There is a greater reality than that which I see and hear."

"Something, or Someone, exists above or below me in the universe."

Some forty thousand years ago the early spiritual teachers, the gifted shamans or medicine people, crawled back into the great painted caves, possibly under the influence of mind-expanding and consciousness-raising hallucinogens, and began to imagine a world far bigger than any other animal species ever did. They reproduced that image on the cave walls.

Was it simply a made-up reality? Was it only in their heads?

Modern physics seems to have discovered that was not the case at all. As Dumbledore observed to Harry Potter, it may have been in their heads, but that doesn't mean it wasn't real. It was just outside their sensory reality, that's all. It took a mind-expanding experience just to catch a glimpse. But anyone who has ever had an out-of-body or near-death experience will insist that it is more real than reality itself. Even the Apostle Paul who, in II Corinthians 12, described his own out-of-body experience, admitted in I Corinthians 13 that in this life we can only "see (as if) through a window, dimly." That window consists of our senses.

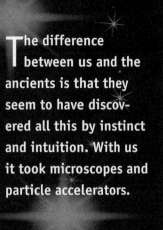

The difference between us and the ancients is that they seem to have discovered all this by instinct and intuition. With us it took microscopes and particle accelerators.

We are just beginning, in our day, to face the fact that our senses filter out much of what is real—light, for instance, and sound and vibration. That doesn't mean things such as ultraviolet light or supersonic sound waves aren't real. It just means we can't perceive them in the particular material perception realm we inhabit in these bodies.

The difference between us and the ancients is that they seem to have discovered all this by instinct and intuition. With us it took microscopes and particle accelerators. We publish our findings in scientific, peer-reviewed journals. They developed myths.

The myths tell us that the time called Eden, Paradise, the original Home of the Gods, Atlantis and Mu or Lemuria, was a good time. An important time. A time of exploration and achievement. It wasn't for everybody. All humans weren't created equal. There were Stone Age peoples and advanced intellectual societies both inhabiting the planet. But that's the case today as well.

The advanced, technical cultures seem to have developed the first civilization. It was a time of exploration. Humankind had awakened to the greater world around them. They had become aware. So they set out to "fill the earth and subdue it" (Genesis 1:28).

Did they send out the equivalent of diplomats or emissaries to seek out new worlds and establish a beachhead on foreign soil? Did they try to communicate with Stone Age people in distant places? Did explorers go searching for natural resources that could help the homeland? At the very least, were there ambassadors of goodwill sent out to expand their horizons?

We'll never know for sure, of course. But that's what we do. Why wouldn't they have done the same thing? Just because they were ancient doesn't mean they were any different from us.

Trouble in Paradise

The whole enterprise was to receive a devastating blow some 12,800 years ago. Like the dinosaurs before us, we are not immune to the whims of the cosmos.

A segmented comet blew up in our atmosphere, almost crushing the newfound human experiment we now call civilization. The weather, moderating quite nicely since the close of the previous ice age had opened up things for exploration, suddenly returned to bitterly cold conditions. The Younger Dryas reared its ugly head and wreaked its vengeance upon the earth.

Wherever the fledgling civilization called home, be it Atlantis or something very much like it, the people discovered a bitter truth: You can't go home again.

They were cast out of Eden and had to make their way into the world.

The people must have asked why. In their view, the attack by what the Edfu temple texts called the serpent from above seemed like retribution for their sins. In short, they blamed themselves. What had they done wrong?

They decided it was probably tied up with hubris. They had wanted to "be like God" (Genesis 3:5). They had, just as in their story about Icarus, tried

When their homeland—perhaps Atlantis—was destroyed by the Younger Dryas event, the ancients who lived there traveled to places where more primitive peoples lived and tried to teach them through stories that became mythology.

to fly too close to the sun. Their reach had exceeded their grasp. They had played with toys that proved much too dangerous.

How could they warn future generations about their mistake? What could they say to a future civilization that might, for instance, destroy the atmosphere with technology powered by burning fossil fuels, or release unthinkable energy by splitting the atom, or populate themselves out of existence?

Well, they could tell stories. And they did just that.

But they could also warn their descendants to search the skies, lest the Great Leaping One, the serpent of old, returned. To that end they built megalithic astronomy structures, in which they encoded mathematical formulas that could someday be discovered by anyone smart enough to follow in their footsteps. "Look up," they seemed to say. "Watch your heads. But always remember. What you see up there is where you came from. You are children of the stars."

This may well be the essential meaning of the monoliths.

Missionaries

After the destruction of their homeland, now forever closed to them by the "cherubim with the flaming swords" (Genesis 3:24), they set out to recreate the world. Where should the efforts begin? They had to establish some criteria.

First of all, they would have wanted to go to places that were warm. It was the Younger Dryas Ice Age in much of the world. But around the equator the sun still shown and waters lapped warm beaches. The band of pyramids found in equatorial regions around the globe probably didn't happen by accident. Early civilizations in Egypt, Sumer, Indonesia, Turkey, Lebanon, Easter Island, Peru, and Mexico speak volumes about ancient beachheads of civilization. Indeed, if the homeland period of this lost civilization back before 12,800 years ago marked a great beginning, the epoch of the Younger Dryas may have been its Golden Age. The comet would have forced them to go forth and multiply. This they seem to have done. It was a period of expansion and growth that probably marked the world's first growth-based economy based on world trade.

Second, they probably decided to go to places where they had already sent their ambassadors before the comet struck. It only made sense. They had already scouted the territory and perhaps even learned the language.

Maybe that even answers the questions that plague smart-aleck Sunday School kids. Who did Cain marry? He went native. How did he find enough people to build a city? They were already there and willing to go to work. Why was he an agriculturist? He taught the locals how to grow crops instead of hunt and gather. He had to. There are a lot of mouths to feed once you build a city and get people to settle in one place.

Since we're into pure speculation now, try this on for size. Did the murder of Abel by his brother Cain symbolize a basic disagreement between the two about how to proceed with their missionary work? Did the Abel faction represent those who thought it best to simply encourage the natives in what they were already doing? Perhaps this group believed in a hands-off policy—a look-but-don't-touch prime directive to let the locals develop in their own way.

If that's the case, the Cain faction would represent those who wanted to jumpstart local evolution by teaching the native inhabitants new things and actively becoming involved in their evolutionary path. This sense of involvement might also explain why Cain married one of the local women. He became actively involved with the indigenous population.

The two groups could not have both had their way. According to the Genesis myth, the Cain faction killed off the Abel faction. This eventually led to the great explosion of knowledge that occurred shortly after this time, during the period now known as the Neolithic Revolution.

Did the murder of Abel by his brother Cain symbolize a basic disagreement between the two about how to proceed with their missionary work?

Perhaps this even explains some of the mysterious passages in Genesis 6:

"When men began to multiply on the earth...." (Of course they multiplied. Farming insured a stable food supply. The laws of biology tell us that when there is an ample food supply, the species expands.)

"... and daughters were born to them, the sons of God ..." (Cain's folks).

"... saw that the daughters of men ..." (the locals).

"... were beautiful, and they married any of them they chose ..." (hey—missionaries are people, too).

"The Nephilim were on the earth in those days—and also afterward—when the sons of God went to the daughters of men and had children by them. They were the heroes of old, men of renown...." (Apparently we're dealing with real men here, who could reproduce, not aliens who would naturally face problems of biological parts fitting together. And the mixing of the races seemed to produce some pretty healthy offspring.)

Myths from all over the world emphasize this mixing of the races. The gods, folks such as Cain and his ambassador cronies, seem to have created quite an impression. But it is always thus. Things happen.

But it cannot be denied that the mixing of the races, in ways both beneficial and worrisome (the two seem to go hand in hand), also furthered civilization. Look what happened according to Genesis 4:16–26.

City Building—"So Cain went out from the LORD's presence and lived in the land of Nod, east of Eden. Cain made love to his wife, and she became pregnant and gave birth to Enoch. Cain was then building a city, and he named it after his son Enoch."

Population Expansion—"To Enoch was born Irad, and Irad was the father of Mehujael, and Mehujael was the father of Methuselah, and Methuselah was the father of Lamech."

Bigamy among the Missionaries?—"Lamech married two women, one named Adah and the other Zillah."

Animal Husbandry—"Adah gave birth to Jabal; he was the father of those who live in tents and raise livestock."

The Arts—"His brother's name was Jubal; he was the father of all who play stringed instruments and pipes."

Industry—"Zillah also had a son, Tubal-Cain, who forged all kinds of tools out of bronze and iron. Tubal-Cain's sister was Naamah."

Dark Clouds Arise—"Lamech said to his wives, 'Adah and Zillah, listen to me; wives of Lamech, hear my words. I have killed a man for wounding me, a young man for injuring me. If Cain is avenged seven times, then Lamech seventy-seven times.'"

Religion—"At that time people began to call on the name of the LORD."

The Other Shoe Drops

All this seems to have taken place during the Younger Dryas, a period that lasted for about 1,200 years. That's a long time. The myths, by their very nature, seem to present the story as a quick occurrence. But the time spans presented are really vast.

Now fast forward to about 11,600 years ago. The end comes with a bang. For reasons no one fully understands, the Younger Dryas ended as abruptly as it began. The geologic record indicates that global warming arrived seemingly overnight. The melting of the ice caps drastically raised ocean levels, broke apart ice dams that held in place inland seas bigger than the size of Texas, resulting in huge inundations all around the globe. The time of Noah's flood had arrived. It didn't cover the whole Earth. But flooding was so widespread it must have felt like it. The myths are in complete agreement. Wherever you lived on Earth 11,600 years ago, you had to head for high ground.

For reasons no one fully understands, the Younger Dryas ended as abruptly as it began. The geologic record indicates that global warming arrived seemingly overnight.

The Russian city of Nizhnevartovsk is underwater in this 2015 photo. People tend to build cities on coastlines and along rivers. Today they are at risk from global warming, just as coastal cities were when extensive flooding happened after the end of the Younger Dryas cold period.

This was the second tragedy for our mysterious, lost civilization. It appears to have been a seafaring enterprise. Coastal cities were its hallmark. And coastal cities were the first to go when rapid sea level rise became the order of the day.

In our day and age, given the advance of undersea exploration technologies, it seems as though a week doesn't go by without someone, off the coast of some continent with ancient roots, finding evidence of underwater ruins. From Malta and Egypt in the Mediterranean to India, from the South Pacific to the coasts of America, from Japan to Australia, come reports of mysterious ruins drowned beneath the sea that will require further exploration.

Could these be the evidence, the smoking gun, that points to a worldwide network of an advanced civilization that we have forgotten ever existed? Perhaps it is even the source of the Atlantis tradition.

The myths are in complete agreement. In cultures around the world people fled to the hills, took refuge in boats, or perished in the rising waters.

The Aftermath

When the deluge ended and Earth slowly began its step-by-step path to what we call normal, civilization was in tatters. It was a huge double punch that left its mark all over the globe.

But there is evidence that the work of civilizing the world didn't quite die out. It was precisely at this time that the first temple at Göbekli Tepe was built and evidence of agriculture's beginning has been uncovered. Strange symbols involving sky charts, animal effigies, and religion are found there. Great, brooding, multi-ton, megalithic figures are found there, their hands pictured as clasped over their bellies, just like the giant figures found at Peru, Indonesia, Mexico, and the Moai statues of Easter Island.

And then, as soon as Göbekli Tepe was finished, the builders buried it.

Why?

The answer is speculative, of course. But when we want to remember a particular era, we bury a time capsule that will be dug up at a future date to testify to our presence and to remind future people what we were like.

Is Göbekli Tepe a time capsule? Who knows? But if it is, we are the recipients of the message it contains. We need only to apply ourselves to its meaning.

Strange, isn't it, that the Mayan Long Count calendar ends during the same era when a possible Göbekli Tepe time capsule is discovered? There are other indications as well, to be found in Giza and Peru. But, as we said, it is purely speculation.

In the Beginning

We have now arrived at that point of time traditional archeology claims marks the beginning of civilization. It started, according to accepted knowledge, at Göbekli Tepe, spread downstream to Sumer and across the Fertile Crescent, sprang up independently in Egypt, and then, after a few thousand years, took off, again independently, in Mexico and Peru.

Given the obvious, and in some cases glaring, discrepancies of the archeological record, however, is that theory of civilization completely tied up in a neat ball and packaged without blemishes? Is there more hidden beneath the surface? Is it quite as simple as the textbooks claim?

Before we finish with this whole subject, we have two more areas to explore.

The first is an arena that often resists artifact evidence. It is to be found in the philosophical recesses of the mind, heart and, dare we say it, soul.

We are now talking about religion. What did these people believe? Even more important, was there something driving them that exists separate from their belief? Is there indeed a source, a force, a metaphysical ancient god behind humankind's rise to civilization? Are we a product of something beyond ourselves that is driving our evolution? Does this force guide our destiny? And did our ancestors know how to contact it?

Even more important for the subject at hand, whether or not we believe in such a force—an ancient god—did they? This is the subject we will next examine.

ANCIENT RELIGIONS

Has science proved that the rishis were right? I think the most we can say—and it is a lot—is that science and the rishis are consistent with each other. They come from different worlds but see with the same vision—almost. Science is still burdened by spiritual materialism, the belief that any explanation of God, the soul, or the afterlife is valid only if matter contains the secret. This is like saying we can't understand jazz until we diagram the atoms in Louis Armstrong's trumpet.

Deepak Chopra in *Life After Death: The Burden of Proof*

Although similar to states of feeling, mystical states seem to those who experience them to be also states of knowledge. They are states of insight into depths of truth unplumbed by the discursive intellect. They are illuminations, revelations, full of significance and importance, all inarticulate though they remain; and as a rule they carry with them a curious sense of authority for after-time.

William James

Kicking It Up a Notch

So far in this book we have been championing the assumption that our civilization was not the first. Others came before us, but we don't remember them. They lay forgotten in the dust of history, destroyed by, quite possibly, a worldwide, one-two-three impact event—fire, ice, and flood—that in the

Did other universes exist before our present one, or is this the first and only universe to have existed?

"Ancient Catastrophes" chapter we called the Younger Dryas event. We may have found evidence of their existence in the archeological record and in ancient mythology, but to understand who they were and what we might be able to learn from them, we had to go searching for clues. Once we did that, we found they were everywhere. All we had to do was open our eyes and, maybe even more importantly, our minds.

Now it's time to ratchet this concept up to cosmic proportions. So far we have limited the search to our planet and what we can see from it when we gaze into the heavens. For the most part, except for a few inquiries into our origins, we stuck to human history as it has unfolded on this, our home world.

Now let's expand our search. If we are not the first civilization, and if, like the legendary phoenix of old, we rose from the ashes of what came before us, can we ask an even more probing question? Is this the first universe, the first cosmos, to exist? Has our universe, like our civilization, arisen from the ashes of a parent universe? Is the Big Bang event that marks the beginning of all that exists in the material cosmos simply an infinitely larger version of the Younger Dryas event that marked the beginning of our civilization? And did our distant ancestors know it? They might not have had access to our radio telescopes and space probes, but did they utilize another means of perceiving what modern cosmology is just discovering? Did the Old Ones intuit what we have deduced? Way before we learned anything about big bangs, infinite multiple universes and quantum theories that render our rock-solid material surroundings into sensory illusions, had our ancient ancestors already come to the same conclusions that our cutting edge physicists are now beginning to explore?

A Cosmic Metaphor

The principal creation metaphor of Hinduism, one of the world's oldest religions, goes something like this:

> Brahman meditates on the lotus blossom growing from the navel of Vishnu, who sleeps on the cosmic ocean made up of the remains of the last universe before this one. When Brahman opens his eyes to look around, a world comes into existence. One

day in the life of Brahman is four billion, three hundred and twenty years, or one world cycle. Then he closes his eyes and the world disappears. When he opens them again, another cycle begins. All this goes on forever.

Jim and Barbara Willis in *Armageddon Now*

That sounds suspiciously like a poetic interpretation of the latest version of Multiverse or Membrane theory. But it is a story that has been told and retold for five thousand years! And, as we shall soon see, it's not the only one. Stories very much like this have been told down through the centuries all over the world.

Limits

When we begin a study this broad, we need to limit ourselves. We can't simply walk through an open door into enough subject matter for a whole new book. So we are going to stick to what the Old Ones thought about all this. Just because they may have arrived at their conclusions through intuition rather than scientific study doesn't mean their findings aren't as valid, or perhaps even more valid, than ours. As we shall soon see, results from the study of out-of-body and near-death experiences, to say nothing of ancient shamanic and meditation techniques, indicate that when freed from the physical shackles of the body, the mind can, and often does, penetrate areas where even telescopes and particle accelerators cannot follow.

Religion or Spirituality?

This brings up an important point. Are we delving into the religion of these ancient people, or their spirituality? The two terms are not synonymous.

For our purposes, we're going to have to agree on a definition of the two. It might not be the same as anyone else's definition, but it's the one we're going to use in this book:

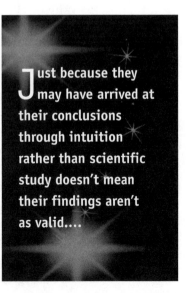

Just because they may have arrived at their conclusions through intuition rather than scientific study doesn't mean their findings aren't as valid....

- Spirituality refers to the sense of wonder and awe we experience when we contemplate what I like to call the Great Mystery, especially when we, in essence, feel a unity with it.

- Religion is the human infrastructure, including doctrines, traditions, buildings, and priesthoods that grow up around spirituality.

In that sense, when an individual has a spontaneous OBE (out-of-body experience) in which he or she

An example of a spiritual event is an out-of-body experience in which one holds the universe in his hands.

becomes aware of holding the entire universe in the palm of their hands, it is a spiritual experience. If they gather a group of followers and teach them how that experience can be replicated, they have to be very careful to ensure that a religion doesn't form around them.

Jesus, Moses, the Buddha, and Muhammad were no doubt spiritual people. But years later we now consider them all to be founders of a religion. (We cannot help but wonder whether or not they would have approved, but that's another story.)

Methods

There is no way we can authentically step back into the shoes of the Ancient Ones. We don't know what they were thinking and feeling. But we can look at the traditions that grew out of their experience, the religions they began, the culture that formed around the cult, and possibly discover clues about what they knew.

This isn't as far-fetched as you might think. If a person has a big, bold spiritual experience, they will want to memorialize it with a big, bold temple. As we have already seen, some of those temples still exist. If their vision includes the cosmos, they probably would want to build a laboratory from which to view the heavens. Those laboratories are being unearthed all over the planet. If they discover meditative techniques that enable them to go outside themselves in awe and wonder, those techniques might still be practiced and memorialized. And, as we shall see, they are.

In short, what we are about to do is attempt to delve into the very soul of those who have gone before us. Some of them were no doubt, generations after their death, revered as ancient gods who brought wisdom to humankind. Their hidden truths might go a long way toward enlightening us. We might even discover that even though they used different techniques than we employ in this scientific age, they were able to penetrate the greatest mystery of all—the mystery of our origins.

Is this the first cosmos to come into existence, or has it been going on forever? Are we just the latest, most evolved, sentient beings to come down the pike, or have there been others? And, as unbelievable as it sounds, have those others attempted to leave clues behind so that intelligent beings in the next cosmos, perhaps our cosmos, can discover them when a species arises that is smart enough to find and interpret them?

Did the Ancient Ones explore the answers to these questions using methods and employing abilities that have atrophied in us, because of disuse? That's what we'll try to figure out in this chapter. We'll begin by looking at modern metaphysical interpretations of contemporary theories involving everything from quantum theory to the God Particle. This field is rapidly turning into the religion of the twenty-first century. But just because we are newly discovering these concepts doesn't mean we are inventing them. If quantum theory, for instance, is true today, it was just as true in the time of the ancients. If it proves to offer adequate explanations of how the cosmos came to be, that explanation was just as available to the Old Ones. They might not have had the use of our modern science toys, but we shall soon discover they may well have had other means at their disposal—methods we are just now beginning to acknowledge.

After perusing some of the concepts of what I am calling the new religion—the culture forming around the cult of modern science—we will delve into some of the most ancient religious systems known to us. The similarities just might astound you.

AKASHA

The wisdom of the mystics, it seems, has predicted for centuries what neurology now shows to be true: In Absolute Unitary Being, self blends into other; mind and matter are one and the same.

Andrew Newberg, M.D., in *Why God Won't Go Away*

Origins

Any questions about ancient civilizations tend to ignore a basic starting point. If one civilization arises from another, who was first? Where do we come from? Where do we go? How did humankind, or any life, for that matter, begin in the first place? Subatomic particles zip into our reality and then zip out again. From where? To where? Cells are constantly replaced. There is not a single cell in your body now that was there when you were born, yet you still feel like you. Why? What existed before the Big Bang began the cosmos we see around us? Could it be that we owe our very being to the collapse, not of another civilization, but of another whole cosmos? Have there been previous universes? Was there any time? Was there any space? Was there anything at all? If so, what was it? And, just as happens when one civilization replaces another after a catastrophe and is capable of passing on some information from what came before, has a previous cosmos passed on to us some bit of information that we someday might come to learn is responsible for our very existence?

What existed before the Big Bang began the cosmos we see around us? Could it be that we owe our very being to the collapse, not of another civilization, but of another whole cosmos?

These are the greatest origin questions of all. They go back to the time when, in the beginning, the whole cosmos began. Physicists lose sleep over this stuff, but they keep trying to figure it out with mathematical computations that grow more and more complex. "Brane" (Membrane) Theory, String Theory, Big Bang Theory, Multiverse—it seems as if the list grows every year.

The ancient Hindu rishis (wise men) used a different method. Theirs was not the path of math and science. They followed their intuition and inner guides to the source. They called it the Akashic Field. In the words of the *Rig Veda*:

Sages who searched with their heart's thought discovered that what exists is kin to the non-existent.

By searching with their hearts, the rishis found that what exists, the Hindu expression for the material world, is *maya*—illusion. In other words, everything that we think is real is, at its root, an illusion—not what it seems.

The funny thing is, though, that the findings of science are beginning to merge with the visions of the ancient mystics. Listen, for instance, to a quote from Robert Jastrow, an eminent American astronomer, physicist, and cosmologist, in his response to discovering the background radiation that appears to prove the theory of an initial Big Bang:

For the scientist who has lived by his faith in the power of reason, the story ends like a bad dream. He has scaled the mountains of ignorance; he is about to conquer the highest peak; as he pulls himself over the final rock, he is greeted by a band of theologians who have been sitting there for centuries.

This isn't a knock on scientists. We stand in awe of them. (Well, most of them.) It's wonderful that science and religion aren't, in most cases, fighting like they used to. That being said, what can we bring from both perspectives to the great mystery of Akasha?

Do We Know What We Know?

"I know what I saw!"

No, you don't. Get over it. Experiment after experiment in the field of law enforcement has proved beyond the shadow of a doubt that six eyewitnesses to an event will probably produce six different versions of what happened. When it comes to describing something we have experienced, we are notoriously unreliable.

How could it be otherwise? Our brains are absorbing far more input than we can possibly process. If we were consciously aware of every small bit of information that is coming to us via our senses, we would never get anything done. Add to that the TV signals, radio signals, other electromagnetic signals, light waves, sounds both above and beyond the ability of our ear to register, temperature fluctuations—well, you get the idea. To help us function in this wild and woolly world of sensory input, we have evolved to make use of an area of our brain called the hippocampus. That's a small but important staging area that stores short-range memories. It helps us function in the present moment. The trouble is that the hippocampus will only store information for about twenty seconds. That's why it is so difficult to remember a long string of numbers. By the time you start to memorize the ones at the end, the ones at the beginning have begun to fade. After the information moves to the process station of some hundred billion neurons in another portion of the brain that stores long-term memory, the hippocampus moves on to process the new material that is streaming into its staging area. But the longer material is stored in our long-term memory banks, the more it is subject to fading and distortion. That's why police are so adamant about questioning witnesses as soon as possible after an incident.

Studies have proved the unreliability of eyewitnesses in police investigations, so how reliable are we when describing spiritual experiences?

Something really sinister begins to happen quite quickly after we process information. The brain has a conversation that goes something like this:

- I saw a red car.

- The car wasn't red, it was blue. And it was a van.

- But I seem to remember a car rather than a van. Could it have been a van? If not, it was an awfully big car.

- So—it must have been a van. Maybe it was a small van that looked kind of like a car. That's it—it was an SUV! And it was blue. Or was it red? Something says blue. So maybe it was really a small blue SUV.

- That's it. I saw a blue SUV!

Do you see what just happened? Our memory began to fade and get confused, so our imagination kicked in and helped out. Our red car is now a blue SUV.

If you want to have some fun at your next family reunion, have your siblings describe a specific incident that everyone remembers as if it were yesterday. You'll be amazed at how the stories vary, but it will help understand why old, old myths become garbled so.

What all this says is that our brains operate in ways we are still trying to understand. A lot of work is being done on this subject, and it will be fascinating to see what is discovered in the future. But when it comes to trusting our brain's interpretation of sensory input, we have to go slow and remain open. It's too easy to just say, "That's out of my experience, so I don't believe it!" It's not surprising at all that when faced with the feelings these energies evoked, the ancients wanted to anchor them in stone monuments.

With that as an introduction, we now have to tackle a very difficult subject. It has to do with how our minds, brains, and bodies function—with how they interface with the multidimensional field of reality that Hindu wise men called Akasha. If this information holds true now, it was also true in the time of our ancient ancestors.

Ervin László and the Zero-Point Field

CJ Martes is an Akashic field theorist and founder of Akashic Field Therapy™ (AFT). In an excerpt from an article she wrote for her website (www.cjmartes.com), she had this to say:

> Quantum scientists recently discovered a new area of time and space called the quantum vacuum. There are newly discovered properties of time and space happening all the time but it seems clear now that this vacuum is a super dense cosmic frictionless medium that carries light and all the universal forces of nature. A well-known scientist and philosopher named Ervin László, in his recently published book, *Science and the Akashic Field* shows that it may not only be a super dense sea of frictionless energy but also a sea of information conveying the historical experience of matter.

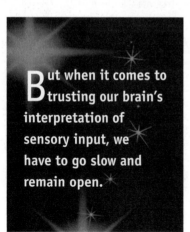

But when it comes to trusting our brain's interpretation of sensory input, we have to go slow and remain open.

She goes on to quote László's theory that the quantum vacuum essentially "generates the holographic field that is the memory of the universe."

So—who is this Ervin László and why is he so important?

We often hear about the so-called Theory of Everything that Stephen Hawking claims is the holy grail of the contemporary physicist. Well, Ervin László claims to have found it. Or, at least, he can describe what it will look like when it is found. It lies at the center of his Akashic Field Theory, released to the world in his 2004 book, *Science and the Akashic Field: An Integral Theory of Everything.*

László, born in Budapest, Hungary, in 1932, has written more than seventy-five books and published hundreds of scientific papers, among his many other accomplishments. He is a heavyweight in the field of quantum reality even though he began his career as a classical pianist. He has since branched out into such fields as philosophy of science, integral theory, and systems theory. When he talks about developing a holistic perspective on the world, a view he labels quantum consciousness, he certainly knows what he's talking about. He is a brilliant synthesist, well-versed in many disciplines.

Using math and the tools of the physicist, he claims to have discovered a field of in-formation, for lack of a better word, that he calls the zero-point field, a place (which is really not a place at all) from which all energy forms existence. Existence, then, is constantly being formed. It is in-formation. The zero-point field is ground zero in terms of being that particular point from which every single ripple of quantum energy originates. It is the mysterious field that eludes and tantalizes the scientists at CERN's Large Hadron Collider in Switzerland. It is home—the mind of God—the place that is both originator and receiver of particles that spring into existence from nowhere and go back to somewhere just as quickly. It is our home as well—the alpha and omega, the beginning and the end, of our existence.

But to better describe this field he turns to that most spiritual of languages, ancient Hindu Sanskrit. Akasha is a word meaning space. In his book he suggests that the Akashic Field, or the quantum vacuum, is a field supporting all the fundamental energy and bits of information that manifest themselves as material objects in the cosmos. (That means you and me as well as all stars and atoms everywhere.) But he goes farther than that. He believes the Akashic Field supports not only this cosmos, this

A former classical pianist, Ervin László is a systems theorist and philosopher of science who has advocated for the idea of quantum consciousness.

> In other words, Akasha is the mysterious realm from which everything originates. It is an infinite wave of potential awaiting incarnation in matter.

universe, but all universes, past and present, discovered and undiscovered. (You can use the words Multiverse or Meta-verse here.)

In other words, Akasha is the mysterious realm from which everything originates. It is an infinite wave of potential awaiting incarnation in matter. Every symphony Beethoven wrote, every painting Picasso created, every possible outcome to any choice you ever made, every idea you ever had—all existed in potential in Akasha. When Beethoven, Picasso, or you plucked your elected idea out of Akasha, they, or you, gave it life through intention. Akasha is the home of the Muse, but much, much more. It is the source, the ground of being. In short, it is consciousness itself.

If that last paragraph wasn't enough to discourage you, it gets even more complicated. The theory continues. Once a manifested, material thought or experience enters the field of Akasha, it remains there as a permanent fixture. In that sense, Akasha is a black hole of physically manifested consciousness. It absorbs everything—every bit of information and experience.

So if the universe emerges from Akasha as a reincarnation of a previous cosmos, something from the physical experience of that cosmos remains with us and helps form us in ways we do not comprehend. It's as if a previous cosmos, a previous civilization, if you will, has experienced a catastrophe, perhaps something like a big crunch, and then re-formed as a new cosmos or civilization—us!

Akasha Is Consciousness Itself!

A basic premise of quantum reality is that an electron does not come into existence until someone looks for it. A possibility wave of potential does not appear until we tease it out by giving it our attention.

That's Akasha in a nutshell. According to László's way of thinking, Forrest Gump was right. At the end of the movie starring Tom Hanks, Forrest speculates about predestination and free will. He wonders which theory is correct. He winds up saying, "I think it's both." And in typical Forrest fashion, he stumbles on the truth. Everything exists in potential. In that sense, everything is predestined. But it manifests itself only when we choose to collapse it into our existence. That's called free will. And the moment you choose the elected manifestation, thereby bringing it into our universe—our perception realm—another you in the infinite Multiverse, or Metaverse, chooses another possible manifestation, until all potential possibilities are manifested somewhere, somehow.

If this seems confusing, listen to Stephen Hawking and Ervin László. Or maybe Morgan Freeman. He'd gladly take you through this wormhole.

Your skepticism is understood. I have it, too. The problem, however, lies in the fact that we are so dependent on our five senses. We've grown used to them. Up to now in life, they've been very reliable. But they don't work out there.

The math, however, implies all this, and physicists are having symposiums on this material. They don't attend such gatherings just for the food. Ask some physicists to describe the Higgs field in layman's terms, for example, and watch them start to giggle hysterically.

There's no doubt about it. Akasha, or the zero-point field, is a hot concept. You know that to be the case when no less a *New York Times* bestselling author than Clive Cussler makes it the critical plot contrivance in his thriller *Zero Hour*.

Perhaps Deepak Chopra explains it best. In his book *Life After Death*, he talks about consciousness being a kind of three-layer cake. The outside layer is the dimension of physical matter. This is the world of concrete objects we encounter through the five senses—the one scientists observe and measure, quantify and study.

Inside that is the dimension of subtle objects. This is the world of dreams and visions, imagination and inspiration.

Finally comes the dimension of pure consciousness itself, the field of Akasha. This is the mysterious realm that gives birth to everything there is—the ground of our very being—consciousness aware of itself. The Bible calls it the dimension of I Am. When Moses asked the burning bush who was sending him on his mission of freedom, the voice responded, "Tell them I Am sent you." Jesus later said, "Before Moses was, I Am!"

Down to Earth

Let's come down from the lofty heights of quantum fields for a minute and try to get a handle on some of this.

When I taught courses on world religions, I always began my first lecture with an explanation designed to put religion in

New Age thinker Deepak Chopra describes our consciousness as having three layers: one of physical matter, one of dreams/visions/inspirations, and one of Akasha, the realm of real awareness.

its proper place. I spoke about the two prevailing human opinions as to why religion existed.

The first position was that expressed by Karl Marx. He believed religion to be a human invention designed to salve over the human need to solve questions about the great Unknown:

> Man makes religion, religion does not make man…. Religion is the sigh of the oppressed creature, the heart of a heartless world, and the soul of soulless conditions. It is the opium of the people.

The rest of the course was based on the second explanation. That is the view that postulates an "Other," another side out there. People who subscribe to this hypothesis believe that there really is a great Unknown, and that we can communicate with It, and It with us. I used to illustrate it as a yin and yang symbol with one side being the material and the other being spiritual, as shown in the illustration.

The circle represents all that is. The curved line separates the material world, the world of atoms and all that we see and touch, from the spiritual world, a world beyond the reach of test tube and microscope. I emphasized, however, that this line was not really solid—that religions (and that includes other things people believe in, such as the ideas of Schrodinger, Bell's theorem, Planck, Bohr, Heisenberg, Entanglement theory, the Copenhagen interpretation, and quantum theory itself) are doors and windows that allow us to see through the line, opening up vistas between the two worlds.

It's a good teaching aid and it served its purpose. I suppose it still has value. But it also limits understanding if it becomes too ingrained. If we allow it to become an untested presumption, it can really cause harm in growth because there comes a point when we have to understand, not just as an intellectual exercise but in the very fiber of our being, that the circle has no perimeter, and that the line is an illusion.

Quantum reality has uncovered something that, even for the great Albert Einstein, has proved to be a rather nasty but inescapable fact, even if it's a fact that is not new at all. The ancient Hindu mystics knew about it thousands of years ago.

Here it is. Duality is just as much a human invention as religion and science. There is no circle. There is no line. It's all an illusion. Consciousness is not on one

The author's representation of a world that is half material and half spiritual.

side of a line. Consciousness doesn't even exist within the circle. Consciousness creates the circle. The whole circle. Every bit of the circle. The circle exists in consciousness. There is no separate world where angels live or fear to tread. There is no place where God is not. Words attributed to Jesus said it best: "The realm of heaven is among (and within) you!"

So did something exist before the Big Bang? Both spiritual tradition and quantum physics answer with a thundering "Yes!" Physics calls it a zero-point field. Religion calls it Akasha. But it's the same thing. The old-timers beat us to it. They were talking about this thousands of years ago.

Levels of Experience

Deepak Chopra, in his *The Book of Secrets*, has brilliantly summarized all this. He points out that we are multidimensional people living in a multidimensional world.

Think about the many dimensions, the layers of consciousness, that vibrate in your life. They are there. You normally just don't listen for them. This is how Dr. Chopra describes them:

- Physical Body: The domain of sensation and the five senses.

- Emotion: The domain of feelings.

- Reason: The domain of logic, science and mathematics.

- Imagination: The domain of creative invention.

- Intuition: The domain where the mind understands the subtle mechanics of life.

- Myth and Archetype: The collective patterns of society. This is the domain of gods and goddesses, heroes and heroines, male and female energy.

- Knowingness: The domain of inner intelligence.

- Love: The motivating force of nature.

- Conditioned Bliss: The domain of awareness as it begins to become conscious of its own existence.

- Pure Being or Akasha: The domain of the Absolute, pure Awareness before it acquires any qualities at all. The state before creation. This is not actually a separate domain since it permeates everything.

A quick perusal of this list will strike a few familiar chords, I am sure. We are all well aware, for instance, of experiencing something real to the five senses and then moving down the list to the realm of emotion. We have all had times wherein we have experienced emotions, for instance, and then

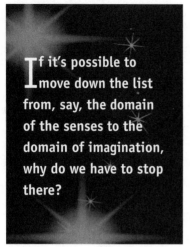

If it's possible to move down the list from, say, the domain of the senses to the domain of imagination, why do we have to stop there?

moved down the list to the domain of reason in order to control them. There are times when we have felt imagination triumph over reason. Just ask Steve Jobs or Bill Gates about that one. Both were able to imagine something others thought unreasonable.

Here's the point. If it's possible to move down the list from, say, the domain of the senses to the domain of imagination, why do we have to stop there? Why not allow our consciousness to go all the way to the experience of Pure Being—Akasha?

The reason most people won't take that leap is because they have not experienced it yet. Perhaps they will when they die. But to attempt such a process while still living requires effort, faith, belief, practice, and discipline. Every founder of every religion ever known made that leap. Jesus was said to have spent forty days in the wilderness doing just that. Moses went up his mountain. Muhammad entered his cave. Paul had a near-death experience on the road to Damascus. The list goes on and on. But most of their followers haven't experienced that same vision. They are too busy living their lives in the world of the five senses called the normal life. They may venture by accident into intuition or love, but they don't stay long. It's uncomfortable. It requires a suspension of normal reality. So they hot-foot it back home as soon as possible and create a religion around the experience.

Perhaps, however, it is more than possible, indeed, maybe even normal, to go all the way. It's just not usual. This is the message of many ancient religions. The Ancient Ones seemed to intuit all this. Perhaps it is becoming the message of the new scientists as well.

AKHENATEN AND THE BIRTH OF MONOTHEISM

Israelite monotheism developed through centuries of discussion, declarations of faith and interactions with other societies and other beliefs. In contrast, Akhenaten's monotheism developed very largely at the behest of a single, absolute monarch presiding over an isolated land, where the pharaoh's word was divine and secular law. It was an experiment that withered on the vine.

Brian Fagan, *Biblical Archeology Review* magazine

From Idea to Religion

Once you postulate a Prime Mover, a Being or Beings who are up there somewhere, separate from the cosmos, there are only two ways to proceed. Either there is one god (monotheism), or there are many gods (polytheism). For much of human history it seems as though our ancestors were polytheistic. They saw ancient gods everywhere and tried to discern the assigned tasks each of them had undertaken.

The first religion generally considered to be monotheistic was Judaism, but that is a very nebulous claim. When early psalmists of Judaism wrote, as in Psalm 95:3, "For the Lord (*YHVH*) is a great God, a great King above all gods," it certainly doesn't sound like monotheism. It sounds more like "my God can whip your god!"

Indeed, there is a case to be made that Judaism didn't really become monotheistic until after the Hebrew people returned from the Babylonian captivity where they encountered Persian Zoroastrianism, which is a fiercely monotheistic religion.

Still, there are those who claim Moses thought of it first. That's why the discovery in 1922 of the religious zealotry of Pharaoh Akhenaten caused such interest in the world of biblical archeology. Although he only ruled in Egypt for a brief fourteen years, from 1352 to 1338 B.C.E., which was close to the time of Moses, he apparently caused quite a furor. He spent the better part of his reign destroying polytheistic religion and installing monotheism. To attempt to overthrow an entire religious system in such a short time must have ruffled some feathers, to say the least. His mysterious death at an early age, according to Egyptian records, has never been fully explained. Claims of murder, leprosy, malaria, or snake bite have all had their day in the sun. One theory even says he fell off his chariot and was run over, explaining the broken leg found when his mummy was examined.

But perhaps the real cause was something even more strange. His death may be tied to his vision of one God.

Now things get interesting.

One theory holds that Moses was the first to come up with the concept of monotheism.

A Vision of Unity

First off, Akhenaten's statues all feature an elongated skull. In keeping with our study of elongated skulls back in the first chapter, that's enough to raise some interesting questions. The plot thickens when we learn that his children shared many of his physical traits, including a long neck, thick features, and what is sometimes called a feminized body—that is, large breasts and hips.

No, this doesn't mean he was a gay crossdresser. It means he may have suffered from a type of temporal lobe epilepsy which often is accompanied by those bodily features. People who suffer from this disease often report that it is triggered by exposure to bright sunlight, which brings on seizures.

As reported in the September 5, 2012, edition of *This Week* magazine, Hutan Ashrafian, a surgeon at Imperial College London, thinks that Tutankhamun, the famous boy king known as King Tut, son of Akhenaten and the equally famous Nefertiti, suffered from the same disease. As did Tuthmosis IV, another Pharaoh of the eighteenth dynasty. He was the one to whom the final work on the great Sphinx of Giza is attributed.

> Akhenaten ... saw, somehow, that God was One, and he spent the next fourteen years overhauling the entire Egyptian religious establishment to express it.

According to the *Dream Stele*, an ancient Egyptian inscription, Tuthmosis's most famous seizure happened on a sunny day and was accompanied by a deeply spiritual, mystical vision. Could this be an example of mystical visions accompanying temporal lobe seizures? MRI scans report that epileptic seizures fire up in the exact same area of the brain as mystical visions and out-of-body experiences. That's not to say that one causes the other. It just means they find expression in the same area of the brain.

But as deeply spiritual as was the vision of Tuthmosis, it didn't have nearly the same results as the same thing experienced by Akhenaten. His vision included a huge leap from polytheism to monotheism. He saw, somehow, that God was One, and he spent the next fourteen years overhauling the entire Egyptian religious establishment to express it.

It may sound silly to say that an epileptic seizure marked the birth of monotheism, but it's not necessarily that far-fetched. Stranger things have happened with even greater results, once the mind is expanded a little.

Other Examples

In July 2004, Francis Crick, co-discoverer of the double helix structure of DNA molecules, died at the age of eighty-eight. Soon after his passing, a little-known fact about his accomplishment surfaced. It was revealed that when Crick was working at the Cavendish Laboratory in Cambridge, England, during the 1950s, he frequently used LSD as a thinking tool. The drug was legal back then, but few knew about it. Timothy Leary hadn't yet been exposed to the general public.

It was on one of Crick's LSD-fueled trips that, in his words, he "perceived the double helix shape" of DNA and began to unravel its structure.

In other words, one of the greatest discoveries in the history of biology happened because someone expanded his mind, opening up the very same area of the brain where epileptic seizures occur.

Apparently, the famous co-discoverer of the structure of DNA, Francis Crick, was taking LSD, which may have helped open his mind to the possibility of discovery.

Earlier we said that one theory advanced about humankind's Great Leap Forward in the great painted caves of Europe some 35,000 years ago, the first expression of symbolic, or religious, thought, was that shamans ate hallucinogenic mushrooms and experienced mind-altering spiritual visions.

The Apostle Paul, in the New Testament book called *The Acts of the Apostles*, told about having some kind of seizure in which he was knocked right off his horse, struck blind, and yet somehow saw the risen Christ. He was thus inspired to begin what we know as the religion of Christianity.

Muhammad experienced a night vision in which he was transported through the seven levels of heaven. Was this an OBE?

It certainly appears as though mind-altering experiences have entered into the human evolutionary experience more often than the conspiracy of silence would care to admit. No one wants to talk about it, but there it is.

The Monotheistic Principle

Having put forth the suggestion that monotheism could very well have come about because of a mind-altering experience, the questions naturally follow: "So what? Does it make any difference? I don't believe in a 'Being from Above' anyway! Why should I care about something that happened in Egypt more than three thousand years ago?"

Those are good points. But stick with me for a minute. This is important.

Do you remember back in the early part of this chapter when we differ-entiated between spirituality and religion? Religions always form around spiritual visions. It's not fair, or even helpful, to judge the original vision by the religion it attracts. Religions, by their very nature, tend to distort spirituality by heaping on traditions and rules. So if Akhenaten experienced a vision of One-ness, of unity, of monotheism, it might be important to examine it.

There are three explanations that are usually used to explain the reality of consciousness and spiritual thought. Dean Radin sums them up nicely in his book, *The Conscious Universe*:

- The first is that mind and matter both exist. Neither causes the other. Matter is studied by scientists in the laboratory. Mind is studied by psychiatrists, religionists, or others of their ilk. This is called dualism.

- The second is that consciousness rises up from below, so to speak—from the physical world of matter manifested in the body. It is a product of a human mind, arising out of the chemicals firing off neurons in the brain. In other words, matter forms mind, which is simply a function of the brain. The building blocks of all matter are therefore stuff that can be measured and explored. This view is called materialistic monism. We've moved into the field of unity (monism) but still locate it in the physical world of matter.

- The third is that mind is primary and not to be confused with brain at all. It can even be said that mind causes matter, or that consciousness is the base for all that exists. Matter exists because it is an expression of consciousness. This is called transcendental monism.

When I wrote to Dr. Radin and asked him to explain this concept, he immediately emailed me this reply:

This view suggests that physical reality as we experience it is manifested, top-down, by a "universal consciousness." It is not a bottom-up emergence from mindless matter/energy. This viewpoint is the opposite of prevailing scientific assumptions, so of course it is quite controversial.

Now let's apply all this.

The Vision of Monotheism

Up to the time of Pharaoh Akhenaten, our ancient ancestors had been in the habit of visualizing their spiritual concepts in terms of various gods out there: metaphysical beings who existed independently of humans and, for that

Does matter generate mind, or does the mind generate matter?

matter, all of matter and existence. They may have been pictured as having bodies, but they certainly weren't material bodies subject to the dictates of physical life as we know it. Spirits inhabited everything. Every rock, tree, animal, star, and moon were animated by spirit. Thus, the religion that grew around this spiritual vision was called animism. It was polytheistic in the sense that there were many gods surrounding us.

For a brief time, Akhenaten changed all that. He saw unity where others saw duality. However it happened, whether by epileptic seizure or spiritual insight, for one, brief moment he became, as far as we know, the first human to see all life as a unity rather than a separate plurality. The result became the religion of Monotheism. God was still out there. God was a Being rather than Being Itself. But it was a first step. It would eventually find expression in Hinduism's unity concepts, the monotheistic religions of Judaism, Christianity, and Islam, and even the Gaia Principle, the idea that our whole planet is one interconnected organism.

Humankind was on its way to a different way of understanding the essential nature of existence. We were on our way to unity.

Not bad for one mind-altering moment on a sunny day!

THE GOD PARTICLE AND THE MATERIAL UNIVERSE

This day and age we're living in
Gives cause for apprehension
With speed and new invention
And things like fourth dimension.
Yet we get a trifle weary
With Mr. Einstein's theory.
So we must get down to Earth at times
Relax, relieve the tension.

"As Time Goes By," words and music by Herman Hupfeld

Something Old, Something New

What makes up the basic substance of the universe? Where did we come from? Did the ancients understand intuitively—and maybe pass on to us—something that we are just beginning to understand with our new discoveries in science? Are we finally beginning to learn the lessons they tried to teach us, lessons they mathematically encoded when they built the monumental religious edifices that have all along been hiding in plain sight? Long ago, had they uncovered concepts we are now rediscovering?

Maybe so, because out of the laboratories of science comes a new gospel that permeates ancient religions. Nothing is as it appears to be! The ancient Hindu rishis taught that life is an illusion. What do modern scientists say?

$$E = mc^2$$

In 1905 a groundbreaking paper was published by Albert Einstein. It was titled "Does the Inertia of a Body Depend upon Its Energy Content?" and was the final installment of four papers he submitted that year to the journal *Annalen der Physik,* completing what is surely the most significant year in the history of physics. The first paper explained what he called the photoelectric effect. The second offered experimental proof that atoms really existed. The third introduced the theory of special relativity. The last and final paper of the series introduced what has become the most famous equation in physics: $E = mc^2$. It looks simple, but what it says is that nothing, absolutely nothing, is what it appears to be. In effect, Einstein's equation says that contrary to the evidence suggested by our five senses, life is but a dream—an illusion.

Albert Einstein's work in physics has been legendary and paradigm-shifting, showing how things like light, energy, and mass are related to each other.

It was a watershed moment. In 1904, it appeared to our senses that time and space and mass and energy were all separate. But in 1905 everything changed. By linking these seemingly unrelated elements together, first into the concept of space-time, then in the equation $E = mc^2$, Einstein completed his theory of special relativity. It defies the senses. Our minds tell us one thing; math tells us something else. Special relativity is perhaps one of the least intuitive theories ever conceived in the history of science, yet it is at the core of modern physics.

This isn't New Age religion. It comes right out of the science lab. Here it is: You are not at all what you appear to be. None of us are. We never were. You seem to be solid and real. But you're not. Take your skin, for instance. It appears to keep everything inside your body. But look closely. It's composed of many millions of cells that are constantly falling off and being replaced by new growth. (The dust that you vacuum up in your house consists mostly of dead skin cells. Aren't you glad you read this far?) But the skin cells aren't solid either. They are composed of atoms, all whirling around at the speed of light. And not even the atoms are solid. They are composed of subatomic particles. (Now we are in the field of quantum reality.) And those subatomic particles come and go, some of them surviving for far less than a second. Where do they come from? Where do they go? No one knows.

What does all this mean? The mass of your body, and everything else our senses tell us is real and solid—the m of $E = mc^2$, is really energy—the E of the equation. Mass is energy. Energy is mass. Mass and energy are the same

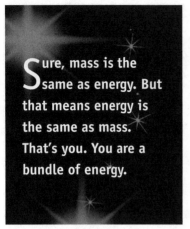

Sure, mass is the same as energy. But that means energy is the same as mass. That's you. You are a bundle of energy.

thing. You can say that your body is composed of mass. That's true, but only in one sense. It is just as valid to say that you are nothing but a seething mass of energy that came from who knows where and is on a journey back home. Before Einstein, mass was something. After, it was seen to be nothing. That's right. Despite the obvious evidence of your existence within reality, the very message that your senses insist is correct: you are nothing, at least as far as the tangible, rock-solid world of mass is concerned.

Yes, life is but a dream. With one simple equation, $E = mc^2$, Einstein concluded that mass and kinetic energy are the same thing, since the speed of light, c^2, is constant. In other words, mass can be changed into energy, and energy can be changed into mass. And it's not a matter of one becoming the other. Both are present and equal at the same time.

The first process is demonstrated by the production of nuclear energy. Particles are smashed and their energy is released.

The second process, the conversion of energy into mass, is demonstrated by the process of particle acceleration, in which low-mass particles zipping through a particle accelerator such as CERN's Large Hadron Collider in Switzerland, collide to form larger particles. But both are equal and present all the time. Whether we see mass or energy depends not on the presence of one or the other, but in how we choose to see them. So, is it mass—or energy? You decide. You'll find whichever you choose to look for.

Of course, the first to latch onto the implications of this discovery was the military. If you can convert the mass of an atom into the energy of an atomic bomb, why not use it to end a war? It would be a way to save countless lives by destroying countless lives … or something.

But look, for a minute, at the other side of the equation. Sure, mass is the same as energy. But that means energy is the same as mass. That's you. You are a bundle of energy. Or perhaps, more accurately, vibration.

This has extreme relevance to those involved in the process of trying to figure out what life is all about. If we can't trust our senses, but still dare to imagine other ways to explain the facts, all kinds of possibilities exist, including the possibilities that humans have flirted with these concepts before, much to our detriment. Here's another one of them.

You're on Candid Camera!

Imagine that you are watching a movie on TV. You are, first and foremost, engaged in a story. It moves you, emotionally. You are fully involved.

But wait a minute! What are you really watching? You're watching a bunch of pixels on a screen. Suppose for a moment that you can merge with them. What do you see? Only a bunch of little dots of energy. They seem to make no sense at all. It all seems like chaos. Just bursts of energy appearing and then disappearing. You can't figure it out. So you move out a little. Now the energy dots appear to have color. There's a group of red ones over here and a group of blue ones over there. So you move out a little more. The energy pixels take on form. They appear to be people, interacting with one another. Move out some more and you are out of the screen and back in your living room, enjoying the story again. The TV screen has become a living universe, boxing in a moving story.

Now, does the story originate within the TV screen? Is the TV the source of the movie that has captured your attention? Of course not! A group of real actors, somewhere, had their mass converted into TV waves, changed into electromagnetic pixels, bounced off a satellite or two, and converted into a picture on your home theater equipment. As a matter of fact, if you have multiple televisions in your house, you can watch alternate shows that all take place at the same time. You are viewing a multiverse of TV shows, and none of the actors in one TV know that the others exist, even though they are only a few feet away from one another.

But wait! Are the actors on your TV screen aware of their own existence, let alone the others? Not on the TV. The real actors were conscious, of course, but after they finished their gig, the physics of the whole thing took over. The actors on your screen are simply bundles of energy who appear to be carrying out their actions in real time.

Down to Earth

Now look at your life with Einstein's equation running through your mind and the voice of ancient Hindu rishis echoing in your ear. You, too, are a mass of pixels called subatomic particles. How do you explain your existence? These particles are coming from somewhere, no one knows where, constantly appearing and disappearing. And yet you feel real, even though, scientifically speaking, you are no more substantial than the pixels on your TV screen. Did real actors, from, perhaps, the future, or another dimension, play out the role you are now experiencing? Are you simply the product of someone's imagination—some far-off scriptwriter? If so, whose? And what about the fact that you are conscious of yourself, something the TV pixels are not? How did that come about? Imagine it: computer-created images that have somehow become conscious of being computer-created images! (Sounds like a *Star Trek* episode, doesn't it? Which way is the holodeck?)

I understand your concern and skeptical frame of mind. You don't feel like a holographic projection. It doesn't feel as though you are simply bundles

Are you sure you are real? Could it be possible we are all some type of holographic projection? How would we know?

of pixilated energy. But physicists assure us that this is actually the case. Can you ever again trust your feelings? Are your senses really reliable?

"THIS IS REAL," you scream! "I know what I feel!"

But according to Einstein and his followers, your senses have evolved to serve you very well, but only in this reality. As Sir Arthur Eddington once wrote, "The universe is not only stranger than we imagine, it is stranger than we *can* imagine."

The Tao of Physics

$E = mc^2$ led to a whole new branch of physics, even though Einstein himself refused, for a long time, to believe it. When confronted with the logical outcome of some of his discoveries, he made his famous reply, "God does not play dice with the universe!"

To which Stephen Hawking has since answered, "God not only plays dice with the universe—he sometimes throws them where they can't be seen!"

In the *Tao of Physics*, theoretical physicist Fritjof Capra wrote these words, which simply reek of spirituality:

> I 'saw' cascades of energy coming down from outer space, in which particles were created and destroyed in rhythmic pulses; I 'saw' the atoms of the elements and those of my body participating in this cosmic dance of energy; I 'felt' its rhythm and I 'heard' its sound, and at the moment I knew that this was the dance of Shiva, the Lord of Dancers, worshipped by the Hindus.

Here's the point. We are not just discovering these things in our day. It is a concept that goes back thousands of years, at least as far as the Hindu rishis, wise men who first wrote about Shiva. In response to this ancient vision, these pulses of energy, the ancients wrote enigmatic texts and raised standing stones. How did they do it? Who taught them?

A Theory of Everything

With the reality dam of the senses unequivocally broken, physicists began to imagine a flood of new ideas that before were thought impossible. Ideas such as:

- A multiverse rather than a single universe.
- Other dimensions (the theoretical string theory postulates at least nine of them!).
- Our reality being just one manifested possible reality stretched out over one of an infinite number of membranes, each perhaps less than an inch away from the others but unknowable to each other because they vibrate on completely different frequencies.
- The possibility of an infinite number of physical manifestations breaking off into an infinite number of alternate realities whenever you make a choice and carry it out.

Anyone who has ever watched the Science Channel, the History Channel, Morgan Freeman's *Through the Wormhole*, or any of the new science fiction shows is familiar with such ideas.

Faced with all this science, even laypeople are now free to ask themselves some big questions:

What If?

What if there existed, somewhere in the parallel realms of philosophy, science, religion, and spirituality, an answer to questions that have taunted humanity for as long as there have been conscious humans to ask them?

- Does life have intrinsic meaning, or are we a cosmic accident?
- Is there a real God, a Universal Consciousness, a sublime Other, at the root of all religions?
- Do the world's great religions open the door on another reality?
- Is there a Grand Unified Theory—a Theory of Everything— that makes sense of the material universe?
- Is there an eternal reason for our being born?
- What happens to us when we die?

These questions, and many more, make up the philosopher's quest, a search that has often been vilified or otherwise ridiculed. Perhaps such questions provoke derision because there doesn't seem to be any intrinsic way to ever prove their speculative answers. Following their trail through the myriad labyrinthine pathways of religion, philosophy, and history seems a futile journey. After all, there are more immediate and pressing things to do with one's time.

But still:

- What if the philosopher's quest were attainable?
- What if meaning and purpose lay within our grasp?

• What if the answer proved to be right in front of us, taught to our ancestors by those who had already struggled with these questions thousands of years ago, but hidden from our allegedly rational minds only by our demonstrably egocentric prejudices that convince us we are the first to consider them?

If the response to any of these questions is that it is possible, we may well be dealing with lost histories and hidden truths.

GUT Theories

Many physicists have written about GUT (Grand Unified Theory)—a theory that explains everything. No less an authority than Stephen Hawking said it this way, in his book *A Brief History of Time*:

> If we do discover a complete theory, it should in time be understood in broad principle by everyone, not just a few scientists. Then we shall all, philosophers, scientists and just ordinary people, be able to take part in the discussion of the question why we and the universe exist. If we find the answer to that, it would be the ultimate triumph of human reason, for then we would know the mind of God.

Read Dr. Hawking's words again, slowly. He has gone beyond science and ventured into the world of the philosopher and the religionist. He's not

just talking about the how, the realm of the scientist. He has slipped over into why, the stuff of spirituality. "For then we would know the mind of God," he says. That's a pretty powerful statement. A preeminent physicist using God language!

But here it's important to remember that when human beings of our current civilization first began to consider these things, they used God language, too—the language of ancient India, Sumer, Babylonia, and Egypt. Why did they all start seeking these truths at the same time, a time that just happened to follow the last great cataclysm on planet Earth?

Brilliant contemporary physicists such as Stephen Hawking have been advancing so far into theoretical territory about the nature of reality as to enter what previously has been thought of as territory reserved for religious speculation.

Searching Questions

Perhaps it is time to ask some searching questions:

- What if there is a universal myth to which every major world religion refers—a myth that remembers a time when those who came before us tried to pass on to us their wisdom, before it died with them?

- What if this teaching encompasses a Theory of Everything, posited now by the scientific method but which has long echoed down the corridors of time in myth and legend?

- What if each world religion, including science itself, is a repository for this myth?

- What if the answer has been right there, under our very noses, the whole time?

Is it possible that we are about to finally come to discover something we already knew, and re-remember the hidden truths of the ancients?

✳ ✴ ✳

HINDU VEDAS AND THE UPANISHADS

There are four Vedas, the Rig Veda, Sama Veda, Yajur Veda and Atharva Veda. The Vedas are the primary texts of Hinduism. They also had a vast influence on Buddhism, Jainism, and Sikhism. Traditionally the text of the Vedas was coeval with the universe. The Vedas contain hymns, incantations, and rituals from ancient India. Along with the Book of the Dead, the Enuma Elish, the I Ching, and the Avesta, they are among the most ancient religious texts still in existence.

Archive, http://www.sacred-texts.com/

The Problem with Textbooks

Quite a few years ago I began what amounted to a second career as a college professor. The first subject I taught at that level was Comparative Religion. I presented an entry level course designed to help students understand the Big Five world religions of Judaism, Christianity, Islam, Hinduism, and Buddhism. Along the way, of course, we broke off into many other expressions of faith, but it took an entire semester to even begin to navigate our way through the fascinating subject of religious expression.

At the time I wasn't as familiar with Hinduism as I am now, so it was pretty exciting for me to study and learn myself as I tried to stay ahead of my students.

I carefully borrowed from various texts, bounced basic ideas off a friend who was born and raised in India, and converted all that to language familiar to American students who had no basic background in the subject. The experience eventually led to my first big book for Visible Ink Press: *The Religion Book: Places, Prophets, Saints, and Seers*, which is an extended version of the glossary of terms I developed for that course.

To any former students who may find themselves reading these words: It was a lot of fun and I stand by everything I told you concerning the religion of Hinduism. But when it comes to what I said concerning the peopling of India and the origins of the Sanskrit language, I owe you a huge apology. None of it is now considered to be factual. Thank goodness it wasn't on the final exam.

> The whole field has turned upside down, and the ones who brought about the change are, bless their hearts, the traditional, mainstream scholars.

In a way, it wasn't really my fault. I was simply passing on what I garnered from the textbooks. And most of them were written prior to 1999. I think I'm on pretty safe ground when I say that virtually no competent scholars today accept much of what was written before then about this subject. The whole field has turned upside down, and the ones who brought about the change are, bless their hearts, the traditional, mainstream scholars. I've had some rough things to say about traditionalists throughout the course of this book, but in this case, to their everlasting credit, they bit the bullet and rewrote the texts when lost histories and hidden truths could be ignored no longer.

Mistake #1: The Mt. Toba Eruption

When I was teaching, the accepted story of how the basic texts of Hinduism, the Vedas and the Upanishads came about went something like this: As we discovered back in the chapter "Ancient Catastrophes," 75,000 years ago the Mt. Toba super eruption pretty much destroyed everyone and everything in India. It plunged the whole world into an ice age that may have lasted as long as 1,800 years. The importance of this event was that it effectively explained why there is less genetic diversity today than one would expect, given the age of humanity. Any biological changes would have begun to develop only 75,000 years ago, as opposed to the 200,000 years we have been on the planet. Since all humans in India at the time would have been killed, any indigenous population must be less than 75,000 years old.

The problem with this theory is that in 2009 an archeological team led by Michael Petraglia from Oxford did archeological digs reminiscent of the Pompeii excavations under layers upon layers of Mt. Toba ash. They found stone implements and artifacts under the ash. That was to be expected. But they also found artifacts right above the ash, proving that humans must have survived the extreme conditions and somehow managed to bounce back.

Thus, in one excellent study, the indigenous population of India was pushed back indefinitely into the past.

That was my first mistake as a teacher. The next is even worse.

Mistake #2: The Aryan Invasion

For a lot of technical reasons, mostly revolving around what was then known as the so-called Indo-European language of Sanskrit, it was thought that the original population of India, mostly dark-skinned aboriginal and Dravidian (people from southern India) tribes consisting of Stone Age primitives, was invaded by a light-skinned, blue-eyed Aryan race sometime during the second millennium B.C.E. They entered the India subcontinent from the northwest through the famous Kyber Pass, bringing with them a superior European language that, when mixed together with the local tongue, produced that most spiritual of languages so beloved by Joseph Campbell, Sanskrit. This was the language of the ancient texts known today as the *Vedas,* followed later by the Upanishads. More about them in a minute.

This Aryan invasion theory, which resulted in a sudden upshift of sophistication both intellectually and biologically, found its ultimate expression in the beliefs of Adolf Hitler and resulted in his Final Solution in the fires of the Nazi concentration camps.

Unfortunately, in a supreme case of too little, too late, the truth is now known. There was no Aryan invasion. There wasn't even an Aryan race. The whole thing was a matter of misinterpreting the Sanskrit word *Aryas* and the European assumption that the original people of India were too primitive to have built the sophisticated civilization unearthed by archeologists.

What this meant was that the old-school method of dating the earliest and possibly most poetically sublime religious texts in the world, the Vedas, was now out the window. If the Vedas were written after an Aryan invasion that took place in the second millennium B.C.E., they couldn't be older than some 3,500 years. But if the assumed invasion never took place, if Sanskrit was developed by the people of the Indus Valley who had been there since at least the Mt. Toba eruptions and maybe even long before, the sky was now the limit. The Vedas might be 3,500 years old or they might be 30,500 years old. Who knew?

Obviously it's time to examine the texts to see what they have to say in the light of these new revelations. But when we do, guess what emerges? Of course! An epic story of catastrophes, floods, and fire, with new civilizations arising out of the ashes of what had come before. From the Bible to the Hopi legends, from the Mayan *Popol Vuh* to the Incan myths, from Indonesia to Japan, from Easter Island to Antarctica, we've heard this song before.

A page from the Vedas, written in Sanskrit, was originally thought to have been written by an Aryan race that had invaded the Indian subcontinent, but this proved to be very wrong, indeed.

The Vedas and the Upanishads

Hinduism is based on oral tradition and the oldest expressions of that tradition are found in the poems of the Vedas. They consist of *Samhitas*, which are collections of hymns. There are four of them:

- *Rig Veda*, which is the oldest and probably the most revered
- *Sama Veda*
- Yajur Veda
- Atharva Veda

It was assumed that these were composed around 1500 B.C.E. Now it is assumed that was when they were finally written down for the first time. The tradition in India was, and in some cases still is, that the texts lose their force when they are captured on paper. They are meant to be spoken aloud. The prodigious feats of memory performed by some Hindu holy men are amazing. The Vedas might very well have survived intact for millennia before finally being committed to parchment.

The Upanishads are usually called the *Vedanta*, a Sanskrit word that generally means either the "last chapters" of the Vedas or the "highest purpose" of the Vedas. They offer a philosophical commentary, so to speak, and best articulate the basic concept of Hinduism: *Tat tvam asi*—"Thou art That."

This is the famous expression that says our innermost being (*Atman*) is one with the inexpressible Absolute (*Brahman*).

(A much deeper exploration of all this is found in *The Religion Book*, listed at the end of this book in Further Readings.)

The Unending Circle

Together, the Vedas and the Upanishads offer many lifetimes' worth of study, but one aspect concerns us now. A basic teaching contained in these works is that there are four great world ages that are repeated over and over again throughout an unending history. These ages are called Yugas.

- Krita Yuga: This age is a Golden Age "in which abounds righteousness."
- Treta Yuga: This age witnesses a decline in morals in which "virtue fails."

- Davapara Yuga: "Lying and arguing expand, minds fall short, and truth declines."
- Kali Yuga: "Men turn to wickedness and value is degraded. Decay flourishes and the human race approaches annihilation."

At the end of each Yuga comes a catastrophe, either fire or flood. Then the next Yuga arises, built on the remains of the preceding one.

According to Hindu belief, we are currently living in the final days of the Kali Yuga, the last age. It is an age marked by progressively worse behavior:

> People will be greedy, take to wicked behavior, will be merciless, indulge in hostilities without any cause, unfortunate, extremely covetous for wealth and world desires.

From the *Bhagavata Purana*

Anything there sound familiar?

Manu and the Seven Rishis (Sages)

There are other concepts found throughout the texts that are, by now, familiar to anyone who has read through this book from the beginning. One of the most striking is that of the Hindu Noah figure, Manu, the Father of Humankind.

According to the *Rig Veda*, Manu, accompanied by seven sages, was spared when the previous Yuga was destroyed by a great flood. He was told by Vishnu to build an ark and gather two of every kind of seed which would be spared by the rising waters. When he and his company landed in the Himalayas, they eventually descended and went about rebuilding civilization. Their purpose was nothing less than "repromulgating the knowledge inherited by them, as a sacred trust, from their forefathers."

Now, are we to believe that a worldwide flood actually covered the Himalayan mountains? Geology pretty much rules that out. But if your civilization is a coastal one, and the waters are rising, you might flee in that direction.

According to some versions of the story, the original Vedas were destroyed. What we have today is a version reproduced by the sages, first orally and then, much later, written down.

> According to Hindu belief, we are currently living in the final days of the Kali Yuga, the last age.

This is now the fifth verse of a familiar song. First in Sumer and Egypt, then in Peru and Mexico, now in India, we have the story of a cataclysm, a flood, a destruction, and a rebuilding of civilization by a mythical ancient god

Manu and the Seven Rishis (sages) are protected from the Great Flood by Vishnu in the form of a fish (Matsya). Manu would then preserve the knowledge of the past and pass it on to the survivors who could rebuild civilization.

and his cohorts. In Sumer it was the Anunnaki. In Egypt it was the Zep Tepi committee of civilization bringers. In Peru it was the Viracochas. In Mexico, Quetzalcoatl and his helpers. Now in India, Manu and the seven sages. All brought civilization to the indigenous people. For that matter, all are depicted wearing "fish-garbed" uniforms and all are pictured carrying what author Graham Hancock has called a "man-bag" type briefcase of some kind—perhaps a sign or tool of a sacred office. I infer that we might even suppose it was the bag in which these early shaman-like figures carried their stash. They all seem like mind-expanding guys and, as we shall soon see, the use of psychedelic drugs are common to shamanism. Who knows?

If that isn't enough, the seven sages of India are said to be represented in the heavens by the seven stars of the constellation we call the Big Dipper, lending an astronomical component to the story that is reminiscent of Egyptian and Sumerian cosmology. All three myths are set at relatively the same time in history, some 13,000 years ago or so.

Is all this coincidence? Did cultures from all over the world make this stuff up? Or, given the recent discovery of ancient cities found drowned beneath the waves in both northwest and southern India, is there more here than meets the eye? Do the myths depict a poetic historical memory as well as a spiritual text? Do the Vedas represent lost histories and hidden truths of a previous civilization's spirituality, around which grew the religion of Hinduism? Has a religious culture grown up around a foundational cult?

These are questions that need answering. Perhaps they are finally peeking out from under the conspiracy of silence so as to tweak our curiosity.

JUDAISM/CHRISTIANITY

Jesus answered, "The most important commandment is, 'Hear, O Israel, the Lord our God is one.'"

Mark 12:29

A Bridge between Worlds

I was on a bus from Jerusalem to Cairo, with a view of the Mediterranean Sea out my right window and the Sinai to my left, when it struck me, for the first time emotionally rather than intellectually, that anyone who, during the last 5.3 million years since the Mediterranean formed, walked from Egypt or, for that matter, the entire African continent, to anywhere else in the world, they would have walked exactly where I was now. The curtain of time suddenly pulled back for a moment. I saw Stone Age families, smiling as their children played in the waves, pause to admire the view. I saw Ethiopian chariots making their way west, perhaps passing Persian caravans going in the other direction. I even saw, for one terrible minute, Jewish tanks engaging Egyptian commandos.

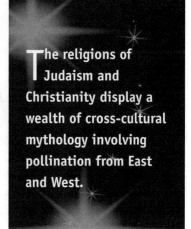

The religions of Judaism and Christianity display a wealth of cross-cultural mythology involving pollination from East and West.

There is no doubt about it. For thousands of years, Israel and its surrounding lands formed a bridge between the continents of Africa, Europe, and the lands to the east. I already knew all this, of course. But what struck me now was how much information shuttled through here along with the trade goods.

The religions of Judaism and Christianity display a wealth of cross-cultural mythology involving pollination from East and West.

Think about it for a minute. The story of Abraham, the father of the Jews, begins all the way over in ancient Sumer. Abraham was an immigrant who followed the Fertile Crescent up and over to the land of the Canaanites. That's what the Phoenicians, that greatest of ancient seafaring people, called themselves. Once he got there, he barely paused before heading west to Egypt for a while. East meets West. Cultures unite.

Two thousand years later, in the Christian story, when Jesus is born, the early writers had to work at it a bit, but they got Jesus to migrate to Egypt because of an edict issued by a Roman ruler. Of both Abraham and Jesus the Bible has God declaring, "Out of Egypt have I called my son." Before the holy family travels west, however, they are visited by stargazing astronomers from the east, that is, ancient Sumer.

Both Jewish and Christian scriptures are chock full of towers from Babel, floods in Mesopotamia, a paradise in either Turkey or Iraq, legends right out of Egyptian mythology, echoes of Persian Zoroastrianism, and cosmopolitan missionaries who were at home in both Palestine and Rome.

East met West in Israel, both figuratively and literally. Even the central Christian icon pictures a man suspended between heaven and Earth, while reaching out his arms to embrace East and West in an ultimate, if horrible, symbol of reconciliation.

Josephus was a Hebrew slave of the Romans who later wrote two important histories of the early Jews that remain valuable resources to scholars for information not found in the Old Testament.

It is only natural, therefore, that the ancient texts embraced by both religions are overshadowed by an even more ancient wisdom that is to be found in Egyptian, Asian, and European folklore.

Josephus

One of the most famous, or infamous, depending on whom you talk to, historians of ancient Israel was the Jewish patriot-turned-Roman writer Joseph ben Matityahu. As a young man he fought against the Romans. Apparently, however, he was enough of a historian to recognize a lost cause when he saw one. He defected to the Romans and was received with open arms after he claimed that it was written in the stars that Vespasian would soon become emperor. When that, indeed, happened, Joseph found himself with a friend in the highest possible place. Vespasian decided to spare Joseph's life and made him a slave and interpreter. Eventually he granted the talented writer his freedom. In gratitude, Joseph took Vespasian's family name as his own. He became Titus Flavius Josephus. Today we know him as Josephus, the historian. The works that cemented his place in history are known as *The Jewish War* and the classic *Antiquities of the Jews*. Together they reveal a lot about early Jewish history that is not mentioned in the Bible.

> Josephus ... mentions that these early astronomers were concerned that their wisdom might be lost in the coming catastrophe.

In the "Ancient Civilizations" chapter of this book, we looked at another non-biblical Hebrew text called the *Book of Enoch*. There it was said the great deluge we call Noah's flood was prophesied ahead of time to the mysterious Enoch, a direct ancestor of Noah. There were obviously other legends that survived down to the first century. Josephus, an educated man, knew about them. Here's one of them, in his own words:

> It is told about the children of Seth, the son of Adam, that they were the inventors of that peculiar sort of wisdom which is concerned with the heavenly bodies and their order. And that their inventions might not be lost before they were sufficiently known, they made two pillars upon Adam's prediction that the world was to be destroyed at one time by the force of fire and at another time by the violence and quantity of water. The one was of brick, the other of stone, and they inscribed their discoveries on both, that in case the pillar of brick should be destroyed by the flood, the pillar of stone might remain, and exhibit these discoveries to mankind and also inform them that there was another pillar, of brick, erected by them.

In "Ancient Astronomers" we saw that an early culture of astronomy marked our distant past. It seems as if Josephus remembered that culture as well. He mentions that these early astronomers were concerned that their wisdom might be lost in the coming catastrophe.

One would be very tempted to wonder if the pillar of stone built to commemorate that wisdom might be something akin to Göbekli Tepe, the pyramids of Giza, Stonehenge, or someplace like them.

Josephus is also quick to point out that flood myths are not unique to Judaism. In his words:

> All the writers of barbarian histories make mention of this flood and of [Noah's] ark, among whom is Berosus the Chaldean Hieronymus the Egyptian ... Mnaseas and a great many more.

In other words: "Hey! Don't take my word for it! I'm just one among many!"

Christian Echoes

Epic catastrophes seem to be a major theme of the ancients. Even Christianity foretells such an event. The concluding book of the Bible, the Revelation of St. John, ends with a bang:

> And I saw a new heaven and a new earth: for the first heaven and the first earth were passed away; and there was no more sea.

> Revelation 21:1

We ended our discussion of the Hindu Vedas with a passage from the *Bhagavata Purana* that talked about the disparaging attitude of humans on Earth when a great cataclysm swept them all away. Compare that passage with these verses from the New Testament:

> First of all you must understand that in the last days scoffers will come ... they will say, "Ever since our fathers died, everything goes on as it has since the beginning of creation." But they deliberately forget that long ago ... the world of that time was deluged and destroyed ... the present heavens and earth are reserved for fire.

> 2nd Peter 3:1–7

A glance through the wisdom literature of Israel, home to ancient wisdom and bridge to many worlds, reveals a compilation of stories that come from both East and West. Are these memories of hidden truths that were accepted by many cultures some two thousand years ago, but that are glossed over today in our preoccupation with technological modern life? Are we the generation of scoffers Peter mentions? It might be good for us to consider, the next time we hear the old "life goes on" clichés, that there was, perhaps, a time when it didn't.

SHAMANISM

> The high civilizations of ancient Egypt and of the ancient Maya maintain an air of occult mystery. We would like to know what made them tick, get inside their souls.... The ultimate origins of these great and mysterious religions of antiquity, one in the Old World, one in the New, are lost in time, but it is certain that at some stage, and for a very long while, shamanism, the techniques of shamanism, the experiences of shamanism, and the discoveries of shamanism played a central role in the evolution of both of them.

> Graham Hancock in *Supernatural*

Old Explorers for New Territories

The newly discovered Higgs Field has opened up whole territories for scientists to explore. As we saw when we looked at the God Particle and the field of Akasha, energy takes on mass when it passes through the Higgs Field and into our realm of perception.

Scientists are in the business of measuring things. That works fine on our side of the Higgs Field. Over here on our playing field, where matter reigns supreme, we can measure to our heart's content. As a matter of fact, there are still scientists who swear that unless we can measure something, it doesn't exist. Matter, according to them, is where it's at! They even claim that reality begins when energy takes on mass. Until then, it's only potential. Potential becomes real when it collapses into our observation window.

The way of negotiating the energy territories on the other side of the Higgs Field, then, is with math and probability studies. We can't measure energy potential, but we can estimate its probability quotient. It's the only way we can ever learn about existence outside our perception realm.

Or is it?

One of the supreme ironies of modern human existence is that in order to see what's on the other side of the Higgs Field, the material fence that separates us from other realms of existence which don't consist of matter and particles, is to employ the talents and skills of a member of a fraternity consisting of perhaps the oldest spiritual practitioners known to humankind—those who are familiar with the art of the shaman. They've been journeying back and forth from this reality to other realities for thousands of years. As a matter of fact, the first shaman might very well have been contemporaneous with the first modern human.

If you have any preconceived ideas about what a shaman is, based on some picture you once saw in an old copy of your parents' *National Geographic*, do your best to disassociate from them. They are, without a doubt, false and an insult to the craft. A modern shaman doesn't have to live in Peru, South Africa, or Siberia, although many of them do. You might even sit next to one in a bus on your morning commute and talk about the results of the latest football game without ever realizing you are

Nobel laureate Peter Higgs first proposed the existence of a particle, now called the Higgs boson, that was essential for explaining how particles achieve mass.

with a unique individual. Being a shaman is almost always a part-time position. You can't go to the metaphysical neighborhoods they visit and stay there. It would probably drive you mad. After a shamanic journey, no matter how vivid and spectacular the trip, you have to come home and do the dishes. That's just the way it is.

Definitions

First, understand that the word "shaman" itself is a bit of a misnomer. It is a Siberian term that has since been applied to all indigenous practitioners who we once called medicine men, priests, or even (shudder!) witch doctors. It is a catchall phrase employed by outsiders. As such, it is probably not a very good label. But it's out there, so we'll use it.

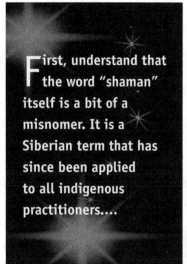

First, understand that the word "shaman" itself is a bit of a misnomer. It is a Siberian term that has since been applied to all indigenous practitioners....

That being the case, it would probably be best to agree on a good definition of what a shaman is. For that we turn to Michael Harner who, in the 1980s, opened the eyes of the world with his groundbreaking book, *The Way of the Shaman*. He didn't gain his insights by learning about shamanism, as was the custom of that time when it came to doing research in the field. Back then you were expected to remain aloof and unattached when studying foreign cultures. "Observe, don't participate," was the academic mantra. "Remain objective!"

Harner was a scientist. But he was open-minded enough to understand that studying shamanism required active participation simply because a typical shaman couldn't possibly teach you anything just by lecturing about it. He quickly discovered that learning about it wouldn't cut it. The most that method could accomplish would be a physical description of someone experiencing an inward journey—a worthless endeavor. That's why shamans don't usually write anything down about their practices. It is an oral tradition and has been since the beginning.

Harner wrote *The Way of the Shaman* in 1980. Its genius lay in the fact that he was able to synthesize shamanistic tradition and package it in a way Americans could grasp. He didn't write his next book, *Cave and Cosmos*, until 2013, and the only reason he wrote the second book at all was that he considered the inevitable approach of death and felt it would be advantageous to share some of the work in core shamanism he had accomplished at his Foundation for Shamanic Studies in Mill Valley, California.

According to Michael Harner, in his book, *Cave and Cosmos*:

While the work of shamans encompasses virtually the full gamut of known spiritual practices, shamanism is universally characterized by an intentional change in consciousness to engage in two-way interaction with spirits. Its most distinctive feature, which is not universal, is the out-of-body journey to other worlds. It should be noted that in some indigenous societies, there are shamans who do not journey at all, and others who journey only in the Middle World or, if they journey beyond the Middle World, may not go to both the Upper and Lower Worlds. What they all do share is disciplined interaction with spirits in non-ordinary reality to help and heal others.

Core Shamanism

Let's break that down a bit. A core teaching of shamanism is that there is more than one reality. The reality we live in consists of matter and extends to the end of the universe. You may travel, as has been reported by those who have experienced a typical out-of-body experience, to the farthest reach of the cosmos and hold the universe in the palm of your hand, but you still haven't left the Middle World. The Middle World is the world of the scientists. It consists of matter that can be measured. It is bound by the Higgs Field. Harner calls it "ordinary reality."

Shamans recognize that territories exist across the fence on the other side of physical matter—realms that exist in what Harner calls "non-ordinary reality." They also believe those realms are just as present here as they are there. If shamanism spawned a religion, it was probably the religion known as Animism—the belief that everything made of matter, rock, tree, and person, is animated by spirit. It is alive, as opposed to what one of my shaman friends refers to as the dead-stick philosophy.

Ordinary reality, then, is what we experience in what I have elsewhere called our "perception realm," a term coined by my wife, Barbara. But there are realms we cannot perceive with the five senses, even though we walk, run, and live amongst and in them. Perhaps Jesus said it best in Luke 17:21: "The realm of God is within (or amongst) you." We have deduced the existence of these

In shamanism, there is the belief that we just live in one reality, but there are others we cannot perceive with our ordinary five senses.

realms through the math of quantum physics but cannot experience them physically except in rare cases of splash-over that we often attribute to emotions, déjà vu or metaphysical enigmas. This is the country of nonordinary reality.

In traditional shamanism there are worlds on both sides of our perceptions.

- First is the Lower World, usually associated with animal spirits. This was probably the world experienced by the ancient shamans who went into the great caves of Europe and rendered, in vivid pigments, artistic images of the animal envoys they met there.

- Second is the Upper World, usually associated with images of fairies and angels found in mythologies everywhere. In other words, it is associated with flight.

At this point, if your knowledge about shamanism is limited to a few articles picked up from the Internet, you are probably ready to throw up your hands in disgust and turn to the next chapter.

But wait! There's more!

Describing the Indescribable

Suppose you see something completely outside your experience and attempt to explain it to someone. How are you going to do it? They haven't seen it, so all you can do is tell them what it's like.

- "I saw this beautiful flower that only grows in India. It's different from anything I've ever seen. It was kind of red and gold, with a gorgeous petal like...."

- "Dude, I saw this guy do a totally radical move on his surfboard. He did like a 360 with a kind of backward flip and then tucked into a ball and landed on his feet. Oh man, you had to have been there!"

- "The music was unbelievable—kind of a cross between Led Zeppelin and Barry Manilow, you know, with some Beethoven orchestrations behind it that sounded like Shostakovich on steroids!"

Well, you get the idea. It's hard to describe something unless your listener has a common point of reference.

Next, suppose you have the good fortune to expand your consciousness to the point of seeing a totally different reality. Words were invented to describe experiences in this reality. How are they possibly going to work over there?

It gets even more complicated. Forget trying to explain it to someone else. How are you going to process it? You are seeing something that is totally outside of the realm that language was invented to explain.

Have you ever tried to describe a dream? Difficult, isn't it? The images are very real to you. But the poor person you're trying to tell about it just sits there with a blank face.

The problem lies in the fact that your right-brain intuitive neurons are experiencing something that can only be processed by your left brain analytical memories. The left brain has to sort through your entire rolodex of experiences to come up with something that the image looks like.

You probably didn't see a two-headed eagle with the body of a fish, but that's the only image your left brain synapses could come up with that looked remotely like the image you did see, which was, by the way, an entity encountered in a perception reality completely devoid of physical matter.

> **W**ords were invented to describe experiences in this reality. How are they possibly going to work over there?

Is it any wonder that shamans may have difficulty expressing that which is, by its very nature, inexpressible?

Therein lies both the problem and the practice. But cheer up! The only faith you have to have in the whole process is backed up by what physics and metaphysics have already proved: that parallel universes, or nonordinary realities, actually exist and that it may be possible to experience them directly.

Beginnings

How did it all start? When did our ancient ancestors first discover the existence of other realms that were outside of this one but still very much real?

The speculation, by no means proven, is that mind-expanding or consciousness-raising journeys, or trips, to use a term from the 1960s, began the same way they sometimes occur today—by ingesting chemicals found in plant derivatives that open up areas of the brain that we seldom use in day-to-day life.

Our brains have evolved to bring order to the world we live in. That only makes sense. It doesn't mean other realities don't exist. It just means we have forgotten how to access them. Estimates have been advanced that some 2% of the human race is born with the correct amount of naturally occurring chemicals in the brain to spontaneously experience other realities and to see with sacred eyes. For the rest of us the windows and doors are still there, hidden in the recesses of our minds, but as we age we've learned to just close them.

Please don't think that all shamans are druggies, however. Some, indeed, are famous for their use of *ayahuasca* and psychedelic mushrooms. When used correctly they are ingested in a sacred manner after much preparation and are overseen by experienced shamanic practitioners. It is considered to be a sacred, ritualistic journey, not a recreational trip.

But there are other methods employed in shamanic journeying. Perhaps the most universal is the use of drumming, often accompanied by rhythmic dance. It produces the same kind of effect in modern cultures completely divorced from shamanism, such as is expressed in the well-known song of some years back:

Give me the beat, boys, to free my soul,
I wanna get lost in your rock 'n roll and drift away....

"I Want to Get Lost in Your Rock and Roll": Dobie Gray

Others practice intense meditation. American Indian tribes were famous for inducing discomfort and even pain through deprivation, such as in the vision quest or, even more extreme, the sun dance.

Purpose

All this is not to say, however, that the purpose for shamanic journeying is to experience a kind of personal ecstasy. That happens sometimes, it is true.

Psilocybe semilanceata is a species of mushroom that may be used for inducing a "psychedelic", spiritual experience.

But the core of shamanism is to obtain information and assistance to help others. Shamans are not priests. Their primary purpose is not to lead ritualistic pageants. Instead, they share more in common with healers. Their purpose is to journey out for help and return with healing.

They are the oldest religious practitioners known to humankind. They are familiar with the landscape of other worlds. They practice to serve. Perhaps the time has now come for scientists, for all of us, to abandon long-held prejudices and turn to the folks who have the experience to explore where test tubes and microscopes cannot go—the subtle world we have finally discovered that lies beyond the Higgs Field.

Old meets new—a marriage made in heaven!

STRUCTURES, STONES, AND INTUITION

Historians of religion divide the use of sacred stones into four categories, giving them technical names drawn from Celtic terminology. A single upright stone is known as a "menhir." A circle formed from such standing stones is called a "cromlech," the most famous example being the magnificent Stonehenge in England. Flat stones placed on the top of pairs of upright stones are called "dolmens" and are frequently associated with burials. Finally, memorials formed from large heaps of stones are called "cairns." Archeologists and historians have found examples of all these types of sacred stones in nearly all cultures of the world, from Neolithic times to the present.

William L. Hamblin and Daniel C. Peterson
in *Deseret News*, October 7, 2012

The Stones Cry Out

Portal tombs, passage graves, galleries, menhirs, stone circles, henges, dolmens, barrows, cairns—these are only a few of the terms used to describe the more than fifty thousand magnificent, mysterious, enigmatic stone structures found scattered across the landscape from Asia to Great Britain, from South America to the frozen arctic of Canada, and from the islands of the Pacific to the outback of Australia. Most were built during the Golden Age of megalithic construction, 4500 to 1500 B.C.E., but their architectural roots can be found much earlier, and their lineage continues into modern times. It is, as we have seen throughout this book, a worldwide phenomenon, built by arguably the least-understood peoples of ancient times, who were, perhaps, taught by an even older culture—a forgotten culture with a lost history.

> It is, as we have seen throughout this book, a worldwide phenomenon, built by arguably the least-understood peoples of ancient times....

Constructing stone monuments is a custom often overlooked in religious circles that read the following passages from the Bible without the words really registering:

> Jacob set out for Haran.... When he reached a certain place he placed a stone under his head and lay down to sleep. He had a dream in which he saw a stairway resting on the earth, with its top reaching to heaven, and the angels were ascending and

descending on it…. He was afraid and said … "this is the gate of heaven." And he set the stone up as a pillar and called it Bethel … the "House of God."

Genesis 28:10–19

Ever since then, Sunday School kids have been singing "We Are Climbing Jacob's Ladder."

Then there's this strange command from the book of Exodus, the same book of the Bible that gives us the Ten Commandments and provides a blue-print for building the Ark of the Covenant, a device so important that it repeats the instructions in triplicate:

If you make an altar of stones for me, do not build it with dressed stones, for you will defile it if you use a tool on it.

Exodus 20:25

Obviously stones are big throughout history!

How and Why

The "How did they do it?" question is only part of the mystery. Small standing stones are easily moved by a few strong men. Temples, on the other hand, are simply mystifying. Pyramids even more so.

But even more elusive is the why. Why did our ancestors feel the need to move megaton boulders across their landscape? Why are the monuments built in particular locations, even when those locations are sometimes very difficult to access? Why did the builders find it necessary to select stones of a particular composition, even when those stones sometimes weighed several tons and could only be found hundreds of miles away? How did they manage to order their society so as to secure proper cooperation and motivational spirit, even when the construction of these edifices may have required hundreds of years?

And what meticulous care they took!

The Megalithic Yard

When Dr. Alexander Thom, a Scotsman born in 1894 who dedicated much of his life to studying megalithic sites in Britain and France, mapped and charted more than six hundred stone circles and buildings, he discovered something quite remarkable.

Although his theory has been questioned, he reasons that it was as if the builders went about their task armed with a megalithic yardstick. Our modern yardstick measures 3 feet, or 36 inches, long. The megalithic yardstick measured 2.72 feet, or just a smidgeon more than 32.5 inches (to be exact, 32.64 inches). Over and over, at every site he studied, he discovered that it was as if the ancient builders had all carried this basic ruler with them and used it to mark off dimensions.

To put this in contemporary terms, every house constructed today is built to certain specific measurements. Two-by-four studs are placed every sixteen inches. Building materials such as sheetrock and plywood are measured to fit at four-foot intervals, four two-by-fours to the piece. If you went out and measured a thousand houses, you could deduce that all the carpenters who built them carried a ruler to keep these measurements uniform. And they did. It's

One of the many stone circles studied by Dr. Alexander Thom, "Long Meg and Her Daughters" in Cumbria, England, dates to the Stone Age. Its original purpose is still a matter of conjecture.

called a carpenter's square, and you can't build a house without one. It's a tool that is simple and uniform, having been used for years and years. It's got no moving parts and is used to determine everything from the pitch of your roof line to the inset of the stringers supporting your front steps. It's so simple and versatile that it will probably be around for thousands of years.

What Dr. Thom discovered was that early stone circle builders used what we might call a megalithic carpenter's square. The only thing different from our modern one was the length of the markings on its surface. Over and over, this measurement and its multiples appeared consistently throughout his study of stone structures.

Why do the dimensions of monuments located thousands of miles apart, on continents scattered throughout the world, all seem to be built using multiples of a universal measurement that we call a megalithic yard? Is it coincidence?

Don't dismiss this line of thinking too quickly. This has great implications because it might begin to answer questions about the spirituality of ancient stone builders. Throughout this book we have raised the possibility that the "Why?" question might be answered by a wisdom that was passed down by a forgotten civilization, consisting of hidden truths that we have since forgotten. But there remain questions about why the monuments were constructed the way they were. Is there a message hidden within their very measurements?

In short, what was the motivation of our ancient ancestors? What on earth were they thinking? Were they trying to teach us something? The fact of their efforts cannot be disputed. The evidence is right before us, written in stone. But the reason—ah, there's the rub!

Walking in the Moccasins of the Old Ones

We've been talking about stone megaliths. Let's consider, for a moment, something easier to grasp. Maybe that will help us walk in the footsteps of our ancestors.

Hold in your hand a stone projectile point, ax, or gardening tool. Try to bond with it and put yourself in the place of the person who made it—the person who used it.

Consider an ancient hoe, for instance. It might be a few thousand years old. It was used to plant and cultivate vegetables. This tells you that the people were staying in one place for a sufficient period of time in which to grow a crop. That's important. But it tells you so much more if you develop the ability to think with creative imagination.

> In short, what was the motivation of our ancient ancestors? What on earth were they thinking? Were they trying to teach us something?

Why does a person plant a garden? He or she wants to feed a family. What feelings does the word family produce in your mind? Just think about your last Thanksgiving family gathering. You will remember feelings expressed by words like love, security, nostalgia, and fondness. But, if you are honest, you will probably also think of words such as squabbles, anger, or resentment. They are all part of the same experience. Not all families are like the Waltons, and not all family issues are resolved within a sixty-minute timeframe, with time out for commercials.

Thus it has always been. That's simply the human condition. Why should these folks have been any different from us? They might have turned to a higher power in thanksgiving or for help through difficult times, just as many do today. They might have sung the equivalent of the Christian hymns, "We Gather Together to Ask the Lord's Blessing," or "Come, Ye Thankful People, Come." They cried when they were hurt. They laughed when they were happy. Their children sometimes made them proud and sometimes let them down. They must have felt the encroachment of the years on their tired bodies. They must have sometimes wondered, "God, why did You allow this to happen?" They probably celebrated weddings and funerals, were sometimes afraid of the dark, and welcomed the warming of spring every year.

Intuition and Revelation

Here's the point. Sometimes, if you are quiet for long enough and can sit still in meditation while gazing at the artifacts the Old Ones left behind, you can make a journey through the centuries and feel at one with the ancients. The illusion of time beaks down. The scales fall away.

And why not? The blood of our ancestors flows in our veins. We are what they became. They once were what we are today.

Now extend your vision upward to include the great temples, standing stones, pyramids, and structures from around the world, all built to a similar scale of measurement. There is a consistency to the whole thing. It is as if they all followed a central, accepted, handed-down blueprint even as they stamped their own individuality on it.

Think of it this way. My house doesn't look like your house, but both are built to the same, standard specifications. Why is that?

Because the folks who built our houses were part of a long tradition of craftsmen who knew how to build things and passed down their knowledge from generation to generation for centuries.

Can you imagine what it would be like to have accomplished what the Old Ones did? Can you think of any clues that might reveal the reasons behind their carefully executed tradition?

Listen for the echo of their forgotten voices. Perhaps they were saying, "We were here. Don't forget us!" Even though they might not have been consciously thinking along these lines, it doesn't mean their plea wasn't somewhere buried in their subconscious.

Perhaps they were saying, "We were here. Don't forget us!"

I recently built the house in which I now live and type these words. While I was working, I wasn't consciously thinking of how posterity might view my efforts. I was too busy concentrating to have time for lofty thoughts. At least, most of the time. But somewhere down deep I certainly wanted the finished product to stand forever and reveal my competence and values. I wanted to be proud of my work. I wanted to send a message down through the ages: The person who built this house was a person who cared. He built it with love! He was deeply sensitive to both function and beauty. He was a good person!

Is it possible that our so-called primitive ancestors built with the same sense of the future? Can we imagine that they were, indeed, sending us, their descendants, a similar massage? If we can imagine it, who is to say that it isn't at least one of the answers to the "Why?" question? After all, how can you imagine something that doesn't exist?

If we are correct in our assessment, we have just heard them speak to us. Their message has been received. They have communicated with us even after all these millennia have passed. They can finally say, "Mission accomplished!"

And if we can hear this message, who can say there are not others?

The Proof

All this won't convince an archeologist, of course. "Where's the proof?" he would say. "How do you know you're not making all this up?"

Well, the proof lies in the artifact you hold in your hand and the fact that people are people, wherever, and whenever, you find them. We know, for instance, that they used stone tools. We know they built great temples and stone structures. They mapped the world. They searched the heavens. We've found the evidence they left behind. This is unequivocal fact. They were dreamers and planners. They searched for answers to questions that must have been similar to the ones we ask today. "Where do we come from? Where do we fit into the great scheme of things? What is the meaning of our existence? How should we live?"

If all this is true, maybe they discovered something about life that we need to know lest we follow in their footsteps down a path that could lead to oblivion.

Isn't it the height of hubris to somehow assume that the people who accomplished these wonderful, ancient projects were somehow inferior in philosophy and intellect to us?

Yet another example of megastructures left by the ancients is the Nubian pyramids located in present-day Meroë, Sudan. Perhaps such creations were left behind merely from the urge to say, "We were here."

It's true that our technologies are different. They would probably require some real adjustment to live in our world. But we would almost certainly die in a week if we were suddenly transported back to theirs. They were tough, imaginative, inventive, and intelligent. They had to be to do what they did and survive.

Why is it so very far-fetched to imagine an equinox ceremony at Stonehenge, for instance, in which men and women danced together, forming long conga-like lines, making their way closer and closer until they mingled together to rejoice in the simple things of life—the planting of a new crop, the marriage of their maturing children, or the hope of a new and better tomorrow for their grandkids?

Answers

Is this scientific? Does it help answer our questions?

Well, it's true that we can't prove anything like what we have suggested ever happened. But we can't prove gravity exists either. Or electricity. Or anything else. We can't prove we all didn't wake up into existence yesterday, each of us sharing the same synchronized dream. But we have the evidence of the artifacts, the standing stones and temples, that prove the Old Ones were heavily invested in the outcome of their labors. We have the contemporary experience of being alive and human. It's how we would probably act. What we have described is no different from a modern wedding or church ceremony, when you come right down to it. Wouldn't we want to pass something of who we were down to future generations?

Who is to say that intuitive imagination, much like Albert Einstein's famous thought experiments, can't take us nearer to the truth than anything else? And who is to say that we can't get into the minds and hearts of the Old Ones through a process called empathy? If we can imagine what the pain of a friend feels like, even though he or she is going through something we never experienced, what difference does it make if that friend lives today or a few thousand years ago? Empathy is what spiritually evolved people do.

Or perhaps creative intuition is a better phrase. It's how we share another's experiences, both good and bad. It's how we creatively solve problems. It's how we create great art. It's what makes us one.

This is not just a New Age metaphysical concept. Creative intuition has been used in the scientific community ever since, according to the account of the first century B.C.E. Roman architect Vitruvius, "Archimedes, on getting into a tub, observed that the more his body sank into it the more water ran out over the tub." This leap of insight solved a scientific conundrum he had been working on involving displacement theory. He immediately jumped out of the

Perhaps it's time to open our minds and hearts in a different way, and listen for voices from the past.

tub and ran naked through the town, crying with a loud voice, "Eureka! Eureka!"—"I found it! I found it!"

Every innovative scientist worth his or her salt has stories to tell about a flash of insight that occurred only after study and hard work failed to get the job done. Then while doing something else—bang!—the breakthrough occurred.

Can this kind of intuitive insight lead us into worlds beyond our comprehension? I've come to believe that it's the only thing that can get us there. But if the Old Ones have, indeed, passed a lost wisdom down to us in the projects they left behind, we need to approach the whole matter with a different attitude. Perhaps it's time to open our minds and hearts in a different way, and listen for voices from the past. They might have even greater messages—hidden truths—to reveal.

From Ancient Religions Come Ancient Gods

Spirituality is about music, not spreadsheets. It is about understanding and compromise, not rules and regulations. It is poetry, not prose. But it can infuse spreadsheets, rules, regulations and prose with meaning. In the end, what gives life purpose and makes it worth living is spirituality. And that is our hope.

Jim Willis in: *Faith, Trust, & Belief: A Trilogy of the Spirit*

The more I study ancient religions and read about new concepts about the nature of the material universe, the more I come to believe that modern discoveries are not new at all. They are simply up-to-date, left-brain, scientific explanations of concepts that the ancients knew about by means of their inner spiritual journeys and subtle intuitive insights. As we have seen, vocabulary from thousands of years ago is often borrowed and used to talk about brand new scientific theories. Akasha and the God Particle, the Hindu Vedas and quantum physics, an old pharaoh named Akhenaten and a contemporary idea called transcendental monism, Jewish/Christian scriptures and shamanism—in many ways they tell the same story.

And why not? The cosmos our ancestors lived in is the same cosmos we inhabit. Its basic structure hasn't changed. Neither have we, except for outward superficialities. We think the same way they thought. We ask the same questions. The main thing that separates us is time. A lot of time. We have used that time to develop new religions, but they still address the same old questions and suggest the same spiritual observations.

Out of the ancient past have come ancient religions. From those ancient religions we learn about founders who have been transformed into mythical ancient gods. From those ancient gods we've discovered hidden truths. Those hidden truths hint of lost histories. But underneath it all, once we strip away superficialities such as dress and cosmetics, language and ideas about behavior, are we not the same? Dress our ancestors in contemporary clothing, teach them our language and customs, and you couldn't tell them apart from anyone on the street today. Whisk us away in a time machine, teach us how to behave in an era of different social standards, and we would fit right in.

Lessons of the Past

A few years ago I wrote a book called *Faith, Trust & Belief: A Trilogy of the Spirit*. It was an extended reflection on the Greek word *pistis*, which is usually translated by using one of the three words in the title. In it I wrote about old myths, old religions, and new concepts:

> Early cultures, we are often told, understood myths literally. They believed, physiology to the contrary, that a snake once talked to Eve in a garden. They thought Apollo carried the sun through the sky in his chariot and that Zeus threw thunderbolts down from Mt. Olympus.
>
> But in this "scientific" age, in this "rational" age, in this "intellectual" age, we know better. So mythology has come to be a catch-all term for stories that are not, and never have been, true. They are lies, told by ignorant, primitive people who were trying to explain that which they did not understand. Mythology was the science of the "gaps," the things which primitive humans hadn't yet figured out. Now that we understand about the course of the heavens, the reason for thunder, and the age of the earth, we don't need mythology anymore. So we stopped believing.
>
> But when we threw out the dirty bathwater of mythology, wisdom's baby went with it, right out the window.
>
> There is great insight in the earliest chapters of Genesis, and it matters not whether a historical Adam and Eve ever existed. The story of Passover has much to say to our modern culture, whether or not Moses ever parted the Red Sea. Myths about George Washington have nothing to do with cutting down cherry trees with small hatchets. That's not the point. It never was. Early generations of humans didn't make up stories because they were too dumb to know any better. We misread and dismiss them because we are too dumb to know any better! Mythology exposes

our lack of understanding, not theirs. We have, in our scientific, cultural arrogance, quite simply missed the point.

If there is anything to learn from ancient religions, it is that our ancestors were much more intelligent and thoughtful than we usually give them credit for. Their thinking, revealed both by the mythologies that informed their religions and the structures they built to practice them, is deep, penetrating and insightful.

You may ask, "So what? Why should I care about the primitive superstitions of people long dead?"

Well, if your idea of personal fulfillment is personified by the vacuous models on television that feign eternal happiness because they've discovered a new skincare product, or if you think your life has become more meaningful because the new cell phone you just bought represents the latest technological toy, you probably don't care. Go ahead and live your life. Knock yourself out. If it makes you happy, more power to you. The world needs more happy people.

But if you ever catch yourself gazing up at the night sky and wondering about your place in the universe, you might want to seek out spiritual enlightenment wherever you can get it. Since our ancient ancestors lived life at a much slower pace than we do, since they had time to contemplate life instead of catching up on the latest *NCIS* rerun, since they lived much closer to nature, which is the very source of life itself, they might be able to teach us something that will greatly benefit modern civilization.

When you listen to the latest news from around the world, it's not as if modern humans have it all figured out. There are serious, serious problems out there and many of them we have brought about by our own shortsightedness.

> At the root of many ancient religions lie stories that seem to say the Old Ones felt the same way. When their world collapsed, they thought it was their fault.

At the root of many ancient religions lie stories that seem to say the Old Ones felt the same way. When their world collapsed, they thought it was their fault. How do we know that? Because the early religions tell stories about human sin that led to catastrophe. Whether or not sin really caused a collision with a comet or an exploding volcano isn't important. The important thing is that they thought it did, which means they recognized their shortcomings.

Human sin probably won't bring about another asteroid strike. That's probably beyond our control. But sins such as greed and the exercise of political power can cause devastation enough on their own. The last century of wars and rumors of wars and the current spate of death because of power struggles, mostly blamed on religion and politics, was and is entirely preventable.

In this chapter, have we been reading a message in a bottle, written by a doomed and forgotten civilization? Did they, by the very act of creating enigmatic stone structures and mythologies for religious reasons, toss the message into the sea of time that we call history? When we find it and open it, when we read the message from afar, what is it saying?

Perhaps the message written by those who have been transformed by myth and legend into ancient gods is simply this: It happened to us. Don't let it happen to you!

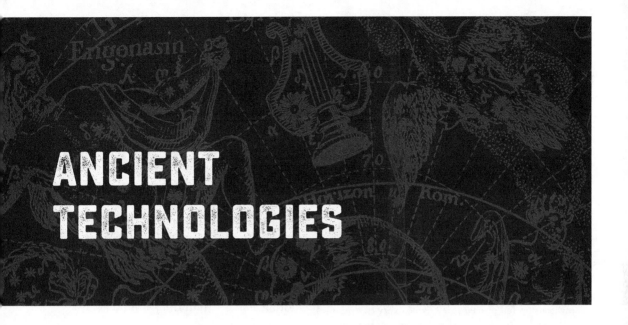

ANCIENT TECHNOLOGIES

Any sufficiently advanced technology is indistinguishable from magic.

Arthur C. Clarke

Even though technology's final product is most evident, it is the spirit of Man that turns ideas into concepts, and concepts into knowledge, which through engineering brilliance, turns science into technology and makes life more efficient and comfortable. Every product ever made began with someone's inspiration and creativity. So, spirit and technology are really different aspects of the same human endeavor.

Edward F. Malkowski

Recognizing the Obvious

The academic community suffers from a refusal to consider, let alone accept, any theories about ancient technologies. "Where is the evidence?" they ask. "Show me the proof!"

Yet the evidence is right in front of them. There stands the proof, right before their eyes. The technology remains a mystery, but the results of a technology are certainly apparent.

Take the pyramids, for instance. If you consult Egyptologists who study such things, they will tell you that there are more than two dozen theories as to how the ancients got the job done.

It would have taken a hundred thousand slaves working nonstop and placing a new stone every two minutes to build the Great Pyramid of Giza in twenty years.

- The most common is that they used ramps composed of brick and earth to build inclined planes pitched at a gradient of about one foot of rise for every ten feet of length.

That would have required a ramp almost five thousand feet long and more than three times the amount of material as is used in the pyramid itself. There is absolutely no evidence of the disposal of such material to be found anywhere at all in the vicinity of Giza and modern engineers have proved that such a ramp would collapse of its own weight unless it was built more massively than the pyramid itself.

The Great Pyramid of Giza alone consists of tens of thousands of blocks weighing fifteen tons or more, and another few-odd millions of blocks weighing only about a few tons each. Given the estimated time of construction, masons who worked ten hours a day, 365 days a year, would have had to place one block every two minutes in order to complete the pyramid in twenty years. The tolerances they achieved sometimes do not permit even a thin knife blade between blocks. Anything less would have collapsed of its own weight thousands of years ago. And, they insist, all this was done during only three months of work every year, because the workers were needed in the fields the rest of the time. But we are told they drank a lot of beer in the process. It was part of their pay. Given that time constraint, the schedule would now call for placing about four blocks every minute, or some 240 every hour. Pity the poor crew who mishandled a two-ton block and dropped it from a hundred courses up on the structure!

- Another theory, put forth in *Discover* magazine, is that a combination of just the right amount of water added to just the right amount of sand makes for a slippery slope, enabling big blocks of stone to be moved quite easily.

The problem here is that building a pyramid involves so much more than simply moving big blocks of stone. And even if that were all there was to it, a slippery slope works both ways—uphill and down. On the level it might work just fine. But how would you like to be the guy on the downhill side of one of those blocks once you start them up a ramp, especially when you get up fifty or sixty feet off the ground?

And then you have to fit them, with no margin of error, close enough so that a piece of paper can't even be inserted between them.

I'm a carpenter and have fitted untold boards together side by side to form floors and walls. In the old days, before we had the kind of joiners and electric sanders we have today, it involved much more than measuring and cutting. Sometimes it would take an hour or so of fine-tuned handwork with a plane to get a fit anywhere near what the ancient builders accomplished. And I'm talking about two eight-foot boards, not mega-ton blocks that, after being worked at the quarry, were then transported hundreds of yards and fitted together so closely that the tolerances achieved are amazing even thousands of years later. Even if a crew of a hundred men could transport such a monster up an inclined plane, there would inevitably have to be minor adjustments made at the site. And there

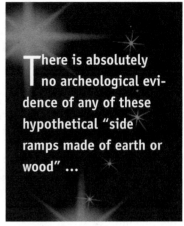

There is absolutely no archeological evidence of any of these hypothetical "side ramps made of earth or wood" ...

wouldn't be room for a hundred men to jockey the block back and forth, assuming they could even accomplish that feat, while the final work was being done, no matter how much the proper mixture of sand and water allowed for adjustments to be made quite easily.

Having stood on the pyramid myself and inspected the work with a carpenter's sensibilities, I can't help but feel that this theory was put forth by people who never really built a pyramid. They may have moved a few blocks, but that's nowhere near the same thing!

- One of my favorite explanations comes out of Cornell University. Their statement says that "the only mystery surrounding the pyramids is why people still believe their origin is a mystery." (That got my attention!) They believe that "many people, misled by mystery-mongering books (presumably that means this one), websites and TV shows, believe that the pyramids are a classic unexplained mystery." (Now I'm all ears!) Here's their explanation. "There are several ways that heavy blocks could have been added to the top. Side ramps made of earth or wood could have been built along the sides of the pyramids, or the workers might have simply built an earthen ramp against one side and dragged the blocks up on logs."

This theory smacks of so much naiveté that it boggles the mind. There is absolutely no archeological evidence of any of these hypothetical "side ramps made of earth or wood," no dumping ground where the supposed building material was discarded and no mention of any of these methods in any early records.

At least the author of this statement had the grace to conclude his article with this note: "It was an incredible amount of work, and required tens of thousands of workers over decades."

I would certainly think so!

- Indiana State University's Dr. Joseph West proposes that the builders may have strapped three wooden beams to each side of the stone blocks to "transform the square prism into a dodecagon which can then be moved more easily by rolling than by dragging."

Maybe so. But you've still got to get them to the top and then fit them together.

On and on it goes, proving that it's much easier to build a pyramid from the comfort of your living room chair than it is to actually get out and do it.

In short, when you stand in front of the Great Pyramid of Giza and listen to some poor guide deliver his story twenty times a day without ever a shrug or a wink, you have to wonder how the so-called experts ever got their doctorates.

To be fair, Egyptologists must have to spend a lot of time dealing with the many quack theories generated by New Age fringe groups. So maybe we need to cut them a little slack from time to time. But of course the builders had different technologies than we can imagine. They had to have them. Any other conclusion is simply preposterous. This doesn't mean they weren't completely appropriate to the cultures of that day. It just means we don't know what they were.

"Where is the evidence?" scream the Egyptologists. "There are no ancient electric wires hanging around waiting to be dug up. There are no rusting machines under the Egyptian desert. This is how they had to have done it because we can't imagine anything else!"

Well, there's the evidence, right out in plain sight. There stands the Great Pyramid prominently on the Giza plateau. If the Egyptologists want to prove their theories I invite them to round up a few thousand of their friends, without the use of cell phones, computers, newspapers, radios, TVs, or public media, and then motivate those friends sufficiently to build a pyramid from the ground up, using only their bare hands and such tools as they can manufacture from scratch. Then build another one, and another. While they're at it, drag megaton boulders across England to build Stonehenge. And travel to Central America to construct Machu Picchu, and to Turkey to build Göbekli Tepe.

Common Sense

You get the idea. The point is this. The ancients had to have had building technologies of which we are not yet aware. It's obvious. We don't know what they were, but the evidence is right in front of us. Instead of proposing such outlandish theories as gangs of workers building mysteriously missing inclined planes and moving four multi-ton blocks every minute while drinking a lot of beer, let's use some common sense and start to search for evidence of technology that we haven't yet imagined.

These people were brilliant! How did they do it? The reason there are so many theories floating around is obvious. We just don't know!

But think of it this way. Our recent ancestors would be baffled by how we do things today. Two hundred years ago electricity would have been considered a fool's dream. Automobiles? Magic. The Internet or sending a man to the moon? Anyone suggesting such things would have been laughed out of town. If this is the case in such recent times, how much more so if we add five thousand years to the equation?

Our technologies came to pass because a few people dared to look in the right places and do the imaginative work required to produce magic. So maybe, just maybe, the old-timers did the same thing. Maybe, just maybe, they knew something that we have forgotten. Given the evidence, it sure seems that way. Maybe, just maybe, they can teach us something if we open our eyes and, more importantly, our minds, and start to look.

In the following pages we're going to consider the roots of what might be called forgotten technology. We're not going to propose a definitive solution because, quite frankly, no one knows how the old-timers did what they did. But maybe we can at least start to look in new directions.

One of those directions, an important one, is to consider what we will call psychic technology. Don't get spooked by this. As we shall soon see, it's not magic. It just appears that way to us. There is science behind it. It doesn't involve the use of wires and cables, machines or exotic materials, none of which are found in the archeological record. It is probably best described as mind over matter. This is not as exotic as you might think. Places such as The Monroe Institute in Virginia, the Institute of Noetic Sciences in California, and even the United States Army have done extensive research in this area. Their findings are, quite frankly, astounding.

Is it possible that our ancient ancestors, free from our acculturated prejudices, stumbled on powers that are inherent in every human being but lie dormant in modern folks because of, for lack of a better word, unbelief? Are we capable of much more than what we consider to be normal lives?

Let's consider the evidence.

DOWSING

> The Lord said to Moses, "Take your rod in your hand and I will go before you to the rock at Horeb. Strike the rock and water will come out of it for the people to drink."
>
> Exodus 17:5–6

Dowsing for Fun and Prophet

Did Moses employ dowsing technology? Can you find water with dowsing rods?

The British Society of Dowsers, formed in 1933, is the leading organization for dowsers in the United Kingdom. Its stated purpose is "to encourage the study and enhance the knowledge of dowsing in all its forms amongst members and the public." According to their publications, dowsing is:

> A technique for bringing information from the intuitive or subconscious senses to the attention of the rational mind, it has potential value in almost every area of human endeavor, research and activity, and dowsing practitioners find it a valuable tool in both their work and their everyday lives.
>
> www.britishdowsers.org

Until relatively recent times, dowsing was primarily known as an ancient technology for finding water. Although many well-drilling companies won't admit it, and they certainly don't publicize it, they often employ dowsers to check out a site before going to the trouble and expense of bringing in heavy equipment and setting up drilling rigs. It's not uncommon at all to see an old-timer with a forked willow or hazel stick slowly walking back and forth over a potential site while trucks idle quietly a few hundred yards away. What happens next, if one is unprepared for it, can sometimes appear quite shocking.

Dowsing can be performed with rods, sticks, a pendulum, or this wishbone-like stick. It is an ancient art used to find water or other valuable items, but it can also be a tool for divination.

Suddenly, for no apparent reason, the stick, or wand as it is called, will quite forcefully be drawn toward the earth, dipping down toward the ground, seemingly out of control. The dowser will try a few more angles, sometimes mumbling in deep concentration. He or she may walk away a few steps, turn and come back slowly to the original point, sometimes changing dowsing equipment to a pendulum or an L-shaped rod held in each hand. Different tools produce different effects. The pendulum will swing around in a circle, often very fast and almost perpendicular to the ground. The L-rods will suddenly either cross or separate, with no discernible movement of the dowser's hands.

After a while, the dowser will mark a spot on the ground, often placing a stone or stick at a particular place that looks no different from any other spot of ground on the landscape, and announce that there is a good vein of water to be found right there at, for instance, 250 feet below the surface.

The trucks move in, begin to drill and, lo and behold, strike water within a few feet of the predicted depth!

How is this possible?

A Mysterious Technology

The truth is, no one really knows. Not even the dowser. But it has happened so often, so predictably, so consistently, and through so many years of history that people who have witnessed the phenomenon simply accept it. It saves too much money, time, and effort to question the process. Simply put, you don't have to understand it. It just works. You don't have to buy sensitive equipment. There are no moving parts to speak of, and it doesn't take a lot of time and effort. All you need is a sensitive, experienced dowser and a little faith. And even the faith comes by experience. Do it often enough, and you stop thinking of it as faith. You don't believe any more. You know.

No less an authority than Albert Einstein admitted to believing in it, while not understanding how it worked. In a letter to Herman E. Peisach of Connecticut, dated February 15, 1946, Mr. Einstein admitted that although the art of dowsing was often "regarded on the same mystical level as astrology," he explained it as a "way of using the human nervous system to detect factors that are unknown to us at this time."

(At this point I simply have to include a brief parenthesis. Without any foreknowledge at all, I entered the above paragraph into this text on February 15, 2016. I was born in 1946. It somehow seems appropriate that without any advanced planning at all, whenever I pick up my dowsing rods, I now know exactly what Albert Einstein was thinking about my activities exactly seventy years ago on this date during the year of my birth. I choose to believe that represents the serendipitous nature of advanced technology … I think … maybe.)

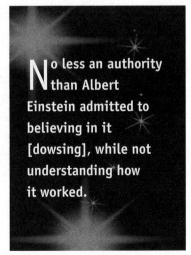

No less an authority than Albert Einstein admitted to believing in it [dowsing], while not understanding how it worked.

Dowsing is not a new phenomenon. Its usefulness and practicality have been recognized not just for generations, but for thousands of years. Even very early examples of writing talk about it.

Its usefulness is not limited to finding water. Early geologists employed dowsers to locate tin mines on the coast of Wales. Dowsers have been hired to search for gold and other precious minerals, as well as oil, in California.

Although modern police departments usually don't want the practice publicized, they often have dowsers on hand to search for lost people. A dowser will sit in a back room of a police department, miles away from the scene, and hold a pendulum on a short string over a topographical map showing the area where the person was last seen. The pendulum will begin to change the direction and intensity of its swing when it passes over a particular mountain range or stream course. Often enough, the person will be found in that area.

Healers, too, sometimes use dowsing with a pendulum to find out exactly what is going on inside the human body—a practice that is entirely noninvasive and requires no preparation on the part of the patient.

The question is, of course, how does it work?

Although no one can answer that question finally and unequivocally, there seems to be a gathering consensus among dowsers that is at once highly sophisticated yet very simple to understand. Ancient folklore, brain research, and quantum physics seem to have come together to offer an elegant hypothesis that goes something like this....

The Basics of Mass = Energy

As we saw when we looked into the God Particle, on June 30, 1905, Albert Einstein, a former patent clerk, submitted a paper on mass-energy equivalence that, when published, told the world that mass and energy are the same thing. This was the famous equation, $E = mc^2$. To review what we said earlier, it says that energy (E) equals (is the same as) mass (m) times the speed of light (c) squared (multiplied by itself). It is probably the most famous and accepted equation in physics. What it means is that mass is the physical manifestation of energy in motion.

Our bodies, along with every other material thing in the universe, be it rock, plant, animal, planet, moon, or sun, consist of mass—that is, everything is made of atoms, particles, and subatomic particles, or particles that are smaller than atoms. This mass equals, or is the same as, energy. They are two forms of the same thing. The closer we look—the farther down we go—the less we can see. Skin consists of cells, for instance. We can see these, and even vacuum them up every day when they slough off our skin. But cells consist of atoms. Atoms consist of particles. Eventually we get down to nothing. Keep peeling away the skin of the onion and what do we find at the bottom? Nothing! We are something that is made up of nothing!

There are many who will read these words and scoff, saying, "I know what I see!" No one will ever convince them that the world may be, at bottom, completely different than it appears—that it is, really, an illusion that they have bought into. It is difficult to grasp that Einstein was saying that mass is nothing more than a three-dimensional manifestation of energy. But such is the power our senses have over us. How strange it is that truth itself appears as an illusion.

Here's the point. Like it or not, realize it or not, believe it or not, we live in, and consist of, a cosmic sea of energy. Energy is everything. Asking whether we recognize it or not is like asking a fish if it believes in water or asking a flower if it believes in air. But we really can't live our daily lives if we're constantly thinking about all this. It's just too complex. So our brains have learned to deal with the world in what seems to us to be a rational way. We take in certain bandwidths of energy and filter out the rest.

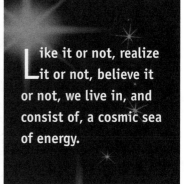

Like it or not, realize it or not, believe it or not, we live in, and consist of, a cosmic sea of energy.

Our eyes, for instance, see light waves that range through a spectrum of red, orange, yellow, green, blue, indigo, and violet. That doesn't mean we see the entire range of light. We know that light waves range way above what we can see and way below. Visible light, as a matter of fact, is only a very narrow band of the entire spectrum.

It's the same with sound. Dogs, for example, hear whistles that sound way above what we can hear, while whales converse in sound waves far below our range of hearing. Ultrasound and subsonic sounds are real. They surround us. They fill our world, but we are not aware of them. Our senses don't perceive them.

Even our sense of smell is focused on a much narrower band than that of most of the animals that live around us. They can smell the scent of other animals that totally escape our attention.

That doesn't mean we can't perceive these other wavelengths of sound, hearing, and smell. They are there, after all, and we constantly walk through them. It's just that sometime in our evolutionary past we developed in such a way that now our brains don't recognize them, so they don't register on our consciousness. If our physical equipment ever had been sensitive enough to register sensations beyond the present, familiar wavelengths, it isn't anymore. So we need technology to register microwaves or subsonic sound. Besides that, in many cases when it comes to perceiving such things, a lifetime of experience has taught us to ignore them. Because we don't need such sensitive perceptions, we filter out that which we don't use. Eventually, the ability to perceive such wavelengths atrophies, so we don't even use the abilities we do have.

Human Perception

This brings us to a quick study of how we perceive things.

Simply put, the human brain is divided into two hemispheres. According to a compelling theory which is, of course, not universally accepted, the right hemisphere, or right brain, is in charge of things like feelings, emotions, intuition, and our emotional response to art and music. This is the part of the brain that seems to concoct wild, symbolic dreams, for instance, or appreciate beautiful music or art without being able to quite express why it is beautiful.

But have you ever noticed in a dream, for instance, that you may be given a book, be able to see the words on a written page, but be unable to read them? That's because the left hemisphere of the brain is the one in charge of things like reading, science, and math. That's our practical, down-to-earth side. It is logical and scientific. During dreams, it is either asleep or relegated to the background, mostly out of use.

(For you *Star Trek* fans—the emotional McCoy is the right-brained type. Logical Spock is left-brained. That's why they can't get along. On the other hand, although both sexes use both hemispheres of their brains, left-brained traits have been, for good or bad, traditionally associated with male thinking. But as most women will say, women are right! At least right-brained, that is. This is the basis for the term women's intuition.)

In order for us to perceive something in its entirety, the hemispheres have to work together. The right hemisphere can simply appreciate a Beethoven symphony, for instance. But the left hemisphere will try to explain why it's beautiful.

Put simply—the right hemisphere perceives. The left hemisphere translates that perception into language. We can never really describe a sunset, for example. All we can say is what the sunset is like. The closest the left hemisphere can come to describing things is to use metaphor: "Skiing down the mountain was a rush!" "Scoring that goal put me on top of the world!" "I felt like a million bucks!"

That kind of thing.

Zen masters understood this exercise. Their intention was to circumnavigate the intellectual process and allow the right hemisphere to function without the need of left-brained rationalization. Their *koans* were designed to literally stifle the left hemisphere. "What is the sound of one hand clapping?" for instance, although probably never used by a real Zen master, asks a question that has no rational answer. Or perhaps the answer is so profound as to elude explanation. When a Zen student

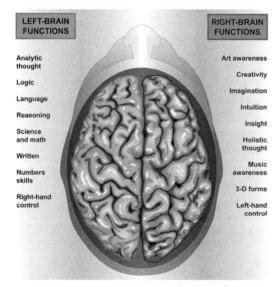

LEFT-BRAIN FUNCTIONS

Analytic thought

Logic

Language

Reasoning

Science and math

Written

Numbers skills

Right-hand control

RIGHT-BRAIN FUNCTIONS

Art awareness

Creativity

Imagination

Intuition

Insight

Holistic thought

Music awareness

3-D forms

Left-hand control

It is widely accepted as fact that our brains are divided into two hemispheres and that each hemisphere supports different functions and attributes of the mind.

reached *satori*, enlightenment, he couldn't explain what he had accomplished, and he wasn't expected to. He had understood something that could not be put into words. That was the whole point of his training.

Truth, to the Zen Buddhist, is beyond rational thought or explanation. It consists of unexplainable, but fully experienced, intuition.

A Theory of Dowsing

Now we come to the crux of what dowsing might be. It seems to be a way to transfer intuition into waking consciousness.

What is intuition? Simply put, it's the process by which right-brain-hemisphere experiences are translated into left-brain-hemisphere consciousness. How did you know that your friend was going to call? How did you know something special was going to happen? How did you know to turn right in order to get to your destination?

The answer is simple. Somehow you perceived something below the level of conscious thought and transferred that perception into action carried out by the cognizant, decision-making part of your brain. You acted on instinct. The right hemisphere felt something and then sent a message to your left hemisphere to act intentionally, even though it might not have known why.

Athletes do it all the time. It's called visualization. Jazz musicians, too, know what notes someone else is going to play, sometimes even before that person knows himself. They don't think about the chord changes or the rhythmic riffs they are using. They just play. When they're in a groove, they don't even know what's going to come out until they hear it. It's not that they don't understand the framework of the music. It's just that the harmonic structure, the key signature, the time signature, the phrasing, is so instinctual, so much a part of their subconscious being, that they are not aware of it. And until music gets to be that instinctual, it sounds stilted.

Many believe this is exactly how dowsing works. There is nothing magic in the dowsing rods themselves. They are not moved by mystical forces from paranormal realms. They are the instrument by which the music of the spheres is translated into visible signals. The body, a receptor for consciousness itself, experiences something below, and maybe even above, the level of conscious thought. By concentrating on the rods in their hands, dowsers see those feelings converted into a visible sign. The rods tell them what it was that they were experiencing that didn't register within the left hemisphere of their brains. The dowsers read the energy through which they move even though they are not fully conscious of it. Are small muscles, beyond the conscious awareness of the dowser, actually moving the rods? Possibly. But that's not the point. The body is acting apart from the conscious awareness of the dowser. That's the important thing to know.

> There is nothing magic in the dowsing rods themselves.... They are the instrument by which the music of the spheres is translated into visible signals.

According to this theory, dowsing rods are a gauge, a visible way to register an impression of energy all around you, even though it is not consciously perceived and thus translated by your left brain's language skills. In the words of The British Society of Dowsers, they are tools "for bringing information from the intuitive or subconscious senses to the attention of the rational mind."

Think of it in this way. Those of you old enough to remember when television consisted of a small, black-and-white box with rabbit ear antennas on the top probably also remember a time when you discovered that if you stood in a certain spot with the antenna in your hand, the picture improved. What was happening?

Well, your body was serving as an antenna. It was picking up the broadcast waves and transferring them to the TV set. Until you saw this demonstrated on the screen you had no idea that the very air you breathed was awash with television signals—that they were, in effect, going right through you all the time.

Then the TV became, in effect, your dowsing rod. It proved, beyond the shadow of a doubt, that unseen forces filled your environment. You could see them right there on the television screen. In the left hemisphere of your brain you weren't consciously aware of any such broadcast waves. But your body knew they were there, and proved it the first chance it got. It showed them on TV.

In the case of TV and radio band signals, technology has simply produced an electronic dowsing rod.

Dowsing through the Years

The present-day world is filled with examples of these phenomena Sometimes we ignore them because, for the most part, modern culture tends to denigrate activities usually associated with, for example, shamanism or aboriginal religion. But this is exactly the kind of experience much of the drug culture of the 1960s and 1970s was seeking. Magic mushrooms and synthetic psychedelics both were used for the same purpose. They were an attempt to bring about an altered state of reality, to bypass the traditional way of processing the world, to view life from an intuitive, rather than a rational, perspective.

It seems as though humans have been experimenting with dowsing earth energies, water, or even paranormal or metaphysical energies for a long time.

In 1949, for instance, a group of French explorers, while traveling through the Atlas Mountains of North Africa, found a system of caverns now called the Tassili Caves. Many of the cave walls were decorated with prehistoric murals. One of them seems to depict a dowser who holds a forked branch in his hand, possibly searching for water. He is surrounded by a group of, presumably, tribesmen. The paintings were carbon dated and yielded an age of at least eight thousand years.

No one can tell, of course, exactly what prehistoric artists meant to portray, but etchings from Egyptian temple walls that are four thousand years old seem to show similar scenes. And although there are many uses for pendulums, the Museum of Egyptian Antiquities in Cairo has displays featuring ceramic pendulums from thousand-year-old tombs. Are they dowsing implements or merely plumb-bobs? No one knows.

In historical, but still very ancient, times, records from Greece refer to dowsing, and the art was practiced on the Isle of Crete as early as 400 B.C.E. Some dowsers even believe the Oracle of Delphi used a pendulum to help answer questions posed by pilgrims.

Bible scholars don't have any idea what the mysterious Urim and Thummin were that appear so often in Old Testament texts such as those found in Exodus, Ezra, and I Samuel, but they seem to be some kind of dice which, when thrown, were believed to indicate the will of YHVH, Jehovah God. And the prophet Ezekiel reported that King Nebuchadnezzar of Babylon first consulted dowsers, or diviners, as they were also called, before deciding whether or not it was wise to attack Jerusalem.

In Germany, during the 1400s, miners used dowsing rods to search for valuable minerals. They referred to the forked sticks they used as *Deuter*, a German word meaning to show, to indicate, to point out, to auger, or to strike.

Closer to home, it's interesting to note that the first official use of the words "dowsing rod" is attributed to John Locke, a writer whose ideas inspired the framers of the United States Constitution. In 1650, Locke wrote an essay in which he said that through dowsing one could discover not only water but precious minerals as well. He

The Museum of Egyptian Antiquities in Cairo houses a number of ancient pendulums that some speculate might have been used for dowsing.

coined the term by employing English words from the old language of Cornwall. The Cornish *Dewsys* meant goddess. *Rhod* was the word for tree branch. Hence the term dowsing rod, and thus it remains to this day.

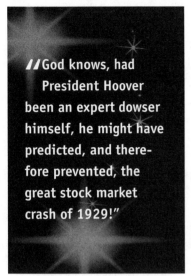

//God knows, had President Hoover been an expert dowser himself, he might have predicted, and therefore prevented, the great stock market crash of 1929!"

Even more interesting is the fact that the 1912 edition of *Mining Magazine*, published in London, England, produced the first translation of a Latin work into English. It was called *On Metals* and had been written 356 years earlier. The translator was a professional American mining engineer who went on to become the thirty-first president of the United States—Herbert Hoover. Author Christopher Bird, who wrote *The Divining Hand*, has noted, "God knows, had President Hoover been an expert dowser himself, he might have predicted, and therefore prevented, the great stock market crash of 1929!"

In 1959, Verne Cameron of California issued a challenge to the United States Navy. He offered to pinpoint the position of every U.S. submarine, using only a map and pendulum. The Navy accepted the challenge. Mr. Cameron was successful, and he threw in a bonus. He located the Russian fleet as well! Speaking of the armed forces, it is rumored that some U.S. Army soldiers in Vietnam were trained to dowse for landmines.

Why aren't these activities widely reported? Well, dowsing, like music and effective public speaking, is as much art as science. Even very experienced dowsers sometimes get it wrong. You probably wouldn't want to follow a dowser into a minefield any more than the dowser would want you to. Furthermore, we have to remember that no one fully understands how dowsing works. It can be an inexact process, even at best. But it has proven to be so reliable over the course of its long, long history that it certainly is worth studying.

Earth Magic

Perhaps the most important outcome of the dowser's craft is an enhanced appreciation of what the ancients might have called earth magic. Hamish Miller, until his death in 2010, was England's most well-known, and certainly most beloved, dowser. The founder of the Parallel Community, an online group of likeminded souls, and the author of many books and articles, Miller was drawn to dowsing after a near-death experience in 1982. In his 1989 book, *The Sun and the Serpent*, written with Paul Broadhurst, he expresses his appreciation of the art with these words:

> The question of meaning arises … in connection with modern discoveries of aligned sacred sites ('leys') throughout the world, of temples orientated astrologically to receive light and energies

from certain heavenly bodies, of the mystical science of geomancy and of the cosmological patterns of formulae which sustained ancient civilizations. Revelations abound.... Together they amount to a statement, given directly by nature; a statement that our present way of understanding and treating the earth is wrong, that we inhabit a living planet and must give it the respect due to any living creature. From that follows a quite different perception of our relationship to nature, leading to a rediscovery of the ancient spiritual sciences. We do not know why serpentine energies spiral around the course of the line of St. Michael sites from the far west to the far east of England. Others before us have recognized the phenomenon, and they have made their sanctuaries and pilgrimage routes in relation to the earth energies. The ancients, as Plato reminds us, were simple people. They did not ask reason from nature but accepted things as they were. Plato also emphasizes that everything, all human science, knowledge, and wisdom originates from divine revelation.

If dowsing teaches us to experience the magic of life itself, if the use of rod, wand, or pendulum helps us to visualize or make manifest Earth energies through which we move, it changes our whole concept of our relationship to Earth—to our place in nature itself. The earth becomes a living, breathing, life-supporting organism, named Gaia, perhaps, rather than a simple manufacturer of resources. Mother Earth not only gives birth to her children, she sustains them throughout their physical existence and receives them back at the end. Earth and Earth's species become one in a cosmic dance of life energy, manifested on this physical plane.

Will dowsing give you the ability to build a megalith? No. But if dowsing opens a window to what might best be called metaphysical realities, what else might be possible? Perhaps, with faith in such realities, the ancients really could move mountains.

* ✳ *

ENTANGLEMENT THEORY

Entanglement insults our intuitions about how the world could possibly work. Albert Einstein sneered that if the equations of quantum theory pre-

Dowsing may teach us to modify our relationship with Mother Earth, to see her as a living, breathing, nurturing being, rather than just a collection of resources to be used.

dicted such nonsense, so much the worse for quantum theory. "Spooky actions at a distance," he huffed to a colleague in 1948.

David Kaiser in the *New York Times Sunday Review*,
November 14, 2014

Diffusionism Revisited

Throughout this book we have regularly assumed the archeological position known as diffusionism. That is the theory that if two cultures, separated by a great distance, both develop similar technology, there must have been contact between them. If one builds a pyramid here, and another builds one there, the folks from here probably traveled there to teach them how. It seems the easiest way to explain the many examples of such phenomena found all around the world.

Having said all that, there remains another possibility. It involves the theory known as quantum entanglement, or simply entanglement theory. To understand how it works we have to once again enter the wild and wacky world of quantum physics.

Quantum Theory

Let's let David Kaiser, writing for the *New York Times Sunday Review* on November 14, 2014, explain it for us:

> Fifty years ago the Irish physicist John Stewart Bell submitted a short, quirky article to a fly-by-night journal titled *Physics, Physique, Fizika*. Though the journal he selected folded a few years later, his paper became a blockbuster. Today it is among the most frequently cited physics articles of all time. Bell's paper made important claims about quantum entanglement, one of those captivating features of quantum theory that depart strongly from our common sense. Entanglement concerns the behavior of tiny particles, such as electrons, that have interacted in the past and then moved apart. Tickle one particle here, by measuring one of its properties—its position, momentum or "spin"—and its partner should dance, instantaneously, no matter how far away the second particle has traveled. The key word is "instantaneously." The entangled particles could be separated across the galaxy, and somehow, according to quantum theory, measurements on one particle should affect the behavior of the far-off twin faster than light could have traveled between them.

Entanglement theory is now a universally accepted phenomenon. Admittedly, it's weird. Even Albert Einstein didn't accept it at first. But it has withstood the rigors of the scientific method time and time again. It's counter-intuitive. It defies common sense. But it seems here to stay.

What can we say? The world is a strange place and is getting stranger by the minute. But what does that have to do with lost histories and hidden truths?

Here we go.

Entangled Minds

If entangled particles interact instantly at great distances, what about the objects made up of those particles? In short, what about human brains? Can one person communicate with someone else through mental power alone, even if they are separated by great distances? Do our individual brains give us instantaneous access to a universal, cosmic mind?

"Of course not," huff the scientists. "We don't believe in telepathy!"

But if particles do it, and if human brains are made up of particles, why not? Is this yet another case of the Ancient Ones discovering something long before modern science tweaked it out of their mathematical equations? After all, if it's possible, you don't need to understand how it works in order to discover and use it. (I don't know how a cell phone works, but I use one from time to time. And don't get me started on automobiles!)

Could our ancestors, through their ancient practice of yoga, meditation, and mental discipline, have chanced upon the phenomenon of telepathy? Were they able to communicate with each other over great distances? Was that ability yet another tool in their metaphysical toolkit?

Before you quickly assign such speculation to the conspiracy of silence, beware. There exists anecdotal evidence galore that the practice is still with us in Aboriginal cultures—people who have not succumbed to modern doctrines of impossibility surrounding such ideas. Most of us have had the experience of reaching for the telephone to call a close friend, only to have it ring and discover that person has just called us. Countless experiments have been done with identical twins which indicate they share a special, entangled relationship.

> Could our ancestors, through their ancient practice of yoga, meditation, and mental discipline, have chanced upon the phenomenon of telepathy?

It may even be that we have invented a similar technology that is in use today. Were it not for the difference in hardware, there is a great similarity between what I have called entangled minds and what we now call cloud computing.

The Cloud

My introduction to cloud technology came from a man who installed the sound system in our new house. I call him Mel the Installer Guy. He's really into these things and was trying to describe to me how far the whole computer/MP3/handheld/Kindle/Blackberry/gizmo culture has evolved since the Internet went public back in the dark ages of, oh, 1990 or so. I had voiced my fear of losing my stuff if my computer ever crashed. But he informed me that he could throw his entire computer in the nearby lake and not lose a thing. (I told him I've had the same thought many times!)

"Where's all your information, your pictures, your tunes?" I asked him. "How do you back them up?"

"They're in the cloud," he said.

"What cloud?" I wanted to know.

That was my introduction to what, apparently, everybody else in the world but I understood. So I looked it up online, thereby using the cloud to tell me what the cloud is. Here's what I discovered, courtesy of Eric Griffith in *PC Magazine* (www.pcmag.com):

> In the simplest terms, cloud computing means storing and accessing data and programs over the Internet instead of your computer's hard drive. The cloud is just a metaphor for the Internet. It goes back to the days of flowcharts and presentations that would represent the gigantic server-farm infrastructure of the Internet as nothing but a puffy, white cumulonimbus cloud, accepting connections and doling out information as it floats.

Pardon me for being naïve here, but it sounds to me as if we humans have invented something that sounds suspiciously like what I already said earlier about Akasha. According to both the ancient Hindu mystics and the contemporary theories of Ervin László, all information (or what we would call bits today) is out there in Akasha. It's called consciousness. We access it through our brains, the hardware of the analogy. The software, I suppose, would correspond to the various religious/philosophical/meditative outlooks we espouse. We even call it the same thing—memory.

The analogy is perfect, except that our cloud, the Internet, is an invention of humankind. The other cloud is the Great Mystery, or God, or Akasha. (Fill in your own word here.) In other words, when we created the Internet, we might very well have been copying a cosmic model that already exists. The only difference is that, in this analogy, people's brains become individual computers, which in turn access the cloud, or the field of Akasha.

"But the Internet cloud is a product of intelligence," you insist. "It had a creator. Us!"

Right, with one important difference. Akasha didn't just have a creator. Akasha is the Creator—the Alpha and Omega of all existence. And then we came along, made in the image of the Creator, and were able to not only

In cloud technology, information from many sources is stored remotely in many outside locations. Analogous to this is the idea of Akasha, an omnipresent consciousness stores information of who we all are—it connects us to one another.

access information, but were able to do it in full consciousness while being aware of the fact that we were doing it! Consciousness accessing consciousness while being fully conscious. It's beautiful. That's Akasha!

"Now, hold on," you shout. "The 'information' that you're talking about isn't really hanging around in a 'cloud.' It exists in millions of computers that are sitting around out there in every country on Earth. It's accessed by the electromagnetic, quantum grid that connects every computer on the Internet to every other computer. It's real. It's a verifiable fact!"

Exactly! Each and every human being, everything in all of creation, is connected, or entangled, through what we call psychic vibrations, telepathy, or clairvoyance. The suggestion here is that our ancient ancestors could consciously experience those connections at will. We usually stumble upon it by accident and call these occasions physic mysteries.

Exchanging Information

Think about it this way. If information exists in a universal field, an Information Field that Carl Jung labeled the collective unconscious and Ervin

László dubbed the Akashic field, it must be a power field, the ground of our being—a mystical field that is at the same time magical and real, but totally accessible if we can only learn how to do so.

Einstein accessed it. What do you think he was doing when he engaged in thought experiments? So did Newton, Socrates, Brahms, Mozart, the builders of ancient monuments, dowsers, Hindu mystics, and every other genius who ever lived.

Could it be that the reason people built similar pyramids in Egypt, Indonesia, and way over in Central America was that they were accessing the same information field? Is it possible that the reason societies started doing the same things with stone at the same time was because they were all tuned in to the same source?

Perhaps when it appears in Akasha, everyone, everywhere, has access to it. If this is true, then the reason human civilizations evolve in bumps and jumps and punctuated equilibrium is best stated by the old Cialis commercial: "When the time is right, you'll know it!"

> Could it be that the reason people built similar pyramids in Egypt, Indonesia, and way over in Central America was that they were accessing the same information field?

What goes around comes around. We, the participants and recipients of imaginative wisdom, have invented our own version of this reality. We have created "God," the sum total of our wisdom, in our own image and called it the Cloud. May the Force be with you!

According to this analogy, the personal expression of its human counterpart sits right in front of me on my desk as I type these words. Me and my computer. Two peas in a cosmic pod. Each of us is a physically manifested expression of a possibility wave that originates either in the Cloud or in Akasha.

The ironic thing is that most people alive today are just about as ignorant of all this as their computers are ignorant of their own individual identity. At least I don't think computers are aware that they exist. Not yet, anyway. (Maybe the next upgraded models will.) And if computers ever do obtain consciousness—that is, awareness of their own existence—they will have completed the journey that our first ancestors began when they stood up, walked over to the nearest fruit tree and decided to "fill the earth and subdue it."

The ancients probably hadn't worked this all out, of course. They just sensed that they were in the presence of something bigger than themselves, and it worked. The ones who most felt its energy coursing through them like blood through an artery, the ones who were connected, or entangled, and were able to communicate through this seemingly mystical power, the shamans, were eventually called ancient gods.

What a concept. A Vulcan mind-meld, but at a distance!

The Proof

Is there any proof of this theory?

None whatsoever. Make no mistake, though, entanglement is real. Similar technologies existing within civilizations separated by great distances are real. Telepathy is still being investigated and alternately accepted or rejected depending on previous opinions held by those who are doing the investigation. Clairvoyance is still considered to be a form of entertainment. Presently all this line of thinking offers is a lot of fun. But who knows what the future holds? If clairvoyance, a feature of entangled minds, is ever proved, according to the strict protocols of the scientific method, it might change our whole approach to understanding our past.

OUT-OF-BODY EXPERIENCES

Some would say that we pass from spirit into the physical at birth and conversely pass from the physical world into spirit at death. I say that we never pass from the spirit, that our reverie of the world around us is just that. The physical world is only a silhouette, a shadow without substance. Everyday life is a mere reflection of spirit experienced as an intention to become aware of *All That Is*. Spirit does not journey through (nonexistent) space/time but across the vastness of knowledge itself, a dimensionless realm of *All That Is*. We are always spiritual beings, even when having a physical experience. Our spiritual selves, enlightened souls, share concurrently what we experience in the physical world with *All That Is*.

"Skip" Atwater in *Captain of My Ship, Master of my Soul*

A Journey into Reality

If you don't have a lot of background dealing with the subject of out-of-body experiences (OBEs) or near-death experiences (NDEs), what follows will seem at best a little out there or, at worst, unbelievable. If the latter is the case, I urge you to keep an open mind. It may prove difficult to believe at first, but some very high-powered researchers and institutions, including the U.S. Army, have studied this field and uncovered phenomena that, although contrary to the waking world most of us inhabit most of the time, have stood up to

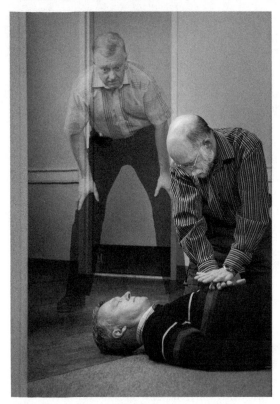

There are many reports of near-death experiences in which those who experienced it were able to describe scenes accurately that occurred while they were "dead."

strenuous tests and experiments. That, coupled with experiential anecdotes of thousands of people now living and even more examples left behind by those who have passed on, raises the possibility that the ancients may have employed by intuition that which is now being discovered by the scientific method.

To put it bluntly, nothing, absolutely nothing in the material world around us, is what it seems to be. Once that is accepted wholeheartedly and without reservation, a human being can accomplish virtually anything, including building giant megalithic structures and advanced civilizations.

Let's be clear. Are we saying that if you experience an OBE or an NDE you can then go out and build a pyramid? Of course not. What we are saying is that if it is possible to separate individual consciousness and awareness from material flesh and blood—your soul from your body—then who knows what else might be possible?

In other words, OBEs and NDEs cannot, by themselves, allow people to accomplish the things we have been studying in this book. But they are part of something much bigger—call it a psychic technology, or psi—that might account for them.

Take electricity, for example. Simply having access to electricity won't let you build your own house. But it is part of a package, including power tools, knowledge, experience, and an infrastructure that can supply material, that all work together to make the job possible. An archeologist who lives ten thousand years in the future would have to have an understanding of electricity and its uses before he or she could adequately explain the tools needed to build a house. Without that knowledge the project might appear quite magical. With it, it's just another ordinary accomplishment that happens every day.

In the same way, we need to have at least a surface understanding of the components of what I have called psychic technology in order to understand how such a thing might be possible. We've seen some of these components in action when we looked at Entanglement Theory, the Akashic Field and, to a lesser extent, dowsing. We'll go into it in more detail in a few moments when we consider siddhis. But for now, let's pause for a minute to ask if our ancient ancestors might have lived in, worked with, and experienced for themselves a source of power quite different from the one we perceive in our waking consciousness.

Welcome to the world of reality, where anything is possible.

Traveling Out of Body

Where do we begin? Well, let's start by learning about getting out of our bodies and thus free from the reality filters we call the five senses—the filters that make the world around us seem so very, very real. Once you experience reality by means of something other than the five senses, the world of consciousness proves to be quite a different kind of place.

"Hold on," you say! "Consciousness is a product of neurons reacting to a chemical soup in our brains. Mind equals brain equals consciousness. They're all the same thing!"

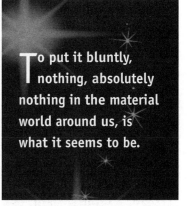

To put it bluntly, nothing, absolutely nothing in the material world around us, is what it seems to be.

Are they? Although over the last hundred years this may have been the standard doctrine, and may still be the majority opinion, it is a belief system that is starting to crack apart at the seams. There is significant evidence beginning to pile up that indicates mind and brain are not the same thing— that the brain is a physical organ that receives and interprets mind, rather than generating it—and that both are independent from consciousness, which is the ground of being out of which both ultimately spring.

We have to be careful here. This is opening a window unto a vista which could easily generate a whole new book. At this point we will simply assume OBEs to be real and within the reach of everyone reading this book. (All it takes is a half hour a day for thirty days and you, if you are like countless thousands who have tried, can have an out-of-body experience yourself. The technique is simple and outlined in William Buhlman's book *Adventures Beyond the Body*. Once you have experienced the phenomenon for yourself, you won't just believe in the possibility, you will know. Don't scoff until you've tried it. Thirty days, thirty minutes a day. Only then will you be entitled to objections.)

The Experience of a Pioneer

The reason we raise the possibility of an extinct civilization well versed in psychic technology that might have been capable of the archeological mysteries found around the world today is that an out-of-body pioneer named Robert Monroe claims to have visited at least one of them.

Bob Monroe is the inventor of Hemi-Sync technology. Let's let him explain it:

Refined with over 50 years of research and development, and supported by numerous independent studies, reports, and articles, the patented Hemi-Sync® technology has been scientifically and clinically proven to be effective. This unique audio-guidance process works through the generation of complex, multi-layered audio signals, which act together to create a resonance that is reflected in unique brainwave forms characteristic of specific states of consciousness. When you hear these through stereo headphones or speakers, your brain responds by producing a third sound (called a binaural beat) that encourages the desired brainwave activity. The result is a focused, whole-brain state known as hemispheric synchronization, or Hemi-Sync®, where the left and right hemispheres are working together in a state of coherence.

http://www.hemi-sync.com/?gclid=CJ3B8uafk
8sCFdgUgQodve4Okw

What this means is that Monroe invented an audio technology that manages to make possible in a very short period of time what used to take serious students of meditation years to achieve on their own. It leads to what he called the Mind Awake/Body Asleep state that allows you to experience, while fully awake and in control, the source world, some might call it the dream world, to which you return while asleep. This is the destination of a shamanic journey—a parallel dimension.

Besides all this, Bob was the founder of The Monroe Institute in Virginia which studies, among other things, the science of OBEs and similar experiences. The Institute is at the forefront of both teaching and research, offering weeklong seminars and workshops in the field. Their graduates number in the thousands. Although Bob has passed on, his books remain top sellers, including *Ultimate Journey*, in which he recounts one of his more spectacular trips back in time to view a lost civilization from long ago. They weren't the ones responsible for building some of the architectural wonders we have discussed. They preceded that time by thousands of years. But it raises interesting possibilities, to say the least.

Others who have been connected with The Monroe Institute include "Skip" Atwater, who, in his book *Captain of My Ship, Master of My Soul*, discusses his work with remote viewing and OBEs while working for the US Army's secret counterintelligence remote-viewing operations at Fort Meade, Maryland.

Perhaps the world's foremost teacher in the field is William Buhlman, who offers workshops several times a year at The Monroe Institute, as well as teaching seminars on OBEs around the world. His book we already mentioned,

Adventures Beyond the Body, is probably the bible when it comes to practicing the OBE phenomenon.

It will, at the very least, open your eyes to the possibility.

A Quick Dream Tutorial

I was already familiar with OBEs when I attended Bill's workshop, but I can personally vouch for his skill as a communicator and facilitator. What he taught was fascinating.

The deep, dark secret of human consciousness is this: We don't return to the field of consciousness, the field of Akasha, only when the material body dies. You were there yourself, just a few hours ago. You visit the home place every night when you sleep. Sometimes you even remember a jumbled version of what you experienced. You usually can't make heads or tails of it because straightforward English just doesn't cut it. Language, after all, is a product of your left brain. Remember, the left brain operates in language. The right brain operates in images. Symbolic images. Mythological images. Dream images.

Joseph Campbell once said that dreams are a great source of spirit. Talk to any shaman worth his or her salt, and he or she will tell you the same thing. In his book *Dreamgates*, Robert Moss, who leads dream workshops all over the world, has this to say:

> Our physical reality is surrounded and permeated by the vigorous, thrumming life of the realms of spirit and imagination to which we return, night after night, in dream. There is no distance between the Otherworld and its inhabitants and our familiar, sensory reality; there is a difference in frequency.

In this age of amazing, awesome, and awe-inspiring scientific revelations about how the body works, in this age of discoveries concerning mitochondrial DNA and cell reproduction, in this age of technicolor NASA flights and Mars Rovers, an amazing fact stands out above all else. At least it seems amazing to me. We have been sleeping and dreaming for millions of years, and no one yet knows why. That's right. No one. In spite of comprehensive research coming out of thousands of sleep clinics found coast to coast and around the world, the first and greatest

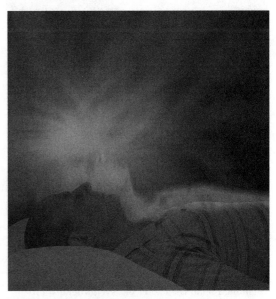

We don't go to the realm of Akasha only when we die, but also when we sleep.

commandment of sleep research is still this: No one knows why we sleep. And the second is like unto it: No one knows why we dream, either.

Dream Study

Sigmund Freud was the first modern psychiatrist to bring the study of dreams to the attention of the general public. He still has a large following. His theory of dreams was that they were a representation of unconscious desires, motivations, and thoughts. He came to believe that we are driven by sexual and aggressive instincts that, because of social pressures, we repress from our conscious awareness. Because these thoughts are not consciously acknowledged, they find their way into our awareness through dreams. (Hence the oversized boxing gloves you used to find in the offices of Freudian psychologists. They were for expressing those aggressive feelings.)

In his book *The Interpretation of Dreams*, Freud wrote that dreams are "disguised fulfillments of repressed wishes." He went on to say that there are two different contextual categories of interpretation that need to be addressed during dream analysis. Manifest content pertains to the actual images, thoughts, and content contained within the dream. Latent content refers to the hidden psychological meaning of the dream. (Of course, "a cigar is sometimes just a cigar." Sometimes there is no hidden meaning. It depends on the latent content lurking, or not lurking, in our psyche.)

Dream research didn't stop with Freud. Here are just a few examples of current schools of thought:

The Activation-Synthesis Model

This theory was proposed by J. Allan Hobson and Robert McCarley in 1977. They believed that circuits in the brain come alive during rapid eye movement (REM) sleep, causing areas of the limbic system that are involved in emotions, sensations, and memories to become active. The brain synthesizes and interprets all this activity in an attempt to find meaning, which results in dreaming. This model, in other words, suggests that dreams are a sym-

Sigmund Freud, the Father of Psychotherapy, proposed that dreams expressed our suppressed desires and fears.

bolic interpretation of signals generated by the brain during sleep. The symbols, if interpreted correctly by a trained analyst, can reveal clues to understanding what is going on in our subjective unconscious.

A variation on this theme is that dreams are the result of our brains trying to make sense out of noises that are happening around us. A car driving by an open window might become a stimulus for a car appearing in our dream. A song on the radio might become part of a story the brain makes up in order to produce nonverbal, symbolic images.

The Computer Model

When your home computer sleeps at night—in other words, when you're not using it—some programs automatically kick in that spend time cleaning up and organizing clutter. (At least they do if you keep the darned thing turned on. I shut mine off. What does that mean, Sigmund?) They defragment and systematize things so the computer will work more efficiently. This dream model speculates that your brain operates in the same way. When you shut down in sleep, your brain goes to work organizing all the thoughts and external stimuli you encountered that day.

The Quiet Therapist

This model proposes that dreams operate as a kind of therapeutic psychotherapy session. The brain tries to make sense out of things while you sleep in the safe environment of your bed, somewhat akin to a therapist's couch. Things that happen to you are analyzed for meaning and projected on the wall of your conscious mind when you wake up and remember. Your emotions help make sense of the symbols.

We might very well discover that one or more of these models is correct. Perhaps the truth lies in combining parts of all of them. But for thousands of years shamans and mystics have taught that in dreams our normal waking consciousness is let out to play. It separates from its confines within the material body and brain and returns to its mystic union with the One in the creative, ground zero, imaginative, zero-point field of Akasha. That is the purpose of sleep, they remind us. Without this daily renewal, life in this material world would simply be too hard to endure.

Modern sleep-deprivation and dream-deprivation studies seem to indicate that this is, indeed, the case. When we are tired and deprived of sleep, our creativity goes first. Then we start to forget things. Finally we go completely mad and die. In this day and age we may not

> When we are tired and deprived of sleep, our creativity goes first. Then we start to forget things. Finally we go completely mad and die.

fully understand what sleep and dreaming are all about, but we know that the material body ceases to function without them. Death is the result. That seems a pretty good indication that the ancients knew something. Indeed, traditional wayside hosts of the old road hostels in Britain, the keepers of the shrine, used to pronounce the final words of the evening to the gathered guests: "May the gods send you a dream."

But shamans went even further. They claimed that when released from the normal bounds of restraints of the waking, analytical hemisphere in our brains, our true nature, our consciousness, returns to the source. They believed that with practice we can actually follow along while fully conscious.

Back to the Subject

What does this mean in terms of hidden truths from the past?

Simply this. Once you accept the idea that it is possible to access realms of wisdom not readily available through the normal five senses, all kinds of knowledge become possible, including technologies that may be entirely unknown to us at this time.

Thomas Edison, in his journals, reveals that he often catnapped during the day for the sole purpose of attaining hidden insights. He would fall asleep in his chair while deliberately holding a handful of ball bearings. When he began to drift off, the bearings would rattle to the floor and bring him back to full consciousness. The brief span of time between consciousness and sleep would provide the state he needed for his "Aha!" moments.

Many famous inventors confess to the same techniques. Sudden insights—"Eureka" moments—are universally attributed to sudden bursts of intuition in like manner. The inventions that followed are now commonplace and accepted. But before they arrived, their use would have seemed quite magical.

Who knows what technologies might have become apparent to our ancestors if they discovered a simple but effective way to access ideas that might seem very simple and obvious if rediscovered today? Once again we have to remind ourselves that much of what we consider commonplace would have seemed magical to folks who lived just a few generations back.

Famous inventor Thomas Edison once revealed that sleeping would allow him to gain insights to create new things.

SIDDHIS AND THE *YOGA SUTRAS*

Until the recent rise of scientific authority, siddhis were not considered controversial. They were accepted as fact, along with many other types of miracles that are accepted on faith within most religions today. But because scientific theories have superseded religious doctrine as the arbiter of truth in the modern educated world, and because science has yet to develop theoretical explanations for such phenomena, this creates a conflict.

Dean Radin in *Supernormal*

A Different World

It's time now to enter a different world—a world so far removed from the experience of most of us that it is virtually unbelievable to any modern, educated, Western-oriented person today. It is a world in which a virtually unexplored technology could exist that would easily explain the enigmatic stone structures found around the world. It could also explain the disappearance of a civilization that built those structures.

"Great!" you say. "Bring it on! Two great questions answered with one theory!"

But there's a problem. Aside from the fact that mysterious structures from a lost civilization exist, there is only one thread of evidence to support the theory, and it lies in the mythological remnants of religion and culture. There are very few scientists willing to study this theory using approved scientific methods and protocol, and the conspiracy of silence reigns supreme regarding their work. It appears to be a field in which almost everyone seems to be interested, but no one will admit it.

This will take some explanation.

The *Yoga Sutras*

Two thousand years ago, a rishi from India named Patanjali wrote a treatise now called the *Yoga Sutras*. It consists of four short sections called *Padas*. Written in Sanskrit, they offer an extended teaching concerning meditation and enlightenment:

Aside from the fact that mysterious structures from a lost civilization exist, there is only one thread of evidence to support the theory, and it lies in the mythological remnants of religion and culture.

- The *Samadhi Pada* is concerned with one-point meditation wherein we free ourselves from the chattering monkey-brain that most of us experience as soon as we sit quietly and begin to meditate. Incessant thoughts swirl around in our minds and we find it very difficult to settle down and concentrate.

- The *Sadhana Pada* shows the way out of this confused stream of consciousness and teaches meditative habits that relieve confusion and subsequent internal turmoil.

- The *Vibhuti Pada* describes supernatural powers called siddhis that become available to the one who reaches this state. Everything from telepathy and telekinesis to levitating and "leaping tall buildings at a single bound" can be experienced and demonstrated by the one who attains this state because he or she has managed to pierce through the illusion that objects we see and feel in our perception realm are, in fact, real. A person who achieves this level recognizes experientially that the nature of reality is, in fact, what science has now proven

A group of Indians practice patanjali yoga on June 21, 2016, which is International Yoga Day. Many Americans view yoga as merely a form of exercise, but it is actually a spiritual practice.

beyond the shadow of a doubt: Life is but a dream. Matter is not solid. What we call reality is an illusion manufactured in our brains because we experience it through the filters of our five physical senses.

- The *Kaivalya Pada* is the final section that concerns itself with *moksha*, the final freedom which is the basic aim of Yoga. Here the practitioner is able to see the world as it really is—a total unity.

Now go back to the third section—the *Vibhuti Pada*. This is the part that particularly concerns us in this book. It's the world of siddhis—miracles such as walking on water and healing the sick, supernormal abilities such as those displayed in comic book characters, unexplained physic abilities, teleportation, ESP, OBEs—and moving great boulders magically across the landscape.

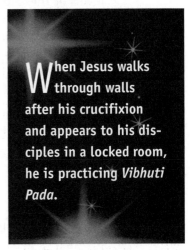

When Merlin is said to have erected the standing stones of Stonehenge using music, he is practicing *Vibhuti Pada*. When Jesus walks through walls after his crucifixion and appears to his disciples in a locked room, he is practicing *Vibhuti Pada*. When the Buddhist monk levitates or the Hindu practitioner bends a spoon with his mind, they are practicing *Vibhuti Pada*. This is the world of the mystic.

When Jesus walks through walls after his crucifixion and appears to his disciples in a locked room, he is practicing *Vibhuti Pada*.

The Proof

"What proof do you have? How can you make such claims?"

Well—none, and I'm not. And to make things worse, numerous psychological studies have been published that indicate if you don't believe in this stuff, the few words that I write in this book are not going to change your mind. You are a skeptic. And if you do accept such things, no skeptic is going to convince you otherwise. You are a believer.

So let me make the argument and then the two of you—skeptic and believer—can fight it out amongst yourselves.

Yoga is ancient beyond anyone's definition of the term. Carved figurines that portray people in typical Yoga postures predate the religion of Hinduism, if that is at all possible, by thousands of years. So these techniques were discovered and practiced way back in human history. In order to follow the ancient instructions eventually written down by Patanjali, you need extreme devotion, passion, spiritual discipline and, above all, quiet. These are all attributes which are in short supply in today's bustling world.

The image of the yogi escaping to a secluded mountaintop in order to meditate is an accurate one. The stories of Moses ascending the mountain,

Jesus going into the desert, Mohammad retreating to his cave, Buddha sitting beneath the Bodhi Tree, Christian monks moving to secluded monasteries, and native Americans going on vision quests are all rooted in fact. You don't achieve such mystical states by going on a weekend retreat or taking a walk. They require sustained meditation. It's all or nothing—and it takes a lifetime. It is extremely difficult, if not impossible, for those of us whose lives are infused with television, cell phones, and the Internet to attain the sublime levels of the Old Ones. That's not to say it can't be done. But those who devote themselves to such a life today practice far from the technological world most of us inhabit, understand, and experience.

Yet historical myths and descriptions of these states are universal. If true, do they imply that some adept masters accomplished what we now consider to be impossible? Did they supervise and assist in the construction of the megalithic enigmas of antiquity? A bountiful wealth of anecdotal evidence insist they did just that.

How? By utilizing a technology of mind over matter.

The Trap

Siddhis, supernatural powers, come with a trap. The *Vibhuti Pada* makes it clear that they are a byproduct of meditation, not an end. They easily hinder spiritual development because they lead to an unhealthy ego, the desire to show off, and the establishment of religious cults focused on personality rather than spirituality. In short, the public, ego-driven practice of displaying so-called supernatural powers leads to hubris, which is precisely the sin that the ancient myths all claim was the cause of the catastrophes that brought about the demise of civilization in the past. To refresh your mind, read Genesis 6 again. There we read that God sent the flood to punish humankind because of their inflated view of themselves.

> The people found new ways to destroy and conquer. They sought to enhance their personal power at the expense of others. Some even invented flying shields, capable of carrying them to villages far away, where they could attack, pillage, and return so quickly that no one knew where they had gone. Sotuknang knew he could not allow this way of life to continue. So he warned Spider Woman that he would again destroy the people, this time with a great flood.

Also—and here's the kicker—siddhis are easily faked. The temptation to pad your resume with spectacular effects has always been with us. It is so prevalent that fraudulent mystics and psychics have given the whole field a bad name.

Real practitioners are warned not to demonstrate their abilities to anyone, not even their closest followers. If you bend a spoon with your mind as a result of meditating, or levitate, or move the living room sofa across the room—fine. It's normal. But it doesn't mean you're enlightened. It just means you're on the right path. These things happen because you recognize that all matter is illusion. All you've done is prove that the scientists are correct when they tell us nothing is solid and everything is entangled. You've pierced through the illusion and seen reality as it is. To those of us who sense only a material world it seems like a big deal. But it's not. It's just another layer of reality peeling away from the mystery of life. Don't tell anyone! First of all, they won't believe it. More importantly, it will distract you from your real purpose, which is spiritual growth.

The temptation to pad your resume with spectacular effects has always been with us. It is so prevalent that fraudulent mystics and psychics have given the whole field a bad name.

The Theory

Now comes the application. Could it be possible that our ancient ancestors, as a result of seriously applying themselves to the study of the great mystery called life, discovered that they could indeed levitate great blocks of stone or perhaps heat them to high temperatures and mold them into place? Could they mentally transport themselves across great distances and build a civilization based on these spectacular, but normal (albeit supernormal to most of us) powers? And did they then fall into the trap of misusing them, thereby following a misguided road of meditative practice, bringing their abilities to a screeching halt while forcing us, their descendants, into the position of wondering about such things as lost histories and hidden truths? Was their failure so complete that we have allowed inherent abilities that are real, but forgotten, to atrophy? In other words, are we physically capable of the same things they were? Have we developed amnesia concerning how to go about restoring our innate talents? Is being human much more complex than we think? Is this what the Bible means when it says in Psalm 82:6, "Ye are Gods"?

Let's summarize:

- If a civilization ever existed that was able to mentally accomplish many of the same things we are able to do through modern technology, that civilization would leave behind the fruits of their labors, the megaliths, but not any evidence of how they were able to accomplish any of it, because theirs would have been a wireless, fuel-less technology. It was all accomplished through intense mental development.

- If such a civilization were destroyed by, say, a comet from on high, the survivors might well have recognized, perhaps for quite some time before the catastrophe, that their psychic powers were being misused. The wise men, the rishis, might have recognized the same errors their descendants would later call hubris and egocentrism. Perhaps they would even call it sin, and attribute their destruction to their actions. (Much the same thing is happening today. We are in the process of using our technology to destroy our planet. We see it coming but seem powerless to prevent it. At some point we will probably want to warn our descendants—"Don't do what we did!" They, in turn, might turn it into a religion. "They angered the gods and brought about a global calamity!")

- The surviving members of this civilization would very probably have been considered gods by the Stone Age people who somehow survived the tragedy. This would account for the many myths about gods mating with humans and God destroying the world because of sin.

- The intense yogic work needed to perfect such psychic powers would no doubt have been impossible to continue following such a cataclysm. The Stone Age survivors, with no background in meditation, would probably forget the methods and remember only the strange, god-like people who were considered to be the bringers of civilization. Within a generation or two, the only thing left would have been the curious megalithic structures, mythic memories concerning their construction, and, compared to what once was, a pale religion.

Could It Be?

I know it's pretty far out there, but it does explain the great megaliths, the mystery surrounding their construction, the wealth of mythology about the subject of miracles found in our sacred scripture stories, and the disappearance of, but widespread anecdotal evidence for, abilities that surge in our imaginations whenever we pick up an adventure comic book or contemplate the latest X-Men episode. Superman will never die!

If this theory is true, the current interest in yoga surfacing in the West might be a latent memory emerging to the surface of our experience. Our dreams of flying might be more than fantasy. Our youthful imagination concerning heroic deeds might be a recollection of what once was commonplace. These might be memories of what once was possible—and could be again.

I know full well what most of you are probably thinking. It sounds outlandish. But think of it this way. The theory, as unbelievable as it sounds, does fit the evidence. It explains everything about lost histories and hidden truths. It even accounts for ancient gods.

There is only one sticking point. Although the theory explains our forgotten past, according to our current experience it seems impossible. Such super powers don't exist in our world.

I feel the same way sometimes. I say to myself, "I just don't believe it!"

Then I hear the voice of my inner Yoda: "That is why you fail!"

Consider siddhis and present-day comic book characters.

This is by no means a new way of thinking. Our imaginations love to soar when it comes to super powers. Consider the following examples:

The internationally popular superhero Batman is actually Bruce Wayne, who studied Eastern philosophy, according to the back story.

- Superman was an alien.
- Wonder Woman, in her first incarnation, was an Amazon. When she moved to television her homeland was moved to Atlantis, where she might have known another famous Atlantian, the *Homo aquaticus* superhero Aquaman.
- Bruce Wayne, in his movie persona, traveled to the East where he studied Eastern spirituality before perfecting his gymnastic skillset as the Batman.
- The Flash came from the future.
- Captain America came from the past to defend the present.

Every one of these fictional, god-like figures was connected to a place or time we have studied in this book as we looked at lost civilizations. If anyone back in ancient times exhibited even a minute portion of the siddhis associated with our modern comic book equivalents, they would certainly have been transformed through myth and time into ancient gods.

Next time you view pictures of the pyramids or other such mysterious ancient building projects, think about how such things were accomplished. Let your imagination soar.

In the end, you need to decide for yourself how they came to be.

Hidden Truths

On Nov. 24, 1907, *The New York Times* published an article headlined "Photographs by Telegraph: Television next?" The reporter was hopeful: "It seems not improbable," the article said, "that someday, we may be able to see distant views through the aid of a telephone wire in the same way that we can now hear distant sounds."

"I can't believe that!" said Alice.

"Can't you?" the Queen said in a pitying tone. "Try again: draw a long breath and shut your eyes."

Alice laughed. "There's no use trying," she said: "one can't believe impossible things."

"I daresay you haven't had much practice," said the Queen. "When I was your age, I always did it for half-an-hour every day. Why, sometimes I've believed as many as six impossible things before breakfast!"

Lewis Carroll in *Alice in Wonderland*

Everyone loves a good mystery. When you sit on a rock and contemplate Stonehenge, when you gaze upward at the pyramids or consider the enigmatic structure called Göbekli Tepe, when you climb a Peruvian hill only to discover it is made by humans, you are engulfed in mystery.

The technologies we have discussed in this chapter are, for the most part, mysterious. Whether we group them together under such headings as psi, metaphysical, siddhis, hidden truths, noetic science, or psychic technology, the truth remains that whether you believe in such things or not, they don't generally form a part of most people's daily experience.

If you, just like Alice in the quote that begins this section, are having trouble accepting the reality of such abilities, maybe what comes next will help.

Future Tech

The technology that fills our lives today was incomprehensible to our ancestors. My grandfather had to work hard at just accepting the idea of television. He never lived to see a remote control device, but I'm sure, knowing him as I did, that he probably would not have wanted one in his house because he would have worried about the possibility of its being a fire hazard.

In the same way, technology is advancing so rapidly today that twenty years from now we will no doubt be considered antiques by our children, if they don't already harbor such notions. Scientists from NASA are even now working on ideas based on entanglement theory which might lead to guiding future Mars Rovers using nothing but the power of the mind. Dowsing is an old but very accepted technique that is practiced all over the world. No longer is it limited to simply finding water. Out-of-body workshops are gaining in popularity. Siddhis are being studied under laboratory conditions.

All these techniques are part of what I have called a psychic toolkit. Alone, they are not sufficient to explain ancient technologies that built pyramids, megaliths, and other enigmatic structures of the past. But they might point to powers and abilities that could. It's important to note that these technologies are not magic. They are all based on state-of-the-art mathematics drawn from current theories about quantum reality. "Beam me up, Scotty," is not a phrase limited to science fiction. Teleportation is theoretically possible. People are actually working on such concepts. Someday we'll do it. We just don't know how yet.

The technology we enjoy on a daily basis today would have been considered magical, even supernatural, by people in the past. A generation or two from now, technology will likely astound us even more.

But here's the point. When we do invent these marvels that will certainly be part of our future, people will be able to effectively employ them whether they understand them or not. I don't understand how my computer works, but I use it. The science on which technology is based is real, whether or not we know how to figure it out. It consists of principles and laws that have been around since the universe first formed. Electricity existed way before Thomas Edison. He didn't invent it. He discovered it.

Ancient Psi-Tech Discoveries

Could it be that the technologies we are in the process of harnessing today were first discovered by our ancient ancestors a long time ago? They might not have deduced them through left-brain intellect. But they might have stumbled on them and employed them through a process we can only call intuitive psychic ability.

It's important to note that we are not the first to come up with the idea of a psychic toolkit and the concept of mind over matter. It's found in all the great religious traditions, hiding in plain sight for thousands of years.

Read Matthew 17:20 in whatever version of the Bible you might have access to. There, Jesus tells his followers that if they have even a small amount of faith—as much as a tiny mustard seed—they will be able to move a mountain. Presumably that includes stone megaliths as well as Peruvian pyramids. We are used to reading that passage metaphorically. But what if we change our perspective a little? Might he have possibly been speaking quite literally?

"Why did humans lose this ability?" you ask.

When people are surrounded by TVs, iPods, iPhones, Smartphones, and other technology, it seems no one just sits and takes time to think anymore. This has, perhaps, caused our ability to focus to atrophy.

Well, we just don't know. It might have been because of the collapse of a civilization due to natural catastrophe, such as a collision with a comet. Perhaps the powers they demonstrated got out of hand, bringing about the very results we fearfully envision today involving the use of nuclear energy. It could have happened because such powers required more mental discipline than most people possessed. Meditation is something that has to be learned through a long period of personal dedication. Most people just don't want to take the time.

Also, and this might cause some psychological discomfort, the truth is that some technologies tend to produce a shortened human attention span. Many people report that the more they concentrate on their computer, for instance, the less they read books. The more they listen to their tunes, the less comfortable they are just sitting and thinking. This probably doesn't help the development of mental discipline required for serious psychic or spiritual growth. Perhaps the ability to focus sufficiently has simply atrophied.

Ask yourself this question. Does the thought of sitting for an hour or two by yourself, alone in a room without books, computers, phones, magazines, or anything else of that nature, seem like a blessing to be cherished or a punishment to be endured?

Now extend those few hours out over the course of a lifetime. That's probably what it would take to learn how to control the feverish monkey-brain that chatters away at us whenever we turn off the distractions of modern technology for a while.

The more we wonder about how the old-timers accomplished some of the things they did, the more we are aware of the great gulf that separates us. They lived in a different world. Maybe a better one, maybe not. But certainly different. Is it any wonder we have a hard time connecting with, or even believing in, what might have been the source of ancient technologies?

CONCLUSIONS

The End of the Matter

Where great feats are performed the wolves will always howl and
the claws of the ravens will strike. This is part of the game.

Sven Hedin to Thor Heyerdahl: *In the Footsteps of Adam*

When I began work on this book I had planned to include many anecdotes gleaned from the history of those who study our origins. I thought their
stories would illustrate how the conspiracy of silence has condemned to the
dustbins of academia many original thinkers who first came up with what are
now fully accepted ideas concerning our early ancestors. I collected dozens and
dozens of such examples. I found them not only in the fields of archeology and
anthropology, but in all the sciences. Music and art yielded a goodly batch as
well—physics and math a treasure trove. It got to the point where I got so
depressed I didn't want to read about them anymore. It seems almost obligato-
ry that when someone comes up with a new idea, he or she must not only be
roundly trumped, but insulted and ridiculed in public.

The above quotation came from Thor Heyerdahl's memoir about the
public trouncing he took after he had completed the *Kon-Tiki* voyage. "Hum-
bug," read the papers, supposedly quoting the experts who said he was guilty of
seeking publicity or even perpetuating a fraud. Erich von Däniken and Barry Fell
would commiserate, I'm sure. Likewise for Graham Hancock and Andrew
Collins. Dean Radin has a Ph.D. and conducts experiments at the Institute of
Noetic Science under the strictest scientific protocols, but has had to endure the
wrath of Internet experts who simply cannot accept the idea that they might not
be qualified to shoot down any hint of psychic phenomena. The research team

of three highly trained geologists who proposed what is now called the Younger Dryas Comet Hypothesis had to endure the many so-called obituaries to their thesis that filled the pages of magazines dedicated to preserving the status quo. All of these pioneers, and many more, were forced to endure public witch trials. As an old friend of mine used to say, "The woodchuck who sticks his head up is the one who gets shot at." The number of good, smart, intuitive thinkers who died before their ideas were accepted is, sadly, depressing.

It seems as though every idea that we now regard as gospel was first denigrated by those who, for some reason, felt threatened. The attacks leveled were both vicious and personal. Politics and religion are not immune from the process, of course.

If you disagree with someone's opinions, it is good and proper to argue your case. But if you attempt to publicly humiliate or attack the character of the one who proposes that opinion, you are not just a bad scientist, you are a bad person.

There is not an idea proposed in this book that has not been scoffed at, ridiculed, deliberately ignored, or, at the very least, suffered that ultimate cowardly putdown—the famous rolling of the eyes.

But plain facts cannot be ignored. First of all, modern civilization is fragile—a lot more fragile than we like to consider. Take away our electricity infrastructure and chaos awaits. Second, our past is mysterious. Evidence of that mystery stands plainly before our eyes in the enigmatic stone structures that dot the landscape of every country on Earth. And no one has yet adequately answered most of the questions we have raised.

Throughout this book we have come down pretty hard on the establishment. Entrenched traditionalists are tough to ignore. But beginning in the glorious mish-mash of the '60s a new breed of specialist began to appear. They have grabbed academia by the proverbial throat and bellowed, like Jacob of Old Testament fame, "I will not let you go until you bless me!" When banished from the halls of institutions devoted to the *status quo* they circumnavigated the establishment and went straight to the public via television and popular books. When banned from peer review, they published in the national press. They stalked the halls of conventions and seminars and braved the scorn of once-revered professors.

May their kind continue to thrive. They are changing the way we think about our past. They are redefining our concept of who we are. They are singing a new song. And many are starting to join in the chorus.

What is at stake is nothing less than the fate of an evolving human species who might yet amount to something wonderful. A reawakening of our past might lead to a re-visioning of our future.

What are these modern prophets telling us?

First: They Are Redefining Our Concept of God

The "Big Five" world religions of Hinduism, Buddhism, Judaism, Christianity, and Islam all began within a relatively short era of history that stretched over a time span of only a thousand years. All are presently showing signs that their founders' definition of "God" might be in need of an update. Although this idea terrifies the religious establishment, a little revolution from time to time might be a good thing.

Is it possible that instead of looking upward for the source of our being, we might actually be better off looking inward? The people labeled ancient gods by our ancestors seem to have practiced a wisdom that originated deep within the human heart. They might very well have been capable of an old spirituality that is surfacing once again, interpreted anew for a modern age. Earlier we said that ancient Hinduism seems to have much in common with new physics. Perhaps the right and left hemispheres of our brains, our intuition and our intellect, had to travel by different paths in order to arrive at the same place.

If it is true that lost histories embodying hidden truths lay buried deep in our forgotten past, the clues our ancestors built into the enigmatic structures that so intrigue us today might indicate a wisdom that encapsulated their spirituality. What might their message have been? Perhaps something like this:

> We are being guided not by ancient gods but by a very present force of some kind which we could rightly call "God" were it not for the modern baggage associated with that term. As philosopher Paul Tillich so eloquently puts it, "God is not a being. God is *being itself*."

Second: They Are Acknowledging Clues Hidden in Mythology

If forgotten civilizations once existed, where did they come from? The word culture is derived from the word cult. For example, the founders established a cult of YHVH, a cult of Osiris, a cult of Muhammad, a cult of Jesus Christ. Each cult built a culture around it.

Aside from enigmatic stone structures, where is the evidence of these supposed ancient cultures? Where did it come from?

For answers to these questions we refer to ancient myths and legends.

If we stay clear of the traditional theory of gradual Uniformitarianism, there are probably only three explanations as to why a universal, worldwide mythology reveals such a similar origin story:

1. The theory put forth in this book—A lost civilization from the past that was destroyed. An Atlantis-type theory that is remembered in myth.

2. Ancient aliens who, having sown the seeds of life, visited to weed their garden and fertilize the soil a bit. We don't find the evidence on Earth because it exists on another planet.

3. People from our own future. This is the theory voiced in the Star Trek movie *First Contact*. Finding themselves marooned in the past, the intrepid crew is told to "Go to Earth and stay out of history's way." We can't find the evidence because it doesn't exist yet.

All three theories are, admittedly, a little hard to swallow unless you, like me, are an incurable romantic. But what else is left? Barring a brand-new concept no one has yet put forth, we are left with the seemingly impossible. But at least these three theories address the riddles traditionalists are reluctant to talk about.

Third: They Are Beginning a Process

To say we can somehow definitively prove the existence of a forgotten civilization or help from out there somewhere is probably too much to ask. But if we can at least acknowledge the possibility of such a thing, some of the unexplained, mysterious, archeological evidence found around the world, backed up by myth and legend, begins to make sense.

The scientific method requires that we begin with a hypothesis before we start to gather experimental proof. Thus, admitting that a hypothetical lost civilization might have existed is the first step in the process. We are still a long way from universal acceptance of that admission, but things are looking up. If enough people make enough noise we might yet accomplish that feat. And if the new books and TV shows are any indication, we are at least on our way.

We began this book with what we called a radical concept that ours is not the first civilization to have inhabited this planet.

You must decide for yourself whether or not we have proved our hypothesis.

If so, there is much work to be done in the fields of archeology, anthropology, mythology, religion, physics, and a host of

God is not a separate being, but being itself. God is everything.

other related disciplines. Stating a hypothesis is just the beginning. The real work begins when you try to prove it.

If not, there remain the questions that prompted this study in the first place. Who built the mysterious stone structures that dot the landscape of the planet? How did they accomplish the feat? How do we reconcile so many similar origin myths? Who are we? Where do we come from?

Today the words of astrophysicist Sir Arthur Eddington ring as true as ever: "Not only is the universe stranger than we imagine, it is stranger than we can imagine." Our journey continues....

Those who cannot remember the past are condemned to repeat it.

George Santayana

APPENDIX:
TIMELINE OF TRADITIONALLY ACCEPTED DATES

(All dates given as BP: *Before Present*, and rounded off for convenience)

Time	Event
3.8 billion years BP	Life begins, DNA originates, or, alternatively, arrives on Earth.
2.5 million years BP	Early human ancestors; *Homo habilis* ("Handy Man") first steps on the scene.
1.9 million years BP	*Homo eergaster* ("Work Man") appears around this time.
250,000 thousand years BP	Neanderthals appear.
200,000 years BP	Birth of modern humans. "Mitochondrial Eve" gives birth to modern humans, probably in Ethiopia. By "modern" we mean that these people had the same features and brain size we do. If they were to spend a day at a spa and put on modern clothes, they would be indistinguishable from us. It is true that if you were to hand them a cell phone and ask them to order a pizza, they wouldn't know what to do. On the other hand, if they were to hand you a spear and tell you to go pick up dinner, you'd be lost.
75,000 years BP	The Mount Toba volcanic eruption violently brings about a severe reduction of the human population, ending what scientists call a genetic "bottleneck." If all humans now living descended from survivors of this catastrophe, genetic evolution effectively began at this time.
50,000 years BP	Evidence of pre-Clovis humans on the Savannah River at the Topper Site in South Carolina.
40,000 years BP	The "Great Leap Forward." Humans first demonstrate the capacity for symbolic (religious) thought by entering the great European caves and producing high art. Although grave sites pre-dating this (going back to

Time	Event
40,000 years BP (cont.)	Neanderthal times) demonstrate a probable belief in the afterlife, and the discovery of what might be a flute hints at the expression of music, the cave paintings reveal a sudden flourishing of spiritual or religious expression. Some theories suggest that the discovery of hallucinogenic, mind-expanding plants led to this giant step on the way to spiritual significance that separated us from our animal predecessors.
25,000 years BP	Solutrean Culture flourishes in southern France and northern Spain. These were the people who may have migrated east to Turkey and west, by boat, to America, where they evolved into the Clovis culture.
26,000 years BP	Gunung Padang is built in Indonesia.
12,800 years BP	Earth collides with a segmented comet that reverses what had been a time of melting glaciers. The result is the Younger Dryas Ice Age that lasts for more than a thousand years and causes the extinction of megafauna around the world.
11,600 years BP	The Younger Dryas Ice Age ends as rapidly and mysteriously as it began. The result is worldwide flooding as the ice cap suddenly releases unimaginable amounts of fresh water into the world's oceans.
11,500 years BP	Göbekli Tepe, thought to be our civilization's first temple, is built.
8,500 years BP	Karahunj, a collection of megalithic menhirs, are erected in present-day Armenia.
8,200 years BP	The 8.2 Kiloyear Event, for unknown reasons, plunges the world into a severe Ice Age.
5,900 years BP	The 5.9 Kiloyear Event, for reasons unknown, brings about severe climate change that eventually turns the Sahara into a desert and causes massive migrations around the world.
5,000 years BP	Major work is completed at Stonehenge, the Majorville Medicine Wheel, and Newgrange.
4,500 years BP	The Pyramids are completed.
4,200 years BP	The 4.2 Kiloyear Event begins a severe, century-long drought that affects weather all over the world. 4,000 years BP the biblical Patriarch, Abraham, makes the journey from the Fertile Crescent into Canaan, honored by all three monotheistic religions (Judaism, Christianity, and Islam).
4,000 years BP	Mystery Hill is built in New Hampshire.

Further Reading

Ashton, John, and Tom Whyte. *The Quest for Paradise: Visions of Heaven and Eternity in the World's Myths and Religions.* New York: Harper Collins, 2001.

Atwater, F. Holmes. *Captain of My Ship, Master of My Soul.* Charlottesville, VA: Hampton Roads Publishing, 2001.

Bauval, Robert, and Adrian Gilbert. *The Orion Mystery.* New York: Three Rivers Press, 1994.

Bolen, Jean Shinoda. *Gods in Every Man.* San Francisco: Harper & Row, 1989.

Broadhurst, Paul, and Hamish Miller. *The Sun and the Serpent.* Cornwall, England: Pendragon Press, 2013.

Buhlman, William. *Adventures Beyond the Body.* New York: Harper Collins, 1996.

———. *Adventures in the Afterlife.* Millsboro, DE: Osprey Press, 2013.

———. *The Secret of the Soul.* New York: Harper Collins, 2001.

Bulfinch's Mythology. New York: Gramercy Books, 1979

Campbell, Joseph. *Transformations of Myth through Time.* New York: Harper & Row, 1990.

Campbell, Joseph, with Bill Moyers. *The Power of Myth.* New York: Bantam, Doubleday Dell Publishing Group, 1988.

Childress, David Hatcher, and Brien Foerster. *The Enigma of Cranial Deformation: Elongated Skulls of the Ancients.* Kempton, IL: Adventures Unlimited Press, 2012.

Chopra, Depak, and Leonard Mlodinonow. *War of the World View: Science versus Spirituality.* New York: Harmony Books, 2011.

Clark, Jerome. *Unexplained! Strange Sightings, Incredible Occurrences, and Puzzling Physical Phenomena,* 3rd edition. Detroit: Visible Ink Press: 2013.

Collins, Andrew. *Göbekli Tepe: Genesis of the Gods.* Rochester, VT: Bear & Co., 2014.

———. *The Cygnus Mystery.* London: Watkins Publishing, 2006.

Cotterell, Arthur, and Rachel Storm. *The Ultimate Encyclopedia of Mythology.* China: Hermes House, 1999.

Dennett, Daniel. *Darwin's Dangerous Idea: Evolution and the Meanings of Life.* New York: Touchstone, 1996.

Durant, Will and Ariel. *The Lessons of History*. New York: Simon & Schuster, 1968.

Ellwood, Robert S., and Barbara A. McGraw. *Many Peoples, Many Faiths: Women and Men in the World Religions*, 7th edition. Upper Saddle River, NJ: Prentice Hall, 2002.

Estes, Clarissa Pinkola. *Women Who Run with the Wolves: Myths and Stories of the Wild Woman Archetype*. New York: Ballantine Books, 1992.

Fell, Barry. *America B.C.: Ancient Settlers in the New World*. New York: Simon & Schuster, 1976.

———. *Saga America*. New York: Times Books, 1980.

Fisher, Mary Pat, and Lee W. Bailey. *An Anthology of Living Religions*. Upper Saddle River, NJ: Prentice Hall, 2000.

Freeman, Gordon R. *Hidden Stonehenge*. London: Watkins Publishing, 2012.

Gaskell, G. A. *Dictionary of all Scriptures and Myths*. New York: Gramercy Books, 1981.

Gould, Stephen J. *Rocks of Ages: Science and Religion in the Fullness of Life*. New York: Ballantine, 1999.

Hancock, Graham. *Fingerprints of the Gods*. New York: Three Rivers Press, 1995.

———. *Magicians of the Gods*. New York: St. Martin's Press, 2015.

———. *Supernatural*. New York: Disinformation Company, 2007.

———. *The Sign and the Seal*. New York: Crown, 1992.

———. *Underworld: The Mysterious Origins of Civilization*. New York: Crown, 2002.

Hapgood, Charles. *The Earth's Shifting Crust*. New York: Pantheon Books, 1958.

———. *Maps of the Ancient Sea Kings: Evidence of Advanced Civilization in the Ice Age*. Kempton, IL: Adventures Unlimited Press, 1966.

———. *The Path of the Pole*. Kempton, IL: Adventures Unlimited Press, 1999.

Harner, Michael. *Cave and Cosmos*. Berkeley, CA: North Atlantic Books, 2013.

———. *The Way of the Shaman*. San Francisco, CA: Harper & Row, 1980.

Harper, Tom. *The Pagan Christ*. Toronto, Canada: Thomas Allen Publishers, 2004.

Hick, John. *Classical and Contemporary Readings in the Philosophy of Religion*. Edgewood Cliffs, NJ: Prentice Hall, 1964

Highwater, Jamake. *The Primal Mind: Vision and Reality in Indian America*. New York: Harper & Row, 1981.

Hitching, Francis. *Earth Magic*. New York: William Morrow and Company, 1977.

Houston, Jean. *The Hero and the Goddess*. New York: Ballantine Books, 1992.

James, Peter, and Nick Thorpe. *Ancient Mysteries*. New York: Ballantine Books, 1999.

James, Simon. *The World of the Celts*. London: Thames & Hudson, 1993.

Jones, Prudence, and Nigel Pennick. *A History of Pagan Europe*. New York: Routledge, 1995.

Joseph, Frank. *Advanced Civilizations of Prehistoric America*. Rochester, VT.: Bear & Company, 2010.

———. *Before Atlantis*. Rochester, VT: Bear & Company, 2013.

Kane, Sharyn, and Richard Keeton. *Beneath These Waters*. Atlanta, GA: National Park Service-Southeast Region, 1993.

Kapra, Fritjof. *The Tao of Physics: An Exploration of the Parallels between Modern Physics and Eastern Mysticism*. Boston: Shambala Publications, 1975.

Kauffman, Stuart A. *Reinventing the Sacred: A New View of Science, Reason, and Religion*. Philadelphia: Basic Books, 2008.

Keck, L. Robert. *Sacred Eyes*. Indianapolis: Knowledge Systems, 1992.

Keen, Jeffrey. *Consciousness, Intent, and the Structure of the Universe*. Victoria, BC: Trafford Publishing, 2005.

Lao Tzu. *Tao Te Ching*, translated by Lau D.C. New York: Penguin Books, 1963.

Laszlo, Ervin. *Science and the Akashic Field: An Integral Theory of Everything*. 2nd edition. Rochester, VT: Inner Traditions, 2007.

———. *The Akashic Experience: Science and the Cosmic Memory Field*. Rochester, VT: Inner Traditions, 2009.

———. *The Whispering Pond: A Personal Guide to the Emerging Vision of Science*. Rockport, MA: Element Books, 1996.

The Lost Books of the Bible [and] *The Forgotten Books of Eden*. New York: The World Syndicate Publishing Co., 1926.

Macrone, Michael. *By Jove!: Brush Up Your Mythology*. New York: Harper Collins, 1992.

Mails, Thomas E. *Dancing in the Paths of the Ancestors*. New York: Marlowe, 1999.

Mavor, James W., and Byron E. Dix. *Manitou*. Rochester, VT: Inner Traditions International, 1989.

Michell, John. *The New View over Atlantis*. New York: Thames and Hudson Inc., 1969.

The Missing Books of the Bible, Vols. 1 and 2. New York: Medium Solutions Services, 1996.

Monroe, Robert A. *Ultimate Journey*. New York: Doubleday, 1994.

Morgan, Elaine. *The Aquatic Ape Hypothesis*. London: Souvenir Press, 1997.

Morris, Desmond. *The Naked Ape*. New York: Dell, 1973.

Mowat, Farley. *The Farfarers*. South Royalton, VT: Steereforth Press, 2000.

Murphy, Carolyn Hanna. *Carolina Rocks! The Geology of South Carolina*. Orangeburg, SC: Sand Lapper Publishing, 1995.

Osborne, Robert. *Civilization: A New History of the Western World*. New York: Pegasus Books, 2006.

Peterson, Robert. *Out of Body Experiences*. Charlottesville, VA: Hampton Roads Publishing, 1997.

Powell, Barry B. *Classical Myth*. Upper Saddle River, NJ: Prentice Hall, 2001.

Prabhupada, A. C. Bhaktivedanta. *Bhagavad-Gita as It Is*. Los Angeles: International Society for Krishna Consciousness, 1984.

Radin, Dean. *The Conscious Universe: The Scientific Truth of Psychic Phenomena*. San Francisco, CA: Harper Collins, 1997.

———. *Entangled Minds*. New York: Simon & Schuster, 2006.

———. *Supernormal: Science, Yoga and the Evidence for Extraordinary Abilities*. New York: Random House, 2013.

Roberts, David. *In Search of the Old Ones*. New York: Simon & Schuster, 1996.

Rolleston, T. W. *Myths & Legends of the Celtic Race*. London: The Ballantine Press, 2011.

Ross, T. Edward, and Richard D. Wright. *The Divining Mind: A Guide to Dowsing and Self-Awareness*. Rochester, VT: Destiny Books, 1990.

Sagan, Carl. *The Dragons of Eden*. New York: Ballantine Books, 1977.

Sassaman, Kenneth E. *People of the Shoals: Stallings Culture of the Savanna River Valley.* Gainesville, FL: University Press of Florida, 2006.

Sitchin, Janet. *The Anunnaki Chronicles: A Zecharia Sitchin Reader.* Rochester, VT: Bear & Co., 2015

Sitchin, Zecharia. *Genesis Revisited.* New York: Avon Books. 1990.

Stanford, Dennis J., and Bruce A. Bradley. *Across Atlantic Ice: The Origin of America's Clovis Culture.* Berkeley and Los Angeles: University of California Press, 2012.

Temple, Robert. *The Sirius Mystery.* Rochester, VT: Destine Books, 1987.

Ulansey, David. *The Origins of the Mithraic Mysteries: Cosmology Salvation in the Ancient World.* New York: Oxford University Press, 1989.

Van Renterghem, Tony. *When Santa Was a Shaman.* St. Paul, MN: Llewellyn Publications, 1995.

Von Daniken, Eric. *Chariots of the Gods.* New York: Penguin, 1968.

Waters, Frank. *Book of the Hopi.* New York: Penguin Books, 1977.

Willis, Jim. *The Dragon Awakes: Rediscovering Earth Energy in the Age of Science.* Daytona Beach, FL: Dragon Publishing, 2014.

———. *The Religion Book: Places, Prophets, Saints and Seers.* Detroit, MI: Visible Ink Press, 2004.

Willis, Jim and Barbara. *Armageddon Now: The End of the World, A–Z.* Detroit: Visible Ink Press, 2006.

Wright, Patricia C., and Richard D. Wright. *The Divining Heart.* Rochester, VT: Destiny Books, 1994.

INDEX

Italic type indicates photos and illustrations.